Artificial Neural Networks and Type-2 Fuzzy Set

Artificial Neural Networks and Type-2 Fuzzy Set

Elements of Soft Computing and Its Applications

Snehashish Chakraverty
National Institute of Technology Rourkela
Department of Mathematics
Rourkela, Odisha, India

Arup Kumar Sahoo
Siksha 'O' Anusandhan Deemed to be University
Department of Computer Science and Engineering
Bhubaneswar, Odisha, India

Dhabaleswar Mohapatra
Siksha 'O' Anusandhan Deemed to be University
Department of Mathematics
Bhubaneswar, Odisha, India

ELSEVIER

MK
MORGAN KAUFMANN PUBLISHERS
AN IMPRINT OF ELSEVIER

Morgan Kaufmann is an imprint of Elsevier
50 Hampshire Street, 5th Floor, Cambridge, MA 02139, United States

For accessibility purposes, images in electronic versions of this book are accompanied by alt text descriptions provided by Elsevier. For more information, see https://www.elsevier.com/about/accessibility.

Publisher's note: Elsevier takes a neutral position with respect to territorial disputes or jurisdictional claims in its published content, including in maps and institutional affiliations.

Notices

Knowledge and best practice in this field are constantly changing. As new research and experience broaden our understanding, changes in research methods, professional practices, or medical treatment may become necessary.

Practitioners and researchers must always rely on their own experience and knowledge in evaluating and using any information, methods, compounds, or experiments described herein. In using such information or methods they should be mindful of their own safety and the safety of others, including parties for whom they have a professional responsibility.

To the fullest extent of the law, neither the Publisher nor the authors, contributors, or editors, assume any liability for any injury and/or damage to persons or property as a matter of products liability, negligence or otherwise, or from any use or operation of any methods, products, instructions, or ideas contained in the material herein.

ISBN: 978-0-443-32894-7

For information on all Morgan Kaufmann publications
visit our website at https://www.elsevier.com/books-and-journals

Publisher: Mara Conner
Acquisitions Editor: Chris Katsaropoulos
Editorial Project Manager: Sangeeta Gaur
Production Project Manager: Punithavathy Govindaradjane
Cover Designer: Greg Harris

Typeset by VTeX

Dedicated to our parents and teachers

Contents

About the Authors xv
Preface xvii
Acknowledgements xix

1. Introduction to soft computing 1
   - 1.1. Introduction 1
   - 1.2. Evolution of soft computing 2
   - 1.3. Soft computing 3
     - 1.3.1. Neural networks 3
     - 1.3.2. Fuzzy set theory 3
     - 1.3.3. Probabilistic reasoning 4
     - 1.3.4. Evolutionary computation 4
   - References 5

PART 1 Artificial neural network

2. Artificial neural network: an overview 9
   - 2.1. Introduction to machine learning 10
   - 2.2. Types of data 10
     - 2.2.1. Data visualization 10
   - 2.3. Training of ML model 12
     - 2.3.1. Hold-out sample validation 14
     - 2.3.2. K-fold cross-validation 15
   - 2.4. The birth and evolution of artificial neural network 15
     - 2.4.1. Topology of ANN 17
     - 2.4.2. Types of learning 17
     - 2.4.3. Applications 18

2.5. Learning rules 18
2.5.1. Backpropagation learning algorithm 19
2.6. Configuration in neural network 19
2.7. Activation functions 21
2.8. Regularization 23
2.9. Optimization 24
2.9.1. Gradient decent 25
2.9.2. Adam 25
2.9.3. L-BFGS 26
References 27

3. Mathematical formulation of the neural network for differential equations 29
3.1. Introduction 29
3.2. Differential equations 30
3.3. Incorporating neural networks into ordinary differential equations 30
3.3.1. Formulation of first-order differential equations with initial conditions 32
3.3.2. Formulation of second-order differential equations with initial conditions 32
3.3.3. Formulation of second-order differential equations with boundary conditions 33
3.4. Example illustration 33
References 34

4. Recent trends in activation functions for solving differential equations 35
4.1. Introduction 35
4.2. Methodology 36

4.3. Simulation results and discussions 36
4.3.1. Experimental setup 37
4.3.2. Model problems 37
4.4. Validation 44
References 44

5. Curriculum learning for an artificial neural network 45
5.1. Introduction 45
5.2. Curriculum Learning 46
5.3. Methodology 46
5.4. Problem statements 47
5.4.1. Lane–Emden equation 47
5.5. Simulation results and discussions 48
5.5.1. Experimental setup 48
5.5.2. Model problems 48
5.6. Validation 52
References 54

6. Symplectic artificial neural network 55
6.1. Introduction 55
6.2. Symplectic artificial neural networks 56
6.3. Methodology 57
6.3.1. Modeling of symplectic artificial neural network 57
6.4. Problem statements 58
6.4.1. Duffing oscillator model 59
6.4.2. Van der Pol–Mathieu–Duffing oscillator model 59
6.5. Simulation results and discussions 59
6.5.1. Experimental setup 59
6.5.2. Model problems 60
6.6. Validation 65
References 70

7. Wavelet neural network 71
7.1. Introduction 71
7.2. Wavelet neural networks 72
7.2.1. Mexican Hat wavelet neural networks (M_hWNN) 73
7.3. Methodology 74
7.3.1. Modeling of Mexican Hat wavelet neural networks 74
7.4. Problem statement 76
7.4.1. Non-linear financial model 76
7.5. Simulation results and discussions 77
7.5.1. Experimental setup 77
7.5.2. Model problems 78
7.6. Validation 86
References 89

8. Physics-informed Neural Network 91
8.1. Introduction 91
8.2. Physics-informed Neural Networks 92
8.3. Methodology 95
8.4. Problem statement 95
8.4.1. Modified Fornberg–Whitham equation 95
8.5. Simulation results and discussions 96
8.5.1. Experiment setup 96
8.6. Model problem 96
8.7. Validation 100
References 101

PART 2 Type-2 fuzzy uncertainty

9. Interval and fuzzy set theory: an overview 105
9.1. Intervals 105
9.2. Interval arithmetic 106

9.3. Fuzzy sets 107
9.3.1. Fuzzy numbers 107
9.3.2. Parametric form of fuzzy numbers 109
9.3.3. Double parametric form of fuzzy numbers 109
9.3.4. Fuzzy arithmetic 110
9.3.5. Derivative of fuzzy valued function 110
9.3.6. Riemann–Liouville fractional integral 110
9.3.7. Fuzzy Riemann–Liouville fractional integral 111
9.3.8. Caputo fractional derivative 111
9.3.9. Caputo fuzzy fractional derivative 111
References 112

10. Preliminaries of type-2 fuzzy sets 113
10.1. Type-2 fuzzy sets 113
10.1.1. Vertical slice of a type-2 fuzzy set 114
10.1.2. $\tilde{\alpha}$-Cut of vertical slice 114
10.1.3. $\tilde{\alpha}$-Plane of a type-2 fuzzy set 114
10.1.4. Footprint of uncertainty 114
10.1.5. Lower membership function and upper membership function of a type-2 fuzzy set 115
10.1.6. Principle set of a type-2 fuzzy set 115
10.1.7. α-Cut of an $\tilde{\alpha}$-plane 115
10.2. Triangularly perfect quasi-type-2 fuzzy numbers 115
10.2.1. Arithmetic of TPQT2FNs 116
10.3. Gaussian triangular type-2 fuzzy number (GTT2FN) 118
10.4. General interval type-2 triangular fuzzy number (GIT2TFN) 118
10.4.1. Perfect interval type-2 triangular fuzzy number (PIT2TFN) 119
10.5. Derivative of type-2 fuzzy valued functions 119
10.6. Riemann–Liouville integral of the type-2 fuzzy valued function 120

10.7. Caputo type-2 fuzzy fractional derivative 121
References 121

11. Uncertain static engineering problems 123
11.1. Introduction 123
11.2. Type-2 fuzzy linear system of equations 125
11.3. Solution procedure for T2FLSEs and FT2FLSEs 127
11.4. Sample problems 129
11.5. Application problems 135
11.5.1. Rectangular sheet 135
11.5.2. Beam structure 137
11.5.3. Truss structure 139
References 144

12. Linear dynamical problems with uncertainty 147
12.1. Introduction 147
12.2. Type-2 fuzzy linear eigenvalue problems 148
12.3. Solution procedure of type-2 fuzzy linear eigenvalue problem 149
12.3.1. Procedure for T2FSEP 149
12.3.2. Procedure for T2GEP 150
12.4. Sample problems 151
12.5. Application problem 157
12.5.1. Spring-mass system 157
References 163

13. Non-linear dynamical problems with uncertainty 165
13.1. Introduction 165
13.2. Type-2 fuzzy non-linear eigenvalue problems 167
13.3. Solution procedure of the type-2 fuzzy non-linear eigenvalue problem 168
13.4. Sample problems 170

13.5. Application problems 178
13.5.1. Damped spring-mass system 178
References 185

14. Type-2 fuzzy initial value problems with applications 187
14.1. Introduction 187
14.2. Problem discussion and proposed methodology 189
14.3. Sample problems 190
14.4. Application problems 198
14.4.1. Logistic model 199
14.4.2. Electric circuit 199
14.4.3. Spring-mass system 204
References 206

15. Type-2 fuzzy fractional differential equations with applications 207
15.1. Introduction 207
15.2. Legendre wavelet method 209
15.2.1. Block-pulse function 209
15.2.2. Fractional-order integration operational matrix 210
15.3. Problem description and implementation of the LWM 210
15.4. Sample problems 211
15.5. Application problems 217
15.5.1. Fractional-order R-L circuit 217
15.5.2. Generalized Bagley–Torvik equation 221
References 228

Index 231

About the Authors

Snehashish Chakraverty has 31 years of experience as a researcher and teacher. Presently, he is working in the Department of Mathematics (Applied Mathematics Group), National Institute of Technology Rourkela, Odisha, as a senior (Higher Administrative Grade) professor. Prior to this, he was with CSIR-Central Building Research Institute, Roorkee, India. After completing graduation from St. Columba's College (Ranchi University), his career started from the University of Roorkee (now the Indian Institute of Technology, Roorkee) and obtained M.Sc. (Applied Mathematics) and M.Phil. (Computer Applications) from the said institute securing the first positions in the university. Dr. Chakraverty received his PhD from IIT-Roorkee in 1993. Thereafter, he did his post-doctoral research at the Institute of Sound and Vibration Research (ISVR), University of Southampton, U.K., and at the Faculty of Engineering and Computer Science, Concordia University, Canada. He was also a visiting professor at Concordia and McGill Universities, Canada, during 1997–1999 and a visiting professor at the University of Johannesburg, Johannesburg, South Africa, during 2011–2014. He has authored/co-authored/edited 33 books, published 482 research papers (to date) in journals and conferences, and two books are ongoing. He is on the editorial boards of various international journals, book series, and conferences. He was the president of the section of mathematical sciences (including statistics) of the Indian Science Congress (2015–2016) and was the vice president of Orissa Mathematical Society (2011–2013). Professor Chakraverty is a recipient of prestigious awards, namely "Careers360 2nd Faculty Research Award" for the Most Outstanding Researcher in the country in the field of Mathematics, Indian National Science Academy (INSA) nomination under International Collaboration/Bilateral Exchange Program (with the Czech Republic), Platinum Jubilee ISCA Lecture Award (2014), CSIR Young Scientist Award (1997), BOYSCAST Fellow. (DST), UCOST Young Scientist Award (2007, 2008), Golden Jubilee Director's (CBRI) Award (2001), INSA International Bilateral Exchange Award ([2010–2011] selected but could not undertake [2015] selected), Roorkee University Gold Medals (1987, 1988) for first positions in M.Sc. and M.Phil. (Computer Application). He is on the list of 2% world scientists (2020 to 2024) in Artificial Intelligence and Image Processing category based on an independent study done by Stanford University scientists. Professor Chakraverty has received an IOP Publishing Top-Cited Paper Award in 2021 and 2022 from India, published across the entire IOP Publishing journal portfolio in the past 3 years, i.e., 2018–2020 and 2019–2021, respectively, for his paper that ranked among the top 1% of the most-cited papers in the materials subject category. In 2020–2021, one of his papers published in ZAMM—Journal of Applied Mathematics and Mechanics (Wiley) was among the most cited papers. He has already guided 25 PhD students and 12 are ongoing. Professor Chakraverty has undertaken around 16 research projects as a principal investigator funded by international and national agencies totaling about Rs. 1.6 crores. He has hoisted around eight international students with different international/national fellowships to work in his group as the PDF, PhD, visiting researchers for different periods. A good number of international and national conferences, workshops, and training programs have also been organized by him. His present research area includes differential equations (ordinary, partial, and fractional), numerical analysis and computational methods, structural dynamics (FGM, nano) and fluid dynamics, mathematical and uncertainty modeling, soft computing and machine intelligence (artificial neural network, fuzzy, interval, and affine computations).

Arup Kumar Sahoo is currently working as an Assistant Professor in the Department of Computer Science and Engineering at Siksha "O" Anusandhan (Deemed to be University), Odisha, India. Dr. Sahoo holds a PhD from the Department of Mathematics, National Institute of Technology Rourkela, Odisha, India. He has also enrolled as a postdoctoral research fellow at the Department of Marine Technologies, University of Haifa, Israel. His PhD research areas include scientific machine learning, differential equations, artificial neural networks and artificial intelligence. He earned his M.Phil. in Mathematics from Utkal University, Bhubaneswar, Odisha, India, and an M.Sc. in Mathematics and Computing from Biju Patnaik University of Technology, Rourkela, Odisha, India. Dr. Sahoo has authored and co-authored 13 research papers and book chapters published in journals and conferences. In 2023, he received the Best Paper Presenter Award at an IEEE conference.

Dhabaleswar Mohapatra is currently working as an Assistant Professor in the Department of Mathematics at the Institute of Technical Education and Research, Siksha "O" Anusandhan (Deemed to be University), Odisha, India. He received his PhD from the National Institute of Technology Rourkela, Odisha, India. To date, Dr. Mohapatra has published 12 research articles in journals and book chapters. His research interests include Type-2 fuzzy uncertainty, static and dynamic problems with uncertainty, numerical and analytical methods, and fuzzy differential and fractional differential equations.

Preface

Soft computing aims to exploit tolerance for imprecision, approximate reasoning, and uncertainty to achieve robustness, tractability, and cost effectiveness for building intelligent machines. Soft computing methodologies include neural networks, fuzzy set theory and logic, genetic algorithms, Bayesian networks, and rough sets, among others. In this regard, neural networks are widely used for modeling dynamic solvers, classification of data, and prediction of solutions, whereas fuzzy sets provide a natural framework for dealing with uncertainty. Artificial Neural Networks and Type-2 Fuzzy Set: Elements of Soft Computing and Its Applications cover the fundamental concepts and the latest research on variants of Artificial Neural Networks (ANN), including scientific machine learning and Type-2 Fuzzy Set (T2FS). In addition, the book also covers different applications for solving real-world problems along with various examples and case studies. It may be noted that a good amount of research has been done on ANN and Fuzzy Set theory/Fuzzy logic. However, Artificial Neural Networks and Type-2 Fuzzy Set is the first book to cover the use of ANN and fuzzy set theory with regards to the Type-2 Fuzzy Set in static and dynamic problems in one place. Artificial Neural Networks and Type-2 Fuzzy Sets are two of the most widely used computational intelligence techniques for solving complex problems in various domains. Both ANN and T2FS have unique characteristics that make them suitable for different types of problems. This book provides the reader with an in-depth understanding of how to apply these computational intelligence techniques in various fields of science and engineering in general, and static and dynamic problems in particular. Further, for validation purposes of the ANN and fuzzy models, the obtained solutions of each model in the book is compared with already existing solutions (in special cases) that have been obtained with numerical or analytical methods.

Snehashish Chakraverty
NIT, Rourkela, India

Arup Kumar Sahoo
S“O”A University, Bhubaneswar, India

Dhabaleswar Mohapatra
S“O”A University, Bhubaneswar, India

Acknowledgements

Professor Snehashish Chakraverty, the first author, extends heartfelt gratitude to his beloved parents, the late Shri Birendra Kumar Chakraborty and late Parul Chakraborty, for their blessings. He also expresses sincere thanks to his wife, Shewli, and daughters, Shreyati and Susprihaa, for their unwavering support and inspiration throughout this project. Appreciation is also extended to the NIT Rourkela administration for their valuable support.

Dr. Arup Kumar Sahoo, the second author, expresses his gratitude to his parents, Shri Antaryami Sahoo and Smt. Jemarani Sahoo, and younger brother, Mr. Swarup Kumar Sahoo. Last but not the least, Dr. Sahoo would like to thank his family members, Shri Ashok Sahoo, Smt. Manjulata Sahoo, Shri Harish Das, Smt. Punam Panda, Dr. Santosh Bej, Smt. Sangeeta Naik, Mr. Soumyaranjan Nayak, Mr. Suraj Kumar Das, Mr. Ankit Sahoo, Mrs. Sasmita Sahoo, Mrs. Mansi Sahoo, Mrs. Srotaswee Jena, and Ms. Prajna Priyadashini for their unwavering love, trust, and moral support.

Dr. Dhabaleswar Mohapatra, the third author, would like to express heartfelt gratitude to his parents, Shri Bhabani Prasad Mohapatra and Smt. Jyotirmayee Mohapatra, and his aunt, Ms. Mamata Dash, for their unwavering support and blessings. Their encouragement and belief in Dr. Mohapatra have been instrumental in achieving this milestone. He cherishes the memory of his late brother, Brahmeshwar Mohapatra, whose guidance and unwavering faith in him were invaluable. His enduring influence and affection continue to inspire and motivate Dr. Mohapatra in every endeavor. He is also deeply thankful to his friends, whose motivation and encouragement provided strength and inspiration, especially during the most challenging phases of this journey.

Furthermore, Dr. Sahoo and Dr. Mohapatra would like to express their sincere gratitude to their doctoral research supervisor Professor S. Chakraverty and his wife Smt. Shewli Chakraverty to encourage them throughout the PhD journey.

The authors extend their heartfelt thanks to the entire team at Elsevier for their support, cooperation, and assistance in facilitating the timely publication of this book. They also express profound appreciation to the authors and researchers whose work is cited in the bibliography and reference sections at the end of each chapter.

1 Introduction to soft computing

Contents

1.1 Introduction ... 1
1.2 Evolution of soft computing ... 2
1.3 Soft computing ... 3
1.3.1 Neural networks ... 3
1.3.2 Fuzzy set theory ... 3
1.3.3 Probabilistic reasoning ... 4
1.3.4 Evolutionary computation ... 4
References ... 5

1.1 Introduction

From apes to Homo-sapiens, humanity has journeyed over millions of years, and continuously striving to shape the world around us to make it more livable. Among mammals, we are the only species that has not only adapted to our environment but has also actively sought to improve it [1]. The development of language played a vital role in this transformation, enabling us to communicate with one another, record our advancements for future, and build on the knowledge of our predecessors. Through this accumulation and transmission of knowledge, we laid the groundwork for progress across various domains. One of the most significant milestones in our development was the invention and utilization of tools. From the stone tools to nuclear machines, technology has evolved with us, empowering our societies to solve complex problems more effectively. This led to the development of different computational approaches, which can broadly be categorized into hard computing and soft computing.

Hard computing techniques depend on precise, deterministic algorithms and traditional mathematical models to deliver exact solutions. These methods are effective for problems with well-defined mathematical solutions. However, many real-world problems are characterized by uncertainty, imprecision, and the need for approximate solutions. This is where soft computing comes into play.

The term Soft Computing was coined by Lotfi A. Zadeh in early 1990s. It encompasses to a collection of computational techniques that aim to model and exploit the inherent tolerance for imprecision and uncertainty in human cognition. Soft computing techniques include neural networks, fuzzy set theory, and probabilistic reasoning. However, latter evolutionary computation, derivative-free optimization techniques such as genetic algorithms, belief networks, and chaotic systems added to it. They provide cost-effective

Artificial Neural Networks and Type-2 Fuzzy Set. https://doi.org/10.1016/B978-0-44-332894-7.00009-5

solutions, making them suitable for tasks like pattern recognition, decision-making, and optimization in complex, dynamic environments. The study of soft computing is essential in today's world as it bridges the gap between traditional computational methods and the demands of modern-day applications, including artificial intelligence, robotics, and data-driven technologies [2].

1.2 Evolution of soft computing

Soft computing has a rich history, starting with the McCulloch–Pitts neuron model in 1943, leading up to the first-ever Nobel Prize win in AI and ML in 2024. Here, we have included some breakthrough inventions in this field [3] [4].

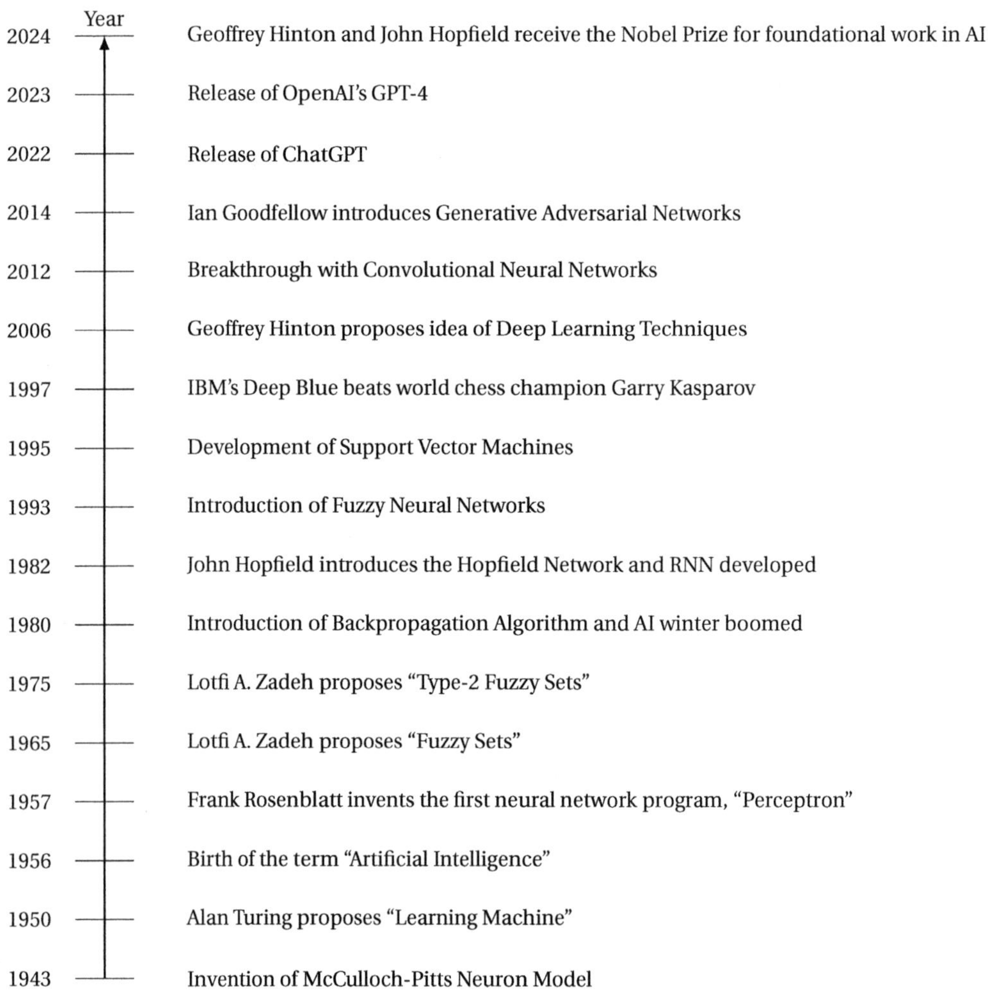

1.3 Soft computing

Here, we have discussed four important aspects of soft computing.

1.3.1 Neural networks

The human brain contains approximately 10^{12} neurons, which rapidly process incomplete information received by perceptrons. It handles visual and auditory information like a parallel computer, performing tasks incredibly faster than modern supercomputers. Inspired by biological neurons, researchers have developed artificial neural network (ANN) models to mimic this information processing capability. Neural networks or connectionist models are considered one of the most significant advancements in the field of artificial intelligence (AI) and have extensive applications in various industries beyond our basic necessities [5].

In the forthcoming chapters of **Unit I**, various ANN models have been studied, and their applications in solving mathematical and physical problems are discussed.

1.3.2 Fuzzy set theory

Fuzzy logic is a kind of reasoning system that imitates human logic, thus it can handle inaccuracy rather than only definite truths as in classical logic. The main idea is that things are not only either true or false, black or white; they may also exist in shades of gray. This is particularly important when modeling real-world systems, as they often contain some vagueness, ambiguity, and fuzziness. Fuzzy logic was initially invented by Lotfi A. Zadeh in 1965 as a tool to depict the uncertainty arising from imprecise information [6]. Zadeh found that many real-world conditions are more complex than binary logic-either true or false can grasp. Fuzzy logic offers a method to capture this kind of in-between "partial" truth.

The concept of basic logic involves fuzzy sets, which are a generalization of classical set theory. A classic set takes an element either into it or not at all. The concept of fuzzy sets differs because elements can partially belong to a set by virtue of having a membership value from 0 to 1. The degree of membership allows an element to relate to the extent that it belongs to a given fuzzy set. For example, suppose we want to classify a group of people as "tall people." Instead of a binary classification where someone is either "tall" or "not tall," a membership is defined, where each person's height is mapped to a membership value between 0 and 1. A person who is 6 feet tall might have a membership value of 0.8 in the "tall" set, while someone who is 5.5 feet tall might have a membership value of 0.4. This gradual transition allows fuzzy logic to more accurately model real-world situations where concepts like "tall" are not strictly defined but rather exist on a continuum.

Furthermore, in fuzzy logic, variables can be described using words (or linguistic variables) rather than precise numerical values. Each linguistic variable can take on one or more fuzzy terms, which are represented by fuzzy sets. For example, a linguistic variable like temperature might have fuzzy terms such as "cold," "warm," and "hot." Each of these terms corresponds to a fuzzy set with its own membership function. The temperature 60°F might belong to the "cold" set with a membership value of 0.3, to the "warm" set with a membership value of 0.7, and to the "hot" set with a membership value of 0.

A fuzzy inference system processes inputs by first converting precise values into fuzzy values through fuzzification, applying fuzzy rules to evaluate outcomes, and then translating the fuzzy output back into a crisp value through defuzzification. This process allows fuzzy systems to make decisions even when the input information is ambiguous or incomplete. Fuzzy logic has a wide range of applications, particularly in control systems, decision-making, and artificial intelligence. It is widely used in systems where precision is difficult to achieve or unnecessary, such as in consumer electronics, robotics, and expert systems. Despite its advantages in handling uncertainty, fuzzy logic systems can be subjective when defining fuzzy sets and rules, and in more advanced versions, like Type-2 fuzzy systems, can increase computational complexity. Nonetheless, its ability to model human-like reasoning makes it invaluable in many fields.

In the subsequent chapters of **Unit II**, various aspects of fuzzy set theory will be explored in depth, including the development of different types of fuzzy sets, such as Type-1 and Type-2 fuzzy sets. Their applications in solving both static and dynamical problems will be discussed.

1.3.3 Probabilistic reasoning

Probabilistic reasoning is a kind of reasoning that deals with uncertainty using principles from the theory of probability. Unlike deterministic reasoning, probabilistic reasoning models situations where one cannot be sure of the truth or an outcome but can represent it in terms of likelihoods or probabilities. Probabilistic reasoning has myriad applications across various fields. It is particularly useful in artificial intelligence and machine learning for predicting outcomes, classifying data, and optimizing choices between two or more alternatives, especially when decisions are made under conditions of uncertainty. For instance, Bayesian networks and hidden Markov models are widely used in natural language processing and robotics, allowing systems to make intelligent decisions based on incomplete or uncertain data. In day-to-day decision-making, probabilistic reasoning can help improve risk assessment and lead to more informed decisions in areas such as financial investment, medical treatment selection, and climate forecasting. By embracing uncertainty, probabilistic reasoning provides a strong framework for operating in complex and uncertain environments through the quantification of uncertainty.

1.3.4 Evolutionary computation

Today's intelligence is not the result of an overnight process; it traces back to the Stone Age, when humans first discovered that round stones were easier to move than other shapes, leading to the first ever invention of mankind, i.e., the wheel. Nature has been guiding us with valuable lessons for millennia, helping us develop machines and tools. Inspired by these principles, AI researchers have sought to replicate aspects of human intelligence in AI, which has led to advancements in evolutionary computation [7].

Evolutionary computation or evolutionary algorithm plays a crucial role in solving optimization problems where traditional heuristic methods may not provide solutions [8]. Techniques like genetic algorithms are commonly used and have been successfully applied to a wide range of problems, from complex engineering designs to machine learning tasks, data mining, and even game development. Additionally, evolutionary strategies and genetic programming are used to solve optimization challenges, particularly in cases where the search space is vast or poorly understood.

Evolutionary computation has proven to be highly effective in various domains, offering robust solutions to complex problems where conventional methods struggle to perform efficiently. It is also conceptually simple and can be represented mathematically as

$$x[t+1] = s(v(x[t])), \tag{1.1}$$

where $x[t]$ represents the population at time t, v is the random variation operator (mutation or crossover), and s is the selection operator, which determines the survival of the fittest individuals in the population. This iterative process continues until an optimal solution is reached.

This simplicity, merged with its adaptability, makes evolutionary computation a powerful tool for handling complex optimization and search problems across diverse fields.

References

[1] D. Khemani, A First Course in Artificial Intelligence, McGraw Hill Education, India, 2013.

[2] J.-S.R. Jang, C.-T. Sun, E. Mizutani, Neuro-fuzzy and soft computing—a computational approach to learning and machine intelligence, IEEE Transactions on Automatic Control 42 (10) (1997) 1482–1484.

[3] Pearson Education, Machine learning, Pearson Education India, 2019.

[4] A.K. Sahoo, S. Chakraverty, Machine intelligence in dynamical systems: A state-of-art review, Wiley Interdisciplinary Reviews: Data Mining and Knowledge Discovery 12 (4) (2022) e1461.

[5] I. Goodfellow, Y. Bengio, A. Courville, Deep Learning, MIT Press, 2016.

[6] L.A. Zadeh, Fuzzy sets, Information and Control (1965).

[7] S.N. Sivanandam, S.N. Deepa, Principles of Soft Computing, John Wiley & Sons, 2007.

[8] A.K. Sahoo, S. Chakraverty, Modeling of Mexican hat wavelet neural network with L-BFGS algorithm for simulating the recycling procedure of waste plastic in ocean, Journal of Engineering Management and Systems Engineering 2 (1) (2023) 61–75.

PART 1

Artificial neural network

Smart things can outsmart us.
Geoffrey Hinton (Nobel Laureate, 2024)

2

Artificial neural network: an overview

Contents

2.1 Introduction to machine learning **10**
2.2 Types of data **10**
2.2.1 Data visualization 10
2.2.1.1 Boxplot 11
2.2.1.2 Histogram 11
2.2.1.3 Scatter plot 11
2.3 Training of ML model **12**
2.3.1 Hold-out sample validation 14
2.3.2 K-fold cross-validation 15
2.4 The birth and evolution of artificial neural network **15**
2.4.1 Topology of ANN 17
2.4.2 Types of learning 17
2.4.3 Applications 18
2.5 Learning rules **18**
2.5.1 Backpropagation learning algorithm 19
2.6 Configuration in neural network **19**
2.7 Activation functions **21**
2.8 Regularization **23**
2.9 Optimization **24**
2.9.1 Gradient decent 25
2.9.2 Adam 25
2.9.3 L-BFGS 26
References **27**

Chapter points

- Discuss the basics of machine learning algorithms and dataset management.
- Discuss bird's-eye view of ANN.
- Discuss various neural network components.
- Basic Python codes are implemented.

Artificial Neural Networks and Type-2 Fuzzy Set. https://doi.org/10.1016/B978-0-44-332894-7.00011-3

2.1 Introduction to machine learning

In 1997, IBM's Deep Blue computer program defeated the world champion, Mr. Garry Kasparov, in a chess match game [1]. This was the time when the most significant number of people began to pay serious attention to the fast evolving field, namely machine learning (ML). However, the desire to create a machine that can think dates back to ancient Greece, when mythical figures like Pygmalion and Daedalus envisioned the creation of life through artificial means [2].

The term ML was first coined by Alan Turing in 1950 [3]. In his historical paper [3], Turing posed the groundbreaking question, "Can machines think?" As of today, ML has become a mature technology, finding its applications in every aspect of life. It powers everything from music recommendations in applications to a medical diagnosis. Though there are many definitions of ML, the most widely accepted one by Professor Tom M.Mitchell, is "*A computer program is said to learn from experience E with respect to some class of tasks T and performance measure P, if its performance at tasks in T, as measured by P, improves with experience E*" [4].

2.2 Types of data

The first step in building ML models, or data-hungry models, begins with the dataset. A dataset is a collection of related information, where each piece of data is characterized by one or more attributes. These attributes provide information about specific characteristics of the data. In Fig. 2.1 an overview of the different types of data is provided.

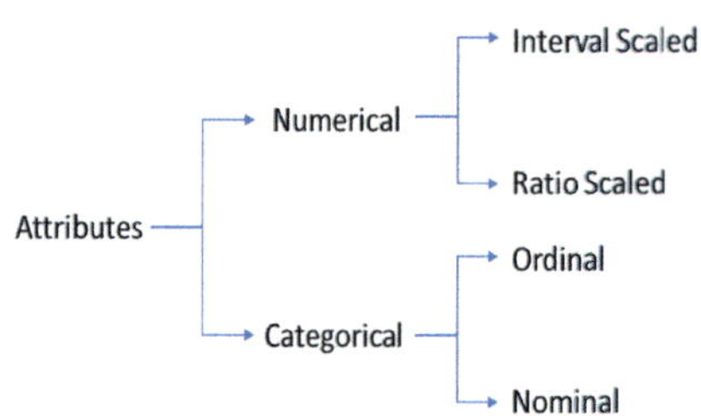

FIGURE 2.1 Types of attributes.

2.2.1 Data visualization

Data visualization is the graphical representation of data through charts, graphs, and maps, making it easier to identify trends, outliers, and patterns. It is particularly essential in the era of Big Data, allowing users to translate complex and high volume data to the non-technical audiences. In our book, we have extensively used boxplot, histogram, and scatter plot to present and compare the obtained solutions with the ground truth and the corresponding errors.

2.2.1.1 Boxplot

A boxplot is also known as box-and-whisker plot. It is a graphical representation of the distribution of a dataset. It is based on a five-number summary of dataset, including "minimum, first quartile (Q1), median (Q2), third quartile (Q3), and maximum" as shown in Fig. 2.2. The *matplotlib* library in Python provides tools to draw boxplots from a dataset. Here is a sample code to draw a boxplot and the corresponding output is provided in Fig. 2.3.

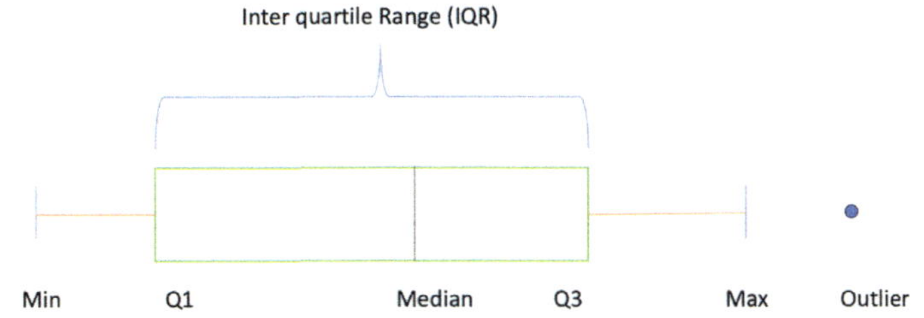

FIGURE 2.2 Schematic diagram of a boxplot.

```
import matplotlib.pyplot as plt

# Sample data set
ds1 = [32,42,44,45,46,47,48,50,60]

# Create a boxplot
plt.boxplot(ds1, vert=False)

# Display the plot
plt.show()
```

Listing 2.1: Creating a boxplot using matplotlib.

2.2.1.2 Histogram

A histogram is a 2D graphical representation of the numerical data. The data is divided into intervals, known as "bins" and the height of each bar indicates the frequency of data points within that bin. It is useful for displaying the general distributional features and shape of the dataset. Below is a sample Python code using the matplotlib library, and the output histogram is shown in Fig. 2.4.

2.2.1.3 Scatter plot

A scatter plot/scatter graph/scatter diagram is a 2D graph and helps to visualize the bivariate relationship through points and dots. One attribute is plotted on the horizontal axis,

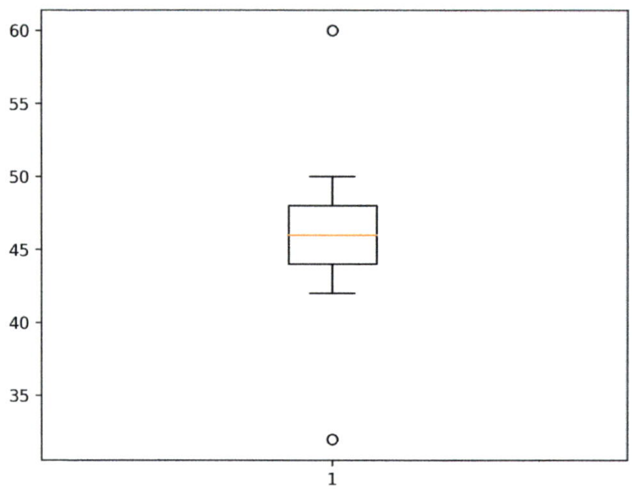

FIGURE 2.3 Output of boxplot for ds1.

```
import matplotlib.pyplot as plt
import numpy as np

# Sample data: Ages of a group of people
ds2 = [22, 23, 25, 25, 26, 30, 30, 32, 35, 35, 36, 38, 40, 42, 45, 48, 50, 50, 52, 55, 60,
    65, 70, 75, 80, 85]

# Create a histogram
counts, bins, patches = plt.hist(ages, bins=10, alpha=0.7, color='green', edgecolor='red')

# Add titles and labels
plt.xlabel('Age')
plt.ylabel('Frequency')

# Display the plot
plt.show()
```

Listing 2.2: Creating a customized boxplot using matplotlib.

while the another attribute is plotted on the vertical axis. It is a widely used data visualization diagram by ML users. Below is the sample Python code by using the matplotlib library and Fig. 2.5 represents the corresponding output of a scatter plot.

2.3 Training of ML model

Machine learning is the study and development of algorithms that can learn from data and make predictions on unseen data. These algorithms work by making decisions through

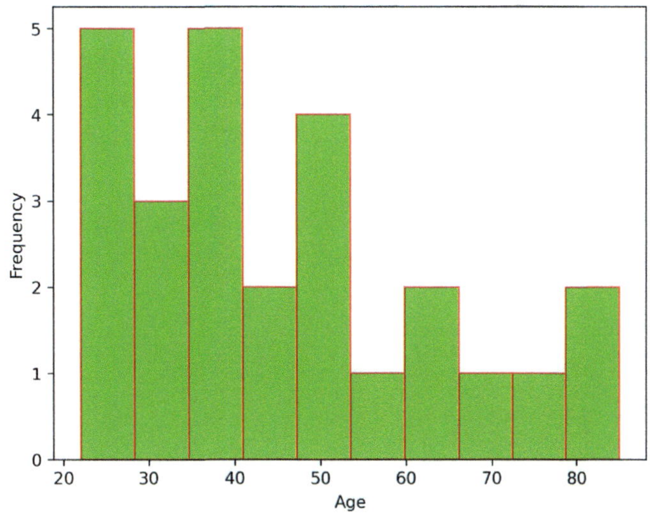

FIGURE 2.4 Output of the histogram for ds2.

```python
import matplotlib.pyplot as plt

# Data: Runs scored, Balls faced, Opponent, and Venue
runs = [85, 55, 16, 103, 95, 0, 88, 101, 51, 117, 54]
balls = [116, 57, 18, 97, 103, 9, 94, 121, 56, 113, 63]

# Create a scatter plot
plt.figure(figsize=(12, 8))
plt.scatter(balls, runs, color='blue', edgecolor='black', s=100, alpha=0.7)

# Add labels and title
plt.title("Virat Kohli's Scores in ODI World Cup 2023")
plt.xlabel("Balls Faced")
plt.ylabel("Runs Scored")

# Display the plot
plt.grid(True)
plt.show()
```

Listing 2.3: Scatter plot of Virat Kohli's scores in the ODI World Cup 2023.

building a mathematical function from training data. Suppose the input variables are denoted as $X = \{x_1, x_2, x_3, ...x_n\}$ and the output variable is denoted by Y. Then the relationship between X and Y may be written as [5]

$$Y = f(X) + e, \tag{2.1}$$

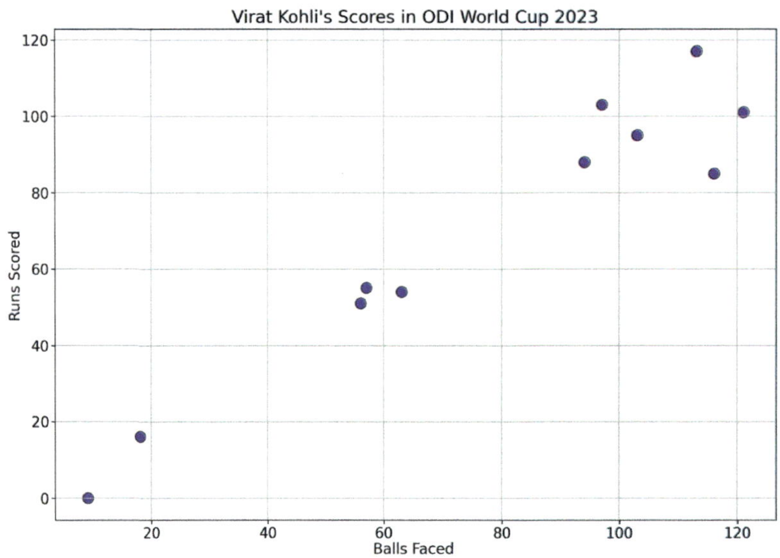

FIGURE 2.5 Scatter plot showing Virat Kohli's runs scored against balls faced in the ODI World Cup 2023.

where f is the target function and e is the error term.

There are various methods to split the data for training and validation of ML models. Here, we will discuss the hold-out sample validation and K-Fold cross-validation methods.

2.3.1 Hold-out sample validation

It is the process of splitting a dataset into two disjoint subsets: the training set and the validation set, for a supervised model. Typically, the labeled data is divided in a $4:1$ ratio (or another ratio depending on the size of data) between training and validation. It is the simplest and is easily applicable algorithm to large datasets. However, it fails when the dataset size is relatively small.

Fig. 2.6 illustrates the schematic diagram of the hold-out sample validation method. The below Python code demonstrates how to split the dataset into training and testing sets using *train_test_split* from *scikit-learn*:

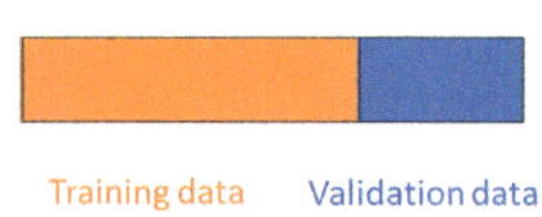

FIGURE 2.6 Schematic diagram of hold-out sample validation.

```
# Importing necessary library
from sklearn.model_selection import train_test_split

# Split the dataset into training and testing sets (4:1)
X_train, X_test, y_train, y_test = train_test_split(X, y, test_size=0.2,
    random_state=40)
```

Listing 2.4: Train-test split for the hold-out method.

2.3.2 K-fold cross-validation

K-fold cross-validation comes to action when the dataset is relatively small. It used to train and validate a ML model by randomly splitting the data into "K" disjoint folds (groups). The model is trained for "K-1" folds and test for 1 fold. This process repeated for "K" times. However, the computational cost of this technique is quite high in comparison to holdout method.

Fig. 2.7 is the schematic diagram of the K-fold cross-validation method for $K = 5$. The below Python code demonstrates the implementation of K-fold cross-validation into the ML model using the `scikit-learn` library.

```
# Importing necessary library
from sklearn.model_selection import KFold

# Define KFold Cross Validation with 5 folds
kf = KFold(n_splits=5, shuffle=True, random_state=42)
```

Listing 2.5: Train-test split for K-fold cross-validation method.

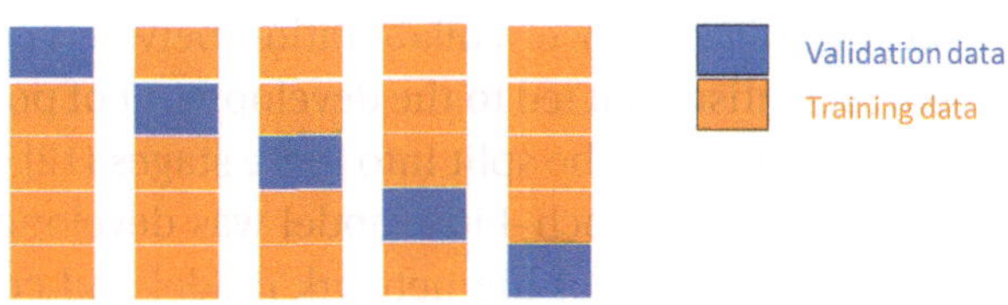

FIGURE 2.7 Schematic diagram of K-fold cross-validation.

2.4 The birth and evolution of artificial neural network

The history of ANN traces back to the early 1940s when researchers began investigating the workings of the brain and how it processes information. In the middle of 20th century, while World War II was still raging, Warren S. McCulloch and Walter Pitts proposed neuron activities that merged the studies of mathematical logic and neurophysiology. In their historical paper [8], they developed the first elementary model of ANN, in which neurons were escorted by the "*all-or-none*" process:

$$\mathbb{R}^n \ni \zeta \mapsto \sigma\left(\sum_{i=1}^{n} w_i \zeta_i\right), \sigma(\zeta) = 0 \text{ if } \zeta < \theta, \text{ else } 1, \tag{2.2}$$

where $\theta \in \mathbb{R}$ is a threshold and $\sigma : \mathbb{R} \to \mathbb{R}$ is an activation function. It brings a revolution in the field of computer science and attracts researchers to work on it.

In 1956 for the first time, John McCarthy coined the term "**Artificial intelligence**" during a famous workshop at Dartmouth College, USA. Later in 1960s, development on the backpropagation (BP) algorithm was started, and it gained popularity by Rumelhart in 1986 [9]. After the development of the BP algorithm, various dynamical problems have been handled using ANN, which may sometimes be difficult to solve using the traditional methods.

In the 1990s, architectures for deep learning (DL) and notable training algorithms commenced to develop [10]. DL is a kind of ANN that uses multiple layers to learn complex patterns from data. It also serves as dynamical solvers having a wide range of applications, including image and speech recognition. During this time, another revolution came in ANN when industries had started using it to provide services such as fraud detection, credit scoring, and speech recognition.

During the 2000s and 2010s, ANN had seen a surge in popularity and was established as a crucial asset in both the academic and industrial sectors [11]. Notably, prominent industries such as technology giants in the MAANG group (Meta, Amazon, Apple, Netflix, and Google) and sensitive research fields like atomic energy, pharmaceutical manufacturing, and stock markets embraced the use of ANNs and invested billions of dollars in its advancement.

Overall, the history of ANNs is a story of collaboration between computer scientists, mathematicians, and neuroscientists that led to the development of powerful tools for understanding and processing data. It may be split into three stages [12]. In the first stage of ANN development in 1960s, the McCulloch–Pitts model was developed [8]. The key feature of that time was the establishment of the network model and compliance with the learning algorithm. Moreover, in the 1980s, the second stage of neural networks development was started to show some significant results. Finally, in 1990s the mature period was started when significant enhancements to the neural networks architecture and theories were produced. With an increase in global requirements, scientists around the world have been working towards the development of various novel and efficient AI techniques.

According to Sahoo and Chakraverty [6], "ANN is a branch of ML that mimics the training process of the human brain to predict patterns from the given historical data. Neural networks are processing devices of mathematical algorithms that can be implemented by computer programming." The basic structure of ANN includes the following.

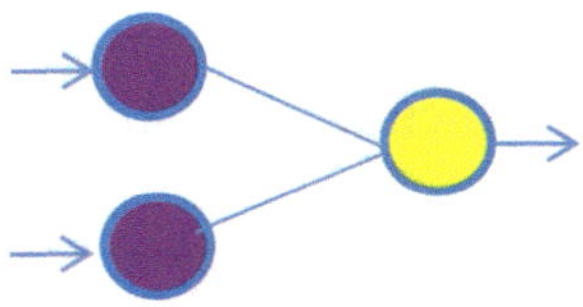

FIGURE 2.8 Architecture of a perceptron.

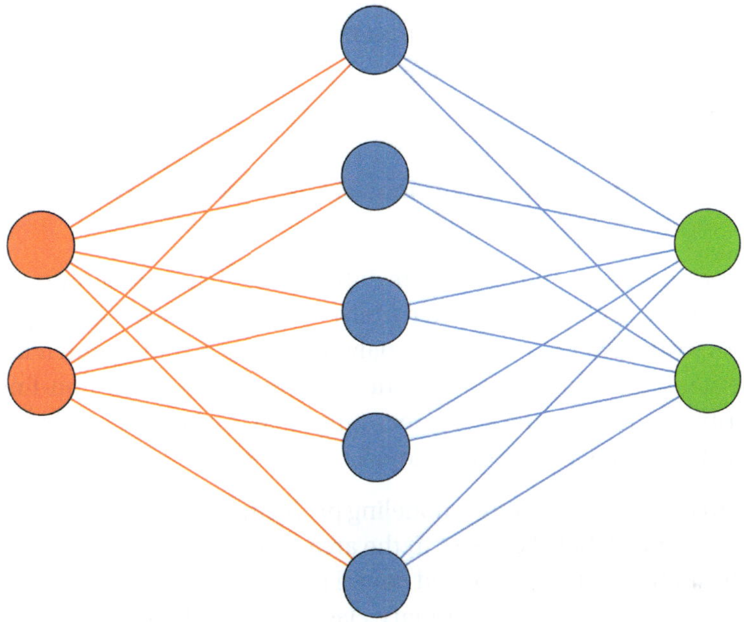

FIGURE 2.9 Architecture of a shallow neural network.

2.4.1 Topology of ANN

ANN is closely related to the ML approach that acquires knowledge from different parameters and learning algorithms [7]. Neural networks are composed of layers and neurons, as shown in Figs. 2.8–2.9. ANN handles data in the same way as the human brain does. It reads input and output values of the training dataset and updates values of parameters to minimize the error of predicted value. One complete cycle of passing the training algorithm and updating parameters is called an epoch. The error is minimized using an optimal number of epochs. But when a network has been trained for a long time, it loses its capacity to generalize. The accuracy of a neural network is improved through hyper-parameter tuning [10].

2.4.2 Types of learning

One of the important characteristics of ANN is their ability to learn from any given domain. The learning methods in ANN are broadly classified into three types:

a) *Supervised learning*: In this paradigm, the network is trained with the labeled data; for instance, classification of objects, prediction of the share value of a company, weather forecast, etc.
b) *Unsupervised learning*: Here, the network is trained using unlabeled data, i.e., only input data is known during the training. Clustering of objects is an example of unsupervised learning.
c) *Reinforcement learning*: It aims to optimize the reward received by the system through trial and error. Here, the machine learns from its own experience. Self-driving cars, ChatGPT are examples of reinforcement learning.

2.4.3 Applications

ANN is a computational model that performs tasks like prediction, classification, decision-making, etc.

Prediction is a non-linear and often quite difficult task that is certainly necessary nowadays. The goal is to anticipate the future pattern of a system based on its prior behavior. Neural networks work better at predictive analytics because of the hidden layers. The advantage of the neural networks model is the capacity to establish non-linear relations among the attributes. The accuracy of forecasting is largely influenced by a comprehensive study of the input data, feature selection, and biases.

Classification refers to a predictive modeling problem where the input data is classified as one of the predefined labeled classes. In the area of data mining, classification is one of the most significant fields of research, and neural networks are one of the most extensively used approaches for classification. In binary classification, there are two neurons in the output layer. Whereas in multi-class classification, the number of neurons in the output layer is equal to the unique classes, each representing 0/1 output for one class.

A **decision** model attempts to anticipate the judgment of humans based on the aspects that he or she considers when making the decision. In most cases, these models have linear functional forms, and they estimate using regression models. Each decision is obtained by a complex process of simultaneous execution of a large number of neurons, which is usually very hard to interpret. ANN is highly suitable to such decision-making areas (such as medical diagnosis, finance) where decision transparency is critical and human experts are unable to explain their decisions.

2.5 Learning rules

Learning constitutes the pivotal process within the architecture of ANNs, involving the essential task of updating the parameters of the model [13]. However, there are different kinds of learning rules that are employed in the neural networks. Among them, the delta learning rule or back-propagation (BP) algorithm is commonly used.

2.5.1 Backpropagation learning algorithm

The Backpropagation learning algorithm or backward propagation of error is a fundamental technique used in multi-layer ANNs. It focuses on updating the parameters of network in such a way that the difference between the ground truth and the predicted output can be minimized. It works by calculating the error and then propagating this error backward through the network to adjust the values of weights by the chain rule. By iteratively adjusting these weights in the opposite direction of the gradient of error, the network learns to approximate complex functions. These iterations are known as epochs. It continues until the stopping criteria is achieved by the network. The BP learning algorithm is a cornerstone of deep learning and has played a crucial role in the success of neural networks in various applications.

2.6 Configuration in neural network

ANN acquires knowledge from different parameters and learning algorithms. It is made up of layers and neurons as shown in Fig. 2.10.

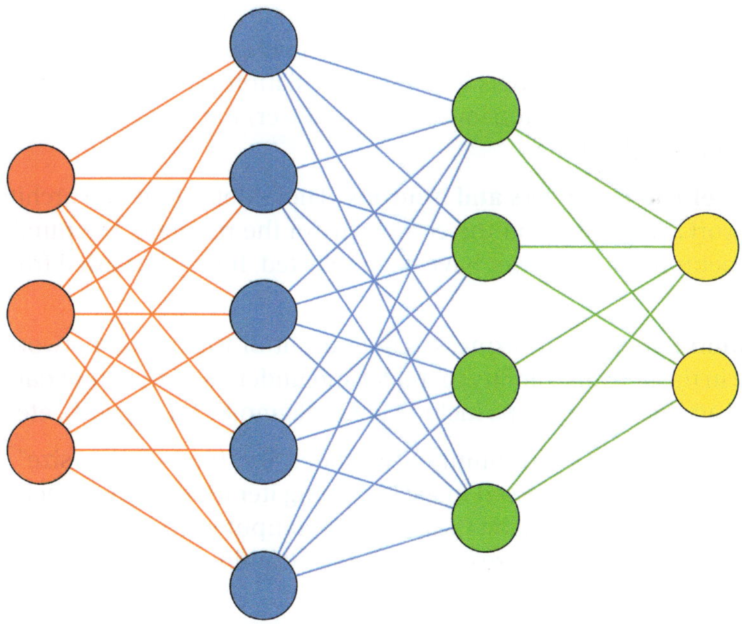

FIGURE 2.10 Architecture of a deep neural network.

The no free lunch theorem [14] states that no ML algorithm is universally superior to all others. In other words, if one algorithm performs exceptionally well on a particular class of problems, there must be another algorithm that outperforms it on a different class of problems. Therefore, selecting the most suitable architecture for solving a specific problem is crucial. In neural networks, there are two key types of configuration settings:

- ***Parameters***
  Parameters are the internal variables that the neural network learns from the training data. It includes the weights and biases of the neural network. The values of parameters are adjusted during the training process using various optimization algorithms. However, the objective of training is to find the optimal values that minimize the error. Parameters are specific to the neural network architecture and are learned automatically through the training process.
- ***Hyper-parameters***
  Hyper-parameters are settings and configurations that are set prior to the training process of neural network. They control various aspects of the architecture and the training process itself. It includes:

  (i) **Learning Rate (η):** It represents the magnitude of the stepsize by which the parameters of model are adjusted in optimization. However, the choice of the learning rate is problem dependent, and it also relies on the optimization algorithm and the architecture of model. Typically, the values of the learning rate range from 0.1 to 0.0001. It may be noted that a higher learning rate (0.1 or higher) may cause the optimization process to diverge, as the steps are too large, leading to oscillations or overshooting the minimum point. A learning rate that is too low (0.0001 or lower) may lead in slow convergence or getting stuck in local optima.

  (ii) **Number of Hidden Layers and Neurons:** These determine the architecture of the neural network. Depending on the complexity of the problem, the number of hidden layers and neurons in each layer have been selected. It may be varied from problem to problem.

  (iii) **Activation Functions:** It expresses the output of the neural network and plays a crucial role in the network's ability to model and understand the input data. Some commonly used activation functions include ReLU, Sigmoid, Tanh, Swish, etc.

  (iv) **Batch Size:** During the training of a model, the term "batch size" refers to the number of data points processed in each training iteration. During each iteration, the parameters are updated based on the gradients computed on the current batch of training data. The choice of batch size can impact the training process and the performance of the neural model.

  (v) **Epochs:** It refers to one complete pass of the entire training dataset through the network. In each epoch, the model iterates over the entire dataset, computes the loss, and updates its parameters using the optimization algorithm. The relation among batch size, iteration, and epoch may be given as

$$\text{Iterations per Epoch} = \frac{\text{Total number of training examples}}{\text{Batch Size}}.$$

(vi) **Regularization:** Regularization refers to any modification made to a learning algorithm to reduce the generalization error, rather than minimizing the training error. It is commonly used to prevent overfitting during the training of the model. Popular regularization techniques include L^1 and L^2 parameter regularizations, as well as early stopping.

Choosing the right hyper-parameters is crucial because it decides the accuracy of the ANN prediction. It often involves experimentation, trial, and error to find the best settings for a particular problem. In summary, parameters are learned from data, while hyper-parameters are set manually and influence the architecture and behavior of the neural network as well as the training process. Accurate tuning of hyper-parameters are crucial to achieving the best performance in neural network models. Next, we will discuss some important hyper-parameters of ANN.

2.7 Activation functions

In the feed-forward neural network, all nodes are fully connected by weights. There exist one or more hidden layers between the input and output layer. The input layer receives the signals, multiplies them by the weights of interneuron connections, then adds them together in order to send one or more hidden layers. The summed value passes through mathematical equations known as an activation function that shapes the output of a neural network. The activation functions have influenced the expressivity of the network. In this regard, some potential activation functions are sigmoid, tanh, arctan, Relu, and Swish, which are defined next:

(i) ***Sigmoid***:

The sigmoid activation function is most commonly used activation function in ANN models having a range in (0,1). It is a bounded, monotonic, and differentiable function. It may be defined as

$$f(x) = \frac{1}{1 + \exp(-kx)}.$$

Fig. 2.11 depicts the sigmoid activation function.

(ii) ***Tanh***:

The hyperbolic tangent function (Tanh) is bounded, monotonic, and an infinitely differentiable function. Tanh activation function is depicted in Fig. 2.12 and may be written as

$$f(x) = \frac{\exp(x) - \exp(-x)}{\exp(x) + \exp(-x)}.$$

The range of the Tanh function is $(-1, 1)$.

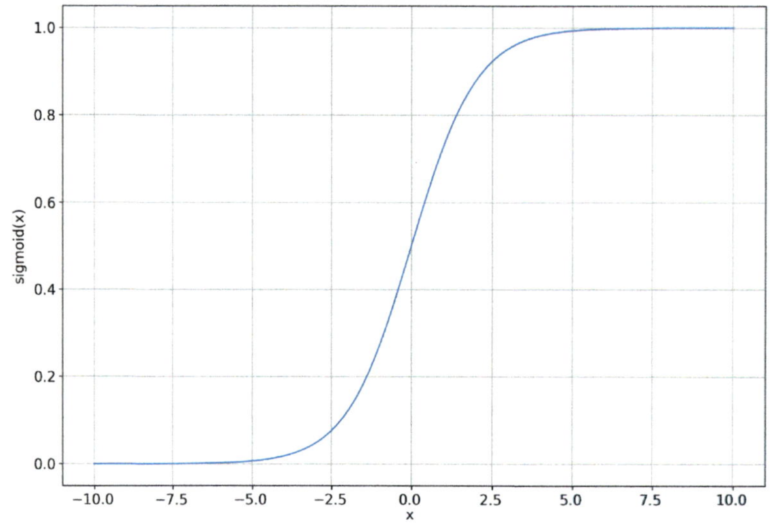

FIGURE 2.11 Sigmoid activation function.

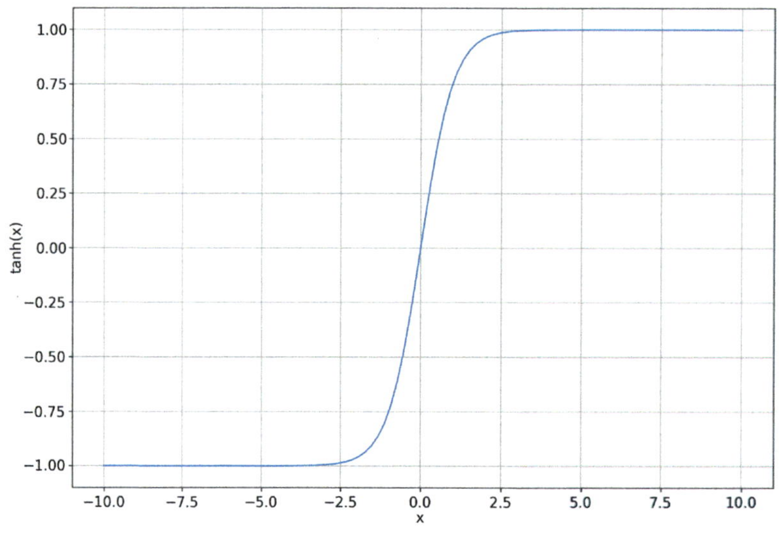

FIGURE 2.12 Tanh activation function.

(iii) ***Relu***:

Relu (Rectifier Linear Unit) is also known as a positive-part function and may be written as

$$f(x) = \max\{0, x\}.$$

The relu activation function is unbounded, monotonic, and differentiable having a range in $[0, \infty)$. It is widely used in the architecture of CNN. Fig. 2.13 represents the graph of the relu activation function.

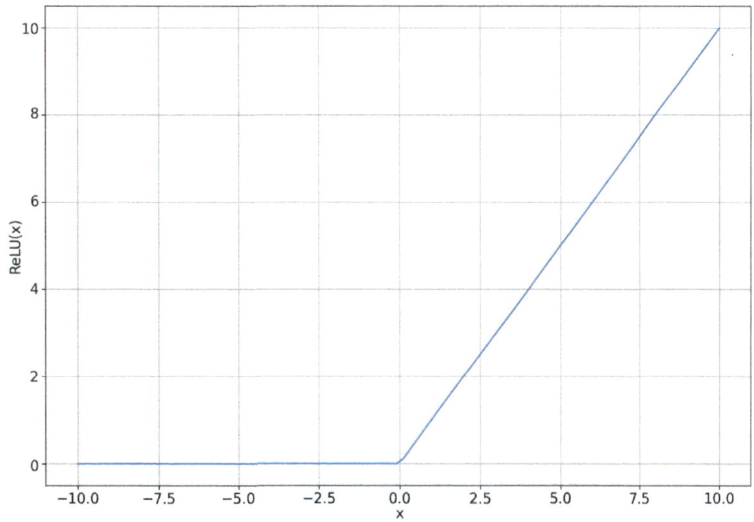

FIGURE 2.13 Relu activation function.

(iv) ***Swish***:

Swish is a state-of-art activation function developed by Google AI lab. It is defined as

$$f(x) = \frac{x}{1 + \exp(-ax)}, a \in [0, \infty].$$

The swish activation function has a range of $(-\infty, \infty)$. It is an infinitely differentiable function on its domain. Fig. 2.14 shows the graphical presentation of the swish activation function.

2.8 Regularization

Regularization techniques are used to prevent ANNs from overfitting and improve the generalization of a model. During training, a model sometimes memorizes the training data, including noise and outliers, instead of learning the underlying patterns. However, this can lead to reduced accuracy during the prediction on unseen data. Regularization introduces a penalty term to the loss function, and avoids it from fitting the training data too closely. Moreover, the three common regularization techniques are L^1 parameter regularization (lasso), L^2 parameter regularization (ridge), and dropout. Below is the Python code to implement activation functions and regularizations in ANN using the Tensorflow deep learning package.

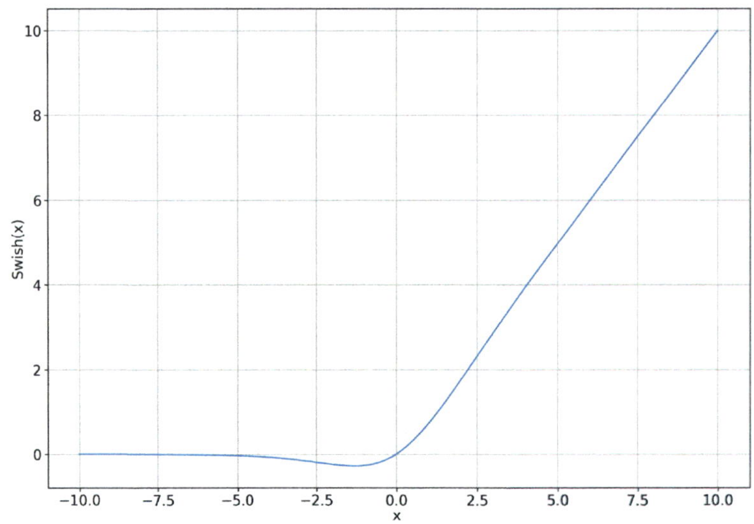

FIGURE 2.14 Swish activation function.

```
import tensorflow as tf
from tensorflow.keras import layers, models, regularizers

# Define a neural network model with L1 and L2 regularization
model = models.Sequential([
layers.Dense(32, activation='relu', kernel_regularizer=regularizers.l1(0.01), input_shape
    =(10,)),
layers.Dense(16, activation='relu', kernel_regularizer=regularizers.l2(0.01)),
layers.Dense(1, activation='sigmoid')
])
```

Listing 2.6: Deployment of L1 and L2 regularization and activation functions in ANN.

2.9 Optimization

Optimization is a fundamental process in the field of ANNs, and it plays a crucial role during the training of ANN models. Optimization algorithms are used to adjust the parameters of the ANN model in order to minimize the cost function. For example, in image classification, the cost function might measure how far off the predicted class probabilities are from the ground truth. Similarly, in NLP, when training a recurrent neural network (RNN) to generate human-like text, optimization is employed to minimize the discrepancy between the machine-generated text and real human-generated text. This optimization process entails the adjustment of ANN parameters, such as weights, with respect to the gradients of the cost function.

Optimization is not limited to neural networks; it is a core concept in ML. Various optimization algorithms, such as gradient descent, Adam, etc., have been developed in recent years. The choice of the optimization algorithm can significantly impact the convergence speed of the ML model. Modern deep learning frameworks such as Pytorch, Tensorflow, etc. provide a variety of optimization algorithms, making it easier to train ANN models. Here, we have discussed gradient descent, Adam, and L-BFGS optimizers.

2.9.1 Gradient decent

Gradient descent is a fundamental optimization algorithm used in ML, DL, and other optimization problems. It minimizes the given loss function by iteratively adjusting parameters of the model in the direction that leads to a reduction in the cost. The key step in the gradient descent optimization algorithm is as follows.

Algorithm 2.9.1. Pseudo-code for Gradient Decent

$$v_t \leftarrow v_{t-1} - \eta \frac{\partial}{\partial v_{t-1}} J(v)$$

Here, η is the learning rate and $J(v)$ is the loss function.

2.9.2 Adam

Adaptive Moment Estimation (Adam) is an advanced optimization algorithm used in ML and DL. It combines techniques from both the RMSprop and momentum methods to achieve faster and more reliable convergence. Here are the key components and features of the Adam optimization algorithm.

Adaptive Learning Rates: It adjusts the learning rates for each parameter individually to enhance convergence and generalization. It computes and stores a separate learning rate for each parameter based on the historical gradient information. This helps to overcome the challenges of manual learning rate tuning.

Momentum: Adam incorporates a momentum term, similar to the traditional gradient descent with momentum. This term allows the optimizer to carry information from previous updates, which may help it to overcome the local optima and achieve faster convergence.

Bias Correction: It performs the bias correction to counteract the effects of initially large moving averages. This correction proves beneficial during the early stages of training when the moving averages are not reliable.

The pseudo-code for Adam optimization algorithm is as follows [15].

Algorithm 2.9.2. Pseudo-code for Adam optimization

$$m_t \leftarrow \beta_1 m_{t-1} + (1-\beta_1)\frac{\partial J}{\partial w_{t-1}}$$

$$m_t^{corrected} \leftarrow \frac{m_t}{1-\beta_1^t}$$

$$v_t \leftarrow \beta_2 v_{t-1} + (1-\beta_2)(\frac{\partial J}{\partial w_{t-1}})^2$$

$$v_t^{corrected} \leftarrow \frac{v_t}{1-\beta_2^t}$$

$$\Delta w \leftarrow \frac{\eta}{\sqrt{v_t^{corrected}}+\epsilon} m_t^{corrected}$$

$$w_{new} \leftarrow w_{old} - \Delta w$$

2.9.3 L-BFGS

The L-BFGS optimization algorithm is an iterative method commonly used for solving unconstrained non-linear optimization problems. L-BFGS belongs to the class of quasi-Newton methods and is especially well suited for optimizing functions that are expensive to compute, as it approximates the Hessian matrix without explicitly computing or storing it. By maintaining a limited memory of past iterations, L-BFGS efficiently adjusts the search direction, making it particularly effective for high-dimensional problems. However, this algorithm maintains a balance between the convergence properties of Newton's method and the memory requirements of traditional BFGS methods. The pseudo-code for L-BFGS optimization algorithm is as follows [16].

Algorithm 2.9.3. Pseudo-code for L-BFGS Optimization

Initialize:

x_0 (initial guess)

m (size of memory)

$k = 0$ (iteration counter)

max_iterations

tolerance (convergence tolerance)

$H_0 = I$ (initial inverse Hessian approximation)

Repeat until convergence or max_iterations reached:

Compute g_k (gradient of the objective function at x_k)

Compute search direction p_k :

If $k = 0$:

$p_k \leftarrow -g_k$

Else:

Compute differences:

$s_i \leftarrow x_k - x_{k-i}$

$y_i \leftarrow g_k - g_{k-i}$

Update the inverse Hessian approximation H_k :

Using s_i and y_i, update H_k

Compute search direction p_k :

$p_k \leftarrow -H_k g_k$

Line search to find step size α_k :

Perform line search to find optimal α_k satisfying Wolfe conditions

Update position:

$x_{k+1} \leftarrow x_k + \alpha_k p_k$

Check for convergence:

If $\|g_{k+1}\| <$ tolerance:

Convergence achieved

Break

Update iteration counter:

$k \leftarrow k + 1$

Return:

x_{k+1} (optimized solution)

g_{k+1} (final gradient)

References

[1] B. Pandolfini, Kasparov and Deep Blue: The Historic Chess Match Between Man and Machine, Simon and Schuster, 1997.
[2] C. Martin, Metamorphoses, WW Norton & Company, 2004.
[3] A.M. Turing, Computing Machinery and Intelligence, Springer, 2009.
[4] T. Mitchell, Introduction to Machine Learning, Machine Learning, vol. 7, McGraw-Hill, New York, 1997, pp. 2–5.
[5] S. Dutt, S. Chandramouli, A.K. Das, Machine Learning, Pearson Education, India, 2018.

[6] S. Kumar, A.K. Sahoo, S. Chakraverty, Comparative study of Chebyshev and Legendre polynomial-based neural models for approximating multidimensional poverty for an Indian state, in: Polynomial Paradigms: Trends and Applications in Science and Engineering, IOP Publishing, Bristol, UK, 2022, p. 13-1.
[7] J. Zurada, Introduction to Artificial Neural Systems, West Publishing Co., 1992.
[8] W.S. McCulloch, W. Pitts, A logical calculus of the ideas immanent in nervous activity, The Bulletin of Mathematical Biophysics 5 (1943) 115–133.
[9] D.E. Rumelhart, G.E. Hinton, R.J. Williams, Learning representations by back-propagating errors, Nature 323 (6088) (1986) 533–536.
[10] I. Goodfellow, Y. Bengio, A. Courville, Deep Learning, MIT Press, 2016.
[11] D. Scherer, A. Müller, S. Behnke, Evaluation of pooling operations in convolutional architectures for object recognition, in: International Conference on Artificial Neural Networks, 2010, pp. 92–101.
[12] C.S. Vui, G.K. Soon, C.K. On, R. Alfred, P. Anthony, A review of stock market prediction with artificial neural network (ANN), in: 2013 IEEE International Conference on Control System, Computing and Engineering, 2013, pp. 477–482.
[13] A.K. Sahoo, S. Chakraverty, An unsupervised wavelet neural network model for approximating the solutions of non-linear nervous stomach model governed by tension, food and medicine, Computer Methods in Biomechanics and Biomedical Engineering (2023) 1–14.
[14] D.H. Wolpert, W.G. Macready, No free lunch theorems for optimization, IEEE Transactions on Evolutionary Computation 1 (1) (1997) 67–82.
[15] S. Chakraverty, S. Mall, Artificial Neural Networks for Engineers and Scientists: Solving Ordinary Differential Equations, CRC Press, 2017.
[16] A.K. Sahoo, S. Chakraverty, Modeling of Mexican hat wavelet neural network with L-BFGS algorithm for simulating the recycling procedure of waste plastic in ocean, Journal of Engineering Management and Systems Engineering 2 (1) (2023) 61–75.

3 Mathematical formulation of the neural network for differential equations

Contents

3.1 Introduction 29
3.2 Differential equations 30
3.3 Incorporating neural networks into ordinary differential equations 30
3.3.1 Formulation of first-order differential equations with initial conditions 32
3.3.2 Formulation of second-order differential equations with initial conditions 32
3.3.3 Formulation of second-order differential equations with boundary conditions 33
3.4 Example illustration 33
References 34

Chapter points

- Discuss the fundamentals of differential equations.
- Explore the application of artificial neural networks in solving differential equations.

3.1 Introduction

Though ANN was invented in the mid-1940s, it was limited to data driven sectors only [1]. However, it became popular among mathematicians in the 1990s after Lee and Kang solved the first-order differential equations (DE) by using a novel Hopfield neural network model [2]. In order to solve DEs, neural networks can be modeled as a constrained optimization problem with the goal to minimize an error function defined by the DE and initial and/or boundary conditions. The neural outputs are incorporated into an approximation solution, which reduces the constrained optimization problem to an unconstrained optimization problem in order to exactly satisfy the initial/boundary conditions. In 1998, Lagaris et al. employed the above concept and proposed a trial solution for DE with regular boundaries, which satisfy the given initial and/or boundary conditions [3]. Nonetheless, these methods were confined to problems with well-defined boundaries.

In the field of ANN modeling for dynamical problems the radial basis function networks (RBFN) and multi-layer perceptron (MLP) are two common feed-forward neural network

Artificial Neural Networks and Type-2 Fuzzy Set. https://doi.org/10.1016/B978-0-44-332894-7.00012-5

models that have been employed to solve DEs [4]. However, the concept of incorporating ANN to dynamical problems was initially proposed in 1998 by Lagaris et al. [3]. In their investigation, 2D and 3D partial differential equations with irregular domain boundaries using a hybrid of MLP and RBFN were addressed successfully. Since then, ANNs have received significant attention from the mathematicians and applied to solve various engineering application problems. Likewise, Hoda and Nagla investigated ANN models for solving a mixed boundary value problem (BVP) using a similar network configuration [5]. In an important work, Mall and Chakraverty proposed a regression-based multi-layer neural network in order to solve DEs. Instead of taking random initial weights, they fixed the values of weights by polynomial regression [6,7].

In recent years, notable developments have been made in the field of ANN for solving various dynamical problems associated with specific properties, including but not limited to lie symmetry DEs [8], stiff DEs [9], delay DEs [10], fractional DEs [11], stochastic DEs [12], fuzzy DEs [13], and singularly perturbed DEs [14].

3.2 Differential equations

Dynamical systems are served as the mathematical backbone for modeling scientific and engineering problems. These mathematical models are typically expressed through DEs, tailored to the specific physical problem at hand. A DE is defined as an equation that involves one dependent variable and its derivatives with respect to one or more independent variables. The following are some examples of DEs:

$$\frac{dy}{dx} = x; \tag{3.1}$$

$$\frac{dy}{dx} + 3x = y; \tag{3.2}$$

$$\frac{d^2y}{dx^2} + \frac{dy}{dt} + y = 0. \tag{3.3}$$

3.3 Incorporating neural networks into ordinary differential equations

General nth-order ODEs can be written as

$$\Gamma\left(t, \phi(t), \phi'(t), \phi''(t), \ldots, \phi^{(n)}(t)\right) = 0, t \in \overline{D} \subset \mathbb{R}^n \tag{3.4}$$

where $\phi(t)$ is the determined solution, $\overline{D}$ the discretized domain over a finite set of points, and $t = (t_1, t_2, \ldots, t_n) \in \mathbb{R}^n$.

Let, $\phi_\tau(t; p)$ indicate the initial ANN approximate solution with adjustable parameters p, then Eq. (3.4) can be rewritten as

$$\Gamma\left(t_i, \phi_\tau(t_i; p), \phi'_\tau(t_i; p), \phi''_\tau(t_i; p) \ldots \phi^{(n)}_\tau(t_i; p)\right) = 0. \tag{3.5}$$

The corresponding error function of ANN can be obtained by converting Eq. (3.5) to an unconstrained optimization problem. It can be written as

$$E(p) = \min_{p} \sum_{t_i \in \overline{D}} \left(\Gamma \left(t_i, \phi_\tau(t_i; p), \phi'_\tau(t_i; p), \phi''_\tau(t_i; p) ... \phi_\tau^{(n)}(t_i; p) \right) \right)^2. \tag{3.6}$$

The initial ANN approximate solution $\phi_\tau(t; p)$ is expressed as the sum of two terms [3]:

$$\phi_\tau(t; p) = \alpha + \Gamma(t, ANN(t; p)), \tag{3.7}$$

where the first part of the approximate solution, i.e., α is associated with the initial and/or boundary conditions, without the adjustable parameters. The subsequent part of the approximate solution $ANN(t; p)$ is an output of ANN that consists of M hidden layers, with k neurons in each hidden layer, and a linear output node for a given input $t \in \mathbb{R}^n$. Fig. 3.1 represents a schematic diagram of a multi-layer neural network for solving DE with a dependent variable t. Weights and biases of $ANN(t; p)$ are adjusted to deal with the minimization of the cost function. The output of ANN can be written as

$$ANN(t; p) = \sum_{j=1}^{k} v_j \sigma(z_j) \tag{3.8}$$

such that

$$z_j = \sum_{i=1}^{n} w_{ji} t_i + b_j. \tag{3.9}$$

Here, v_j, w_{ji} represents the synaptic weights from the hidden unit j to the output unit and from the input unit i to the hidden unit j; respectively, b_j is the biases, k represents the number of neurons, and $\sigma(z_j)$ denotes activation function (swish, sigmoid, tanh, etc.).

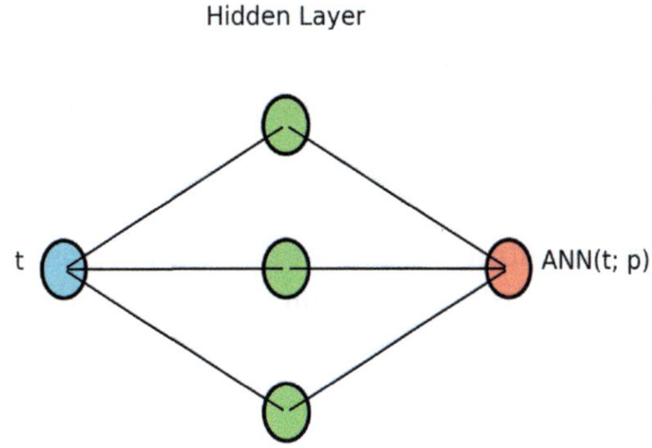

FIGURE 3.1 Block diagram of an artificial neural network (ANN) showing input t and output ANN $(t; p)$.

In particular, let us take swish as an activation function. Then Eq. (3.8) becomes

$$ANN(t;\, p) = \sum_{j=1}^{k} v_j \frac{z_j}{1+\exp(-az_j)},\ a \in [0, \infty). \tag{3.10}$$

3.3.1 Formulation of first-order differential equations with initial conditions

Let us consider the first-order ODE as below:

$$\frac{dy}{dt} = f(t, y) \tag{3.11}$$

with initial condition $y(a) = y_0$.

As discussed above the corresponding initial ANN approximate solution may be written as

$$\phi_\tau(t;\, p) = y_0 + (t-a)ANN(t;\, p), \tag{3.12}$$

where $ANN(t;\, p)$ is the neural network output with input data set t and parameters p. Moreover, $\phi_\tau(t;\, p)$ satisfies the initial condition of the given differential equation.

The error function for the first-order ODE may be calculated as

$$E(p) = \sum_{i=1}^{n} \left(\frac{d\phi_\tau(t_i;\, p)}{dt} - f(t_i, \phi_\tau(t_i;\, p)) \right)^2. \tag{3.13}$$

Here, t_i are discrete points in the domain of t.

3.3.2 Formulation of second-order differential equations with initial conditions

Let us consider the second-order ODE as below:

$$\frac{d^2y}{dt^2} = f(t, y, \frac{dy}{dt}), \tag{3.14}$$

with the initial conditions $y(a) = y_0$ and $\frac{dy(a)}{dt} = v_0$.

Here, the corresponding initial ANN approximate solution may be written as

$$\phi_\tau(t;\, p) = y_0 + v_0(t-a) + (t-a)^2 ANN(t;\, p), \tag{3.15}$$

where $ANN(t;\, p)$ is the FFNN output with input data t and parameters p. The initial ANN approximate solution $\phi_\tau(t;\, p)$ satisfies the initial condition of the given differential equation.

The error function for the second-order ODE may be calculated as

$$E(p) = \sum_{i=1}^{n} \left(\frac{d^2\phi_\tau(t_i;\, p)}{dt^2} - f\left(t_i, \phi_\tau(t_i;\, p), \frac{d\phi_\tau(t;\, p)}{dt}\right)\right)^2. \tag{3.16}$$

3.3.3 Formulation of second-order differential equations with boundary conditions

Let us consider the second-order ODE with two-point Dirichlet BC as

$$\frac{d^2y}{dt^2} = f(t, y, \frac{dy}{dt}), \tag{3.17}$$

with the boundary conditions $y(a) = A$ and $y(b) = B$.

The corresponding initial ANN approximate solution is written as

$$\phi_\tau(t; p) = A(t - b) + B(t - a) + (t - a)(t - b)ANN(t, \theta). \tag{3.18}$$

The error function for the second-order ODE may be calculated as

$$E(p) = \sum_{i=1}^{n} \left(\frac{d^2\phi_\tau(t; p)}{dt^2} - f\left(t, \phi_\tau(t; p), \frac{d\phi_\tau(t; p)}{dt}\right)\right)^2. \tag{3.19}$$

3.4 Example illustration

Let us consider a harmonic oscillator equation:

$$\frac{d^2y}{dt^2} = -ky \tag{3.20}$$

with initial conditions $y(0) = y_0$ and $\frac{dy}{dt}(0) = v_0$. Here, $f(t, y, \frac{dy}{dt}) = -ky$.

Implementing the ANN approach, we will get

$$\phi_\tau(t; p) = y_0 + v_0 t + t^2 \text{ANN}(t; p). \tag{3.21}$$

At $t = 0$, the ANN solution becomes

$$\phi_\tau(t; p) = y_0. \tag{3.22}$$

It may be noted that the initial ANN approximate solution has been selected in a way that it satisfies the given conditions. As discussed above the error function may be written as

$$E(p) = \sum_{i=1}^{n} \left(\frac{d^2\phi_\tau(t_i; p)}{dt^2} + k\phi_\tau(t_i; p)\right)^2. \tag{3.23}$$

In order to adjust the parameters p and minimize error $E(p)$ a suitable optimization technique will be applied. This will result to find an ANN approximate solution to the harmonic oscillator differential equation.

References

[1] S. Chakraverty, S.K. Jeswal, Applied Artificial Neural Network Methods for Engineers and Scientists: Solving Algebraic Equations, World Scientific, 2021.

[2] H. Lee, I.S. Kang, Neural algorithm for solving differential equations, Journal of Computational Physics 91 (1) (1990) 110–131.

[3] I.E. Lagaris, A. Likas, D.I. Fotiadis, Artificial neural networks for solving ordinary and partial differential equations, IEEE Transactions on Neural Networks 9 (5) (1998) 987–1000.

[4] L.S. Tan, Z. Zainuddin, P. Ong, Wavelet neural networks based solutions for elliptic partial differential equations with improved butterfly optimization algorithm training, Applied Soft Computing 95 (2020) 106518.

[5] S.A. Hoda, H.A. Nagla, Neural network methods for mixed boundary value problems, International Journal of Nonlinear Science 11 (3) (2011) 312–316.

[6] S. Chakraverty, S. Mall, Artificial Neural Networks for Engineers and Scientists: Solving Ordinary Differential Equations, CRC Press, 2017.

[7] S. Mall, S. Chakraverty, Comparison of artificial neural network architecture in solving ordinary differential equations, Advances in Artificial Neural Systems 2013 (2013) 12.

[8] Y. Wen, T. Chaolu, X. Wang, Solving the initial value problem of ordinary differential equations by Lie group based neural network method, PLoS ONE 17 (4) (2022) e0265992.

[9] T. Schneidereit, M. Breuß, Computational characteristics of feedforward neural networks for solving a stiff differential equation, Neural Computing & Applications (2022) 1–15.

[10] C.J. Zúñiga-Aguilar, A. Coronel-Escamilla, J.F. Gómez-Aguilar, V.M. Alvarado-Martínez, H.M. Romero-Ugalde, New numerical approximation for solving fractional delay differential equations of variable order using artificial neural networks, The European Physical Journal Plus 133 (2) (2018) 1–16.

[11] M. Shoaib, A.Z. Abbasi, M.A.Z. Raja, K.S. Nisar, A design of predictive computational network for the analysis of fractional epidemical predictor-prey model, Chaos, Solitons and Fractals 165 (2022) 112812.

[12] L. Gonon, C. Schwab, Deep ReLU neural network approximation for stochastic differential equations with jumps, Preprint, arXiv: arXiv:2102.11707, 2021.

[13] M. Mosleh, M. Otadi, Simulation and evaluation of fuzzy differential equations by fuzzy neural network, Applied Soft Computing 12 (9) (2012) 2817–2827.

[14] H. Liu, B. Xing, Z. Wang, L. Li, Legendre neural network method for several classes of singularly perturbed differential equations based on mapping and piecewise optimization technology, Neural Processing Letters 51 (3) (2020) 2891–2913.

4

Recent trends in activation functions for solving differential equations

Contents

4.1 Introduction 35
4.2 Methodology 36
4.3 Simulation results and discussions 36
4.3.1 Experimental setup 37
4.3.2 Model problems 37
4.4 Validation 44
References 44

Chapter points

- Review various activation functions and their impact on the accuracy and efficiency of solving differential equations using artificial neural networks.
- Analyze the computational time of activation functions during the training process.
- Discuss recent advancements in activation functions specifically tailored for solving complex and high-dimensional differential equations.

4.1 Introduction

Activation functions play a crucial role in artificial neural networks (ANN), and acting as the core mathematical mechanisms that enable models to capture complex patterns and nonlinear relationships [1]. As machine learning (ML) techniques have evolved, so too has the need to address more sophisticated problems, such as the solution of differential equations. These equations arise in various domains and often describe dynamic systems that are both time-dependent and nonlinear. Traditionally, solving differential equations (DEs) has relied on numerical methods such as finite difference or finite element techniques. However, the advent of ML, and particularly the growing interest in ANN has opened up new frontiers for addressing these complex problems [2].

In this context, the selection of activation functions has become crucial to the efficacy of neural networks in solving DEs. For decades, standard activation functions like sigmoid, ReLU, and tanh have been widely used, but as the challenges in dynamical modeling have grown, new and modified activation functions have emerged. These innovations aim to improve convergence, stability, and accuracy when dealing with the unique characteristics

Artificial Neural Networks and Type-2 Fuzzy Set. https://doi.org/10.1016/B978-0-44-332894-7.00013-7

of DEs. This chapter explores the latest developments in activation functions, discussing their impact on solving DEs and their potential for advancing fields like robotics, fluid dynamics, and autonomous systems.

4.2 Methodology

Let us consider the first-order ODE as

$$y' = f(t, y), t \in [a, b] \tag{4.1}$$

with the initial condition $y(a) = \hat{\alpha}$. Consequently, the ANN trial solution can be written as

$$\phi_\tau(t; p) = \hat{\alpha} + (1 - e^{-(t-a)})N(t; p), \tag{4.2}$$

where $N(t; p)$ is the output of the Mth hidden layer with one input variable t, and parameters p. The ANN approximate solution $\phi_\tau(t; p)$ satisfies the initial conditions of the given DE. In order to find the cost function, we may need to calculate the gradient of the network $N(t; p)$ with respect to input t. It can be computed as follows:

$$D^m N(t; p) = \sum_{j=1}^{k} v_j w_{ji}^m \sigma^{(m)}(z_j). \tag{4.3}$$

Here, $\sigma^{(m)}(z_j)$ represents the mth-order derivative of the activation function. Differentiating Eq. (4.2) with respect to t, we have

$$\begin{aligned} D^m \phi_\tau(t; p) &= D^m\left[(1 - e^{-(t-a)})N(t; p)\right] \\ &= D^m\left[(1 - e^{-(t-a)}) \sum_{i=1}^{n} \sum_{j=1}^{k} v_j \frac{w_{ji}t_i + b_j}{1 + \exp(-a(w_{ji}t_i + b_j))}\right] \end{aligned} \tag{4.4}$$

Thus the cost function for Eq. (4.1) is written as

$$E(p) = \sum_{i=1}^{n} (D\phi_\tau(t_i; p) - f(t_i, \phi_\tau(t_i; p)))^2. \tag{4.5}$$

4.3 Simulation results and discussions

In this section, some fundamental DEs have been solved in order to show the accuracy of the swish activation function. Here, we have taken two first-order ODEs and one second-order ODE to show the reliability of the swish activation function [3]. The accuracy of the result has been shown in the tables and graphs.

4.3.1 Experimental setup

Our experiments have been carried out in the Google Colab environment using Python 3.0 tailored code developed by the author. Adam optimization exhibits rapid convergence and relatively consistent stability. It computes the gradient of a loss function with respect to the adaptable parameters of neural network and adjusting their values using a stepsize regulated by a learning rate $\eta = 0.001$.

4.3.2 Model problems

Example 4.1. Let us consider an ODE as

$$\frac{du}{dt} = \sin t, \tag{4.6}$$

with initial conditions $u(0) = -1$.

Accordingly, the ANN trial solution may be written as [4]

$$\phi_\tau(t; p) = -1 + (1 - e^{-t})N(t; p)|_{u \to \hat{\alpha} = -1}. \tag{4.7}$$

Here, a multi-layer neural network (MLNN) has been constructed to handle this ODE. The undertaken model consists of one input node, one output node, and three hidden layers, each having 16 nodes. The training dataset contains 50 equispaced points with white noise in $t \in [0, 5]$. The Adam optimizer has been used in order to minimize the loss function Eq. (4.5) with a learning rate of 0.001. Then, the model has been trained for 3,000 epochs with batch size 100.

The training and validation loss against the epochs are delineated in Fig. 4.1. The comparison of exact solutions and the ANN results obtained using different activation functions (swish, sigmoid, and tanh) are presented in Table 4.1 and Fig. 4.2. One may observe that the MAE for ANN predicted results with tanh, sigmoid, and swish activation functions are determined to be 0.033611, 0.002133, and 0.000968, respectively, for 51 testing points. This shows the swish activation function outperforms the other two activation functions.

Example 4.2. Let us consider another benchmark ODE that was solved in the first-ever ANN's paper for solving dynamical problems as follows [5]:

$$\frac{du}{dt} + tu + \left(\frac{1 + 3t^2}{1 + t + t^3}\right) u = t^3 + 2t + t^2 \left(\frac{1 + 3t^2}{1 + t + t^3}\right), t \in [0, 4] \tag{4.8}$$

with initial conditions $u(0) = 1$.

Accordingly, the ANN trial solution may be written as

$$\phi_\tau(t; p) = 1 + (1 - e^{-t})N(t; p)|_{u \to \hat{\alpha} = 1}. \tag{4.9}$$

The problem has been solved by using a MLNN with 16 nodes in each of the four hidden layers. We have trained the network for 100 equispaced points in $t \in [0, 4]$ using different activation functions in particular swish, sigmoid, and tanh activation functions. The Adam

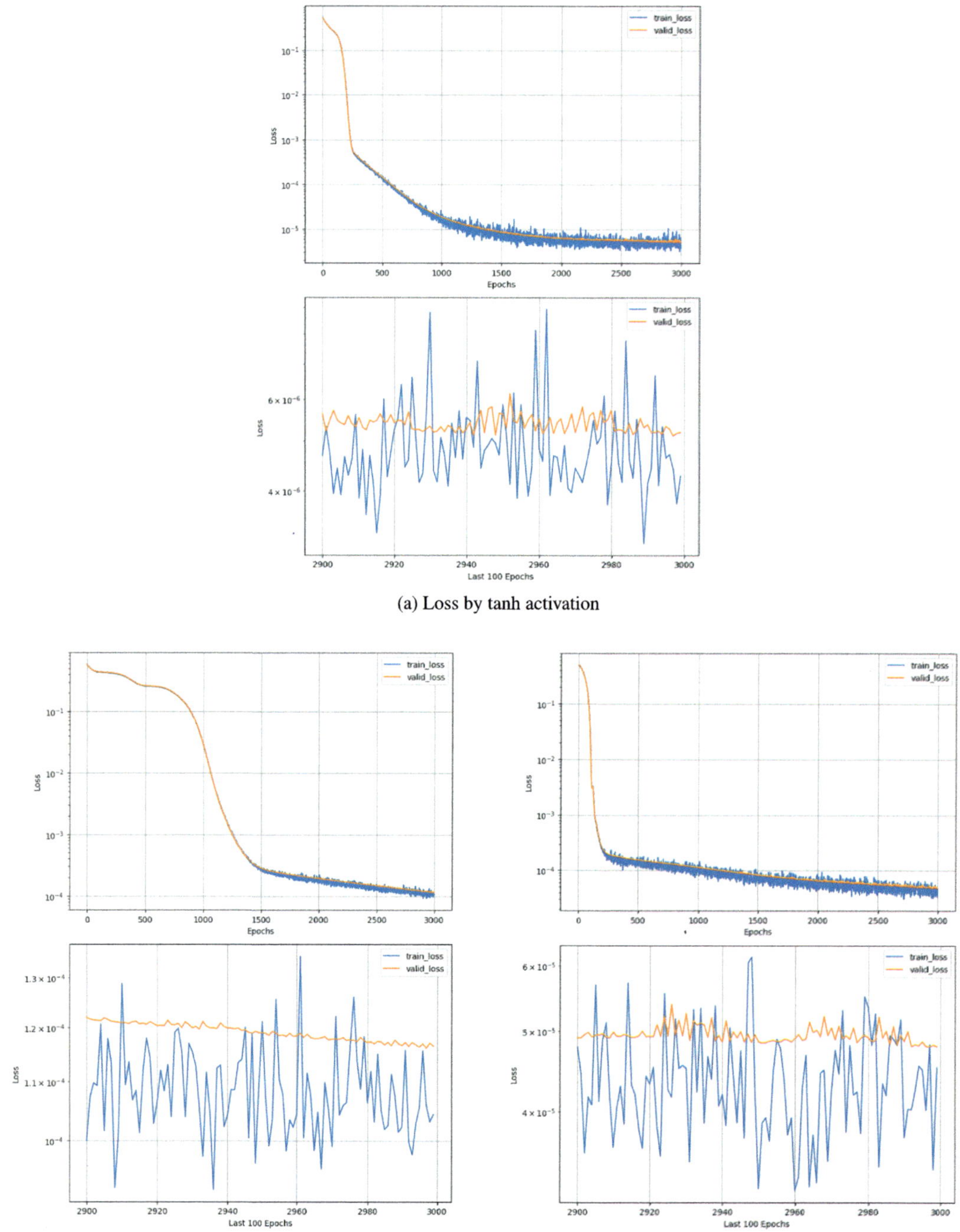

(a) Loss by tanh activation

(b) Loss by sigmoid activation

(c) Loss by swish activation

FIGURE 4.1 Training and validation loss during the learning process of ANN for Example 4.1.

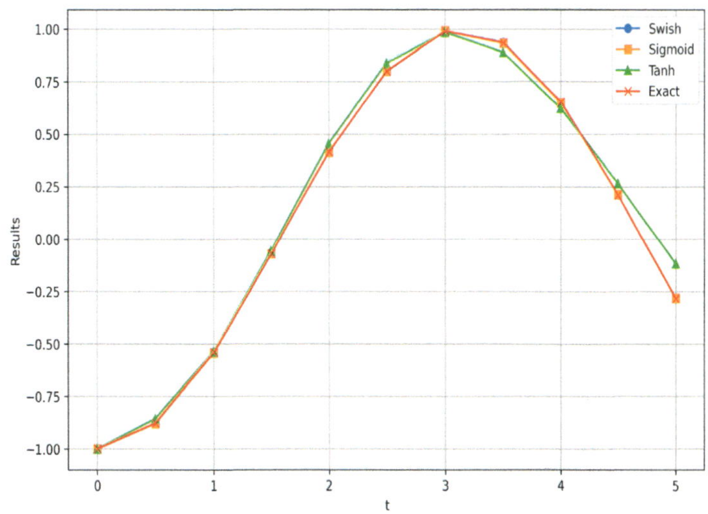

FIGURE 4.2 Comparison of exact and ANN solutions using tanh, sigmoid, swish activation functions for Example 4.1.

Table 4.1 Exact and neural results using tanh, sigmoid, and swish activation functions for Example 4.1.

Input Data (t)	Exact Solutions	Neural Results		
		Swish	Tanh	Sigmoid
0.0	−1.000000	−1.000000	−1.000000	−1.000000
0.5	−0.877583	−0.877733	−0.857186	−0.879666
1.0	−0.540302	−0.540542	−0.537531	−0.542869
1.5	−0.070737	−0.070176	−0.058511	−0.069973
2.0	0.416147	0.416025	0.454092	0.413635
2.5	0.801144	0.800239	0.838221	0.802065
3.0	0.989993	0.991215	0.984749	0.992363
3.5	0.936457	0.937928	0.890023	0.933523
4.0	0.653644	0.651465	0.622978	0.649700
4.5	0.210796	0.211493	0.265551	0.213542
5.0	−0.283662	−0.281852	−0.116924	−0.282420

optimizer has been used in order to minimize the loss function Eq. (4.5) with a learning rate of 0.001. Then, the model has been trained for 6,000 epochs with batch size 50. The loss function of training and validation are contemplated in Fig. 4.3.

Table 4.2 shows a comparison among exact solutions and ANN results using different activation functions. One may very well observe that the swish activation function has better accuracy than the other two activation functions. These results have also been presented graphically in Fig. 4.4. In the context of this problem, the MAE for ANN results with tanh, sigmoid and swish activation functions are obtained as 0.006593, 0.091514, and 0.002213, respectively.

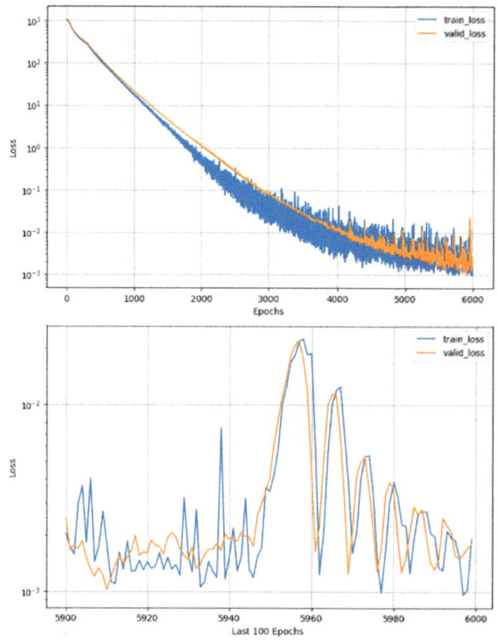

(a) Loss by tanh activation

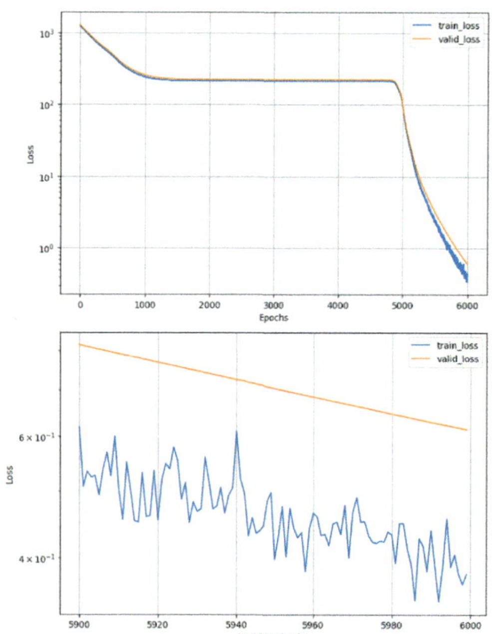

(b) Loss by sigmoid activation

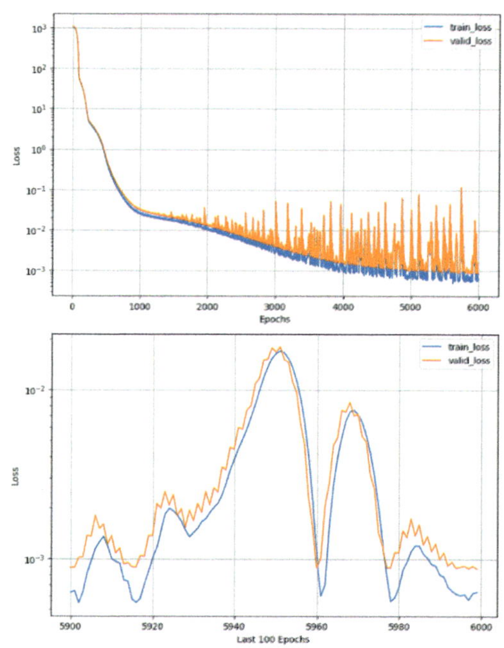

(c) Loss by swish activation

FIGURE 4.3 Training and validation loss during learning process of ANN for Example 4.2.

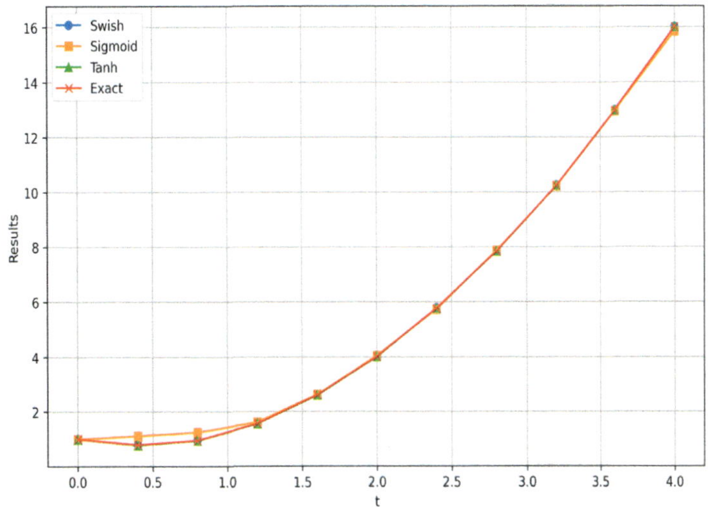

FIGURE 4.4 Comparison of exact and ANN solutions using tanh, sigmoid, swish activation functions for Example 4.2.

Table 4.2 Exact and neural results using tanh, sigmoid, and swish activation functions for Example 4.2.

Input Data (t)	Exact Solutions	Neural Results		
		Swish	Tanh	Sigmoid
0.0	1.000000	1.000000	1.000000	1.000000
0.4	0.790544	0.787635	0.779221	1.116027
0.8	0.954078	0.952345	0.948429	1.249454
1.2	1.563919	1.565384	1.555932	1.618520
1.6	2.601523	2.601765	2.587743	2.616003
2.0	4.012303	4.010789	4.002766	4.045648
2.4	5.763259	5.765523	5.758163	5.722214
2.8	7.840770	7.843517	7.832715	7.866045
3.2	10.240162	10.236738	10.238516	10.220222
3.6	12.960030	12.963239	12.956316	12.940410
4.0	16.000005	15.999987	16.003906	15.853582

Example 4.3. In this example, we consider vibration of a spring-mass system with the $m = 1$ slug. The spring constant is $k = 4\,\text{lb/ft}$, without damping force and the forcing function is $100\cos(\epsilon t)$ for $\epsilon > 0$. The corresponding DE of motion is [6]:

$$m\frac{d^2x}{dt^2} + kx = 100\cos(\epsilon t) \tag{4.10}$$

Substituting $m = 1$ and $k = 4$, we get

$$\frac{d^2x}{dt^2} + 4x = 100\cos(\epsilon t)$$

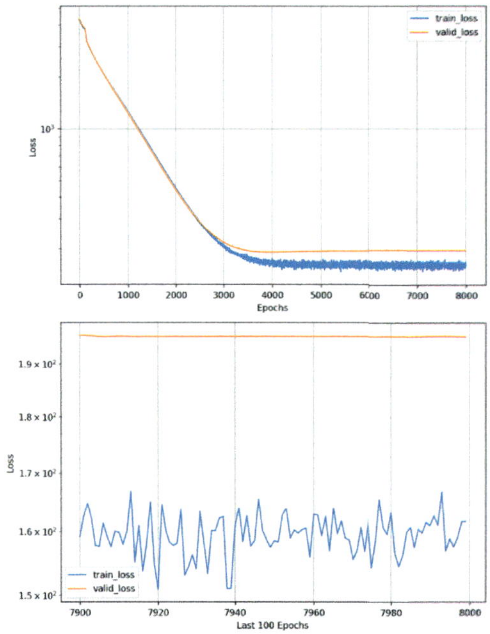

(a) Loss by tanh activation

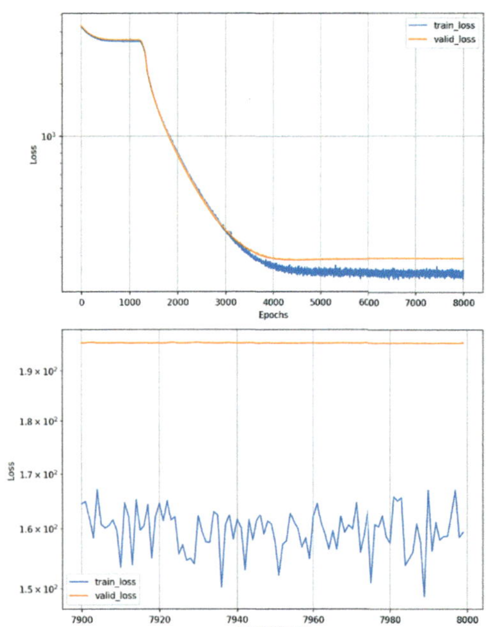

(b) Loss by sigmoid activation

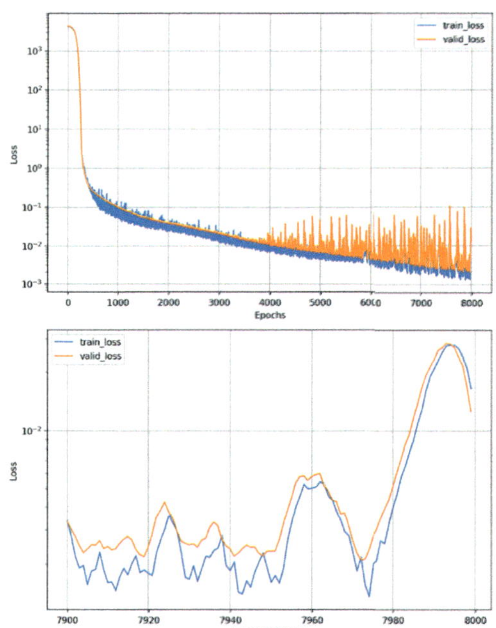

(c) Loss by swish activation

FIGURE 4.5 Training and validation loss during learning process of ANN for Example 4.3.

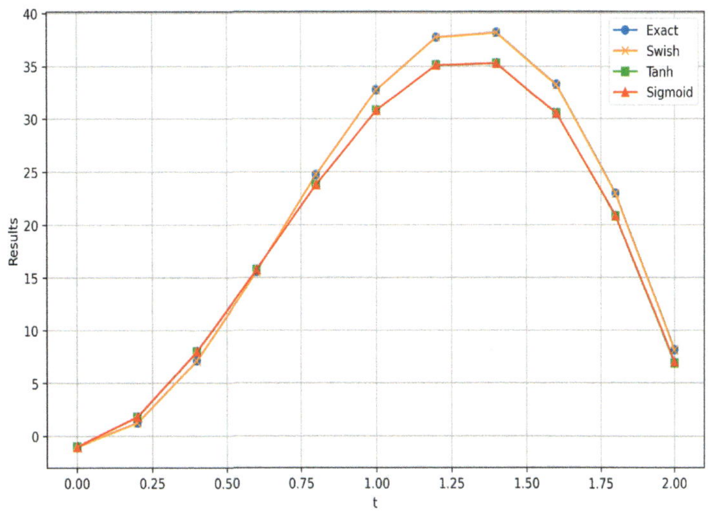

FIGURE 4.6 Comparison of exact and ANN solutions using tanh, sigmoid, swish activation functions for Example 4.3.

Table 4.3 Exact and neural results using tanh, sigmoid, and swish activation functions for Example 4.3.

Input Data (t)	Exact Solutions	Neural Results		
		Swish	Tanh	Sigmoid
0.0	−1.000000	−1.000000	−1.000000	−1.000000
0.2	1.240501	1.240043	1.802876	1.803265
0.4	7.140447	7.137093	8.009741	8.011026
0.6	15.536257	15.529230	15.725744	15.727888
0.8	24.725861	24.714399	23.782082	23.777243
1.0	32.752434	32.737189	30.808957	30.807059
1.2	37.733508	37.714763	35.094598	35.098629
1.4	38.182699	38.159079	35.262499	35.269234
1.6	33.272283	33.240542	30.523064	30.535579
1.8	22.994042	22.952262	20.827717	20.877138
2.0	8.191802	8.142054	6.932398	7.034619

with initial conditions $u(0) = -1$ and $u'(0) = 1$.

Here, we may write the ANN trial solution as

$$\phi_\tau\,(t;\,p) = -1 + t + (1 - e^{-t})^2 N(t;\,p)|_{u \to \hat{\alpha}=-1, u' \to \hat{\beta}=1}. \tag{4.11}$$

This problem has been addressed using a MLNN with three hidden layers, each having 32 nodes. Then, the network is trained for 100 equispaced points in $t \in [0, 2]$ with different activation functions. The training and validation loss against 8000 epochs are plotted in Fig. 4.5. The exact solution and obtained ANN results are presented in Table 4.3, and are also plotted in Fig. 4.6. In this problem, the MAE for ANN results with tanh, sigmoid, and swish activation functions are found to be 1.553848, 1.541827, and 0.017933, respectively.

4.4 Validation

From the experiments conducted above, it is evident that the swish activation function outperforms both the tanh and sigmoid activation functions in terms of accuracy. This conclusion is based on the observation that the swish activation function yields a lower MAE for unseen testing points compared to tanh and sigmoid. This comparison highlights the importance of selecting an appropriate activation function for neural network models when solving dynamical problems, as discussed in the forthcoming chapters.

References

[1] S. Chakraverty, S. Mall, Artificial Neural Networks for Engineers and Scientists: Solving Ordinary Differential Equations, CRC Press, 2017.
[2] A.K. Sahoo, S. Chakraverty, An unsupervised wavelet neural network model for approximating the solutions of non-linear nervous stomach model governed by tension, food and medicine, Computer Methods in Biomechanics and Biomedical Engineering (2023) 1–14.
[3] P. Ramachandran, B. Zoph, Q.V. Le, Searching for activation functions, arXiv preprint: arXiv:1710.05941, 2017.
[4] S. Mall, S. Chakraverty, Comparison of artificial neural network architecture in solving ordinary differential equations, Advances in Artificial Neural Systems 2013 (2013) 12.
[5] I.E. Lagaris, A. Likas, D.I. Fotiadis, Artificial neural networks for solving ordinary and partial differential equations, IEEE Transactions on Neural Networks 9 (5) (1998) 987–1000.
[6] S. Tapaswini, S. Chakraverty, T. Allahviranloo, A New Approach to nth Order Fuzzy Differential Equations, Computational Mathematics and Modeling, vol. 28, Springer, 2017, pp. 278–300.

5

Curriculum learning for an artificial neural network

Contents

5.1 Introduction **45**
5.2 Curriculum Learning **46**
5.3 Methodology **46**
5.4 Problem statements **47**
5.4.1 Lane–Emden equation 47
5.5 Simulation results and discussions **48**
5.5.1 Experimental setup 48
5.5.2 Model problems 48
5.6 Validation **52**
References **54**

Chapter points

- Cover the fundamentals of Curriculum learning.
- Evaluate the effectiveness of employing Curriculum learning to solve dynamical problems.
- Apply an ANN algorithm with a trial solution approach for solving the Lane–Emden equations.
- An unsupervised training algorithm ensures that the undertaken algorithm is a powerful tool to predict solutions of dynamical problems with singularities.

5.1 Introduction

Many modern machine learning (ML) algorithms are inspired by natural processes, biological systems, evolutionary strategies, and collective behaviors found in nature. Researchers take cues from the way organisms adapt, evolve, and mimick these processes to develop algorithms, which may provide robust, flexible, and adaptive solutions to complex computational problems [1].

These systems are known for their efficiency in solving optimization tasks, self-organization, and adaptability to changing conditions. In practice, these ML algorithms can be applied to tasks such as optimization, classification, and pattern recognition, and often outperforming traditional methods in handling dynamical problems. Like the human brain, the neural network provides better accuracy when the user started training from small and then gradually increases the difficulty level. In this investigation, we discuss the effect of curriculum learning in solving DEs.

Artificial Neural Networks and Type-2 Fuzzy Set. https://doi.org/10.1016/B978-0-44-332894-7.00014-9

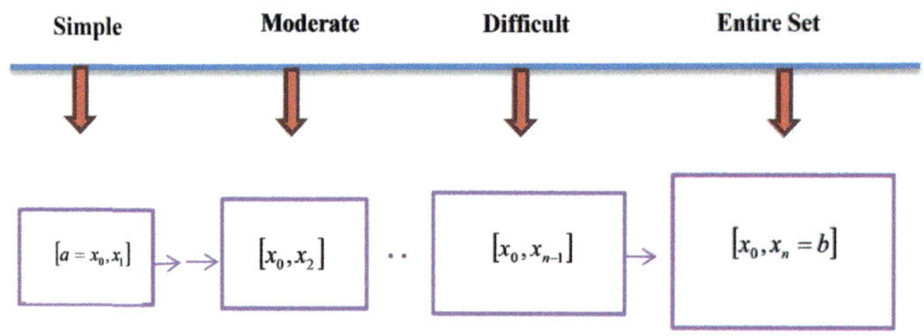

FIGURE 5.1 Framework of curriculum learning in a given domain $[a, b]$ where $a, b \in \mathbb{R}$.

5.2 Curriculum Learning

Learning becomes easier for a student when the teacher starts from basic examples, and subsequently increases the difficulty of the problem. Similarly, the performance of neural networks improve when the input data is presented incrementally instead of the entire data simultaneously. In the context of ML, this is known as **Curriculum Learning**. In 1993, Elman proposed the curriculum learning to increase efficiency of neural network training [2]. Due to the increase in complexity of problems, curriculum learning has recently become popular in the field of ML.

In this chapter, we have used curriculum learning techniques for the training of ANNs in order to solve various types of DEs in the given domain $[a, b]$. With this aim, the domain $[a, b]$ has been divided into $n + 1$ different groups, such as

$$[a, x_1] = [x_0, x_1] \subset [x_0, x_2] \subset [x_0, x_3] \subset \ldots [x_0, x_{n-1}] \subset [x_0, x_n] = [a, b], \tag{5.1}$$

where, $a = x_0 < x_1 < x_2 \ldots x_{n-1} < x_n = b$ and $a, b, x_i \in \mathbb{R}$. First, we trained the network in $[x_0, x_1]$, then trained in $[x_0, x_2]$, and gradually expanded the domain and continued the training process as demonstrated in Fig. 5.1.

5.3 Methodology

Let us consider the following second-order ODE:

$$y'' = f(t, y, y'), t \in [a, b] \tag{5.2}$$

with the initial conditions $y(a) = \alpha$, $y'(a) = \alpha'$.

The corresponding initial ANN approximate solution of Eq. (5.2) such that it satisfies given initial and boundary conditions can be written as [3]

$$\phi_\tau(t; \Theta) = \alpha + \alpha'(t - a) + (1 - e^{-(t-a)})^2 ANN(t; \Theta), \tag{5.3}$$

where $ANN(t; \Theta)$ is the neural output of the FFNN with one input data t and parameter Θ, defined by

$$ANN(t; \Theta) = (z_J \, o\sigma \, o \, z_{J-1} \, o\sigma \ldots \sigma \, o \, z_1)t^0. \tag{5.4}$$

Here, $\phi_\tau(t;\Theta)$, satisfies the initial condition of given DE. The final approximate solution may be predicted by fine-tuning the set of parameters Θ, achieved through minimizing the cost function formed by combining the approximate solution and the given DE. In this regard, we need to calculate the gradient of the network with respect to "t" as discussed in the last chapter.

The cost function for the above second-order ODE is written as

$$E(p) = \sum_{i=1}^{n} \left(\frac{d^2\phi_\tau(t_i;\Theta)}{dt^2} - f\left(t_i, \phi_\tau(t_i;\Theta), \frac{d\phi_\tau(t_i;\Theta)}{dt}\right)\right)^2. \tag{5.5}$$

The epochs will continue until the error is minimized or stopping criteria is achieved.

5.4 Problem statements

In this section, the general form of the singular value problem (SVP) and governing equation of Lane–Emden equations have been discussed.

However, a DE having singularities can significantly influence the existence, uniqueness, and behavior of solutions. So, understanding the type of singularities is crucial for both theoretical analysis and practical applications. The singular points can be further classified based on the behavior of the coefficients near the vanishing point. A special instance of SVP is the Lane–Emden equations, which are commonly employed in astronomy and mathematical physics.

5.4.1 Lane–Emden equation

The general SVP has the form

$$y''(t) + \frac{\alpha}{t}y'(t) + f(t,y) = g(t), t \in D, \alpha > 0, 0 \notin D, \tag{5.6}$$

subject to the initial conditions $y(0) = a$, $y'(0) = b$.

The Lane–Emden equations are a particular case of SVPs whose general form is [4]

$$y''(t) + \frac{\alpha}{t}y'(t) + kf(t,y) = g(t), t \in (0,1], \alpha > 0, \tag{5.7}$$

subject to initial conditions $y(0) = a$, $y'(0) = b$, where α is called the shape factor, $a, b \in \mathbb{R}$, and $D \subseteq \mathbb{R}$ are the given domain.

Historically, the standard Lane–Emden equation is written as [4]

$$y''(t) + \frac{2}{t}y'(t) + y^m = 0, t \in (0,1], \tag{5.8}$$

subject to the initial conditions $y(0) = 1$, $y'(0) = 0$. These Lane–Emden equations have a singularity at $t = 0$ and represent a dimensionless form of Poisson's equation for the gravitational potential of a Newtonian self-gravitating spherically symmetric, polytropic fluid.

5.5 Simulation results and discussions

In this section, the robustness of undertaking ANN model along with curriculum learning is presented for solving various application problems having singularity. Moreover, different global statistical measures are evaluated for convergence analysis of the proposed algorithm based on results at testing points with respect to existing numerical solutions. These results are incorporated in tables and graphs, which indicate the correctness, precision, and efficacy of the neural model.

5.5.1 Experimental setup

The following experiments have been carried out in Python 3.0 under the Google Colab environment. As the Adam optimization algorithm converges faster and is relatively stable, so we took Adam as a training optimizer with a learning rate of 0.001. Initial weights have been generated randomly and set to small numbers in (0, 1]. The state-of-art swish activation function has been taken during the training of the model. However, after selecting the basic framework, the optimal number of hidden layers and the number of nodes in each hidden layer are selected after several experiments. For curriculum learning, we have trained the neural network as shown in Fig. 5.1.

5.5.2 Model problems

Example 5.1. Let us consider an isothermal gas sphere equation by fixing $\alpha = 2$, $k = 1$, $f(t, y) = e^y$, $g(t) = 0$ in Eq. (5.7)

$$y''(t) + \frac{2}{t}y'(t) + e^y = 0, \tag{5.9}$$

with the initial conditions $y(0) = 0$, $y'(0) = 0$.

The approximate polynomial solution by using SRMM is as follows [5]:

$$y(t) = -0.00031099t^6 - 0.00034799t^5 + 0.0085476t^4 - 0.00005321t^3 - 0.166663t^2. \tag{5.10}$$

As discussed in Section 5.3, the ANN trial solution can be written as

$$\phi_\tau(t, p) = (1 - e^{-(t)})^2 ANN(t; \Theta)|_{y \to \alpha = 0, y' \to \alpha' = 0}. \tag{5.11}$$

In order to illustrate the advantages of proposed algorithm, a neural network with a linear input and output node is considered. Furthermore, the network is configured with a depth of three hidden layers, each containing 32 nodes, for the execution of the ANN algorithms. The swish activation function has been used in the hidden layer during the modeling of the network. For traditional training, we trained the network for 100 equidistant points with white noise in [0, 2], and for curriculum training, we first trained the network for 100 equidistant points in [0, 1] with batch size 20, then in [0, 1.5], and finally in the whole domain.

Table 5.1 Analytical solutions and neural solutions at testing points $t \in [0, 2]$, $\triangle t = 0.2$ for Example 5.1.

t	Curriculum Learning	Traditional Learning	Analytical Results
0.0	0.000000	0.000000	0.000000
0.2	−0.006653	−0.006654	−0.006653
0.4	−0.026454	−0.026457	−0.026455
0.6	−0.058941	−0.058946	−0.058944
0.8	−0.103382	−0.103385	−0.103386
1.0	−0.158826	−0.158824	−0.158828
1.2	−0.224159	−0.224151	−0.224157
1.4	−0.298167	−0.298156	−0.298182
1.6	−0.379594	−0.379586	−0.379724
1.8	−0.467202	−0.456203	−0.467722
2.0	−0.559818	−0.539825	−0.561355

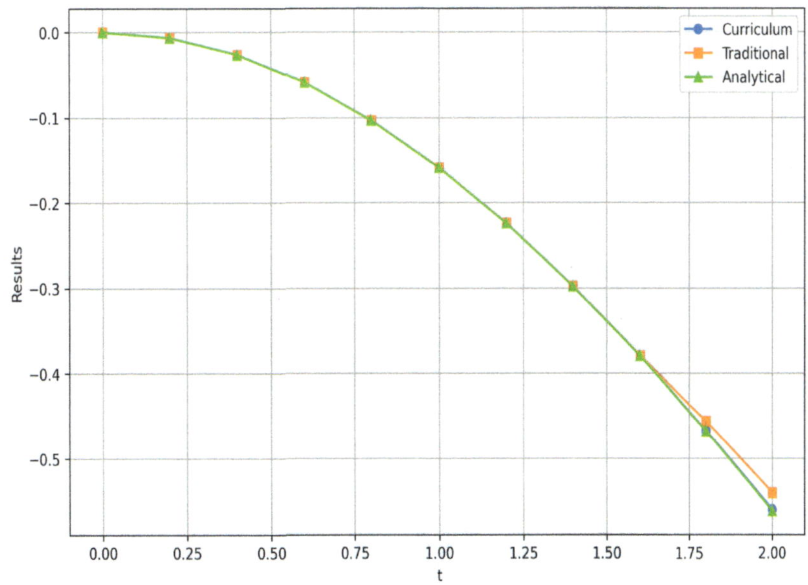

FIGURE 5.2 Plot of analytical solutions and neural network predicted solutions using curriculum learning for Example 5.1.

Then we have predicted the values in a testing dataset of $t \in [0, 2]$, $\Delta t = 0.04$. The comparison among analytical solutions, ANN solutions by traditional training and by curriculum learning are presented in Table 5.1. It is clearly seen that the values of AEs for curriculum learning are in the range of $10^{-04} - 10^{-05}$, with respect to the analytical solution. This establishes the resilience of the proposed neural model. A graphical comparison between the solution provided in literature and the obtained solution by curriculum learning has been given in Fig. 5.2. The training loss graph against 3,000 epochs is plotted in Fig. 5.3, which is constantly decreasing as the number of epochs increases and flattens toward the

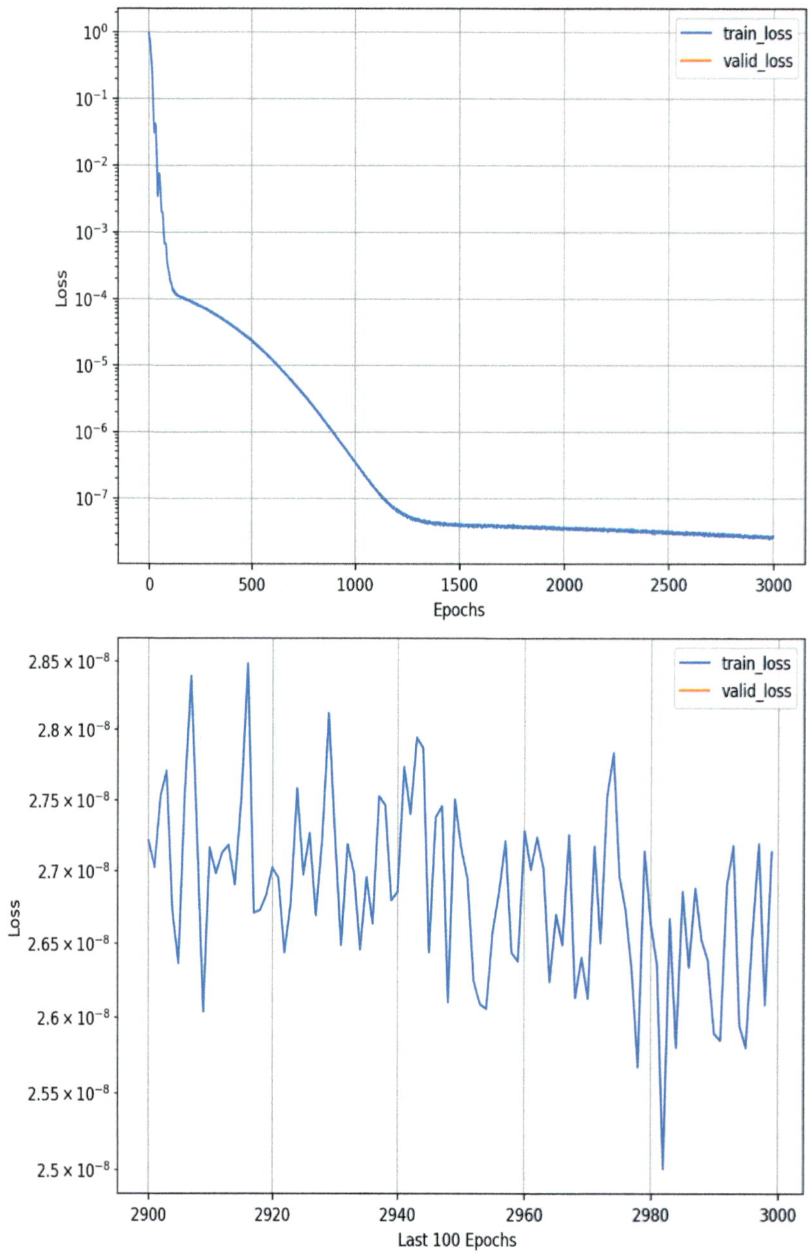

FIGURE 5.3 Training loss during the learning process of ANN for Example 5.1.

Table 5.2 Analytical solutions and neural solutions at testing points $t \in [0, 2.5]$ for Example 5.2.

t	Curriculum Learning	Traditional Learning	Analytical Results
0.00	0.000000	0.000000	0.000000
0.25	−0.010343	−0.010437	−0.010449
0.50	−0.041845	−0.042145	−0.042195
0.75	−0.095783	−0.096190	−0.096483
1.00	−0.174418	−0.175063	−0.175566
1.25	−0.281415	−0.282550	−0.283016
1.50	−0.422317	−0.424415	−0.424180
1.75	−0.605623	−0.609482	−0.606787
2.00	−0.845033	−0.851160	−0.841709
2.25	−1.163837	−1.172147	−1.143862
2.50	−1.605707	−1.615049	−1.533265

end. The global errors like MAE and MSE are found to be 0.000145 and $1.32598E-07$, respectively, for curriculum learning. Moreover, for traditional learning, it has found to be 0.000147 and $1.43697E-06$. From these tabular results and graphs, it is quite clear that curriculum learning has better accuracy than the traditional training.

Example 5.2. Let us consider an equation employed in Richardson's theory of thermionic currents for the study of density and electric force of an electron gas in the neighborhood of a hot body in thermal equilibrium by replacing $\alpha = 2$, $k = 1$, $f(t, y) = e^{-y}$, and $g(t) = 0$ in Eq. (5.7). Then Eq. (5.7) becomes

$$y''(t) + \frac{2}{t}y'(t) + e^{-y} = 0, \tag{5.12}$$

with the initial conditions $y(0) = 0$, $y'(0) = 0$.

The approximate polynomial solution by using SRMM is as follows [5]:

$$y(t) = -0.000850028t^6 - +0.000553538t^5 - 0.00869272t^4 + 0.0000928951t^3 - 0.166673t^2. \tag{5.13}$$

In this case, the ANN trial solution is written as

$$\phi_\tau(t, p) = (1 - e^{-(t)})^2 ANN(t; \Theta)|_{y \to \alpha = 0, y' \to \alpha' = 0}. \tag{5.14}$$

For traditional training, the network has been trained for 200 equidistant points with white noise from $t \in [0, 2.5]$, and for curriculum training, we first trained the network for 100 equidistant points in $t = 0$ to $t = 1.0$ with white noise, then gradually increases the domain. Then we evaluate the performance of proposed model in a training dataset of 51 points in $t \in [0, 2.5]$.

Table 5.2 demonstrates the comparison between the analytical solution and ANN results at various testing points. The analytical solutions are compared with the neural network predicted solutions using curriculum learning and traditional learning in Fig. 5.4. The

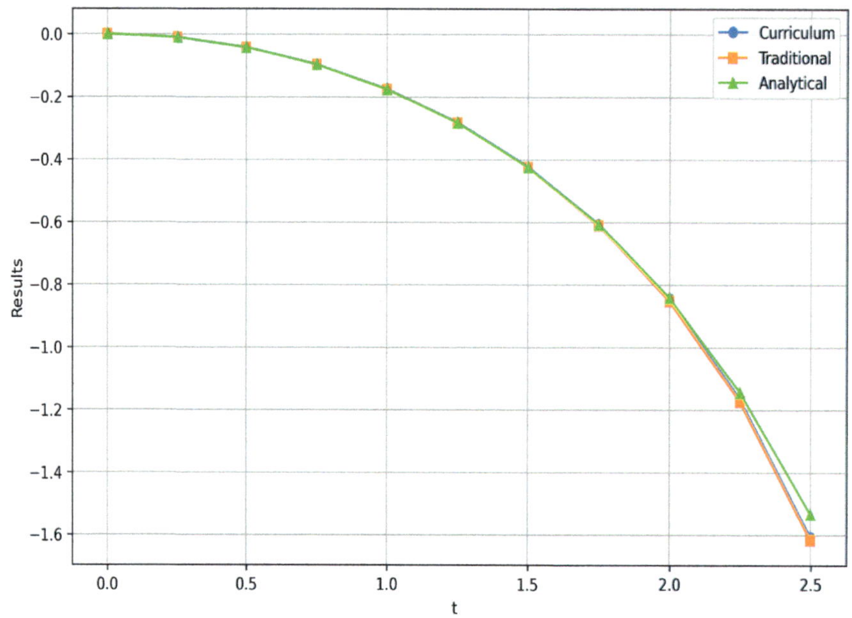

FIGURE 5.4 Plot of exact solutions and neural network predicted solutions using curriculum learning for Example 5.2.

MAE and MSE for traditional learning are found to be 0.008262 and $3.7796E-04$, whereas for curriculum learning MAE and MSE are found to be 0.006527 and $2.59028E-04$. It can be inferred from the error analysis that the curriculum learning outperforms traditional training. Finally, the training loss against 7,000 epochs is plotted in Fig. 5.5, which gradually decreases and converges toward the end of epochs.

5.6 Validation

The neural network predicted solutions are validated here by comparing with the existing one and calculating different types global statistical errors. In the proposed methodology, we assume that the solution of the given problems are unknown to the network. Thus, we adopt an unsupervised training method for solving DEs. In this regard, the network undergoes unsupervised training by using an error function derived from the DE, as well as the trial solution. It is noteworthy that the neural network output is considered as a solution of the DE when the loss function tends to 0.

For the above examples, the accuracy of the proposed algorithm is witnessed through the comparative assessment of ANN predicted solutions and existing solutions by numerical methods. The investigations of the performances based on statistical measures such as MAE and MSE are calculated for the SVP and outcomes are graphically portrayed in the figures. One may see that for curriculum learning, the MAE magnitude lies in close vicinity of $1E-02$. Similarly, the MSE value lies in the neighborhood of $1E-04$. The accuracy rate

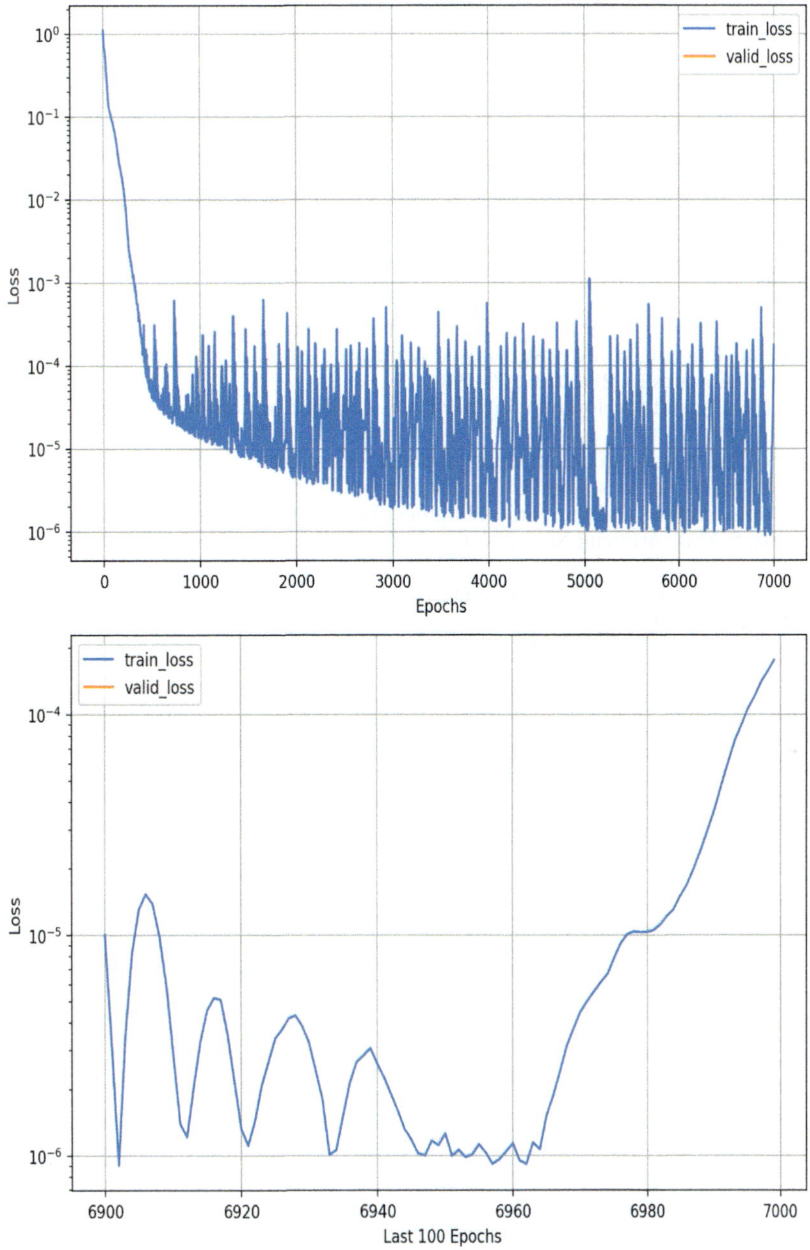

FIGURE 5.5 Training loss during the learning process of ANN for Example 5.2.

of ANN may be visualized from the graphs of training loss against epochs. As the number of epochs increases, the loss value gradually decreases. As the graph of validation and training accuracy are converging, it can be concluded that the obtained model is a robust model.

This chapter manifests the effect of curriculum learning to train ANN for solving Lane–Emden models. The neural model successfully overcomes the singular behavior of the problem. The proposed machine intelligence-based method can be used to solve other types of relevant singular problems emerging in science and engineering applications.

References

[1] A.K. Sahoo, S. Chakraverty, A novel approach to simulate Lane-Emden and Emden-Fowler equations using curriculum learning-based unsupervised symplectic artificial neural network, East Asian Journal on Applied Mathematics 13 (2) (2023) 276–298.

[2] J.L. Elman, Learning and development in neural networks: the importance of starting small, Cognition 48 (1) (1993) 71–99.

[3] A.K. Sahoo, S. Chakraverty, An unsupervised wavelet neural network model for approximating the solutions of non-linear nervous stomach model governed by tension, food and medicine, Computer Methods in Biomechanics and Biomedical Engineering 27 (11) (2024) 1538–1551.

[4] S. Chakraverty, S. Mall, Artificial Neural Networks for Engineers and Scientists: Solving Ordinary Differential Equations, CRC Press, 2017.

[5] B. Căruntu, C. Bota, Approximate polynomial solutions of the nonlinear Lane–Emden type equations arising in astrophysics using the squared remainder minimization method, Computer Physics Communications 184 (7) (2013) 1643–1648.

6 Symplectic artificial neural network

Contents

6.1 Introduction 55
6.2 Symplectic artificial neural networks 56
6.3 Methodology 57
6.3.1 Modeling of symplectic artificial neural network 57
6.4 Problem statements 58
6.4.1 Duffing oscillator model 59
6.4.2 Van der Pol–Mathieu–Duffing oscillator model 59
6.5 Simulation results and discussions 59
6.5.1 Experimental setup 59
6.5.2 Model problems 60
6.6 Validation 65
References 70

Chapter points

- Discuss the integration of symplectic structures into Artificial Neural Networks.
- Explain the fundamental architecture of Symplectic Artificial Neural Networks.
- Evaluate the effectiveness of SANN in solving oscillator dynamical problems.

6.1 Introduction

Symplectic Artificial Neural Networks (SANN) are a type of neural network inspired by the mathematical structure of symplectic geometry, which is used to describe the dynamics of physical problems. SANNs are more efficient than traditional neural networks because they use fewer parameters and require less training data, which makes them well suited for dynamical problems. Moreover, SANN is constructed in such a way that it conserves energy [1,2].

The van der Pol oscillator is a mathematical model that describes the behavior of an electrical circuit, particularly an electronic oscillator. Dutch physicist Balthasar van der Pol introduced this model in 1927 while he was working at the Philips Research Laboratories in Eindhoven, Netherlands [3]. The governing equation of the van der Pol oscillator includes nonlinearity that causes the system to exhibit limit cycle behavior, and complex dynamics. It has received remarkable attention from the research community due to its

Artificial Neural Networks and Type-2 Fuzzy Set. https://doi.org/10.1016/B978-0-44-332894-7.00015-0

various applications in engineering problems, such as the non-linear vibration of beams and plates [4], fluid flow induced vibration [5], magneto-elastic mechanical systems [6], etc.

In a pioneering work, the chaotic behaviors of van der Pol–Mathieu–Duffing Oscillator (VdPM-DO) system under different forms of excitations were excellently presented by Kimiaeifar [7]. For solving VdPM-DO equations, few other numerical techniques have been developed in recent years [8,9]. However, numerical techniques require the repetition of iterations for numerical precision, leading to a significant computing cost.

So, to overcome these limitations, different kinds of ANN models have been developed by researchers. Mall and Chakraverty developed a single-layer Hermite link ANN model to approximate VdP-DO equations [10]. For detecting the weak signals in a strongly coupled Duffing–van der Pol oscillator, Wang et al. proposed a long short-term memory neural network [11]. Yin et al. introduced a combination of fractional FLANN filters for solving VdP-DO equations [12]. In recent research, Bukhari et al. introduced a non-linear autoregressive radial basic function neural network filters for solving the VdPM-DO equations [13].

In this chapter, an unsupervised multi-layer neural model, namely the Symplectic Artificial Neural Network has been proposed to understand the dynamical behavior of linear/non-linear oscillator systems. Moreover, it is more numerically precise and robust method to solve dynamical equations than standard neural networks and numerical methods. This chapter primarily contributes by examining the efficacy of SANN in addressing different kinds of duffing oscillator equations across various excitation functions and parameters.

6.2 Symplectic artificial neural networks

General nth-order ODEs can be written as

$$\Gamma\left(t, \phi(t), \phi'(t), \phi''(t), \dots, \phi^{(n)}(t)\right) = 0, t \in \overline{D} \subset \mathbb{R}^n \tag{6.1}$$

where $\phi(t)$ is the determined solution, $\overline{D}$ the discretized domain over a finite set of points, and $t = (t_1, t_2, \dots, t_n) \in \mathbb{R}^n$.

Let $\phi_\tau(t; p)$ indicates the ANN approximate solution with adjustable parameters p, then Eq. (6.1) can be rewritten as

$$\Gamma\left(t_i, \phi_\tau(t_i; p), \phi'_\tau(t_i; p), \phi''_\tau(t_i; p) \dots \phi^{(n)}_\tau(t_i; p)\right) = 0. \tag{6.2}$$

The corresponding loss function can be obtained by converting Eq. (6.2) to an unconstrained optimization problem. As such, it may be written as

$$E(p) = \min_{p} \sum_{t_i \in \overline{D}} \left(\Gamma\left(t_i, \phi_\tau(t_i; p), \phi'_\tau(t_i; p), \phi''_\tau(t_i; p) \dots \phi^{(n)}_\tau(t_i; p)\right)\right)^2. \tag{6.3}$$

The initial ANN approximate solution $\phi_\tau(t; p)$ may be expressed as the sum of two terms [1]

$$\phi_\tau(t; p) = \alpha + \Gamma(t, SANN(t; p)), \tag{6.4}$$

where the first part of the initial approximate solution, i.e., α is associated with the initial and/or boundary conditions, without the adjustable parameters. The second part is an output of the SANN that consist M hidden layers, with k neurons in each hidden layer, and a linear output node for a given input $t \in \mathbb{R}^n$. Weights and biases of $SANN(t; p)$ are adjusted to deal with the minimization of the loss function. The output of ANN can be written as

$$SANN(t; p) = \sum_{j=1}^{k} v_j \sigma(z_j) \tag{6.5}$$

where $z_j = \mathbf{W}^{(j)}\mathbf{t}^{k-1} + b^{(j)}$, $j = 1, 2, ..., k$.

Here, $p = \{\mathbf{W}^{(j)}, b^{(j)}\}_{j=1}^{k}$ is the set of updatable parameters, $\mathbf{W}^{(j)} = \omega_{ij}$ is set of weights, such that w_{ji} represents from the input layer i to the neuron j such that $i = 1, 2, 3, ...n$ and $b^{(j)}$ is the bias. Here, $\sigma(z_j)$ denotes activation function (swish, sigmoid, tanh, etc.). In particular, let us take swish as an activation function. Then Eq. (6.5) becomes

$$SANN(t; p) = \sum_{j=1}^{k} v_j \frac{z_j}{1 + \exp(-a z_j)}, a \in [0, \infty). \tag{6.6}$$

6.3 Methodology

This section covers the implementation of the SANN algorithm for approximating nonlinear oscillator problems.

6.3.1 Modeling of symplectic artificial neural network

Let us consider the first-order ODE as

$$y' = f(t, y), t \in [a, b] \tag{6.7}$$

with the initial condition $y(a) = \hat{\alpha}$.

Consequently, the symplectic neural network initial approximate solution can be written as [1]

$$\phi_\tau(t; p) = \hat{\alpha} + (1 - e^{-(t-a)}) SANN(t; p), \tag{6.8}$$

where $SANN(t; p)$ is the output of kth hidden layer with one input variable t, and parameters p. The ANN approximate solution $\phi_\tau(t; p)$ satisfies the initial conditions of the given DE. In order to find the loss function, we may need to calculate gradient of the network

$SANN(t;\, p)$ with respect to input t. It can be computed as follows:

$$D^m SANN(t;\, p) = \sum_{j=1}^{k} v_j w_{ji}^m \sigma^{(m)}\left(z_j\right). \tag{6.9}$$

Here, $\sigma^{(m)}\left(z_j\right)$ represents the mth-order derivative of activation function.

Differentiating Eq. (6.8) with respect to t, we have

$$\begin{aligned} D^m \phi_\tau(t;\, p) &= D^m\left[(1 - e^{-(t-a)})SANN(t;\, p)\right] \\ &= D^m\left[(1 - e^{-(t-a)})\sum_{i=1}^{n}\sum_{j=1}^{k} v_j \frac{w_{ji}t_i + b_j}{1 + \exp(-a(w_{ji}t_i + b_j))}\right] \end{aligned} \tag{6.10}$$

Thus the cost function for Eq. (6.7) is calculated as

$$E(p) = \sum_{i=1}^{n}\left(D\phi_\tau(t_i;\, p) - f\left(t_i, \phi_\tau(t_i;\, p)\right)\right)^2 \tag{6.11}$$

Now, consider the second-order ODE as

$$y'' = \mathrm{f}(\mathrm{t}, y, y'),\ \mathrm{t} \in \left[\mathrm{a}, \mathrm{b}\right] \tag{6.12}$$

with the initial condition $y(a) = \hat{\alpha}$, $y'(a) = \hat{\beta}$.

Here, the neural approximate solution is written as

$$\phi_\tau(t;\, p) = \hat{\alpha} + \hat{\beta}(t - a) + (1 - e^{-(t-a)})^2 SANN(t;\, p). \tag{6.13}$$

Weights associated with this multi-layer perceptron are updated by the BP learning algorithm through optimizing the below loss function

$$E(p) = \sum_{i=1}^{n}\left(D^2\phi_\tau(t_i;\, p) - f\left(t_i, \phi_\tau(t_i;\, p), D\phi_\tau\right)\right)^2 \tag{6.14}$$

During the training of the neural network the epochs will continue until the error is minimized. During training the Adam optimizer will update the parameters of the network without affecting the learning rates in order to find the optimum weights.

6.4 Problem statements

In this section, the governing equation of (i) Duffing oscillator models, and (ii) van der Pol–Mathieu–Duffing oscillator models have been discussed.

6.4.1 Duffing oscillator model

The governing form of the damping Duffing oscillator model (DOEs) is written as [14]

$$\gamma''(t) + \alpha\gamma'(t) + \beta\gamma + \eta\gamma^3 = \kappa\cos(\varpi t), \alpha > 0 \tag{6.15}$$

subject to the initial conditions $\gamma(0) = a$, $\gamma'(0) = b$.

Here, κ stands for the magnitude of periodic force, α denotes the damping coefficient, ϖ and t represent the frequency of periodic force and the periodic time, respectively. For $\kappa = 0$, Eq. (6.15) reduces into the unforced damped DOEs.

6.4.2 Van der Pol–Mathieu–Duffing oscillator model

The governing equation of VdPM-DO equations can be written as [7]

$$\gamma''(t) + \varepsilon\left[\left(\mu - \alpha\gamma^2\right)\gamma'(t) + \vartheta\gamma\cos(\Omega t)\right] - \varpi^2\gamma + \beta\gamma^3 - \varepsilon\sigma\gamma\zeta(t) = 0, \alpha > 0 \tag{6.16}$$

subject to the initial conditions $\gamma(0) = a$, $\gamma'(0) = b$.

Here, σ denotes frequency of periodic coefficient, β stands for the coefficient of the cubic non-linearity term, $\gamma(t)$ is displacement from equilibrium position, and ϑ is intensity of periodic coefficient. It may be noted that μ and α in Eq. (6.16) are defined as constant values.

6.5 Simulation results and discussions

In this section, different duffing oscillator problems have been solved by using SANN algorithm. The accuracy of the proposed algorithm has been demonstrated through the presentation of results in tables and graphs.

6.5.1 Experimental setup

Neural network training techniques are often iterative therefore the user must designate a starting point for iterations. Furthermore, for training neural models the initial guess has a significant impact on most approaches. One of the most prominent strategies for the parameter initialization is known as "**break the symmetry**" [15]. So, one may start with arbitrary, small, and distinct real numbers as the initial weights of the network. As such, arbitrary real numbers in $[-1, 1] \setminus \{0\}$ are considered as initial weights in this experiment.

Our experiments have been carried out in the google colab environment using Python 3.0. Adam optimization exhibits rapid convergence and a relatively consistent stability. It computes the gradient of a loss function concerning the network's adaptable parameters, adjusting their values using a stepsize regulated by a learning rate $\eta = 0.001$.

6.5.2 Model problems

Example 6.1. Let us consider a non-linear VdPM-DO equations by fixing the value of $\zeta(t) = t, \alpha = 0.2, \beta = 0.5, \varepsilon = 0.1, \mu = 0.5, \vartheta = 0.1, \varpi = 0.1, \sigma = 0.1, \Omega = 0.5$ in Eq. (6.16) [7]

$$\gamma''(t) + \varepsilon\left[\left(\mu - \alpha\gamma^2\right)\gamma'(t) + \vartheta\gamma\cos(\Omega t)\right] - \varpi^2\gamma + \beta\gamma^3 - \varepsilon\sigma\gamma = 0, \alpha > 0 \tag{6.17}$$

with the initial conditions $\gamma(0) = 0$, $\gamma'(0) = 1$.

As discussed above, the initial neural approximate solution can be computed as follows:

$$\phi_\tau(t,p) = t + (1 - e^{-t})^2 SANN(t,p)|_{\gamma \to \hat{\alpha}=0, \gamma' \to \hat{\beta}=1} \tag{6.18}$$

To solve this non-linear system, we have constructed a multi-layer network with a single input, single output, and three hidden layers, with 32 nodes in each hidden layer. Then the model has been trained for 200 equidistant points with white noise in $t \in [0, 3]$ sec, which are randomly selected at the beginning of each epoch.

Then the network has been trained for 6,000 epochs with a batch size of 200. The obtained neural network predicted solutions has been compared with RK4 numerical solutions for 31 training points at different time steps. Table 6.1 shows the comparison among RK4 and the obtained SANN solutions with 5,000 and 6,000 epochs. From the tabular values, the MSE of SANN is found to be $5.168E - 04$, demonstrating improvement over the existing method.

In Fig. 6.1, the curves of training and validation loss over $6,000$ epochs have been demonstrated. It may be perceived that the loss function is minimized as the training period increases. The time-series plot of SANN solutions is delineated in Fig. 6.2. The absolute error between SANN and RK4 results are compared graphically in Fig. 6.3. It is worth mentioning that the CPU time is 226.79 sec.

Example 6.2. Let us consider a non-linear van der Pol–Mathieu (VdPM) dust plasma model by fixing the value of $\alpha = 0.02$ and $\beta = 0.001$ in Eq. (6.19) [13],

$$\gamma''(t) - (\alpha - \beta\gamma^2)\gamma'(t) - \gamma = 0, \alpha > 0 \tag{6.19}$$

with the initial conditions $\gamma(0) = 1$, $\gamma'(0) = 1$.

Here, the initial neural approximate solution may be written as

$$\phi_\tau(t,p) = 1 + t + (1 - e^{-t})^2 SANN(t,p)|_{\gamma \to \hat{\alpha}=1, \gamma' \to \hat{\beta}=1} \tag{6.20}$$

A multi-layer neural network with a single input, a single output, and four hidden layers, each consisting of 50 nodes, has been designed to demonstrate the effectiveness of the proposed method. Then the network was first trained on 200 equispaced points with added white noise for $t \in [0, 2]$. Subsequently, the network underwent training for 8,000 epochs with a batch size of 20.

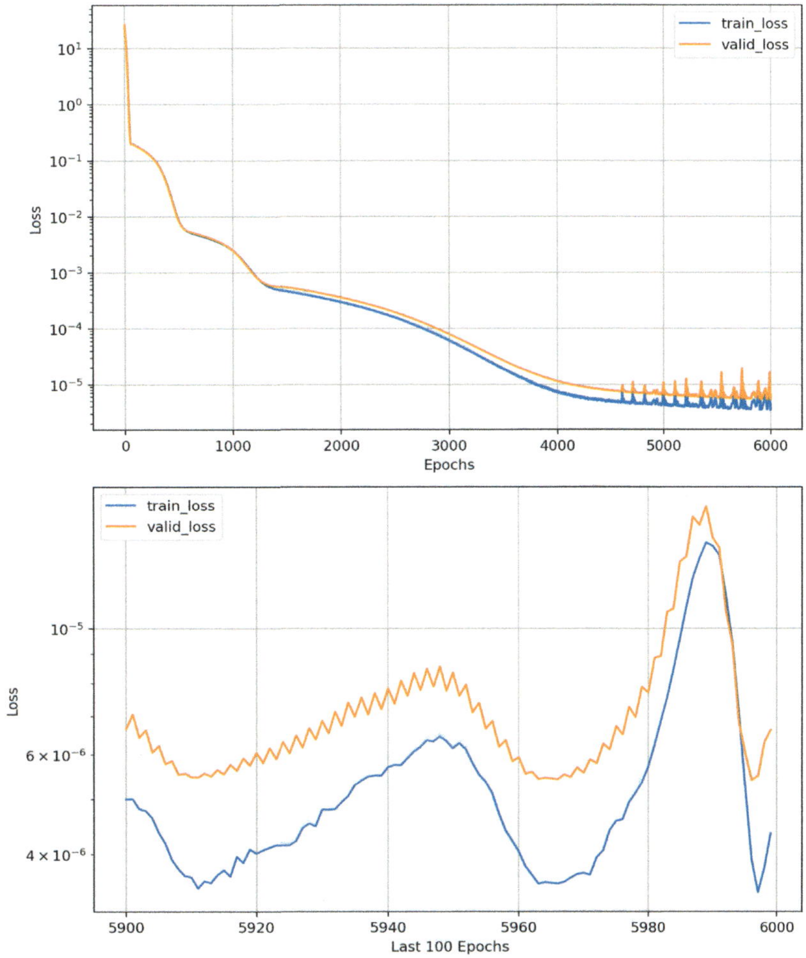

FIGURE 6.1 Training and validation loss during the learning process of SANN for Example 6.1.

The training and validation loss against the epochs are delineated in Fig. 6.4, and the comparison between RK4 solutions and neural solutions are plotted in Fig. 6.5. Robustness of the model increases along with the decrease of the value of cost function. Moreover, the tabular results at different testing points for various training epochs are demonstrated in Table 6.2. It has been found that the solution converges at 8,000 epochs as the MAE is obtained 0.000079. The absolute errors between SANN and RK4 are presented graphically in Fig. 6.6. Furthermore, it may be observed from the error graph that absolute error ranges in $1E-04$ to $3E-04$. The time taken by CPU for training of network is 412.65 sec.

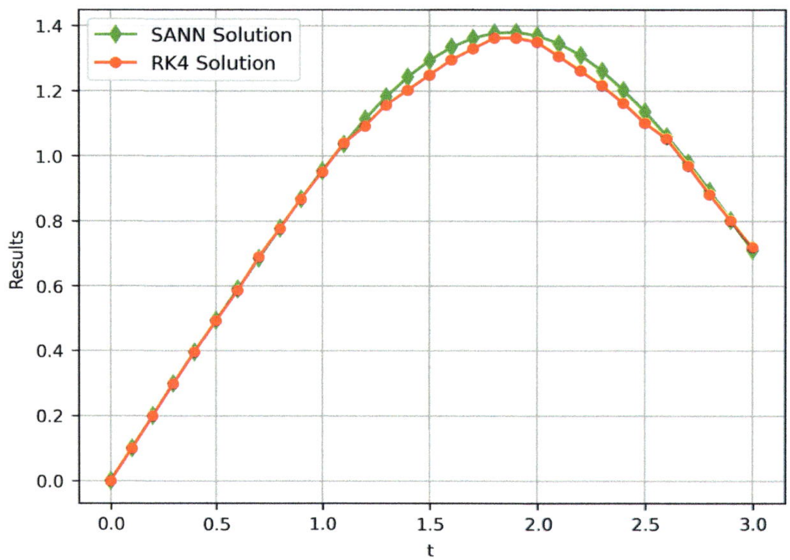

FIGURE 6.2 Comparison of results obtained from SANN with RK4 method at different time steps for Example 6.1.

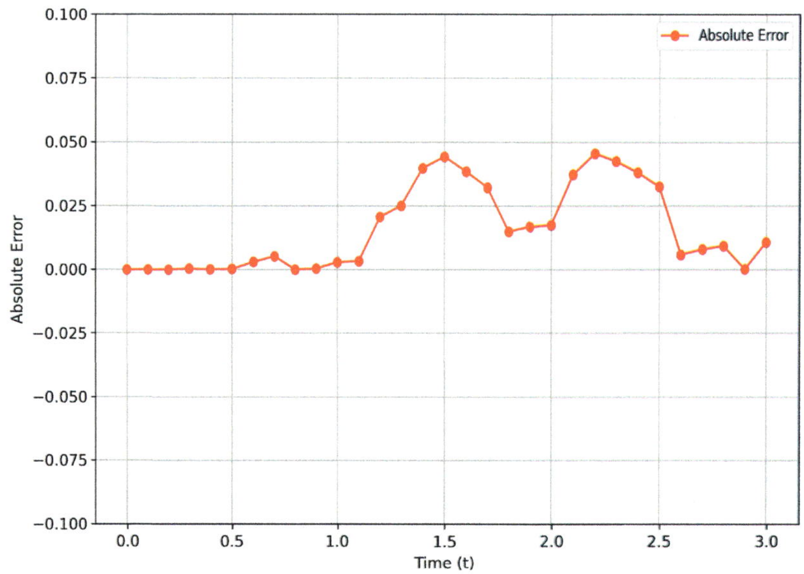

FIGURE 6.3 Plot of absolute error between SANN and RK4 solutions for Example 6.1.

Example 6.3. Let us consider an unforced duffing oscillator problem by fixing the value of $\alpha = 1$ and $\beta = 20$, $\eta = 2$ in Eq. (6.15). Then we have

$$\gamma''(t) + \gamma'(t) + 20\gamma + 2\gamma^3 = 0 \tag{6.21}$$

Table 6.1 Comparison of RK4 and SANN solutions for various epochs for Example 6.1.

Input Data (t)	RK4 Results	SANN Results for 5,000 epochs	SANN Results for 6,000 epochs
0.0	0.00000	0.000000	0.000000
0.1	0.09970	0.099733	0.099748
0.2	0.19890	0.198986	0.198990
0.3	0.29730	0.297741	0.297698
0.4	0.39590	0.395892	0.395794
0.5	0.49340	0.493255	0.493116
0.6	0.58640	0.589557	0.589398
0.7	0.68950	0.684406	0.684243
0.8	0.77702	0.777268	0.777109
0.9	0.86770	0.867444	0.867285
1.0	0.95100	0.954065	0.953896
1.1	1.03930	1.036101	1.035904
1.2	1.09150	1.112375	1.112135
1.3	1.15630	1.181606	1.181312
1.4	1.20250	1.242460	1.242107
1.5	1.24910	1.293613	1.293205
1.6	1.29510	1.333837	1.333382
1.7	1.32960	1.362082	1.361589
1.8	1.36210	1.377557	1.377035
1.9	1.36240	1.379801	1.379257
2.0	1.35050	1.368727	1.368161
2.1	1.30680	1.344625	1.344035
2.2	1.26200	1.308144	1.307525
2.3	1.21710	1.260228	1.259573
2.4	1.16320	1.202039	1.201345
2.5	1.10150	1.134873	1.134135
2.6	1.05330	1.060072	1.059289
2.7	0.97000	0.978957	0.978129
2.8	0.88250	0.892776	0.891906
2.9	0.80210	0.802672	0.801761
3.0	0.71960	0.709662	0.708715

with the initial conditions $y(0) = -0.2$, $y'(0) = 2$.

As discussed above, the initial ANN approximate solution can be written as

$$\phi_\tau(t; p) = -0.2 + 2(t) + (1 - e^{-t})^2 SANN(t; p)|_{y \to \hat{\alpha} = -0.2, y' \to \hat{\beta} = 2}. \tag{6.22}$$

Here, a multi-layer neural network has been constructed with a single input, single output, and four hidden layers, such that each hidden layer contains 32 nodes. Then the

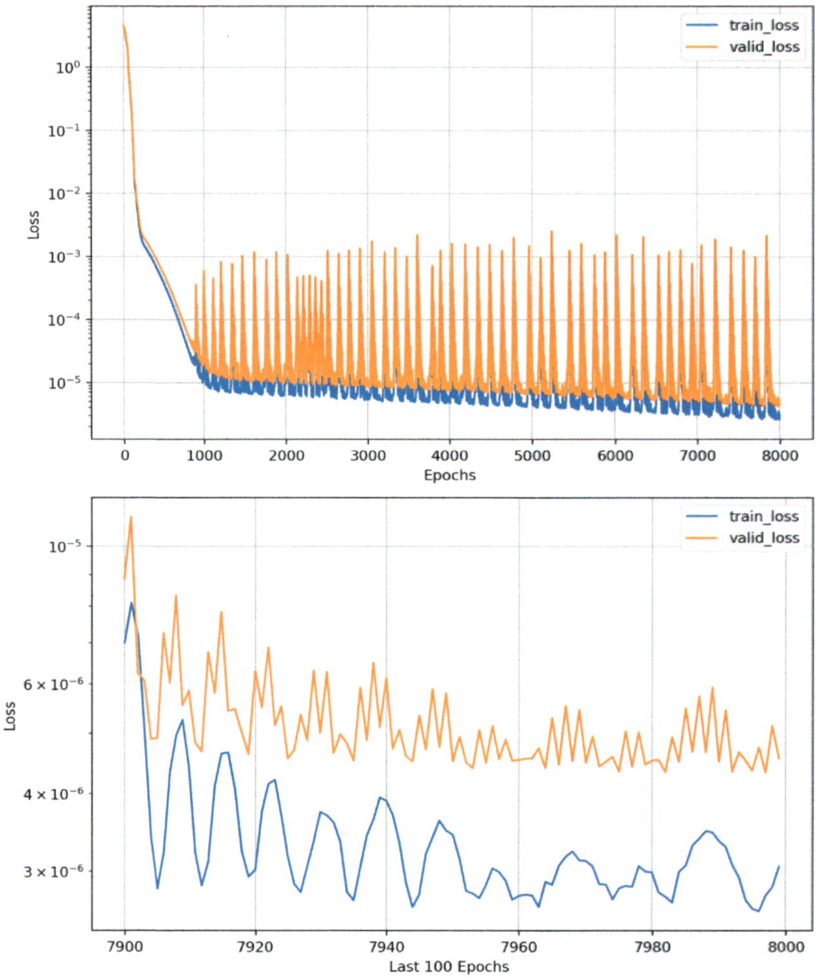

FIGURE 6.4 Training and validation loss during the learning process of SANN for Example 6.2.

network has been trained for 128 equidistant points with white noise from $t \in [0, 5]$ sec. Additionally, the batch size is set to 100, and the model is trained for 9,000 epochs.

A comparison between numerical results obtained by the modified differential transform method (MDTM) by the Pade approximate of [3/3] [16], and SANN results are given in Table 6.3. The loss function of training and validation is contemplated in Fig. 6.7. The time series of SANN results are portrayed in Fig. 6.8, and absolute errors between SANN and MDTM solutions are compared graphically in Fig. 6.9. Moreover, the MAE is obtained as 0.00927 and MSE is 0.000231 that manifest the efficacy of proposed model for solving the DOE. The time taken by CPU for training of this model is 396 sec.

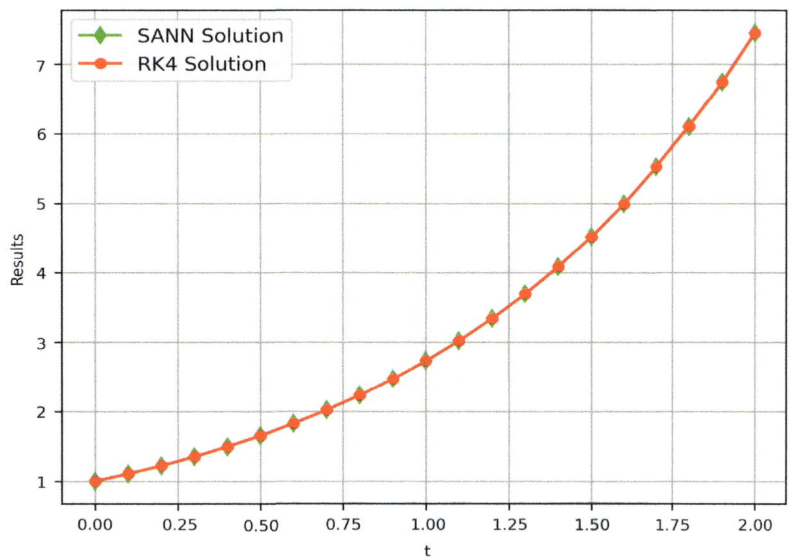

FIGURE 6.5 Comparison of results obtained from SANN with RK4 method at different time steps for Example 6.2.

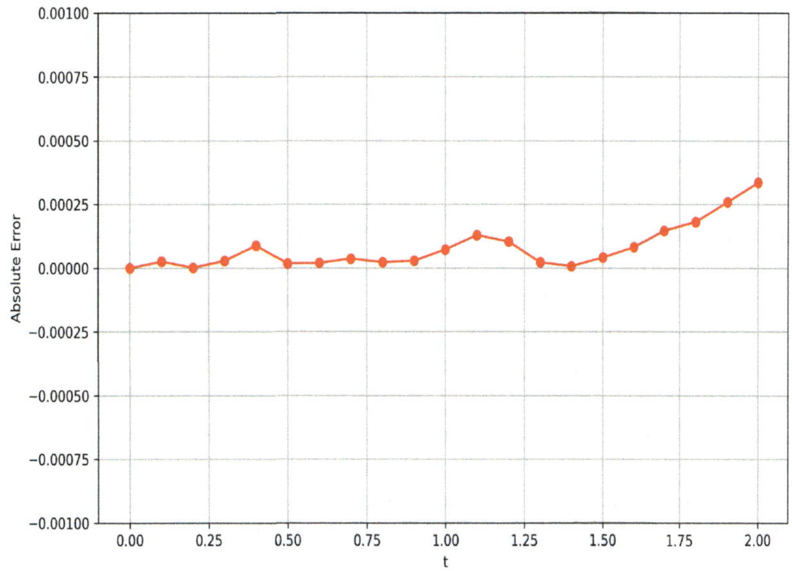

FIGURE 6.6 Plot of absolute error between SANN and RK4 solutions for Example 6.2.

6.6 Validation

In the proposed methodology, the independent variables of DE are used as neural network input. A feed-forward pass on the network gives us the values of the dependent variables

Table 6.2 Comparison of RK4 and SANN solutions for various epochs for Example 6.2.

Input Data (t)	RK4 Results	SANN Results for 6,000 epochs	SANN Results for 8,000 epochs	SANN Results for 10,000 epochs
0.0	1.0000	1.000000	1.000000	1.000000
0.1	1.1053	1.105276	1.105274	1.105272
0.2	1.2218	1.221806	1.221802	1.221795
0.3	1.3508	1.350779	1.350771	1.350756
0.4	1.4936	1.493527	1.493512	1.493482
0.5	1.6515	1.651510	1.651482	1.651427
0.6	1.8263	1.826324	1.826280	1.826190
0.7	2.0197	2.019727	2.019663	2.019530
0.8	2.2336	2.233659	2.233577	2.233395
0.9	2.4702	2.470269	2.470171	2.469936
1.0	2.7319	2.731940	2.731827	2.731536
1.1	3.0213	3.021302	3.021171	3.020821
1.2	3.3412	3.341252	3.341096	3.340682
1.3	3.6948	3.694965	3.694777	3.694294
1.4	4.0857	4.085916	4.085692	4.085133
1.5	4.5176	4.517901	4.517642	4.517005
1.6	4.9947	4.995067	4.994782	4.994070
1.7	5.5215	5.521953	5.521646	5.520872
1.8	6.1030	6.103512	6.103181	6.102363
1.9	6.7445	6.745120	6.744758	6.743911
2.0	7.4518	7.452532	7.452135	7.451275

evaluated at that particular point. Since neural network is differentiable, we can compute the derivatives of the dependent variable (outputs) with respect to the independent variable (inputs) in order to find different derivatives that appear in the original DE. An unsupervised training method has been considered for solving the DE without knowing any solutions in advance. In this regard, an error function has been derived from the given DE, the approximate function and their derivatives. It may be noted that neural network output is indeed a solution of DE when the loss function tends to zero.

From the above experiments, the accuracy of SANN algorithm is witnessed through the comparative assessment of SANN and existing numerical solutions. When compared to the solutions from the literatures, the MAE for Examples 6.1–6.3 are determined to be $5.168E-04$, $7.932E-05$, and $9.274E-03$, respectively. Since these values are close to 0, it confirms the effectiveness of our model in addressing the given problems. The error calculations, displayed graphs, and CPU processing time have been established to produce a comprehensive robustness study for the SANN model. These results clearly indicate that the present unsupervised model is well validated.

These investigations manifest that the presented SANN algorithm for solving the DEs is promising. The accuracy of the proposed model is demonstrated by the remarkable agreement of findings between SANN and existing numerical techniques available in literature.

Table 6.3 Comparison of MDTM and SANN Solutions for various epochs for Example 6.3.

Input Data (t)	MDTM Results	SANN Results for 9,000 epochs	SANN Results for 10,000 epochs
0.0	−0.2000	−0.200000	−0.200000
0.1	0.0031	0.003230	−0.144221
0.2	0.1863	0.187646	−0.067521
0.3	0.3170	0.313786	0.013874
0.4	0.3753	0.384200	0.084453
0.5	0.3565	0.351468	0.131892
0.6	0.2714	0.278934	0.149670
0.7	0.1427	0.136287	0.137734
0.8	−0.0010	−0.018770	0.101477
0.9	−0.1307	−0.145704	0.050288
1.0	−0.2234	−0.221444	−0.004594
1.1	−0.2648	−0.261473	−0.052454
1.2	−0.2519	−0.256923	−0.085238
1.3	−0.1923	−0.191119	−0.098562
1.4	−0.1016	−0.101068	−0.092022
1.5	−0.0002	−0.000751	−0.069350
1.6	0.0916	0.097630	−0.037142
1.7	0.1574	0.103229	−0.002577
1.8	0.1869	0.169524	0.028027
1.9	0.1781	0.164990	0.049679
2.0	0.1362	0.175961	0.059184
2.1	0.0724	0.071757	0.055932
2.2	0.0007	0.005468	0.042264
2.3	−0.0642	−0.029202	0.022761
2.4	−0.1108	−0.110917	0.002639
2.5	−0.1319	−0.124619	−0.013885
2.6	−0.1259	−0.129151	−0.024517
2.7	−0.0965	−0.091228	−0.028894
2.8	−0.0515	−0.048908	−0.028020
2.9	−0.0009	−0.000374	−0.023540
3.0	0.0450	0.019920	−0.017165
3.1	0.0781	0.073430	−0.010320
3.2	0.0931	0.097477	−0.004012
3.3	0.0890	0.080516	0.001159
3.4	0.0684	0.069228	0.004921
3.5	0.0367	0.036147	0.007235
3.6	0.0010	0.008918	0.008211
3.7	−0.0315	−0.037075	0.008042
3.8	−0.0550	−0.052452	0.006966
3.9	−0.0657	−0.069683	0.005227

continued on next page

Table 6.3 (continued)

Input Data (t)	MDTM Results	SANN Results for 9,000 epochs	SANN Results for 10,000 epochs
4.0	−0.0629	−0.069192	0.003066
4.1	−0.0484	−0.023714	0.000705
4.2	−0.0261	−0.022935	−0.001656
4.3	−0.0009	−0.017712	−0.003842
4.4	0.0221	−0.009664	−0.005700
4.5	0.0387	−0.000655	−0.007105
4.6	0.0464	0.047641	−0.007950
4.7	0.0445	0.043980	−0.008149
4.8	0.0343	0.017602	−0.007632
4.9	0.0186	0.018173	−0.006346
5.0	0.0008	0.000657	−0.004247

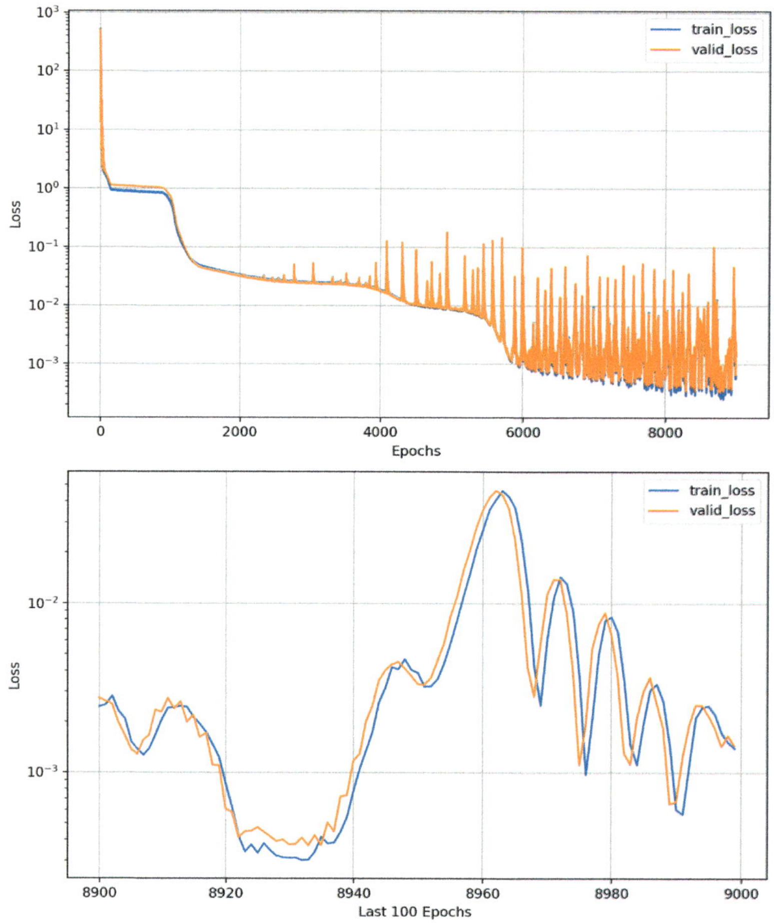

FIGURE 6.7 Training and validation loss during the learning process of SANN for Example 6.3.

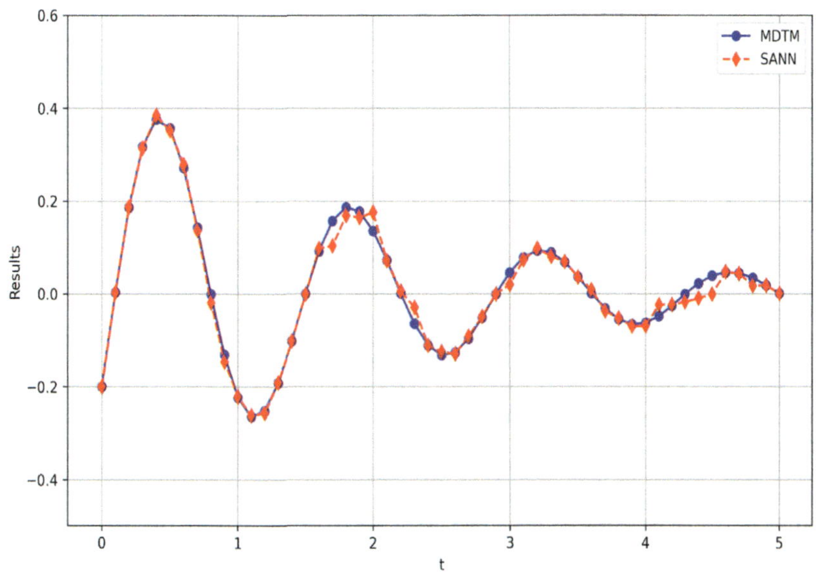

FIGURE 6.8 Comparison of results obtained from SANN with the RK4 method at different time steps for Example 6.3.

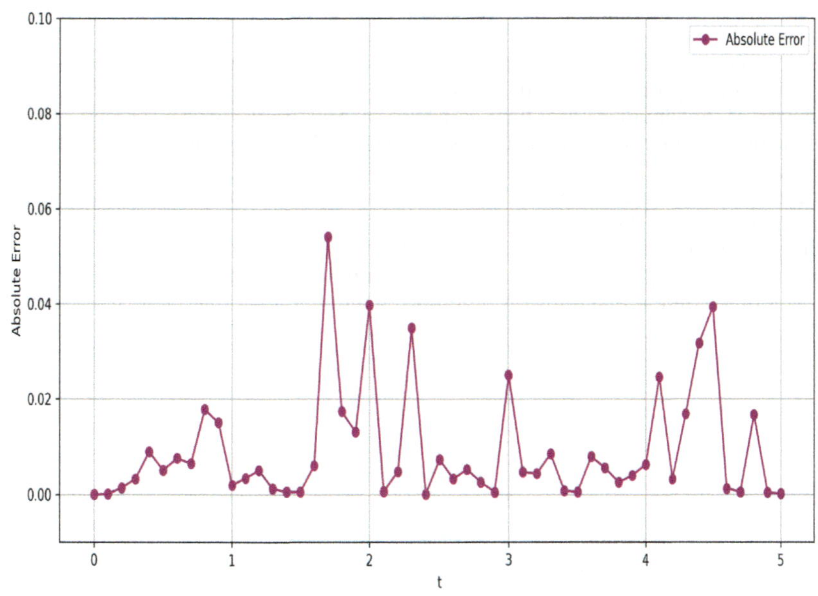

FIGURE 6.9 Plot of absolute error between SANN and MDTM solutions for Example 6.3.

In view of the above, it may also be concluded that SANN is a computationally efficient and generic model.

References

[1] M. Mattheakis, P. Protopapas, D. Sondak, M. Di Giovanni, E. Kaxiras, Physical symmetries embedded in neural networks, arXiv preprint: arXiv:1904.08991, 2019.

[2] A.K. Sahoo, S. Chakraverty, A neural network approach for the solution of van der Pol-Mathieu-Duffing oscillator model, Evolutionary Intelligence 17 (3) (2024) 1425–1435.

[3] M.L. Cartwbight, Balthazar van der Pol, Journal of the London Mathematical Society s1–35 (3) (1960) 367–376.

[4] M.T. Ahmadian, M. Mojahedi, H. Moeenfard, Free vibration analysis of a nonlinear beam using homotopy and modified Lindstedt-Poincare methods, Journal of Solid Mechanics 1 (1) (2009) 29–36.

[5] N. Srinil, H. Zanganeh, Modelling of coupled cross-flow/in-line vortex-induced vibrations using double Duffing and van der Pol oscillators, Ocean Engineering 53 (2012) 83–97.

[6] J. Guckenheimer, P. Holmes, Nonlinear Oscillations, Dynamical Systems, and Bifurcations of Vector Fields, vol. 42, Springer Science & Business Media, 2013.

[7] A. Kimiaeifar, An analytical approach to investigate the response and stability of van der Pol–Mathieu–Duffing oscillators under different excitation functions, Mathematical Methods in the Applied Sciences 33 (13) (2010) 1571–1577.

[8] J. Kalas, Z. Kadeřábek, Periodic solutions of a generalized van der Pol–Mathieu differential equation, Applied Mathematics and Computation 234 (2014) 192–202.

[9] I. Jadoon, M.A.Z. Raja, M. Junaid, A. Ahmed, A. ur Rehman, M. Shoaib, Design of evolutionary optimized finite difference based numerical computing for dust density model of nonlinear van-der Pol Mathieu's oscillatory systems, Mathematics and Computers in Simulation 181 (2021) 444–470.

[10] S. Mall, S. Chakraverty, Hermite functional link neural network for solving the van der Pol–Duffing oscillator equation, Neural Computation 28 (8) (2016) 1574–1598.

[11] K. Wang, X. Yan, Q. Yang, X. Hao, J. Wang, Weak signal detection based on strongly coupled Duffing–van der Pol oscillator and long short-term memory, Journal of the Physical Society of Japan 89 (1) (2020) 014003.

[12] K.-L. Yin, Y.-F. Pu, L. Lu, Combination of fractional FLANN filters for solving the van der Pol-Duffing oscillator, Neurocomputing 399 (2020) 183–192.

[13] A.H. Bukhari, M. Sulaiman, M.A.Z. Raja, S. Islam, M. Shoaib, P. Kumam, Design of a hybrid NAR-RBFs neural network for nonlinear dusty plasma system, Alexandria Engineering Journal 59 (5) (2020) 3325–3345.

[14] S. Chakraverty, S. Mall, Artificial Neural Networks for Engineers and Scientists: Solving Ordinary Differential Equations, CRC Press, 2017.

[15] I. Goodfellow, Y. Bengio, A. Courville, Deep Learning, MIT Press, 2016.

[16] S. Nourazar, A. Mirzabeigy, Approximate solution for nonlinear Duffing oscillator with damping effect using the modified differential transform method, Scientia Iranica 20 (2) (2013) 364–368.

7 Wavelet neural network

Contents

7.1 Introduction **71**
7.2 Wavelet neural networks **72**
7.2.1 Mexican Hat wavelet neural networks (M_hWNN) 73
7.3 Methodology **74**
7.3.1 Modeling of Mexican Hat wavelet neural networks 74
7.4 Problem statement **76**
7.4.1 Non-linear financial model 76
7.5 Simulation results and discussions **77**
7.5.1 Experimental setup 77
7.5.2 Model problems 78
7.6 Validation **86**
References **89**

Chapter points

- Explains the architecture of Wavelet Neural Networks.
- Discuss the structure of Mexican Hat Wavelet Neural Networks.
- Demonstrate the implementation of Wavelet Neural Networks for solving dynamical problems.
- Evaluate the effectiveness of the L-BFGS optimizer in addressing the undertaken financial model governed by a system of differential equations.

7.1 Introduction

ANN is the most successful AI technique, which has influenced science and technology over the decades. In literature, the sigmoid activation function has been extensively used in ANN models because of its stability [1]. However, despite its widespread application, it is not appropriate for all circumstances. As the application areas of ANN are quite diverse, using a *one-size-fits-all* activation function for getting accuracy is difficult.

Traditional neural networks also had incompetence to define local features such as jumps in objective function, discontinuities in curvature, and stuck in local minima [2]. To address this limitation, a group of neural scientists from Sweden and the INRIA laboratory, France headed by Zhang and Benveniste [3] proposed the wavelet neural network (WNN) model, based on the multi-time scale and non-linear properties of the time-series

Artificial Neural Networks and Type-2 Fuzzy Set. https://doi.org/10.1016/B978-0-44-332894-7.00016-2

problems. WNN is based on the combination of some particular wavelet kernels and feed-forward neural networks. It seems to be an effective and strong, approximate model for universal functions. WNNs overcome the above drawbacks of traditional ANNs and convert it into an efficient technique for universal function approximation. WNN has been extensively used by researchers and scientists in various fields such as fault diagnosis [4], daily pan evaporation [5], astrophysical events [6], etc. Additionally, the learning rate of the WNN is relatively faster than that of conventional neural network. The parameters of neural network, i.e., weights and biases of a multi-layer perceptron are replaced by the translation and dilation parameters.

Shoaib et al. [7] introduced a Meyer neuro-evolutionary genetic algorithm for simulating the epidemiological smoking model by employing hybrid Meyer WNNs. Further, to explore the solution of DEs, Rahimkhani and Ordokhani [8] presented two efficient neural algorithms, namely orthonormal Bernoulli WNN-optimization and orthonormal Bernoulli WNN-collocation methods. In a pioneer work, Sahoo and Chakraverty proposed the PWNN model [9] to investigate stomach problems.

A good number of optimization algorithms have emerged during the last few years, marking remarkable advances in both application areas and research. These algorithms can be classified as derivative-based or derivative-free. However, derivative-based optimization algorithms are generally more stable when compared to the derivative-free optimization algorithms [10]. In this regard, some potential derivative-based optimization algorithms are gradient descent (GD), conjugate gradient, stochastic gradient descent (SGD), and Limited-memory Broyden–Fletcher–Goldfarb–Shanno (L-BFGS).

Motivated by the above literatures, efficient WNN algorithms have been proposed in combination of the L-BFGS algorithm to understand the dynamical behavior of the nonlinear financial model.

7.2 Wavelet neural networks

In this section, the background of WNN has been discussed and also recalls some fundamental definitions and theorems related to WNN.

A wavelet is a “small wave” function centered in the neighborhood of “0” and denoted as $\psi(t) \in L^2(\mathbb{R})$ having the following property:

$$\int_{-\infty}^{\infty} \psi(t)\, dt = 0. \tag{7.1}$$

The neural network has fault tolerance, is self-adaptive and strong inference ability where as wavelet basic has the time frequency localization property. The architecture of WNNs is very similar to a feed-forward multi-layer neural network, whose hidden layer consists of wavelet neurons generally known as wavelons. The mother wavelet is made up of two factors, namely translation and the dilation a_i, where i denotes the ith wavelet [12] and written as below:

$$\varphi(t) = \frac{1}{\sqrt{|a_i|}}\psi\left(\frac{t-b}{a}\right), a > 0, b \in \mathbb{R}. \tag{7.2}$$

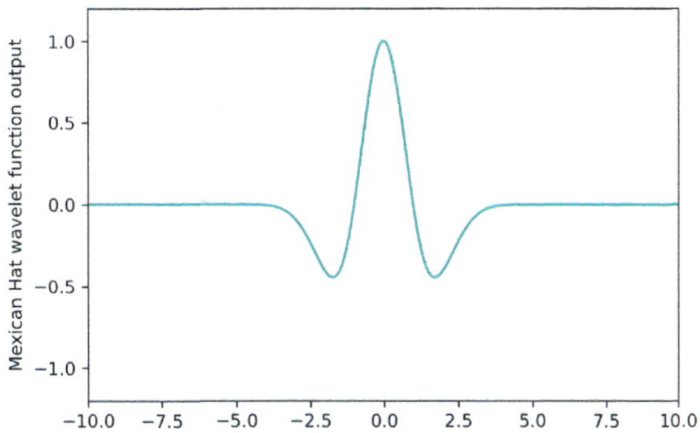

FIGURE 7.1 Mexican Hat mother wavelet function.

In this regard, the following theorems which describe the properties and rate of convergence of WNN may be found in literature.

Theorem 1. *The WNN has L^2 and universal function approximation properties [13].*

Theorem 2. *In a WNN the rate of convergence of above properties can be made rapid if for any $\epsilon > 0$, there is a Sobolev space H_b such that for any $f \in H_b$, there exists a sequence of wavelet networks f_n, where $n = 2^M$ such that [13]*

$$\|f - f_n\|_{sup} = \mathcal{O}(n^{-\epsilon}) \tag{7.3}$$

and

$$\|f - f_n\|_{L^2} = \mathcal{O}(n^{-\epsilon}). \tag{7.4}$$

Proof. For the proof of Theorems 1 and 2, Zhang et al. [13] may be referred. □

Theorem 3. *Let $m, P \in \mathbb{N}$ are dimensions of the input layer and number of hidden layers in the network, respectively. $\psi : \mathbb{R} \to \mathbb{R}$ and $\Theta \subset \mathbb{R}^m$ are the domain of the activation function. Let $\Phi = ((w_{i,j}, b_j), j = 1, 2, ..., P)$ be a neural network with architecture $(m, N_1, N_2, ..., N_P)$ and $\tilde{N_1}, \tilde{N_2}..., \tilde{N_P} \in \mathbb{N}$ such that $\tilde{N_l} \geq N_l$ for all $l = 1, ... P-1$. Then there exists a neural network $\tilde{\Phi}$ with architecture $(m, \tilde{N_1}, \tilde{N_2}..., \tilde{N}_{P-1}, \tilde{N_P})$ and such that $R_\psi^\Theta(\Phi) = R_\psi^\Theta(\tilde{\Phi})$ [14].*

Proof. For the proof, Petersen et al. [14] may be referred. □

7.2.1 Mexican Hat wavelet neural networks (M_hWNN)

The Mexican Hat mother wavelet function can be expressed as

$$\Psi_{MexicanHat} = (1-t)^2 e^{-t^2/2}. \tag{7.5}$$

The Mexican Hat mother wavelet is obtained from the Gaussian function by applying the Laplacian operator and it is continuously a differentiable wavelet. Fig. 7.1 shows the graphical representation of the Mexican Hat wavelet.

The output of M_hWNN is defined as

$$\hat{M}_{NN}(t;\Theta)=\sum_{i=1}^{n}\mu_{i,j}\Psi_i(t_1,t_2,t_3...,t_N)+b_j,\ j=1,2,...,K \tag{7.6}$$

where $\mu_{i,j}$ is the weight from the input unit i to the hidden unit j, b_j is the bias and Θ is the set of trainable parameters.

7.3 Methodology

This section covers the application of the M_hWNN-LBFGS algorithm for approximating an non-linear financial model and evaluates its effectiveness.

7.3.1 Modeling of Mexican Hat wavelet neural networks

This section explains implementation of the proposed M_hWNN-LBFGS algorithm to solve the non-linear financial model as an unconstrained problem.

An autonomous system of non-linear financial model can be written in the vector form as

$$\begin{pmatrix} f_1\left(t,X,\dfrac{dX}{dt}\right)\\ f_2\left(t,D,\dfrac{dD}{dt}\right)\\ f_3\left(t,P,\dfrac{dP}{dt}\right)\end{pmatrix}=\begin{pmatrix}0\\0\\0\end{pmatrix}. \tag{7.7}$$

First, the governing equation (Eq. (7.16)) will be transferred into an approximate solution, as a combination of initial/boundary conditions, a user-defined mathematical expression, and M_hWNN-LBFGS output. Therefore, we have

$$\begin{cases}\widetilde{X}(\mathbf{t};\Theta_x)=a_1+(1-\exp(-t))\hat{M}_{NN}(t;\Theta_x)\\ \widetilde{D}(t;\Theta_d)=a_2+(1-\exp(-t))\hat{M}_{NN}(t;\Theta_d)\\ \widetilde{P}(t;\Theta_p)=a_3+(1-\exp(-t))\hat{M}_{NN}(t;\Theta_p),\end{cases} \tag{7.8}$$

where the first term $a_i, i=1,2,3$ satisfies the initial condition of the given non-linear financial model without adjustable parameters and second term is the neural network output. Let us assume that neural network has $J-1$ hidden layers, such that each hidden layer has k number of neurons. For given input $t\in\mathbb{R}^n$, the unknown function $\hat{M}_{NN}(\mathbf{t};\Theta)$ in the second part of the approximate solution is denoted by

$$\begin{cases}\hat{M}_{NN}(\mathbf{t};\Theta_x)=\left(\sum_{j=1}^{k}\omega_{i,j}^{w}(1-z_j)^2\exp(-z_j^2/2)\right),\\ \hat{M}_{NN}(\mathbf{t};\Theta_d)=\left(\sum_{j=1}^{k}\omega_{i,j}^{m}(1-z_j)^2\exp(-z_j^2/2)\right),\\ \hat{M}_{NN}(\mathbf{t};\Theta_p)=\left(\sum_{j=1}^{k}\omega_{i,j}^{r}(1-z_j)^2\exp(-z_j^2/2)\right),\end{cases} \tag{7.9}$$

where $z_j = \mathbf{W}^{(j)}\mathbf{t}^{J-1} + b^{(j)}$, $j = 1, 2, ..., J$.

Here, $\Theta = \{\mathbf{W}^{(j)}, b^{(j)}\}_{j=1}^{J}$ is the set of updatable parameters, $\mathbf{W}^{(j)} = \omega_{ij}$ is set of weights, such that ω_{ij} represents from the input layer j to the neuron i such that $i = 1, 2, 3, ...k$ and $b^{(j)}$ is the bias.

Let us denote the output of $J - 1^{th}$ layer as

$$\hat{M}_{NN}(\mathbf{t}; \Theta) = O(t_i), \tag{7.10}$$

where $O(t_i) = [o(t_1), o(t_2), ..., o(t_k)]^T \in \mathbb{R}^{k\times 1}$. Then $O(t_i)$ can be obtained from

$$\begin{bmatrix} \Psi(\mu_{1,1}t_1 + b_1) & \Psi(\mu_{1,2}t_1 + b_2) & \dots & \Psi(\mu_{1,J\text{-}1}t_1 + b_{J\text{-}1}) \\ \Psi(\mu_{2,1}t_2 + b_1) & \Psi(\mu_{2,2}t_2 + b_2) & \dots & \Psi(\mu_{2,J\text{-}1}t_2 + b_{J\text{-}1}) \\ \cdot & \cdot & \cdot & \cdot \\ \cdot & \cdot & \cdot & \cdot \\ \cdot & \cdot & \cdot & \cdot \\ \Psi(\mu_{k,1}t_k + b_1) & \Psi(\mu_{k,2}t_k + b_2) & \dots & \Psi(\mu_{k,J\text{-}1}t_k + b_{J\text{-}1}) \end{bmatrix} \begin{bmatrix} \omega_1 \\ \omega_2 \\ \cdot \\ \cdot \\ \cdot \\ \omega_{J-1} \end{bmatrix} = \begin{bmatrix} o(t_1) \\ o(t_2) \\ \cdot \\ \cdot \\ \cdot \\ o(t_k) \end{bmatrix}. \tag{7.11}$$

Let us take the output matrix of $J - 1^{th}$ layer, C and the weight vector ω as follows:

$$C = \begin{bmatrix} \Psi(\mu_{1,1}t_1 + b_1) & \Psi(\mu_{1,2}t_1 + b_2) & \dots & \Psi(\mu_{1,J\text{-}1}t_1 + b_{J\text{-}1}) \\ \Psi(\mu_{2,1}t_2 + b_1) & \Psi(\mu_{2,2}t_2 + b_2) & \dots & \Psi(\mu_{2,J\text{-}1}t_2 + b_{J\text{-}1}) \\ \cdot & \cdot & \cdot & \cdot \\ \cdot & \cdot & \cdot & \cdot \\ \cdot & \cdot & \cdot & \cdot \\ \Psi(\mu_{k,1}t_k + b_1) & \Psi(\mu_{k,2}t_k + b_2) & \dots & \Psi(\mu_{k,J\text{-}1}t_k + b_{J\text{-}1}) \end{bmatrix}, \text{ and } \omega = \begin{bmatrix} \omega_1 \\ \omega_2 \\ \cdot \\ \cdot \\ \cdot \\ \omega_{J\text{-}1} \end{bmatrix} \in \mathbb{R}^{J-1\times 1}.$$

Now let us define the block matrix B of the following form:

$$B(t) = \begin{bmatrix} A_x(t) & 0 & 0 \\ 0 & A_d(t) & 0 \\ 0 & 0 & A_p(t) \end{bmatrix}$$

$$W = \begin{bmatrix} \omega_j^x & \omega_j^d & \omega_j^p \end{bmatrix}^T.$$

$$O = \begin{bmatrix} \hat{M}_{NN}(\mathbf{t}; \Theta_w) & \hat{M}_{NN}(\mathbf{t}; \Theta_m) & \hat{M}_{NN}(\mathbf{t}; \Theta_r) \end{bmatrix}^T$$

Then the above matrix can be compactly written as

$$B(\mathbf{t})W = O. \tag{7.12}$$

Then a training algorithm has been employed to tune the parameters of M_hWNN-LBFGS, which is embedded in the approximate solution. The M_hWNN-LBFGS is trained to predict the solutions of a non-linear financial for any testing point inside the given domain by unsupervised learning. In order to find the objective function, we may need to calculate the derivative of the network $\hat{M}_{NN}(\mathbf{t};\Theta)$ with respect to $\mathbf{t}$. It may be computed as follows:

$$D^{\gamma}(\hat{M}_{NN}(\mathbf{t};\Theta)) = \frac{\partial^{\gamma}\hat{M}_{NN}(\mathbf{t};\Theta)}{\partial \mathbf{t}^{\gamma}} = \sum_{j=1}^{k}\omega_{i,j}\frac{\partial\Psi^{\gamma}}{\partial t^{\gamma}} = \sum_{j=1}^{k}\omega_{i,j}\mathbf{W}^{(j)\gamma}\Psi^{(\gamma)}(t_j), \tag{7.13}$$

where γ is the order of the derivative.

Differentiating Eq. (7.8), we have

$$\begin{aligned}
&D^{\gamma}[\widetilde{X}(\mathbf{t};\Theta_x), \widetilde{D}(\mathbf{t};\Theta_d), \widetilde{P}(\mathbf{t};\Theta_p)] \\
&\quad = D^{\gamma}\left[(1-e^{-x})\hat{M}_{NN}(\mathbf{t};\Theta_x), (1-e^{-x})\hat{M}_{NN}(\mathbf{t};\Theta_d), (1-e^{-x})\hat{M}_{NN}(\mathbf{t};\Theta_p)\right] \\
&\quad = D^{\gamma}[(1-e^{-x})\sum_{j=1}^{k}\sum_{i=1}^{n}\omega_{i,j}^{x}(1-\left(\mathbf{W}^{(j)}\mathbf{t}^{\,J-1}+b^{(j)}\right))^2\exp\left(\frac{-(\mathbf{W}^{(j)}\mathbf{t}^{\,J-1}+b^{(j)})^2}{2}\right), \\
&\qquad (1-e^{-x})\sum_{j=1}^{k}\sum_{i=1}^{n}\omega_{i,j}^{d}(1-\left(\mathbf{W}^{(j)}\mathbf{t}^{\,J-1}+b^{(j)}\right))^2\exp\left(\frac{-(\mathbf{W}^{(j)}\mathbf{t}^{\,J-1}+b^{(j)})^2}{2}\right), \\
&\qquad (1-e^{-x})\sum_{j=1}^{k}\sum_{i=1}^{n}\omega_{i,j}^{p}(1-\left(\mathbf{W}^{(j)}\mathbf{t}^{\,J-1}+b^{(j)}\right))^2\exp\left(\frac{-(\mathbf{W}^{(j)}\mathbf{t}^{\,J-1}+b^{(j)})^2}{2}\right)].
\end{aligned} \tag{7.14}$$

By using the gradient of the approximate solutions and for the given problem, the objective function can be formulated as follows:

$$\mathbb{J}(\Theta) = \begin{cases} \sum_{i=1}^{n}(D\widetilde{X}(\mathbf{t};\Theta_x) - f_1(t_i, \widetilde{X}(\mathbf{t};\Theta_x)))^2, \\ \sum_{i=1}^{n}(D\widetilde{D}(\mathbf{t};\Theta_d) - f_2(t_i, \widetilde{D}(\mathbf{t};\Theta_d)))^2, \\ \sum_{i=1}^{n}(D\widetilde{P}(\mathbf{t};\Theta_p) - f_3(t_i, \widetilde{P}(\mathbf{t};\Theta_p)))^2. \end{cases} \tag{7.15}$$

7.4 Problem statement

In this section, the governing equation of the non-linear financial model [11] has been discussed.

7.4.1 Non-linear financial model

The instability and complexity of the economic system significantly restrict the accuracy of economic forecasts. There are so many different factors that affect it, and they all interact in complicated ways. This is especially true in areas like finance, the stock market, and social economics. By examining patterns over time, various types of changes, and the factors contributing to unpredictability, we can gain insights into the complexities at play. This understanding can inform improved methods for analyzing, forecasting, and managing the economy.

The fluctuations in X are primarily driven by two factors: first, the inherent contradictions within the investment market, specifically the imbalance between investment and savings; and second, structural adjustments stemming from changes in goods prices. The rate of change in D is directly correlated with the rate of investment, and inversely correlated with both the cost of investment and interest rates. Assuming a constant return on investment over a given period, the change in D can be predicted based on these factors. Changes in P are influenced by a combination of supply and demand dynamics within the commercial market and fluctuations in inflation rates. It is assumed that the quantity of goods supplied and demanded remains constant over a certain period, with these quantities inversely proportional to prices. Moreover, the changes in inflation rates are tied to fluctuation in the real interest rate, calculated as the nominal interest rate minus the real interest rate.

The non-linear financial model is represented via three components, i.e., the rate of interest (X), the investment demand (D), and the price index (P) as shown below

$$\begin{cases} X'(t) = P + (D - \alpha)X, & X(\alpha_1) = a_1 \\ D'(t) = 1 - \beta D - X^2, & F(\alpha_2) = a_2 \\ P'(t) = -X - \gamma P, & M(\alpha_3) = a_3, \end{cases} \tag{7.16}$$

where α is the saving amount, β is the cost per investment, and γ is the elasticity of demand of commercial markets. It may be noted that all these three constants are positive. Moreover, $a_i (i = 1, 2, 3)$ are initial conditions for all components of the financial model.

7.5 Simulation results and discussions

In order to manifest the presented M$_h$WNN-LBFGS algorithm, which is promising, the following problems have been addressed.

7.5.1 Experimental setup

Moreover, we uniformly adopt L-BFGS as an optimizer with a learning rate $\eta = 0.001$ to update the parameters. L-BFGS is a potential optimization techniques based from the quasi-Newton family that are widely employed in the field of deep learning. L-BFGS is same as BFGS except for the Hessian matrix updation. However, after selecting the basic framework, hyper-parameter tuning has been done to select the optimal number of hidden layers and the number of nodes in each hidden layer. The simulation workflow of M$_h$WNN-LBFGS for solving non-linear financial model is presented in Fig. 7.2.

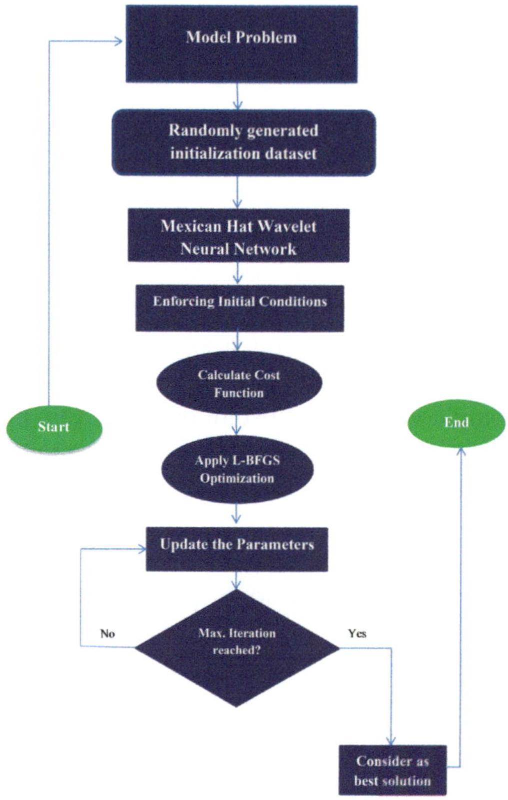

FIGURE 7.2 Workflow diagram of M_hWNNs-LBFGS for approximating the financial model.

7.5.2 Model problems

Example 7.1. Let us consider a non-linear financial model by substituting the values of $\alpha = 3.0, \beta = 0.1, \gamma = 1.0, \alpha_1 = \alpha_2 = \alpha_3 = 0, a_1 = 2, a_2 = 3,$ and $a_3 = 2$ in Eq. (7.16) [11]

$$\begin{cases} X'(t) = P + (D-3)X, & X(0) = 2 \\ D'(t) = 1 - 0.1D - X^2, & F(0) = 3 \\ P'(t) = -X - P, & M(0) = 2. \end{cases} \tag{7.17}$$

In order to apply the M_hWNN-LBFGS algorithm, let us reformulate the above problem into an initial neural approximation solution as

$$\begin{cases} \widetilde{X}(t, \Theta_x) = 2.0 + (1 - \exp(-t))\hat{M}_{NN}(t, \Theta_x)|_{W \to a_1 = 2.0} \\ \widetilde{D}(t, \Theta_d) = 3.0 + (1 - \exp(-t))\hat{M}_{NN}(t, \Theta_d)|_{M \to a_2 = 3.0} \\ \widetilde{P}(t, \Theta_p) = 2.0 + (1 - \exp(-t))\hat{M}_{NN}(t, \Theta_p)|_{R \to a_3 = 2.0}. \end{cases} \tag{7.18}$$

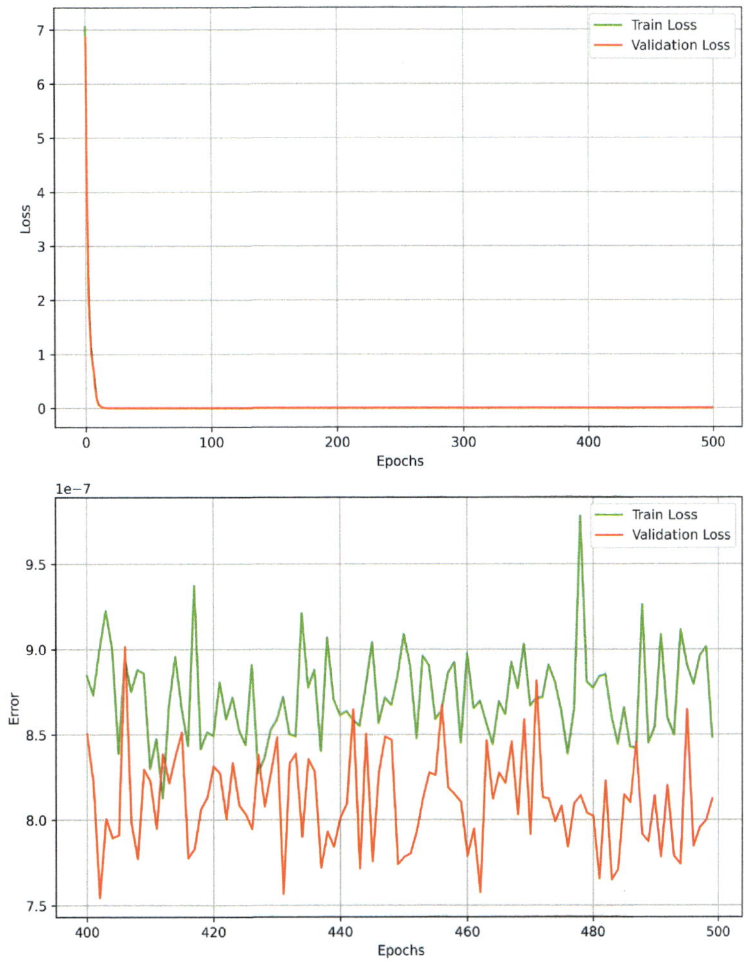

FIGURE 7.3 Learning curves showing the result of training loss vs. validation loss during training process of M_hWNN-LBFGS with respect to epochs for Example 7.1.

A deep neural network has been employed with a depth of 3 hidden layers, such that each hidden layer is set to contain 16 neurons. Then the network has been trained for 100 equidistant points with white noise in $t \in [0, 2]$. During the training of model, we track the learning performance of each epoch through training loss and validating loss. The training and validation loss for the aforementioned example for 500 epochs (last 100 epochs are depicted in subfigure) are presented in Fig. 7.3. In other words, this graph represents the network's capability for solving the WMR model. Both the training and validation losses continue to decrease throughout the learning process, demonstrating the robustness of the proposed model.

In order to demonstrate the effectiveness of the M_hWNN-LBFGS algorithm, it is vital to compare the neural results obtained by the proposed algorithms with the ex-

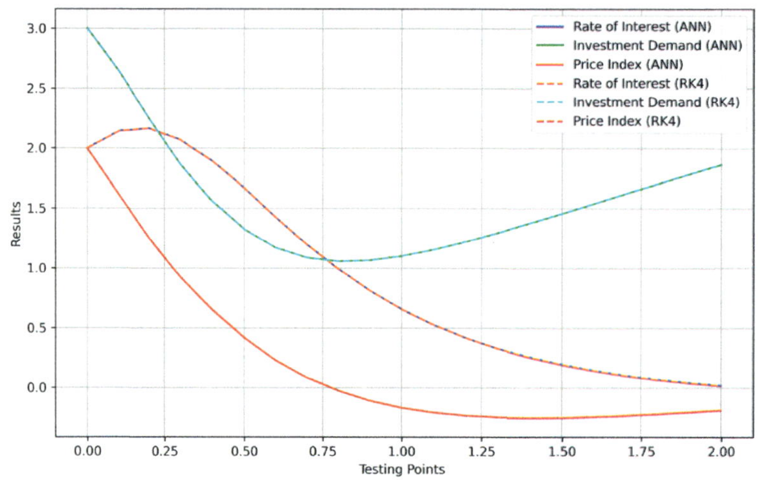

FIGURE 7.4 Comparison between RK4 solutions and M_hWNN-LBFGS solutions of the financial model for Example 7.1.

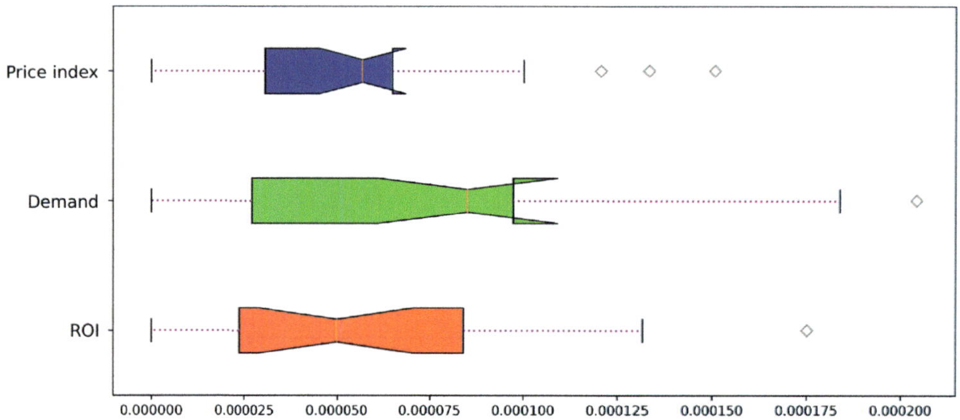

FIGURE 7.5 Box plot of absolute error between RK4 solutions and M_hWNN-LBFGSs solutions for Example 7.1.

isting results at different testing points. Moreover, to compare the M_hWNN-LBFGS algorithm with the conventional methods, we obtained RK4 solutions at 21 different testing points. The predicted solutions are graphically portrayed in Fig. 7.4, that illustrates the efficacy of M_hWNN-LBFGS. From this figure, it can be observed that the neural results are coinsides with the numerical results. Table 7.1 presents the neural network predicted results of non-linear financial models at testing points $t \in [0, 2]$, $\Delta t = 0.1$.

Moreover, the absolute error values are delineated in Fig. 7.5. Different other global statistical errors (NSE, MAPE, TIC, and RMSE) are also evaluated and presented in Fig. 7.6.

Table 7.1 M_hWNN-LBFGS solution for non-linear financial model at testing points for $t \in [0, 2]$, $\Delta t = 0.1$ for Example 7.1.

Index	Testing Points (t)	$X(t)$	$D(t)$	$P(t)$
0	0.0	2.000000	3.000000	2.000000
1	0.1	2.143275	2.638395	1.611470
2	0.2	2.165415	2.245593	1.252143
3	0.3	2.073414	1.872097	0.930589
4	0.4	1.895780	1.558543	0.652745
5	0.5	1.670150	1.325112	0.420831
6	0.6	1.430310	1.171984	0.233435
7	0.7	1.199737	1.087625	0.086463
8	0.8	0.991328	1.056906	−0.025584
9	0.9	0.810024	1.065414	−0.108500
10	1.0	0.655880	1.101133	−0.167665
11	1.1	0.526545	1.154985	−0.207756
12	1.2	0.418861	1.220683	−0.232733
13	1.3	0.329668	1.294052	−0.245931
14	1.4	0.256078	1.372242	−0.250141
15	1.5	0.195497	1.453187	−0.247649
16	1.6	0.145624	1.535404	−0.240242
17	1.7	0.104475	1.617985	−0.229264
18	1.8	0.070458	1.700529	−0.215721
19	1.9	0.042416	1.782857	−0.200448
20	2.0	0.019640	1.864527	−0.184273

Example 7.2. Let us consider another non-linear financial model by substituting the values of $\alpha = 3.0$, $\beta = 0.1$, $\gamma = 1.0$, $\alpha_1 = \alpha_2 = \alpha_3 = 0$, $a_1 = 1$, $a_2 = 2$, and $a_3 = 1$ in Eq. (7.16) [11],

$$\begin{cases} X'(t) = P + (D - 3)X, & X(0) = 1 \\ D'(t) = 1 - 0.1D - X^2, & F(0) = 2 \\ P'(t) = -X - P, & M(0) = 1. \end{cases} \tag{7.19}$$

Accordingly, the initial neural approximation solution can be written as

$$\begin{cases} \hat{X}(t, \Theta_{\hat{x}}) = 1 + (1 - \exp(-t))\mathrm{NN}(t, \Theta_{\hat{x}})|_{X \to a_1 = 1} \\ \hat{D}(t, \Theta_{\hat{d}}) = 2 + (1 - \exp(-t))\mathrm{NN}(t, \Theta_{\hat{d}})|_{D \to a_2 = 2} \\ \hat{P}(t, \Theta_{\hat{p}}) = 1 + (1 - \exp(-t))\mathrm{NN}(t, \Theta_{\hat{p}})|_{P \to a_3 = 1}. \end{cases} \tag{7.20}$$

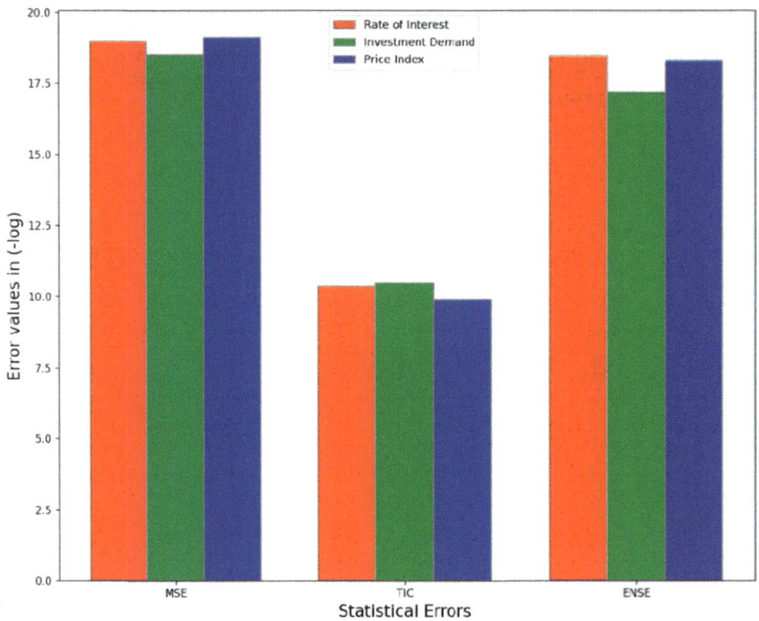

FIGURE 7.6 Performance indices of M_hWNN-LBFGS model based on statistical measures MAPE, TIC, and RMSE for Example 7.1.

Likewise, in Example 7.1, a deep neural network has been constructed. Then the model has been trained for 500 epochs and the history of the loss function is given in Fig. 7.7. The training data set contains a grid of 100 equidistant points with white noise in $t \in [0, 2]$. Here, we have taken learning rate $\eta = 0.001$ during the updation of the trainable parameters.

Since in this case the exact solution is not available, the obtained results are compared with RK4 results at different testing points and those are depicted in Table 7.2. The solutions are also depicted in Fig. 7.8. It can be seen from the figure that the curve of our predicted solution fits the RK4 solution curve very well. However, there are still some errors that can be seen from the error graph in Figs. 7.9–7.10. This result shows the effectiveness of the proposed algorithm in order to solve the financial model.

Example 7.3. Let us consider a non-linear financial model by substituting the values of $\alpha = 1.5$, $\beta = 0.1$, $\gamma = 1.0$, $\alpha_1 = \alpha_2 = \alpha_3 = 0$, $a_1 = 2$, $a_2 = 3$, and $a_3 = 2$ in Eq. (7.16) [11],

$$\begin{cases} X'(t) = P + (D - 1.5)X, & X(0) = 2 \\ D'(t) = 1 - 0.1D - X^2, & F(0) = 3 \\ P'(t) = -X - P, & M(0) = 2. \end{cases} \tag{7.21}$$

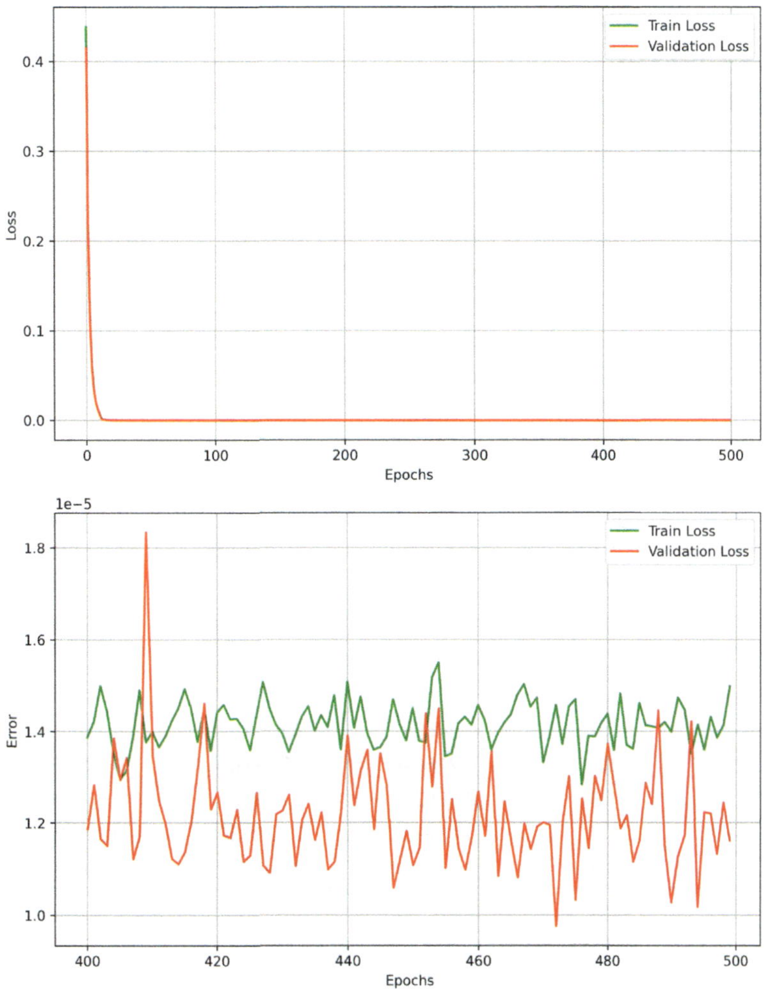

FIGURE 7.7 Learning curves showing the result of training loss vs. validation loss during training process of M_hWNN-LBFGS with respect to epochs for Example 7.2.

Accordingly, the initial neural approximation solution may be written as

$$\begin{cases} \hat{X}(t,\Theta_{\hat{x}}) = 2 + (1-\exp(-t))\mathrm{NN}(t,\Theta_{\hat{x}})|_{X\to a_1=2} \\ \hat{D}(t,\Theta_{\hat{d}}) = 3 + (1-\exp(-t))\mathrm{NN}(t,\Theta_{\hat{d}})|_{D\to a_2=3} \\ \hat{P}(t,\Theta_{\hat{p}}) = 2 + (1-\exp(-t))\mathrm{NN}(t,\Theta_{\hat{p}})|_{P\to a_3=2}. \end{cases} \tag{7.22}$$

Similar to Example 7.1, a deep neural network has been constructed to approximate this problem. Then the model has been trained for 1,500 epochs and monitor the training in Fig. 7.11. Moreover, our experimental studies are reported in two parts. First, the results obtained by the M_hWNN-LBFGS algorithm are compared with RK4 results. Fig. 7.12

Table 7.2 M_hWNN-LBFGS solution for the non-linear financial model at testing points for $t \in [0, 2]$, $\Delta t = 0.1$ for Example 7.2.

Index	Testing Points (t)	$X(t)$	$D(t)$	$P(t)$
0	0.0	1.000000	2.000000	1.000000
1	0.1	0.989427	1.981308	0.810523
2	0.2	0.961802	1.965778	0.639954
3	0.3	0.920364	1.957142	0.489047
4	0.4	0.868978	1.957470	0.357494
5	0.5	0.811350	1.967458	0.244019
6	0.6	0.750560	1.986884	0.146863
7	0.7	0.688933	2.015060	0.064369
8	0.8	0.628129	2.051156	−0.004719
9	0.9	0.569300	2.094351	−0.061410
10	1.0	0.513223	2.143819	−0.106849
11	1.1	0.460389	2.198649	−0.142498
12	1.2	0.411053	2.257798	−0.169965
13	1.3	0.365291	2.320170	−0.190646
14	1.4	0.323056	2.384810	−0.205511
15	1.5	0.284225	2.451095	−0.215162
16	1.6	0.248622	2.518791	−0.220084
17	1.7	0.216044	2.587864	−0.220895
18	1.8	0.186313	2.658101	−0.218442
19	1.9	0.159333	2.728730	−0.213750
20	2.0	0.135144	2.798232	−0.207884

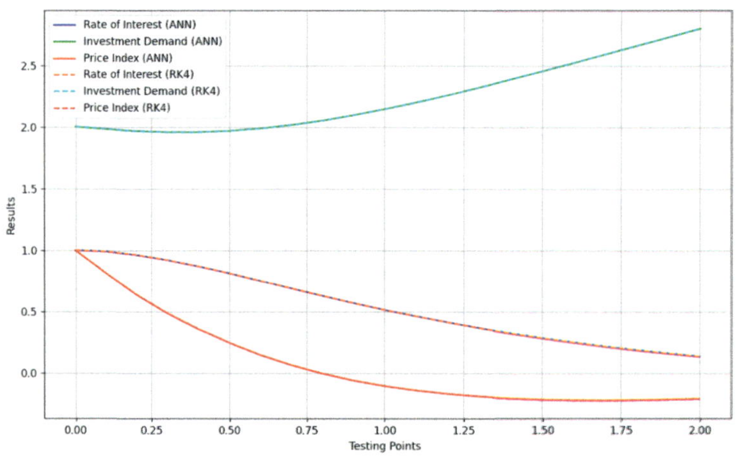

FIGURE 7.8 Comparison between RK4 solutions and M_hWNN-LBFGS solutions of the financial model for Example 7.2.

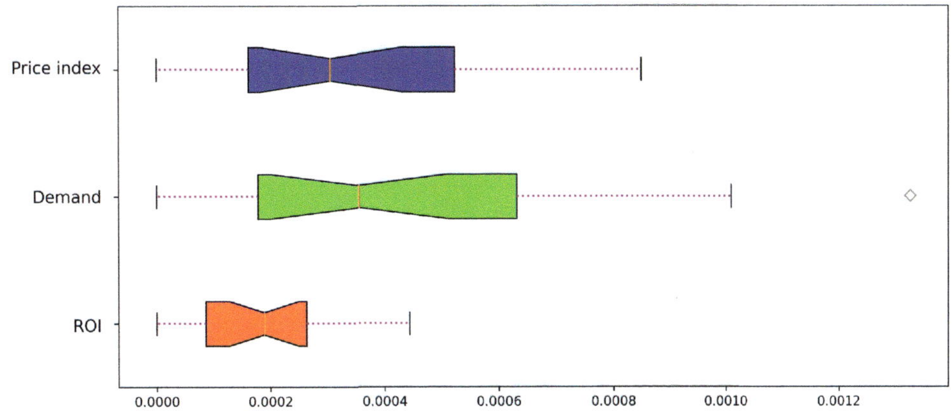

FIGURE 7.9 Box plot of absolute error between RK4 solutions and M_hWNN-LBFGSs solutions for Example 7.2.

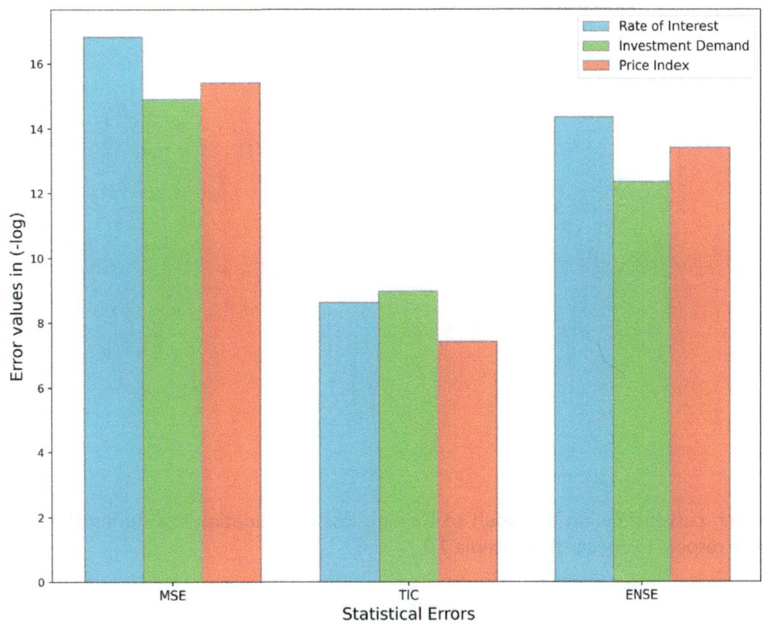

FIGURE 7.10 Performance indices of the M_hWNN-LBFGS model based on statistical measures MAPE, TIC, and RMSE for Example 7.2.

represents the comparison of solutions obtained by using the M_hWNN-LBFGS algorithm with the RK4 numerical solutions of the financial system. Table 7.3 shows the prediction against testing points in $t \in [0, 2]$, $\Delta t = 0.1$. Then statistical measures are reported for convergence analysis. In this regard, different errors are evaluated and depicted in Figs. 7.13–7.14.

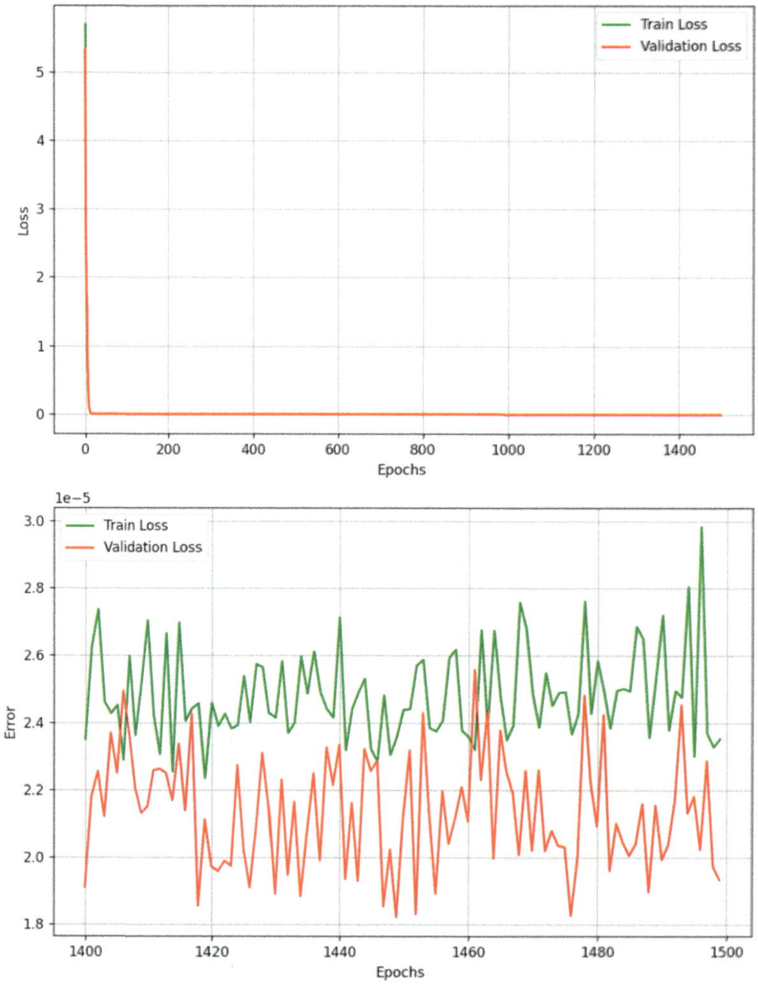

FIGURE 7.11 Learning curves showing the result of training loss vs. validation loss during the training process of M_hWNN-LBFGS with respect to epochs for Example 7.3.

7.6 Validation

This section delves into the validation of the above experiments. Another way to verify WNN performances are based on calculating the global statistical errors.

From the above box plots, we can observe that the mode of absolute error of $X(t)$, $D(t)$, and $P(t)$ classes found in the neighborhood of $5E-05$, $8E-05$, and $5E-05$, respectively, for Example 7.1. For Example 7.2 the mode of absolute error of $X(t)$, $D(t)$, and $P(t)$ classes lies in the vicinity of $2E-04$, $3.5E-04$, and $3E-04$, respectively. Likewise, for Example 7.3 the mode of absolute error of $X(t)$, $D(t)$, and $P(t)$ classes are found to be $4.5E-04$, $3E-04$,

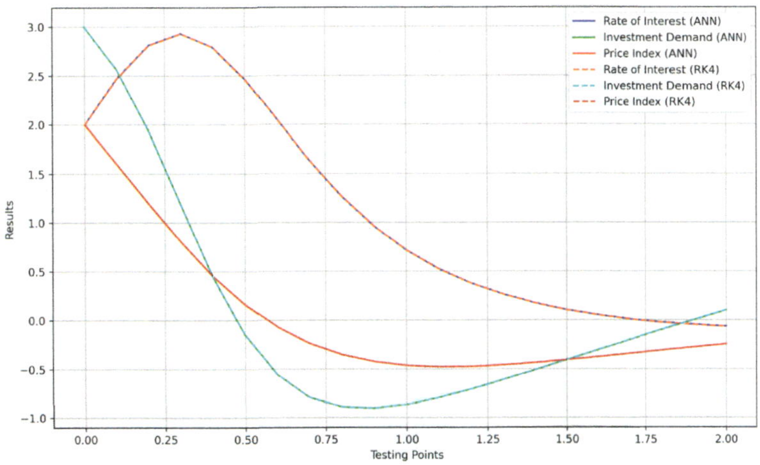

FIGURE 7.12 Comparison between RK4 solutions and M_hWNN-LBFGSs solutions of the financial model for Example 7.3.

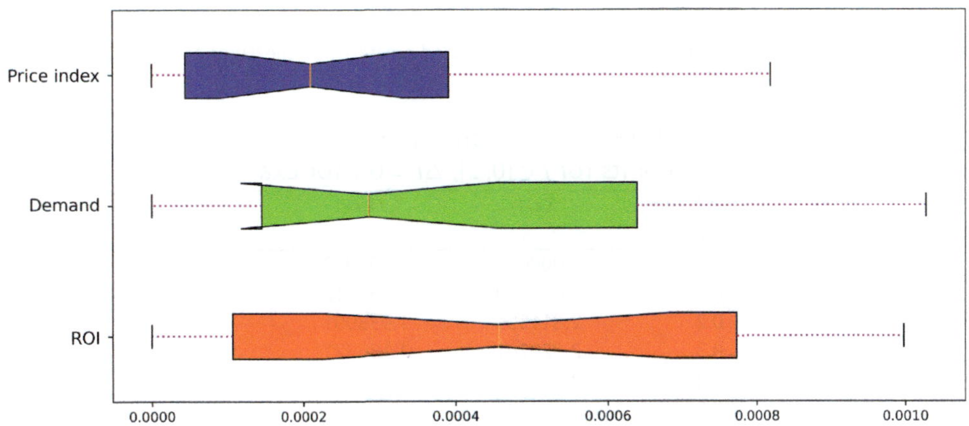

FIGURE 7.13 Box plot of absolute error between RK4 solutions and M_hWNN-LBFGSs solutions for Example 7.3.

and $2E-04$. It demonstrates the efficacy of the designed algorithm M_hWNN-LBFGS for solving the financial model.

The accuracy of proposed algorithm is witnessed through the histograms of MSE, TIC, and ENSE errors portrayed in the Figs. 7.6, 7.10, and 7.14. The bar graphs are used to illustrate the trend of errors. In order for better observation, the errors have been presented in $(-log)$ form. It may be noted that the magnitude of the TIC operator for $X(t)$, D(t), and P(t) lies in the neighborhood of $1E-04$ for Example 7.1, and $1E-03$ for Examples 7.2–7.3. Similarly, the ENSE value lies in the range $1E-06$ to $1E-07$ and the mean performances of RMSE are obtained in the neighborhood of $1E-03$. So, one can evidently observe that

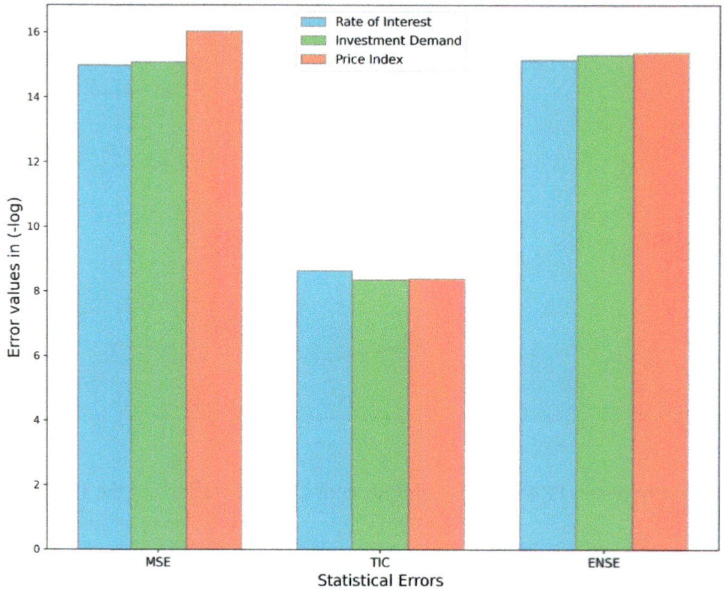

FIGURE 7.14 Performance indices of M_hWNN-LBFGS model based on statistical measures MAPE, TIC, and RMSE for Example 7.3.

Table 7.3 M_hWNN-LBFGS solution for the non-linear financial model at testing points for $t \in [0, 2]$, $\Delta t = 0.1$ for Example 7.3.

Index	Testing Points (t)	$X(t)$	$D(t)$	$P(t)$
0	0.0	2.000000	3.000000	2.000000
1	0.1	2.469519	2.568112	1.596320
2	0.2	2.811559	1.938991	1.190734
3	0.3	2.929741	1.186371	0.802044
4	0.4	2.793389	0.448111	0.452064
5	0.5	2.464228	−0.151468	0.158173
6	0.6	2.047193	−0.559545	−0.071706
7	0.7	1.630157	−0.791092	−0.239464
8	0.8	1.261319	−0.891241	−0.353505
9	0.9	0.956465	−0.904905	−0.424576
10	1.0	0.713547	−0.865514	−0.462890
11	1.1	0.523427	−0.795077	−0.477010
12	1.2	0.375579	−0.707324	−0.473808
13	1.3	0.260602	−0.610573	−0.458658
14	1.4	0.171102	−0.509698	−0.435556
15	1.5	0.101681	−0.407367	−0.407285
16	1.6	0.048402	−0.304832	−0.375734
17	1.7	0.008081	−0.202525	−0.342337
18	1.8	−0.022244	−0.100624	−0.308427
19	1.9	−0.045505	0.000395	−0.275382
20	2.0	−0.064504	0.099239	−0.244550

all these global statistical measures (MAE, TIC, RMSE, and ENSE) are close to 0, indicating the efficacy, correctness, and precision of the M_hWNN-LBFGS model.

By integrating wavelet analysis for feature extraction and deep learning for function approximation, this chapter demonstrated the ability of WNN to capture the intricate dynamics inherent in the dynamical models. The inclusion of graphical and tabular representations add clarity to the results. These visualizations illustrate the precision and effectiveness of the WNNs algorithm for approximating the solutions of time-series problems, where traditional computational algorithms may struggle.

References

[1] S. Kumar, A.K. Sahoo, S. Chakraverty, Comparative study of Chebyshev and Legendre polynomial-based neural models for approximating multidimensional poverty for an Indian state, in: Polynomial Paradigms: Trends and Applications in Science and Engineering, IOP Publishing, Bristol, UK, 2022, p. 13-1.

[2] J. Jin, J. Shi, Feature-preserving data compression of stamping tonnage information using wavelets, Technometrics 41 (4) (1999) 327–339.

[3] Q. Zhang, A. Benveniste, Wavelet networks, IEEE Transactions on Neural Networks 3 (6) (1992) 889–898.

[4] L. Qipeng, Y. Xiaoling, F. Quanke, Fault diagnosis using wavelet neural networks, Neural Processing Letters 18 (2) (2003) 115–123.

[5] H. Abghari, H. Ahmadi, S. Besharat, V. Rezaverdinejad, Prediction of daily pan evaporation using wavelet neural networks, Water Resources Management 26 (12) (2012) 3639–3652.

[6] H. Kaur, R. Mittal, V. Mishra, Haar wavelet approximate solutions for the generalized Lane–Emden equations arising in astrophysics, Computer Physics Communications 184 (9) (2013) 2169–2177.

[7] M. Shoaib, A.Z. Abbasi, M.A.Z. Raja, K.S. Nisar, A. Rafiq, Neuro-computing intelligent networks to analyze Casson nanofluid flow over a curved stretching surface, Waves in Random and Complex Media (2023) 1–20.

[8] P. Rahimkhani, Y. Ordokhani, Orthonormal Bernoulli wavelets neural network method and its application in astrophysics, Computational & Applied Mathematics 40 (2021) 1–24.

[9] A.K. Sahoo, S. Chakraverty, An unsupervised wavelet neural network model for approximating the solutions of non-linear nervous stomach model governed by tension, food and medicine, Computer Methods in Biomechanics and Biomedical Engineering (2023) 1–14.

[10] H. Badem, A. Basturk, A. Caliskan, M.E. Yuksel, A new hybrid optimization method combining artificial bee colony and limited-memory bfgs algorithms for efficient numerical optimization, Applied Soft Computing 70 (2018) 826–844.

[11] M. Jun-hai, C. Yu-shu, Study for the bifurcation topological structure and the global complicated character of a kind of nonlinear finance system (I), Applied Mathematics and Mechanics 22 (2001) 1240–1251.

[12] D. Veitch, Wavelet neural networks, University of UK, 2005.

[13] J. Zhang, G.G. Walter, Y. Miao, W.N.W. Lee, Wavelet neural networks for function learning, IEEE Transactions on Signal Processing 43 (6) (1995) 1485–1497.

[14] P. Petersen, M. Raslan, F. Voigtlaender, Topological properties of the set of functions generated by neural networks of fixed size, Foundations of Computational Mathematics 21 (2) (2021) 375–444.

8 Physics-informed Neural Network

Contents

8.1 Introduction 91
8.2 Physics-informed Neural Networks 92
8.3 Methodology 95
8.4 Problem statement 95
8.4.1 Modified Fornberg–Whitham equation 95
8.5 Simulation results and discussions 96
8.5.1 Experiment setup 96
8.6 Model problem 96
8.7 Validation 100
References 101

Chapter points

- Discuss the basic structure of Physics-informed Neural Networks and help beginners to take the first step toward the field of scientific machine learning.
- Implement the Physics-informed Neural Networks for solving fluid dynamics problems.
- Investigate the role of boundary and initial conditions in training Physics-informed Neural Networks for the Fornberg–Whitham equation.
- Highlight the advantages of using Physics-informed Neural Networks for modeling the complex wave phenomena in the Fornberg–Whitham equation.

8.1 Introduction

In the real-world scenarios, many engineering problems can be effectively modeled using partial differential equations (PDEs) [1]. Traditionally, various numerical techniques such as the finite element method, finite volume method, homotopy perturbation method, homotopy transformation method, and Adomian decomposition method have been employed to solve PDEs [2]. Despite the well-documented success of the aforementioned traditional methods, they often fall short when applied to complex, nonlinear, real-world problems. Moreover, they are also problem-specific and not mesh-free [3]. Recently, the integration of machine learning (ML) techniques into scientific computing, particularly for dynamical problems, has emerged as a rapidly growing area of research. It also opens new avenues for solving challenging non-linear problems and overcomes some of limitations of traditional analytical/numerical methods.

Artificial Neural Networks and Type-2 Fuzzy Set. https://doi.org/10.1016/B978-0-44-332894-7.00017-4

A significant portion of the literature discussing the application of deep learning to approximate DEs based on the Lagaris et al. [4] model or adheres to the supervised learning paradigm [5], which requires extensive sets of labeled data. However, in practical applications, this data is often synthetic or generated through experiments or simulations, which can be highly computationally expensive. Additionally, there may be cases where to train a supervised model and sufficient data is unavailable, or the dataset may be sparse and/or noisy. These factors limit the performance of traditional ANN algorithms. Therefore, it is highly desirable to find ML techniques that can approximate PDEs with minimal or no resiliance on data. Recently developed Physics-Informed Neural Networks (PINNs) by Raissi et al. offer such a framework, precisely addressing these challenges [6].

8.2 Physics-informed Neural Networks

Scientific Machine Learning (SciML) refers to the integration of ML techniques with scientific computing to enhance the modeling, simulation, and analysis of complex scientific systems. In 2019, the idea of leveraging prior knowledge of physics in the learning process of ANNs was introduced by the CRUNCH group from Brown University headed by Raissi et al. [6]. PINNs are a special type of neural networks and a branch of SciML that incorporates physical laws and constraints into its architecture during the training process.

ANN models have a long and successful history since 1990s, for solving dynamical problems governed by differential or integral equations. However, the question arises: Why are we now particularly interested in PINNs, and how do they differ from traditional ANN models?

The answer lies in several key advancements [8]:

- **Rapidly Increasing Data:** The availability of datasets has been exponentially increased, providing the necessary input for ANN models.
- **Advancements in Hardware:** Significant improvements in hardware, such as graphics processing units and parallel computing, have accelerated the training and prediction of ANN models.
- **Matured Deep Learning Libraries:** The development and refinement of deep learning libraries have made it easier to implement and optimize these models effectively.

PINNs are able to take these three advantages, distinguishing themselves from traditional ANN models. It is also capable of providing solutions for both forward and inverse problems with minor modification in codes [9].

The key steps to implement PINNs are:

1. Define the PDE with the initial and boundary conditions;
2. Describe a suitable PINNs model;
3. Design a loss function;
4. Minimize the loss function.

Let us consider a PDE to be approximated by PINNs as

$$\zeta_t + D_{\mathbf{x}}[\zeta] = 0, \mathbf{x} \in \Omega \subset \mathbb{R}^n \tag{8.1}$$

subject to initial and boundary conditions

$$\begin{aligned}\zeta(\mathbf{x}, 0) &= \psi(\mathbf{x}) \\ \zeta(\mathbf{x}, t) &= \phi(\mathbf{x}, t), \mathbf{x} \in \partial\Omega\end{aligned}$$

where $D_{\mathbf{x}}$ is a general linear or non-linear differential operator. Here, $\mathbf{x}$ and t have been considered as the spatial and temporal coordinates, respectively. Ω and $\partial\Omega$ denote the computational domain and the boundary of the given PDE, respectively, whereas $\zeta(\mathbf{x}, t)$ is the solution of PDE with IC $\psi(\mathbf{x})$ and BC $\phi(\mathbf{x}, t)$.

Next, a neural network $NN(\mathbf{x}, t; \theta)$ has been constructed for given independent input vector $[\mathbf{x}, t]^T$ as a surrogate of the solution $\zeta(\mathbf{x}, t)$. Here, $\theta = \{W^{[l]}, b^{[l]}\}$, $1 \leq l \leq L$ is the trainable parameter consisting of weights and biases matrices and L is number of hidden layers. The neural network output $\widehat{\zeta}_{\text{NN}}(\mathbf{x}, t; \theta)$ is denoted by [10]

$$\begin{aligned}
Z^{[1]} &= W^{[1]}X + b^{[1]} \\
\sigma\left(Z^{[1]}\right) &= a^{[1]} \\
Z^{[2]} &= W^{[2]}a^{[1]} + b^{[2]} \\
&\vdots \\
Z^{[l]} &= W^{[l]}a^{[l-1]} + b^{[l]} \\
\sigma\left(Z^{[l]}\right) &= a^{[l]} \\
&\vdots \\
Z^{[L]} &= W^{[L]}a^{[L-1]} + b^{[L]} \\
\sigma\left(Z^{[L]}\right) &= a^{[L]} = \widehat{\zeta}_{\text{NN}}(x, t; \theta)
\end{aligned} \tag{8.2}$$

where X is $n_0 \times m$ input matrix of m data entries and each data entry is of n_0 dimension, L is total number of hidden layers in neural network, $W^{[l]}$ is $n_l \times n_{l-1}$ and $b^{[l]}$ are $n_l \times 1$ matrices of weights and biases, respectively, for layer l, $a^{[l]}$ is the activation for layer l, and $Z^{[l]}$ is weighted sum of the activation of layer $l-1$ and $\sigma(.)$ is an activation function.

The loss function in PINNs can be written as a combination of the residual of PDE and physical characteristics, namely BC and IC of the governing PDE and is defined as

$$\mathscr{L}(\theta) = \mathscr{L}_f + \mathscr{L}_b + \mathscr{L}_i, \tag{8.3}$$

where

$$\mathscr{L}_f = \frac{1}{N_f} \sum_{j=1}^{N_f} \left| \widehat{\zeta}_{\text{NN}_t}(\mathbf{x}_j, t_j; \theta) + D_{\mathbf{x}}[\widehat{\zeta}_{\text{NN}}(\mathbf{x}_j, t_j; \theta)] \right|^2; \tag{8.4}$$

$$\mathscr{L}_b = \frac{1}{N_b}\sum_{j=1}^{N_b}\left|\widehat{\zeta}_{\mathrm{NN}}(\mathbf{x}_j, t_j; \theta) - \phi_j\right|^2; \tag{8.5}$$

$$\mathscr{L}_i = \frac{1}{N_i}\sum_{j=1}^{N_i}\left|\widehat{\zeta}_{\mathrm{NN}}(\mathbf{x}_j, 0; \theta) - \psi_j\right|^2. \tag{8.6}$$

Here, $\mathscr{L}_f$, $\mathscr{L}_b$, and $\mathscr{L}_i$ are the residual loss of the given PDE, BCs, and ICs, respectively. We have taken the N_f arbitrary number of training points in the spatio-temporal domain to obtain the residual information of PDE. Moreover, N_b and N_i, the number of different sample points are taken to obtain information on a given boundary and the initial points, respectively. In addition, if there exists some data inside the domain, an extra loss term $\mathscr{L}_d$ may be taken into account:

$$\mathscr{L}_d = \frac{1}{N_d}\sum_{j=1}^{N_d}\left|\widehat{\zeta}_{\mathrm{NN}}(\mathbf{x}_j, t_j; \theta) - \zeta_{data}\right|^2.$$

In order to update, the gradient of loss function $\mathscr{L}$, we need to compute the derivatives of the outputs with respect to the inputs x by using the chain rule for differentiating compositions of functions. In the early 1990s, computing derivatives of output for the neural network with respect to trainable parameters for hidden layers relied on the manual derivation of the backpropagation algorithm that includes high computational cost [4]. In the PINNs framework, such computations are achieved by using automatic differentiation (AD), which overcome the drawbacks of earlier models. Nowadays, AD is conveniently integrated in ML open source libraries such as TensorFlow, PyTorch, Theano, etc. Fig. 8.1 represents an illustration of the PINNs model.

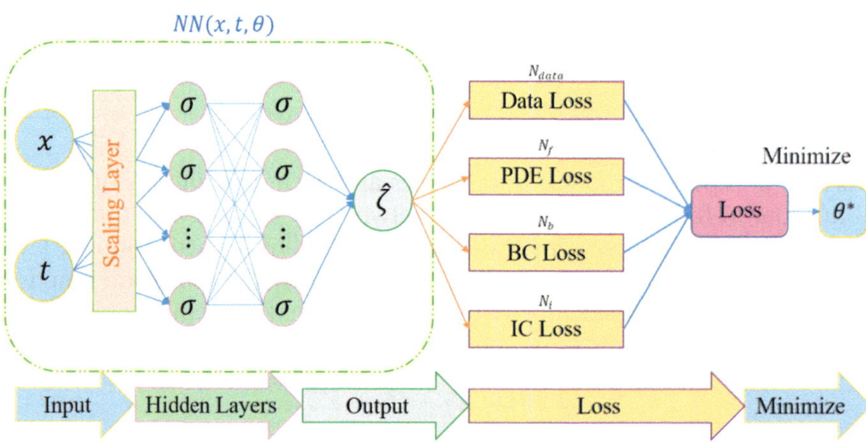

FIGURE 8.1 Schematic diagram of a PINN for solving PDEs. It consists of two parts: (a) The left part is a fully connected neural network with inputs x and t, and output $\widehat{\zeta}_{\mathrm{NN}}(\mathbf{x}, t; \theta)$; (b) The right part is the Physics-informed neural network, where the network output satisfies the physical laws as well as the given PDE.

8.3 Methodology

Here we explore the nuances of the PINN algorithm, custom-designed for addressing the below PDE:

$$\zeta_t - \zeta_{xxt} + (b+1)\zeta^2\zeta_x = b\zeta_x\zeta_{xx} + \zeta\zeta_{xxx}, \tag{8.7}$$

with the initial and boundary conditions,

$$\begin{aligned} &\zeta(x,0) = g(x), \\ &\zeta(0,t) = y_0(t), \\ &\zeta(1,t) = y_1(t), \\ &t \geq 0, x \in (0,1). \end{aligned}$$

In order to train the model and get optimized hyper-parameters, the trainable parameters θ, must be adjusted by minimizing the loss function. As discussed above, the loss function incorporates errors derived from data, the residual of the PDE, and the physical properties, such as BCs and ICs. Mathematically, it can be defined as

$$\mathscr{L}(\theta) = \mathscr{L}_f + \mathscr{L}_{b_1} + \mathscr{L}_{b_2} + \mathscr{L}_{b_3} \tag{8.8}$$

where

$$\begin{aligned} \mathscr{L}_f = \frac{1}{N_f}\sum_{i=1}^{N_f}\Bigg| &\frac{\partial\widehat{\zeta}_{\mathrm{NN}}(\mathbf{x}_i,t_i;\theta)}{\partial t_i} - \frac{\partial^3\widehat{\zeta}_{\mathrm{NN}}(\mathbf{x}_i,t_i;\theta)}{\partial\mathbf{x}_i^2\partial t_i} + (b+1)\widehat{\zeta}^2_{\mathrm{NN}}(\mathbf{x}_i,t_i;\theta)\frac{\partial\widehat{\zeta}_{\mathrm{NN}}(\mathbf{x}_i,t_i;\theta)}{\partial\mathbf{x}_i} \\ &- b\frac{\partial\widehat{\zeta}_{\mathrm{NN}}(\mathbf{x}_i,t_i;\theta)}{\partial x_i} + \widehat{\zeta}_{\mathrm{NN}}(\mathbf{x}_i,t_i;\theta)\frac{\partial\widehat{\zeta}^3_{\mathrm{NN}}(\mathbf{x}_i,t_i;\theta)}{\partial\mathbf{x}_i^3}\Bigg|^2 \end{aligned} \tag{8.9}$$

$$\mathscr{L}_{b_1} = \frac{1}{N_{b_1}}\sum_{i=1}^{N_{b_1}}\left|\widehat{\zeta}_{\mathrm{NN}}(\mathbf{x}_i,0;\theta) - \psi_i(\mathbf{x}_i)\right|^2. \tag{8.10}$$

$$\mathscr{L}_{b_2} = \frac{1}{N_{b_2}}\sum_{i=1}^{N_{b_2}}\left|\widehat{\zeta}_{\mathrm{NN}}(0,\mathrm{t_i};\theta) - \phi_0(t_i)\right|^2 \tag{8.11}$$

$$\mathscr{L}_{b_3} = \frac{1}{N_{b_3}}\sum_{i=1}^{N_{b_2}}\left|\widehat{\zeta}_{\mathrm{NN}}(1,\mathrm{t_i};\theta) - \phi_1(t_i)\right|^2. \tag{8.12}$$

8.4 Problem statement

In this section, the general form of the Fornberg–Whitham (FW) equation has been discussed.

8.4.1 Modified Fornberg–Whitham equation

The FW equation examines the qualitative behavior of wave phenomena and water propagation. It is named after Bengt Fornberg and Gerald Whitham, who contributed to the analysis and understanding of wave behavior described by such equations. The FW equation has traveling wave solutions known as kink-like waves and anti-kink-like waves. It can be derived from a family of equations written as [7]

$$u_t + f(u)u_x + \alpha u_{xxx} = 0, \tag{8.13}$$

with the IC and BC,

$$\begin{cases} u(x,0) = \psi(x), \quad x \in \Omega \\ u(x,t) = \phi_0(t), u(x,t) = \phi_1(t), \\ t \in \gamma, \quad x \in \delta\Omega \end{cases}$$

8.5 Simulation results and discussions

In this section, we have employed PINNs to solve a particular case of the FW equation and then compared it with the exact solutions.

8.5.1 Experiment setup

This experiment has been conducted in the Google colab environment leveraging Python language, and employed the Tensorflow to take advantage of AD. Hyper-parameter tuning is performed to determine the optimal number of hidden layers and the number of nodes in each layer. Unless otherwise specified, a fully connected multi-layer neural network has been constructed with two input nodes, one output node, and three hidden layers, each containing 50 neurons. Then the model has been trained on random points in the temporal-spatial domain, rather than grid points. In this regard, 3,000 random collocation points inside the domain, 100 initial points, and 150 boundary points are selected randomly for training of the PINN as shown in Fig. 8.2.

8.6 Model problem

Example 8.1. Let us consider the following FW equation:

$$u_t - u_{xxt} + u_x = uu_{xxx} - uu_x + 3u_x u_{xx} \tag{8.14}$$

with the initial and boundary conditions,

$$\begin{aligned} &u(x,0) = \psi(x), \\ &u(x,t) = \phi_0(t), \\ &u(x,t) = \phi_1(t), \\ &x \in [-4,4], t \in [0,5]. \end{aligned}$$

The corresponding exact solution may be written as [11]

$$\zeta(x,t) = \frac{4}{3} exp\left(\frac{x}{2} - \frac{2}{3}t\right). \tag{8.15}$$

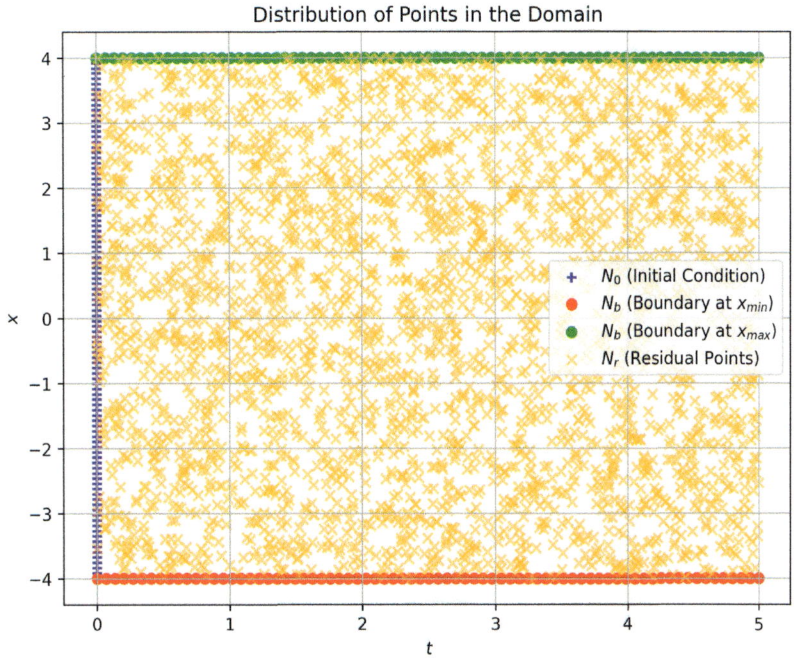

FIGURE 8.2 Residual points inside the domain, initial and boundary points, selected randomly for training of the PINN model for Example 8.1.

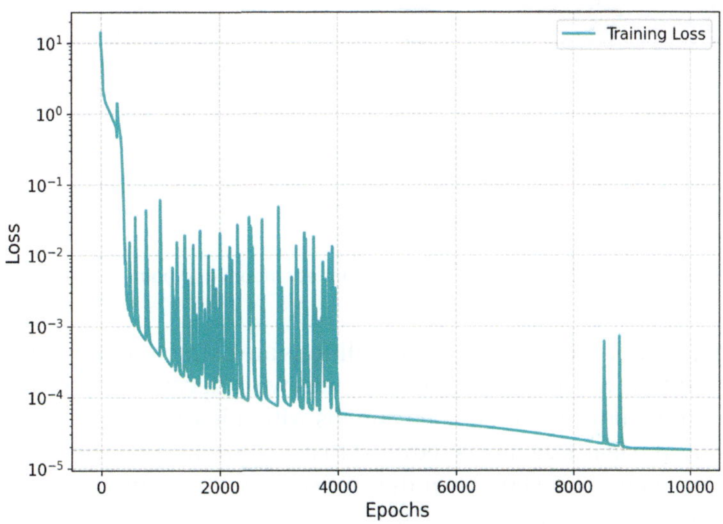

FIGURE 8.3 Learning curves showing the result of training loss during the training process of PINNs with respect to 10,000 epochs for Example 8.1.

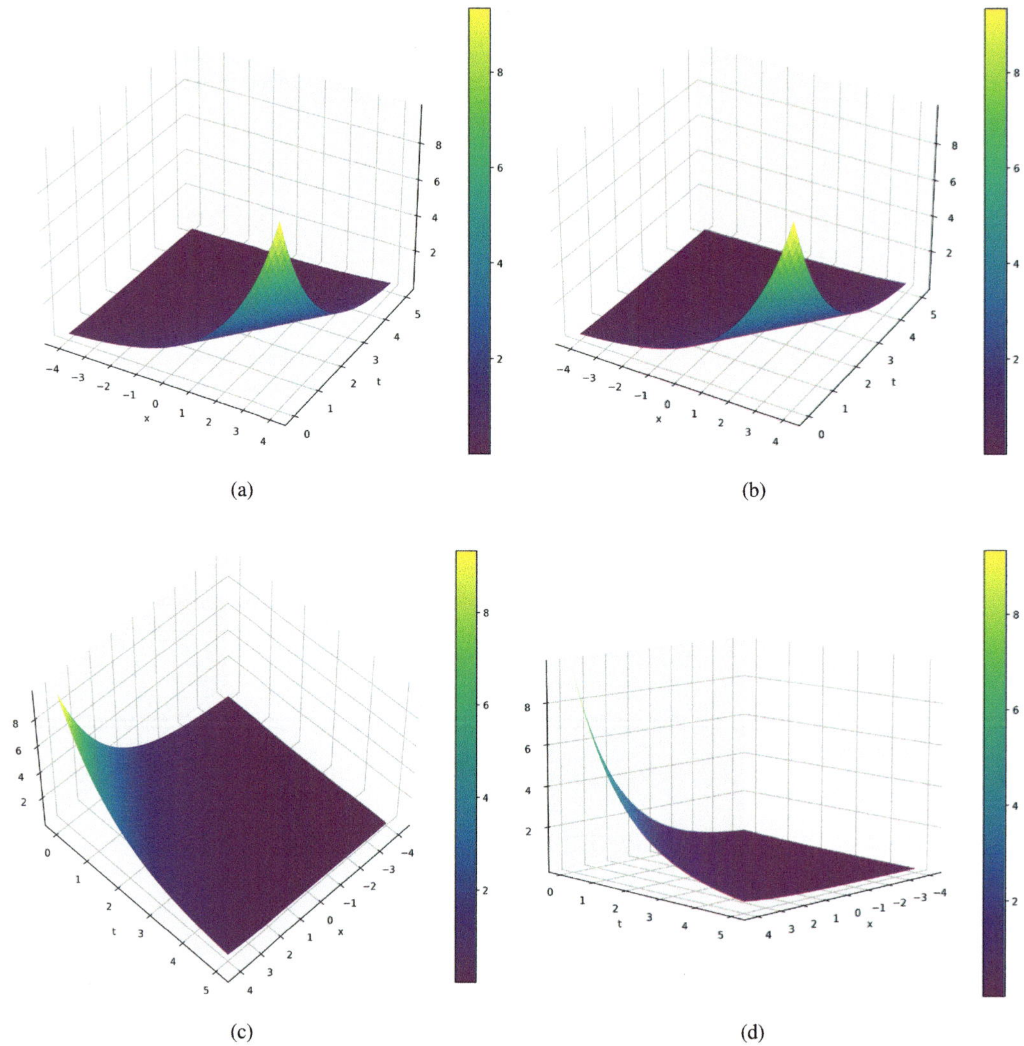

FIGURE 8.4 Comparison of (a) exact and (b, c, d) PINN solutions at random grid points $(x, t) \in [-4, 4] \times [0, 5]$.

For this problem, the boundary and initial conditions are extracted from the exact solution.

Adam optimization has employed with a piecewise decay of the learning rate. The model has been trained for the first 4,000 epochs with a learning rate of $\eta = 0.01$. For the next 5,000 epochs, the learning rate is reduced to $\eta = 0.001$, and for the final 1,000 epochs, it is further decreased to $\eta = 0.0001$. Over the course of 10,000 training epochs, the training loss is monitored, as shown in Fig. 8.3. The figure reflects the ability of PINNs to approximate the FW equation, with the loss stabilizing into a flat line after 9,000 epochs.

To demonstrate the effectiveness of the PINN solution, it is compared with exact solutions at various testing points. This comparative analysis is graphically depicted in Fig. 8.4.

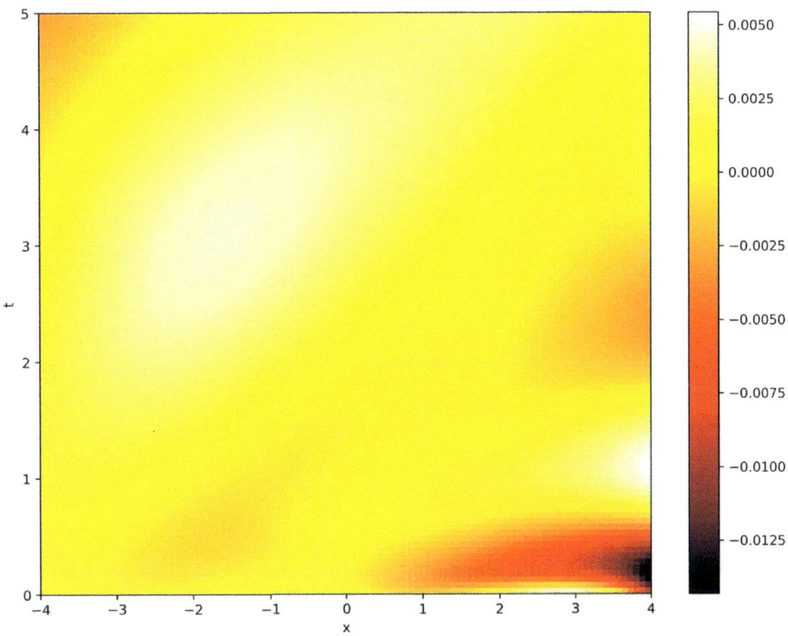

FIGURE 8.5 Heat map of the error graph for Example 8.1.

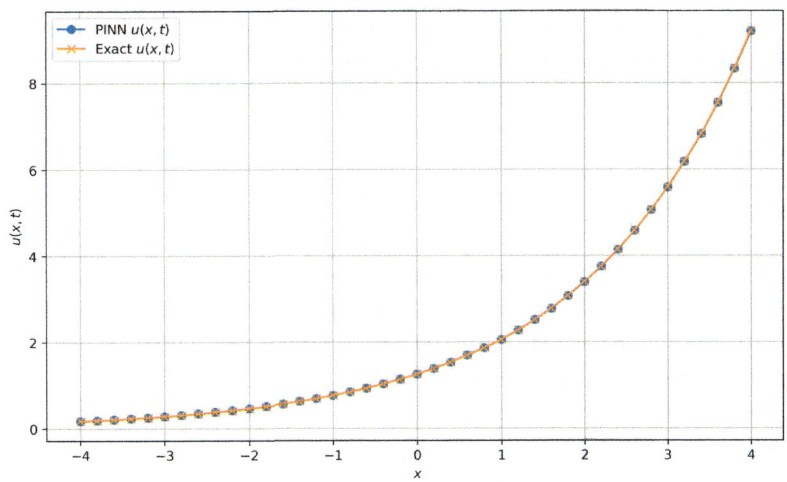

FIGURE 8.6 Plot of ground truth and approximate solutions for $t = 0.1$ and $x \in [-10, 10]$.

Moreover, these 3D figures show that the solution in the given domain exhibits kink-like waves. Notably, in Fig. 8.4 subgraph (a) represents the exact solution, while the remaining three images depict the PINNs predicted solutions from different angles. Although the PINNs predicted solutions closely resemble the exact solution, there are some errors and

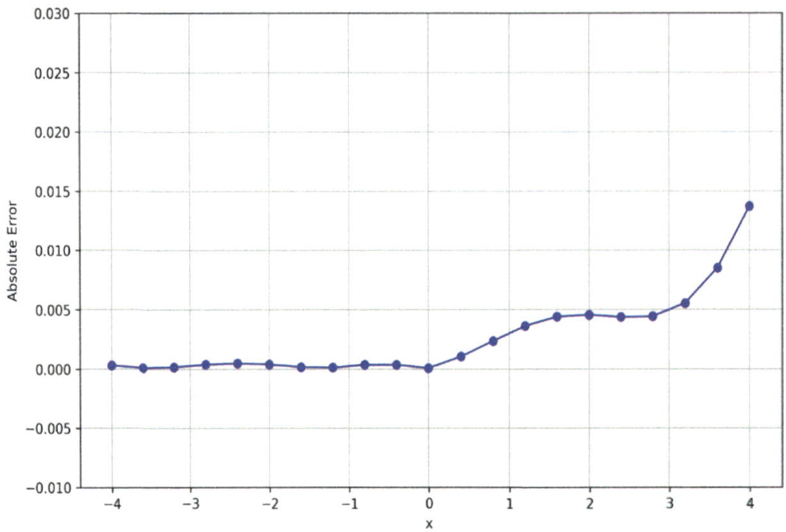

FIGURE 8.7 2D Plot of AE between the PINN approximate solutions and ground truth at testing points for $t = 0.1$ and $x \in [-4, 4]$.

it has been presented in Fig. 8.5. Additionally, a 2D comparison graph for a fixed value of $t = 0.1$ is provided in Fig. 8.6 and corresponding errors are depicted in Fig. 8.7. From these graphs, it is evident that the results predicted by PINNs closely match the exact solutions. It may be noted that the CPU time for training the model is 324 sec.

8.7 Validation

In this section, the results obtained from the PINNs model are validated against the exact solutions in two ways.

First, the solutions are compared in the entire domain, and second, by fixing the specific value of x. The accuracy of the proposed algorithm is demonstrated by the error graph, where the Mean Absolute Error (MAE) is 0.001667, which is very close to zero. This indicates a high level of precision in the PINNs predictions.

Additionally, a comparative analysis of the solutions is presented in Table 8.1 for 21 testing points. Upon close examination, it is observed that the absolute error ranges from 10^{-2} to 10^{-4}. This range further underscores the accuracy of the PINNs model. Both the tabulated data and graphical representations clearly show that the solutions predicted by the PINNs model align closely with the ground truth. This confirms the effectiveness and reliability of the proposed PINNs approach for approximating the solutions of the FW equation.

It is worth mentioning that the undertaken problem is renowned for its complexity, which makes predicting dynamics a daunting task. This complexity often requires substantial computational resources to model the problem. The use of SciMl, particularly in the form of PINNs, offers a promising avenue for advancing research in this area.

Table 8.1 Comparison of PINN and exact solutions with absolute error at testing points by fixing $t = 0.1$.

x	PINN $u(x, t)$	Exact $u(x, t)$	Absolute Error
−4.0	0.169116	0.168809	0.000306
−3.6	0.206279	0.206184	0.000094
−3.2	0.251669	0.251834	0.000165
−2.8	0.307210	0.307591	0.000381
−2.4	0.375221	0.375692	0.000472
−2.0	0.458475	0.458872	0.000396
−1.6	0.560296	0.560467	0.000171
−1.2	0.684681	0.684556	0.000125
−0.8	0.836478	0.836119	0.000359
−0.4	1.021595	1.021238	0.000357
0.0	1.247263	1.247343	0.000080
0.4	1.522462	1.523508	0.001046
0.8	1.858450	1.860817	0.002367
1.2	2.269187	2.272806	0.003619
1.6	2.771618	2.776012	0.004394
2.0	3.386072	3.390629	0.004556
2.4	4.136957	4.141323	0.004366
2.8	5.053800	5.058224	0.004424
3.2	6.172584	6.178129	0.005545
3.6	7.537472	7.545983	0.008511
4.0	9.202956	9.216685	0.013729

References

[1] A.K. Sahoo, S. Chakraverty, Machine intelligence in dynamical systems: a state-of-the-art review, Wiley Interdisciplinary Reviews: Data Mining and Knowledge Discovery 12 (1) (2022) e1461.

[2] S. Chakraverty, S. Mall, Artificial Neural Networks for Engineers and Scientists: Solving Ordinary Differential Equations, CRC Press, 2017.

[3] S. Chakraverty, S.K. Jeswal, Applied Artificial Neural Network Methods for Engineers and Scientists: Solving Algebraic Equations, World Scientific, 2021.

[4] I.E. Lagaris, A. Likas, D.I. Fotiadis, Artificial neural networks for solving ordinary and partial differential equations, IEEE Transactions on Neural Networks 9 (5) (1998) 987–1000.

[5] A. Verma, M. Kumar, Numerical solution of Lane–Emden type equations using multilayer perceptron neural network method, International Journal of Applied and Computational Mathematics 5 (2019) 1–14.

[6] M. Raissi, P. Perdikaris, G.E. Karniadakis, Physics-informed neural networks: a deep learning framework for solving forward and inverse problems involving nonlinear partial differential equations, Journal of Computational Physics 378 (2019) 686–707.

[7] F. Abidi, K. Omrani, The homotopy analysis method for solving the Fornberg–Whitham equation and comparison with Adomian's decomposition method, Computers & Mathematics with Applications 59 (8) (2010) 2743–2750.

[8] S. Kumar, A.K. Sahoo, S. Chakraverty, Physics-informed machine learning framework for approximating the modified Degasperis-Procesi equation, in: Proceedings of the 2023 International Conference on Ambient Intelligence, Knowledge Informatics and Industrial Electronics (AIKIIE), 2023, pp. 1–6.

[9] A.K. Sahoo, S. Kumar, S. Chakraverty, Application of Physics-Informed Neural Networks for Simulating Mass-Spring-Damper Systems, 2024.
[10] S. Kumar, A.K. Sahoo, S. Chakraverty, Comparative study of Chebyshev and Legendre polynomial-based neural models for approximating multidimensional poverty for an Indian state, in: Polynomial Paradigms: Trends and Applications in Science and Engineering, IOP Publishing, 2022, p. 13-1.
[11] S. Shaheen, S. Haq, A. Ghafoor, A meshfree technique for the numerical solutions of nonlinear Fornberg–Whitham and Degasperis–Procesi equations with their modified forms, Computational and Applied Mathematics 41 (4) (2022) 183.

PART 2

Type-2 fuzzy uncertainty

My crystal ball is fuzzy.

Lotfi A. Zadeh (Father of Fuzzy Logic (1921–2017))

9

Interval and fuzzy set theory: an overview

Contents

9.1 Intervals **105**
9.2 Interval arithmetic **106**
9.3 Fuzzy sets **107**
9.3.1 Fuzzy numbers 107
9.3.1.1 Triangular fuzzy number 107
9.3.1.2 Trapezoidal fuzzy number 107
9.3.1.3 Gaussian fuzzy number 108
9.3.2 Parametric form of fuzzy numbers 109
9.3.3 Double parametric form of fuzzy numbers 109
9.3.4 Fuzzy arithmetic 110
9.3.5 Derivative of fuzzy valued function 110
9.3.6 Riemann–Liouville fractional integral 110
9.3.7 Fuzzy Riemann–Liouville fractional integral 111
9.3.8 Caputo fractional derivative 111
9.3.9 Caputo fuzzy fractional derivative 111
References **112**

Chapter points

- Basic concepts are related to interval arithmetic.
- Introduction to fuzzy set theory and related definitions.
- Calculus related to fuzzy valued functions.

9.1 Intervals

An interval is a set of real numbers that includes all numbers between any two given numbers within the set. An interval x^I is denoted by $[x^l, x^u]$ on the set of real numbers $\mathbb{R}$ given by [1,2],

$$x^I = [x^l, x^u] = \{x \in \mathbb{R} : x^l \leq x \leq x^u\}, \tag{9.1}$$

Artificial Neural Networks and Type-2 Fuzzy Set. https://doi.org/10.1016/B978-0-44-332894-7.00019-8

where x^l and x^u are known as the lower and upper bounds of the interval x^I. Various types of intervals are present in literature, such as open intervals, closed intervals, semi-open/semi-closed intervals depending upon whether the end points are included or not.

Let us consider two arbitrary intervals x^I and y^I and are said to be equal, i.e., $x^I = y^I$, if and only if the respective lower and upper bounds are equal, i.e., $x^l = y^l$ and $x^u = y^u$. Further, if the lower and upper bound of the interval x^I are equal, then it is known as a degenerate interval, which is a singleton set, i.e., identical to a real number.

9.2 Interval arithmetic

In interval arithmetic, operations such as addition, subtraction, multiplication, and division are performed on intervals rather than single values. The result of an operation on intervals is itself an interval that bounds the possible outcomes of the operation. That means, when two ideal quantities x and y are contained in their respective intervals x^I and y^I, then after any binary operation $(*)$, the ideal quantity $x * y$ will lie in the interval $x^I * y^I$.

Therefore, $x^I = [x^l, x^u]$ and $y^I = [y^l, y^u]$ are two intervals; then all standard interval arithmetic is defined as [1,2]

$$x^I * y^I = \{x * y \mid x \in x^I, y \in y^I\}. \tag{9.2}$$

1. Interval Addition:

$$x^I + y^I = [x^l + y^l, x^u + y^u]. \tag{9.3}$$

2. Interval Subtraction:

$$x^I - y^I = [x^l - y^u, x^u - y^l]. \tag{9.4}$$

3. Scalar Multiplication:
   For any scalar $k \in \mathbb{R}$,

$$k \times x^I = \begin{cases} [k \times x^l, k \times x^u], k \geq 0, \\ [k \times x^u, k \times x^l], k < 0. \end{cases} \tag{9.5}$$

4. Interval Multiplication:

$$x^I \times y^I = [\min(P), \max(P)], \tag{9.6}$$

   where $P = \{x^l \times y^l, x^l \times y^r, x^r \times y^l, x^r \times y^r\}$.

5. Interval Division:

$$\frac{x^I}{y^I} = x^I \times \frac{1}{y^I} = \begin{cases} [x^l, x^u].\left[\frac{1}{y^u}, \frac{1}{y^l}\right], 0 \notin y^I, \\ (-\infty, \infty), 0 \in y^I. \end{cases} \tag{9.7}$$

9.3 Fuzzy sets

A fuzzy set [3,4] $\tilde{A}$ on the universal set X is a collection of ordered pairs $x \in X$ and $\mu_{\tilde{A}}(x)$, mathematically,

$$\tilde{A} = \{(x, \mu_{\tilde{A}}(x)) | x \in X\}. \tag{9.8}$$

Here, $\mu_{\tilde{A}}(x)$ is the membership function of x.

9.3.1 Fuzzy numbers

A fuzzy set $\tilde{A}$ is said to be a fuzzy number [3,4], if:

1. The membership function is piecewise continuous.
2. The fuzzy set is normalized, i.e., $\exists$ at least one $x \in X$ such that $\mu_{\tilde{A}}(x) = 1$.
3. The fuzzy set is convex, i.e., for any $x_1, x_2 \in X$ and $\lambda \in [0, 1]$, the following condition holds:

$$\mu_{\tilde{A}}(\lambda x_1 + (1-\lambda)x_2) \geq \min(\mu_{\tilde{A}}(x_1), \mu_{\tilde{A}}(x_2)),$$

where $\mu_{\tilde{A}}(x_1)$ and $\mu_{\tilde{A}}(x_2)$ are the membership values of x_1 and x_2, respectively.

There are several types of fuzzy numbers based on the shape of the membership functions, namely triangular fuzzy numbers (TFN), trapezoidal fuzzy numbers (TrFN), Gaussian fuzzy numbers (GFN), exponential fuzzy numbers (EFN), and pentagonal fuzzy numbers (PFN). As such, the basic definition and behavior of TFN, TrFN, and GFN are discussed in this chapter.

9.3.1.1 Triangular fuzzy number

A convex and normalized fuzzy set $\tilde{A}$ defined over the set of real numbers $\mathbb{R}$ with the membership function $\mu_{\tilde{A}}$ as [3,4]:

$$\mu_{\tilde{A}}(x) = \begin{cases} \frac{x - A_l}{A_c - A_l} & \text{if } A_l \leq x \leq A_c, \\ \frac{A_u - x}{A_u - A_c} & \text{if } A_c \leq x \leq A_u, \\ 0 & \text{otherwise,} \end{cases}$$

is called as TFN and it is written as $\tilde{A} = (A_l, A_c, A_u)$. Fig. 9.1 depicts the schematic diagram for a TFN $\tilde{A}$.

9.3.1.2 Trapezoidal fuzzy number

The Trapezoidal Fuzzy Number (TrFN) represents a specific category of fuzzy number written as, $\tilde{A} = (A_l, A_{c1}, A_{c2}, A_u)$, the membership function $\mu_{\tilde{A}}$ of $\tilde{A}$ is defined as

$$\mu_{\tilde{A}}(x) = \begin{cases} \frac{x - A_l}{A_{c1} - A_l}, \; A_l \leq x \leq A_{c1} \\ 1, \; A_{c1} \leq x \leq A_{c2} \\ \frac{A_u - x}{A_u - A_{c2}}, \; A_{c2} \leq x \leq A_u \\ 0, \; \text{otherwise.} \end{cases} \tag{9.9}$$

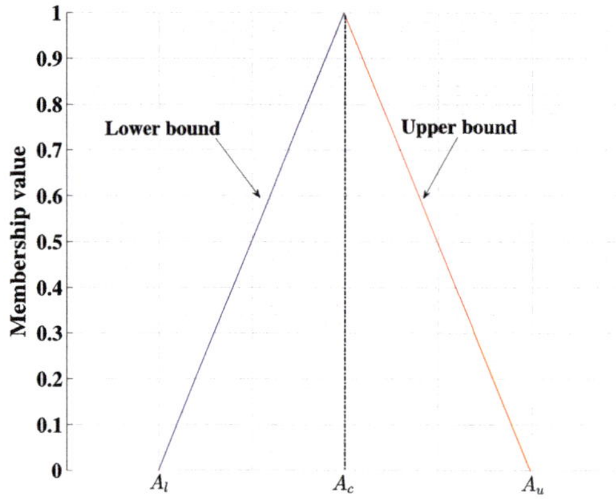

FIGURE 9.1 Schematic diagram of the TFN $\tilde{A} = (A_l, A_c, A_u)$.

In Fig. 9.2, a schematic diagram of the TRFN $\tilde{A}$ is given.

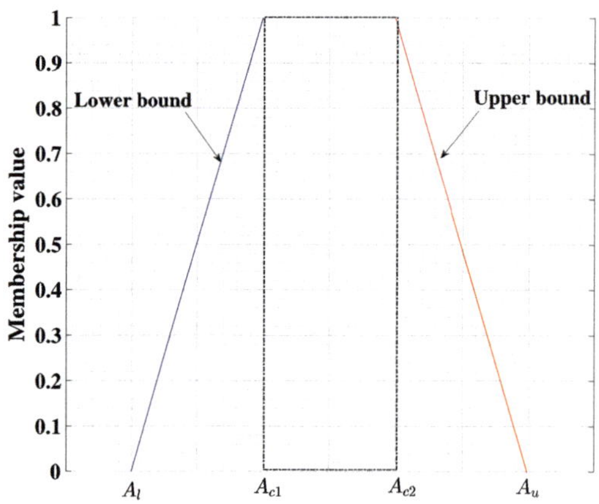

FIGURE 9.2 Schematic diagram of the TRFN $\tilde{A} = (A_l, A_{c1}, A_{c2}, A_u)$.

9.3.1.3 Gaussian fuzzy number

The Gaussian fuzzy number (GFN) is defined as $\tilde{A} = (m, \sigma_l, \sigma_r)$. The membership function for a GFN $\tilde{A}$ is defined as [3,4]

$$\mu_{\tilde{A}}(x) = \begin{cases} exp(-\frac{(x-m)^2}{2\sigma_l{}^2}) \text{ for } x \leq m, \\ exp(-\frac{(x-m)^2}{2\sigma_r{}^2}) \text{ for } x \geq m, \end{cases} \tag{9.10}$$

where m denotes the center and σ_l, σ_r denotes the left and right bounds of the fuzzy number. For $\sigma_l = \sigma_r$, the GFN is called symmetric GFN. In Fig. 9.3, the schematic diagram of the GFN $\tilde{A} = (m, \sigma_l, \sigma_r)$ is shown.

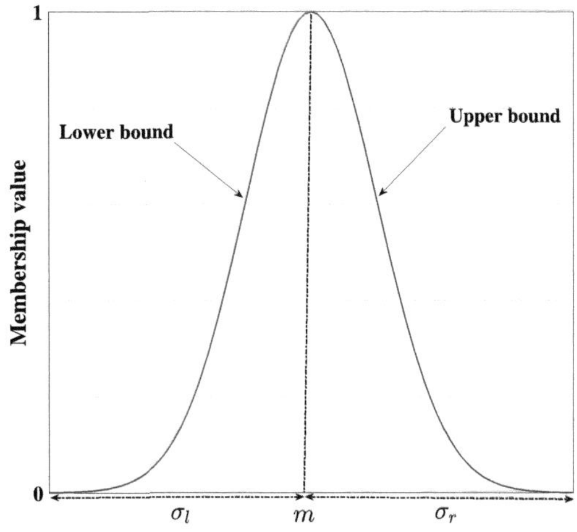

FIGURE 9.3 Schematic diagram of the GFN $\tilde{A} = (m, \sigma_l, \sigma_r)$.

9.3.2 Parametric form of fuzzy numbers

Fuzzy numbers can be expressed as a pair of functions using the α-cut, where $\alpha \in [0, 1]$, as [4,5],

$$\tilde{A}(\alpha) = [\underline{A}(\alpha), \overline{A}(\alpha)], \tag{9.11}$$

which is a standard closed interval, where $\underline{A}(\alpha)$ and $\overline{A}(\alpha)$ are lower and upper bounds, with the following criteria:

1. $\underline{A}(\alpha)$ is a bounded left continuous and non-decreasing function over $[0, 1]$.
2. $\overline{A}(\alpha)$ is a bounded right continuous and non-increasing function over $[0, 1]$.
3. $\underline{A}(\alpha) \leq \overline{A}(\alpha), 0 \leq \alpha \leq 1$.

The parametric forms of:

1. TFN $\tilde{A}$, i.e., $\tilde{A}(\alpha) = [\underline{A}(\alpha), \overline{A}(\alpha)] = [A_l + \alpha(A_c - A_l), A_u - \alpha(A_u - A_c)]$.
2. TrFN $\tilde{A}$, i.e., $\tilde{A}(\alpha) = [\underline{A}(\alpha), \overline{A}(\alpha)] = [A_l + \alpha(A_{c1} - A_l), A_u - \alpha(A_u - A_{c2})]$.
3. Symmetric GFN $\tilde{G}$, i.e., $\tilde{G}(\alpha) = [\underline{G}(\alpha), \overline{G}(\alpha)] = [m - \sigma\sqrt{-2\log\alpha}, m + \sigma\sqrt{-2\log\alpha}]$.

9.3.3 Double parametric form of fuzzy numbers

Suppose $\tilde{A}(\alpha)$ is the parametric representation of a fuzzy number $\tilde{A}$. Then the double parametric form of $\tilde{A}$, i.e., $\tilde{A}(\alpha, \alpha') = \underline{A}(\alpha) + \alpha'(\overline{A}(\alpha) - \underline{A}(\alpha))$, where $\alpha' \in [0, 1]$. The double parametric form helps in order to treat the fuzzy number as a crisp number [6,7]. The lower and upper bounds of the solution in a single parametric form can be obtained by putting $\alpha' = 0$ and 1, respectively.

9.3.4 Fuzzy arithmetic

For any two fuzzy numbers in α-cut form, $\tilde{u} = [\underline{u}, \overline{u}]$, $\tilde{v} = [\underline{v}, \overline{v}]$ along with scalar κ, the fuzzy arithmetic is defined as [4]:

1. $\tilde{u} = \tilde{v}$ iff $\underline{u}(\alpha) = \underline{v}(\alpha) =$ and $\overline{u}(\alpha) = \overline{v}(\alpha)$.
2. $\tilde{u} + \tilde{v} = [\underline{u}(\alpha)) + \underline{v}(\alpha), \overline{u}(\alpha) + \overline{v}(\alpha)]$.
3. $\tilde{u} \times \tilde{v} = [\min W, \max W]$, where $W = \{\underline{u} \times \underline{v}, \underline{u} \times \overline{v}, \overline{u} \times \underline{v}, \overline{u} \times \overline{v}\}$.
4. $\kappa \tilde{u} = \begin{cases} [\kappa \overline{u}, \kappa \underline{u}], \kappa < 0 \\ [\kappa \underline{u}, \kappa \overline{u}], \kappa \geqslant 0 \end{cases}$.
5. $\frac{\tilde{u}}{\tilde{v}} = [\underline{u}, \overline{u}] \times \left[\frac{1}{\overline{v}}, \frac{1}{\underline{v}}\right]$, where $0 \notin \tilde{v}$.

9.3.5 Derivative of fuzzy valued function

Let $\tilde{f}$ be a fuzzy valued function defined on the interval $[a, b] \subseteq \mathbb{R}$. $\tilde{f}$ is said to be differentiable at x_0 [8]:

1. if for $h > 0$ sufficiently close to 0, the Hukuhara differences $\tilde{f}(x_0 + h) - \tilde{f}(x_0)$ and $\tilde{f}(x_0) - \tilde{f}(x_0 - h)$, and the limits

$$\tilde{f}'(x_0) = \lim_{h \to 0^+} \frac{\tilde{f}(x_0 + h) - \tilde{f}(x_0)}{h} = \lim_{h \to 0^+} \frac{\tilde{f}(x_0) - \tilde{f}(x_0 - h)}{h}.$$

or

2. if for $h > 0$ sufficiently close to 0, the Hukuhara differences $\tilde{f}(x_0) - \tilde{f}(x_0 + h)$ and $\tilde{f}(x_0 - h) - \tilde{f}(x_0)$, and the limits

$$\tilde{f}'(x_0) = \lim_{h \to 0^+} \frac{\tilde{f}(x_0) - \tilde{f}(x_0 + h)}{-h} = \lim_{h \to 0^+} \frac{\tilde{f}(x_0 - h) - \tilde{f}(x_0)}{-h}.$$

Here, the limits are considered in the metric space of all type-1 fuzzy number valued functions with metric generated by the Hausdorff metric of the α-cut of the fuzzy valued functions.

Further, using the concept of α-cut representation and the differentiability of $\tilde{f}$ in first and second case, one can write $\tilde{f}'$ as $\tilde{f}'(x, \alpha) = [\underline{f}(x, \alpha), \overline{f}(x, \alpha)]$ and $\tilde{f}'(x, \alpha) = [\overline{f}(x, \alpha), \underline{f}(x, \alpha)]$, respectively [8].

9.3.6 Riemann–Liouville fractional integral

The Riemann–Liouville integral operator I^{β} of order $\beta > 0$ is defined as [7,9]

$$I^{\beta} f(t) = \frac{1}{\Gamma(\beta)} \int_0^t (t - \tau)^{\beta - 1} f(\tau) d\tau, t > 0. \tag{9.12}$$

9.3.7 Fuzzy Riemann–Liouville fractional integral

The Riemann–Liouville fractional integral of order $\beta > 0$ of the fuzzy valued function $\tilde{f}$, based on its α-cut representation is given as [10,12]

$$I^{\beta}\tilde{f}(t;\alpha) = [I^{\beta}\underline{f}(t;\alpha), I^{\beta}\overline{f}(t;\alpha)], t > 0, \tag{9.13}$$

where

$$\begin{aligned} I^{\beta}\underline{f}(t;\alpha) &= \frac{1}{\Gamma(\beta)}\int_0^t (t-\tau)^{\beta-1}\underline{f}(\tau;\alpha)d\tau, t > 0. \\ I^{\beta}\overline{f}(t;\alpha) &= \frac{1}{\Gamma(\beta)}\int_0^t (t-\tau)^{\beta-1}\overline{f}(\tau;\alpha)d\tau, t > 0. \end{aligned} \tag{9.14}$$

9.3.8 Caputo fractional derivative

The fractional derivative of $f(t)$ in the Caputo sense is defined as [11]

$$D^{\beta}f(t) = J^{m-\beta}D^{m}f(t) = \begin{cases} \frac{1}{\Gamma(m-\beta)}\int_0^t \frac{f^{(m)}(\tau)}{(t-\tau)^{\beta+1-m}}d\tau, m-1 < \beta < m, m \in \mathbb{N}, \\ \\ \frac{d^m}{dt^m}f(t), \beta = m, m \in \mathbb{N}. \end{cases} \tag{9.15}$$

9.3.9 Caputo fuzzy fractional derivative

Let $\tilde{f}(t;\alpha)$ be a fuzzy valued function defined on the interval $[a,b]$. The fractional derivative of $\tilde{f}$ of order β is given as [11,12].

1. If $\tilde{f}(t;\alpha)$ is a Caputo-type fuzzy fractional differentiable function in the first form, then

$$D^{\beta}\tilde{f}(t;\alpha) = [D^{\beta}\underline{f}(t;\alpha), D^{\beta}\overline{f}(t;\alpha)]. \tag{9.16}$$

2. If $\tilde{f}(t;\alpha)$ is a Caputo-type fuzzy fractional differentiable function in the second form, then

$$D^{\beta}\tilde{f}(t;\alpha) = [D^{\beta}\overline{f}(t;\alpha), D^{\beta}\underline{f}(t;\alpha)]. \tag{9.17}$$

Here,

$$\begin{aligned} D^{\beta}\underline{f}(t;\alpha) &= \frac{1}{\Gamma(m-\beta)}\int_0^t \frac{\underline{f}^{(m)}(\tau;\alpha)}{(t-\tau)^{\beta+1-m}}d\tau, m-1 < \beta < m, m \in \mathbb{N}, \\ D^{\beta}\overline{f}(t;\alpha) &= \frac{1}{\Gamma(m-\beta)}\int_0^t \frac{\overline{f}^{(m)}(\tau;\alpha)}{(t-\tau)^{\beta+1-m}}d\tau, m-1 < \beta < m, m \in \mathbb{N}, \end{aligned} \tag{9.18}$$

where $\tilde{f}$ is continuous and Lebesgue integrable, $\tilde{f}'(x) = \frac{d\tilde{f}}{dx}$.

References

[1] Ramon E. Moore, R. Baker Kearfott, Michael J. Cloud, Introduction to Interval Analysis, SIAM, 2009.
[2] G. Alefeld, J. Herzberger, Introduction to Interval Computation, Academic Press, 2012.
[3] L.A. Zadeh, Fuzzy sets, Information and Control 8 (3) (1965) 338–353.
[4] S. Chakraverty, D.M. Sahoo, N.R. Mahato, Concepts of Soft Computing, vol. 1007, Springer, Singapore, 2019, pp. 978–981.
[5] H.-J. Zimmermann, Introduction to fuzzy sets, in: Fuzzy Set Theory—and Its Applications, Springer, 2001, pp. 1–8.
[6] D. Behera, S. Chakraverty, New approach to solve fully fuzzy system of linear equations using single and double parametric form of fuzzy numbers, Sadhana 40 (2015) 35–49.
[7] S. Chakraverty, S. Tapaswini, D. Behera, Fuzzy Differential Equations and Applications for Engineers and Scientists, CRC Press, 2016.
[8] Y. Chalco-Cano, H. Roman-Flores, On new solutions of fuzzy differential equations, Chaos, Solitons and Fractals 38 (1) (2008) 112–119.
[9] R. Gorenflo, F. Mainardi, Fractional Calculus: Integral and Differential Equations of Fractional Order, Springer, 1997.
[10] S. Salahshour, T. Allahviranloo, S. Abbasbandy, Solving fuzzy fractional differential equations by fuzzy Laplace transforms, Communications in Nonlinear Science and Numerical Simulation 17 (3) (2012) 1372–1381.
[11] M. Mazandarani, A.V. Kamyad, Modified fractional Euler method for solving fuzzy fractional initial value problem, Communications in Nonlinear Science and Numerical Simulation 18 (1) (2013) 12–21.
[12] S. Chakraverty, S. Tapaswini, D. Behera, Fuzzy Arbitrary Order System: Fuzzy Fractional Differential Equations and Applications, John Wiley & Sons, 2016.

10 Preliminaries of type-2 fuzzy sets

Contents

10.1 Type-2 fuzzy sets ... **113**
- 10.1.1 Vertical slice of a type-2 fuzzy set ... 114
- 10.1.2 $\tilde{\alpha}$-Cut of vertical slice ... 114
- 10.1.3 $\tilde{\alpha}$-Plane of a type-2 fuzzy set ... 114
- 10.1.4 Footprint of uncertainty ... 114
- 10.1.5 Lower membership function and upper membership function of a type-2 fuzzy set ... 115
- 10.1.6 Principle set of a type-2 fuzzy set ... 115
- 10.1.7 α-Cut of an $\tilde{\alpha}$-plane ... 115

10.2 Triangularly perfect quasi-type-2 fuzzy numbers ... **115**
- 10.2.1 Arithmetic of TPQT2FNs ... 116

10.3 Gaussian triangular type-2 fuzzy number (GTT2FN) ... **118**

10.4 General interval type-2 triangular fuzzy number (GIT2TFN) ... **118**
- 10.4.1 Perfect interval type-2 triangular fuzzy number (PIT2TFN) ... 119

10.5 Derivative of type-2 fuzzy valued functions ... **119**

10.6 Riemann–Liouville integral of the type-2 fuzzy valued function ... **120**

10.7 Caputo type-2 fuzzy fractional derivative ... **121**

References ... **121**

Chapter points

- Basic concepts related to type-2 fuzzy sets are discussed here.
- The concept of α-cut of the $\tilde{\alpha}$-plane of triangularly perfect quasi-type-2 fuzzy numbers is discussed, which will be used in handling the type-2 fuzzy parameters in the subsequent chapters.
- The concept of type-2 fuzzy arithmetic is provided.
- Type-2 fuzzy calculus for both integer and fractional-order is presented.

10.1 Type-2 fuzzy sets

Fuzzy sets, or type-1 fuzzy sets, assign a single degree of membership to each element within a set. Whereas type-2 fuzzy sets (T2FS) take uncertainty to a deeper level by introducing the concept of fuzzy sets within the membership function itself. In a type-2 fuzzy set, the membership degree becomes a fuzzy set, allowing for a more nuanced representation of uncertainty.

Artificial Neural Networks and Type-2 Fuzzy Set. https://doi.org/10.1016/B978-0-44-332894-7.00020-4

A T2FS, denoted as $\tilde{\tilde{A}}$ [1], is characterized by a type-2 membership function $\mu_{\tilde{\tilde{A}}}(x, u)$, where $x \in X$ and $u \in J_x \subseteq [0, 1]$, i.e.,

$$\tilde{\tilde{A}} = \{((x, u), \mu_{\tilde{\tilde{A}}}(x, u)) \mid x \in X, u \in U_x \subseteq [0, 1]\}$$

in which $0 \leq \mu_{\tilde{\tilde{A}}}(x, u) \leq 1$, where x is the primary variable, X is the domain of the fuzzy set, and J_x is the domain of the secondary membership function at x. When the secondary membership grade of the type-2 fuzzy set equals unity, i.e., $\mu_{\tilde{\tilde{A}}}(x, j) = 1$ for all $x \in X$ and $j \in J_x$, then the type-2 fuzzy set is called an interval type-2 fuzzy set.

In a similar manner, the concept of type-k fuzzy sets may be defined as "fuzzy sets, which have fuzzy uncertain membership grades of type $k - 1$."

10.1.1 Vertical slice of a type-2 fuzzy set

At each value of x, say $x = x'$, the 2D-plane whose axes are u and $\mu_{\tilde{\tilde{A}}}(x', u)$ is called the vertical slice of $\mu_{\tilde{\tilde{A}}(x,u)}$, which is a type-1 fuzzy set [1,2]. It is given by

$$\mu_{\tilde{\tilde{A}}}(x = x', u) = \mu_{\tilde{\tilde{A}}}(x') = \int \frac{f_{x'}(u)}{u} \text{ where } u \in J_{x'} \subseteq [0, 1],$$

in which $0 \leq f_{x'}(u) \leq 1$.

10.1.2 $\tilde{\alpha}$-Cut of vertical slice

An $\tilde{\alpha}$-cut set of the vertical slice of a type-2 fuzzy set at point $x' \in X$ is defined as [1,2]

$$S_{\tilde{\tilde{A}}}(x'|\tilde{\alpha}) = \begin{cases} \{u \in J_{x_0} | f_{x'}(u) \geq \tilde{\alpha}\}, & \text{for } 0 < \tilde{\alpha} \leq 1, \\ cl\{u \in J_{x_0} | f_{x'}(u) \geq \tilde{\alpha}\}, & \text{for } \tilde{\alpha} = 0 \end{cases} \tag{10.1}$$

where $cl(.)$ denotes the closure of the set.

10.1.3 $\tilde{\alpha}$-Plane of a type-2 fuzzy set

Let $\tilde{\tilde{A}}$ be a T2FS. The union of all secondary domains of the T2FS, whose secondary grades are greater or equal to $\tilde{\alpha} \in [0, 1]$, is called $\tilde{\alpha}$-plane of $\tilde{\tilde{A}}$ [1,2] and denoted by $\tilde{\tilde{A}}_{\tilde{\alpha}}$.

10.1.4 Footprint of uncertainty

Suppose $\tilde{\tilde{A}}$ is a T2FS. The $\tilde{\alpha}$-plane of the set at $\tilde{\alpha} = 0$ is called the footprint of uncertainty of $\tilde{\tilde{A}}$, denoted by $\text{FOU}(\tilde{\tilde{A}})$ [1].

10.1.5 Lower membership function and upper membership function of a type-2 fuzzy set

A type-2 fuzzy set $\tilde{\tilde{A}}$ at level $\tilde{\alpha}$, i.e., $\tilde{\tilde{A}}_{\tilde{\alpha}}$ can be written in parametric form as $\tilde{\tilde{A}}_{\tilde{\alpha}} = (\underline{\tilde{A}}_{\tilde{\alpha}}, \overline{\tilde{A}}_{\tilde{\alpha}})$, where $\underline{\tilde{A}}_{\tilde{\alpha}}$ and $\overline{\tilde{A}}_{\tilde{\alpha}}$ are called a lower membership function (LMF) and upper membership function (UMF) of $\tilde{\tilde{A}}$, respectively, and they both are type-1 fuzzy sets [1].

10.1.6 Principle set of a type-2 fuzzy set

The $\tilde{\alpha}$-plane of the type-2 fuzzy set $\tilde{\tilde{A}}$ at $\tilde{\alpha} = 1$ is called the principle set of $\tilde{\tilde{A}}$, which is a type-1 fuzzy set [3].

10.1.7 α-Cut of an $\tilde{\alpha}$-plane

Suppose $\tilde{\tilde{A}}$ is a type-2 fuzzy set and let $\tilde{\tilde{A}}(\tilde{\alpha})$ be the $\tilde{\alpha}$ -plane representation of $\tilde{\tilde{A}}$, then the α-cut of $\tilde{\tilde{A}}(\tilde{\alpha})$ is defined as [3] the α-cut of LMF and UMF of $\tilde{\tilde{A}}(\tilde{\alpha})$, i.e., $\tilde{\tilde{A}}(\tilde{\alpha}, \alpha) = (\underline{\tilde{A}}(\tilde{\alpha}, \alpha), \overline{\tilde{A}}(\tilde{\alpha}, \alpha))$.

10.2 Triangularly perfect quasi-type-2 fuzzy numbers

A perfect type-2 fuzzy number (T2FN) $\tilde{\tilde{A}}$ [4] is a T2FS, which satisfies the conditions below:

1. LMF and UMF of FOU$(\tilde{\tilde{A}})$ are type-1 fuzzy numbers.
2. LMF and UMF of the principle set of $\tilde{\tilde{A}}$ are also type-1 fuzzy numbers.

Perfect quasi-T2FN [4] is a kind of perfect T2FN, where all vertical slices are T1FNs and piecewise functions of the same kind. A triangular perfect quasi-T2FN (TPQT2FN) $\tilde{\tilde{t}}$ was introduced in [4], as

$$\tilde{\tilde{t}} = (\overline{L}_{t0}, L_{t_1}, \underline{L}_{t0}, p, \underline{R}_{t0}, R_{t_1}, \overline{R}_{t0}), \tag{10.2}$$

satisfying

$$\overline{L}_{t0} \leq L_{t_1} \leq \underline{L}_{t0} \leq p \leq \underline{R}_{t0} \leq R_{t_1} \leq \overline{R}_{t0}. \tag{10.3}$$

The schematic diagram of the TPQT2FN $\tilde{\tilde{t}}$ is shown below in Fig. 10.1.

Now, the $\tilde{\alpha}$, α form [4] is

$$\tilde{\tilde{t}}(\tilde{\alpha}, \alpha) = (\underline{\tilde{t}}(\tilde{\alpha}, \alpha), \overline{\tilde{t}}(\tilde{\alpha}, \alpha)), \tag{10.4}$$

where

$$\underline{\tilde{t}}(\tilde{\alpha}, \alpha) = (\underline{L}_t(\tilde{\alpha}, \alpha), \underline{R}_t(\tilde{\alpha}, \alpha)) \tag{10.5}$$

$$\underline{L}_t(\tilde{\alpha}, \alpha) = L_{t_1}(\alpha) - (1 - \tilde{\alpha})(L_{t_1}(\alpha) - \underline{L}_{t0}(\alpha)) \tag{10.6}$$

$$\underline{R}_t(\tilde{\alpha}, \alpha) = R_{t_1}(\alpha) - (1 - \tilde{\alpha})(R_{t_1}(\alpha) - \underline{R}_{t0}(\alpha)) \tag{10.7}$$

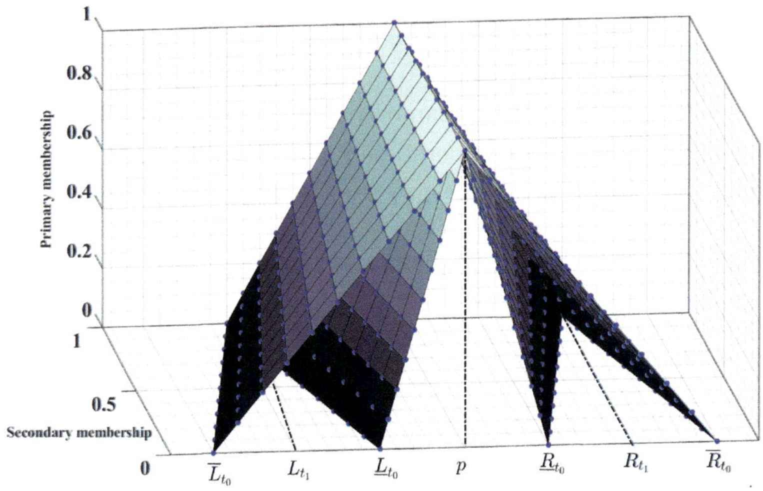

FIGURE 10.1 Schematic diagram of the TPQT2FN $\tilde{\tilde{t}} = (\overline{L}_{t_0}, L_{t_1}, \underline{L}_{t_0}, p, \underline{R}_{t_0}, R_{t_1}, \overline{R}_{t_0})$.

and

$$\overline{\tilde{t}}(\tilde{\alpha}, \alpha) = (\overline{L}_t(\tilde{\alpha}, \alpha), \overline{R}_t(\tilde{\alpha}, \alpha)) \tag{10.8}$$

$$\overline{L}_t(\tilde{\alpha}, \alpha) = L_{t_1}(\alpha) - (1 - r_1)(L_{t_1}(\tilde{\alpha}) - \overline{L}_{t_0}(\alpha)) \tag{10.9}$$

$$\overline{R}_t(\tilde{\alpha}, \alpha) = R_{t_1}(\alpha) - (1 - \tilde{\alpha})(R_{t_1}(\alpha) - \overline{R}_{t_0}(\alpha)) \tag{10.10}$$

Further,

$$\begin{aligned}
\overline{L}_{t_0}(\alpha) &= p - (1 - \alpha)(p - \overline{L}_{t_0}), \\
L_{t_1}(\alpha) &= p - (1 - \alpha)(p - L_{t_1}), \\
\underline{L}_{t_0}(\alpha) &= p - (1 - \alpha)(p - \underline{L}_{t_0}), \\
\overline{R}_{t_0}(\alpha) &= p - (1 - \alpha)(p - \overline{R}_{t_0}), \\
R_{t_1}(\alpha) &= p - (1 - \alpha)(p - R_{t_1}), \\
\underline{R}_{t_0}(\alpha) &= p - (1 - \alpha)(p - \underline{R}_{t_0}).
\end{aligned}$$

10.2.1 Arithmetic of TPQT2FNs

Let $\tilde{\tilde{u}} = (\overline{L}_{u0}, L_{u1}, \underline{L}_{u0}, m, \underline{R}_{u0}, R_{u1}, \overline{R}_{u0})$ and $\tilde{\tilde{v}} = (\overline{L}_{v0}, L_{v1}, \underline{L}_{v0}, n, \underline{R}_{v0}, R_{v1}, \overline{R}_{v0})$ be two TPQT2FNs and $k \in \mathbf{R}$ any crisp number, then [5]:

1. Addition

Addition of $\tilde{\tilde{u}}$ and $\tilde{\tilde{v}}$ is given by

$$\tilde{\tilde{u}} + \tilde{\tilde{v}} = (\overline{L}_{u0} + \overline{L}_{v0}, L_{u1} + L_{v1}, \underline{L}_{u0} + \underline{L}_{v0}, m + n, \underline{R}_{u0} + \underline{R}_{v0}, R_{u1} + R_{v1}, \overline{R}_{u0} + \overline{R}_{v0}).$$

2. **Scalar Multiplication**
   For any scalar $k \in \mathbf{R}$,

$$k\tilde{\tilde{u}} = (k\overline{L}_{u0}, kL_{u1}, k\underline{L}_{u0}, km, kR_{u1}, k\overline{R}_{u0}), k \geq 0$$
$$k\tilde{\tilde{u}} = (k\overline{R}_{u0}, kR_{u1}, km, k\underline{L}_{u0}, kL_{u1}, k\overline{L}_{u0}), k < 0.$$

3. **Subtraction**
   Subtraction of $\tilde{\tilde{u}}$ and $\tilde{\tilde{v}}$ is given by

$$\tilde{\tilde{u}} - \tilde{\tilde{v}} = (\overline{L}_{u0} - \overline{R}_{v0}, L_{u1} - R_{v1}, \underline{L}_{u0} - \underline{R}_{v0}, m - n, \underline{R}_{u0} - \underline{L}_{v0}, R_{u1} - L_{v1}, \overline{R}_{u0} - \overline{L}_{v0}).$$

4. **Multiplication**
   Let $\tilde{\tilde{u}}(\tilde{\alpha},\alpha) = (\underline{\tilde{u}}(\tilde{\alpha},\alpha), \overline{\tilde{u}}(\tilde{\alpha},\alpha))$ and $\tilde{\tilde{v}}(\tilde{\alpha},\alpha) = (\underline{\tilde{v}}(\tilde{\alpha},\alpha), \overline{\tilde{v}}(\tilde{\alpha},\alpha))$, then $\tilde{\tilde{u}}(\tilde{\alpha},\alpha) * \tilde{\tilde{v}}(\tilde{\alpha},\alpha)$ is given by

$$\tilde{\tilde{u}}(\tilde{\alpha},\alpha) * \tilde{\tilde{v}}(\tilde{\alpha},\alpha) = (\underline{\tilde{u}}(\tilde{\alpha},\alpha) * \underline{\tilde{v}}(\tilde{\alpha},\alpha), \overline{\tilde{u}}(\tilde{\alpha},\alpha) * \overline{\tilde{v}}(\tilde{\alpha},\alpha)),$$

   where

$$\begin{aligned}\underline{\tilde{u}}(\tilde{\alpha},\alpha) * \underline{\tilde{v}}(\tilde{\alpha},\alpha) = \Big[&\min\Big(\underline{L}_u(\tilde{\alpha},\alpha) * \underline{L}_v(\tilde{\alpha},\alpha), \underline{L}_u(\tilde{\alpha},\alpha) * \underline{R}_v(\tilde{\alpha},\alpha),\\ &\underline{R}_u(\tilde{\alpha},\alpha) * \underline{L}_v(\tilde{\alpha},\alpha), \underline{R}_u(\tilde{\alpha},\alpha) * \underline{R}_v(\tilde{\alpha},\alpha)\Big),\\ &\max\Big(\underline{L}_u(\tilde{\alpha},\alpha) * \underline{L}_v(\tilde{\alpha},\alpha), \underline{L}_u(\tilde{\alpha},\alpha) * \underline{R}_v(\tilde{\alpha},\alpha),\\ &\underline{R}_u(\tilde{\alpha},\alpha) * \underline{L}_v(\tilde{\alpha},\alpha), \underline{R}_u(\tilde{\alpha},\alpha) * \underline{R}_v(\tilde{\alpha},\alpha)\Big)\Big]\\ \overline{\tilde{u}}(\tilde{\alpha},\alpha) * \overline{\tilde{v}}(\tilde{\alpha},\alpha) = \Big[&\min\Big(\overline{L}_u(\tilde{\alpha},\alpha) * \overline{L}_v(\tilde{\alpha},\alpha), \overline{L}_u(\tilde{\alpha},\alpha) * \overline{R}_v(\tilde{\alpha},\alpha),\\ &\overline{R}_u(\tilde{\alpha},\alpha) * \overline{L}_v(\tilde{\alpha},\alpha), \overline{R}_u(\tilde{\alpha},\alpha) * \overline{R}_v(\tilde{\alpha},\alpha)\Big),\\ &\max\Big(\overline{L}_u(\tilde{\alpha},\alpha) * \overline{L}_v(\tilde{\alpha},\alpha), \overline{L}_u(\tilde{\alpha},\alpha) * \overline{R}_v(\tilde{\alpha},\alpha),\\ &\overline{R}_u(\tilde{\alpha},\alpha) * \overline{L}_v(\tilde{\alpha},\alpha), \overline{R}_u(\tilde{\alpha},\alpha) * \overline{R}_v(\tilde{\alpha},\alpha)\Big)\Big]\end{aligned}$$

5. **Division**
   Let $\tilde{\tilde{u}} = (\overline{L}_{u0}, L_{u1}, \underline{L}_{u0}, m, \underline{R}_{u0}, R_{u1}, \overline{R}_{u0})$ and $\tilde{\tilde{v}} = (\overline{L}_{v0}, L_{v1}, \underline{L}_{v0}, n, \underline{R}_{v0}, R_{v1}, \overline{R}_{v0})$ be two TPQT2FNs (where $\tilde{v} \neq 0$), then $\frac{\tilde{\tilde{u}}(\tilde{\alpha},\alpha)}{\tilde{\tilde{v}}(\tilde{\alpha},\alpha)}$ is given by

$$\frac{\tilde{\tilde{u}}(\tilde{\alpha},\alpha)}{\tilde{\tilde{v}}(\tilde{\alpha},\alpha)} = \left(\frac{\underline{\tilde{u}}(\tilde{\alpha},\alpha)}{\underline{\tilde{v}}(\tilde{\alpha},\alpha)}, \frac{\overline{\tilde{u}}(\tilde{\alpha},\alpha)}{\overline{\tilde{v}}(\tilde{\alpha},\alpha)}\right),$$

where

$$\frac{\underline{\tilde{u}}(\tilde{\alpha},\alpha)}{\underline{\tilde{v}}(\tilde{\alpha},\alpha)} = \left[\min\left(\frac{\underline{L}_u(\tilde{\alpha},\alpha)}{\underline{L}_v(\tilde{\alpha},\alpha)}, \frac{\underline{L}_u(\tilde{\alpha},\alpha)}{\underline{R}_v(\tilde{\alpha},\alpha)}, \frac{\underline{R}_u(\tilde{\alpha},\alpha)}{\underline{L}_v(\tilde{\alpha},\alpha)}, \frac{\underline{R}_u(\tilde{\alpha},\alpha)}{\underline{R}_v(\tilde{\alpha},\alpha)}\right),\right.$$
$$\left.\max\left(\frac{\underline{L}_u(\tilde{\alpha},\alpha)}{\underline{L}_v(\tilde{\alpha},\alpha)}, \frac{\underline{L}_u(\tilde{\alpha},\alpha)}{\underline{R}_v(\tilde{\alpha},\alpha)}, \frac{\underline{R}_u(\tilde{\alpha},\alpha)}{\underline{L}_v(\tilde{\alpha},\alpha)}, \frac{\underline{R}_u(\tilde{\alpha},\alpha)}{\underline{R}_v(\tilde{\alpha},\alpha)}\right)\right]$$
$$\frac{\overline{\tilde{u}}(\tilde{\alpha},\alpha)}{\overline{\tilde{v}}(\tilde{\alpha},\alpha)} = \left[\min\left(\frac{\overline{L}_u(\tilde{\alpha},\alpha)}{\overline{L}_v(\tilde{\alpha},\alpha)}, \frac{\overline{L}_u(\tilde{\alpha},\alpha)}{\overline{R}_v(\tilde{\alpha},\alpha)}, \frac{\overline{R}_u(\tilde{\alpha},\alpha)}{\overline{L}_v(\tilde{\alpha},\alpha)}, \frac{\overline{R}_u(\tilde{\alpha},\alpha)}{\overline{R}_v(\tilde{\alpha},\alpha)}\right),\right.$$
$$\left.\max\left(\frac{\overline{L}_u(\tilde{\alpha},\alpha)}{\overline{L}_v(\tilde{\alpha},\alpha)}, \frac{\overline{L}_u(\tilde{\alpha},\alpha)}{\overline{R}_v(\tilde{\alpha},\alpha)}, \frac{\overline{R}_u(\tilde{\alpha},\alpha)}{\overline{L}_v(\tilde{\alpha},\alpha)}, \frac{\overline{R}_u(\tilde{\alpha},\alpha)}{\overline{R}_v(\tilde{\alpha},\alpha)}\right)\right]$$

10.3 Gaussian triangular type-2 fuzzy number (GTT2FN)

The Gaussian triangular type-2 fuzzy number (GTT2FN) $\tilde{\tilde{A}}$ is denoted as [6]

$$\tilde{\tilde{A}} = (m, \sigma_p, \sigma_s),$$

where m is called the core (mean) of the type-2 fuzzy number, σ_p is the standard deviation in the primary grade to handle the uncertainty in domain space, and σ_s is the deviation in the secondary domain.

The α-cut of a GTT2FN at a $\tilde{\alpha}$-plane is given as

$$\tilde{\tilde{A}}(\tilde{\alpha},\alpha) = (\underline{\tilde{A}}(\tilde{\alpha},\alpha), \overline{\tilde{A}}(\tilde{\alpha},\alpha)), \tilde{\alpha}, \alpha \in [0, 1],$$

where $\underline{\tilde{A}}(\tilde{\alpha},\alpha)$ and $\overline{\tilde{A}}(\tilde{\alpha},\alpha)$ are the LMF and UMF, respectively, and given as

$$\underline{\tilde{A}}(\tilde{\alpha},\alpha) = [(m - 2\sigma_s) + \sigma_s(1-\tilde{\alpha}), (m + 2\sigma_s) - \sigma_s(1-\tilde{\alpha})],$$
$$\overline{\tilde{A}}(\tilde{\alpha},\alpha) = [(m - 2\sigma_s) - \sigma_s(1-\tilde{\alpha}), (m + 2\sigma_s) + \sigma_s(1-\tilde{\alpha})],$$

with $\sigma_s = \sigma_p\sqrt{(-2\ln\alpha)}$. Further, when $\tilde{\alpha} = 0$, the resulting type-1 fuzzy set is called the FOU and when $\tilde{\alpha} = 1$ it is called the principle set (PS) of a type-2 fuzzy set. The schematic diagram of the GTT2FN $\tilde{\tilde{A}}$ is shown in Fig. 10.2.

10.4 General interval type-2 triangular fuzzy number (GIT2TFN)

A general interval type-2 triangular fuzzy number $\tilde{\tilde{B}}$ is written as [7], $\tilde{\tilde{B}} = (b1_U, b1_L, b2_L, b2_U, b3_L, b3_U)$, where $b1_U \le b1_L \le b2_L \le b2_U \le b3_L \le b3_U$. $B_L = (b1_L, b2_L, b3_L)$ and $B_U = (b1_U, b2_U, b3_U)$ are called the LMF and UMF of the interval type-2 triangular fuzzy number

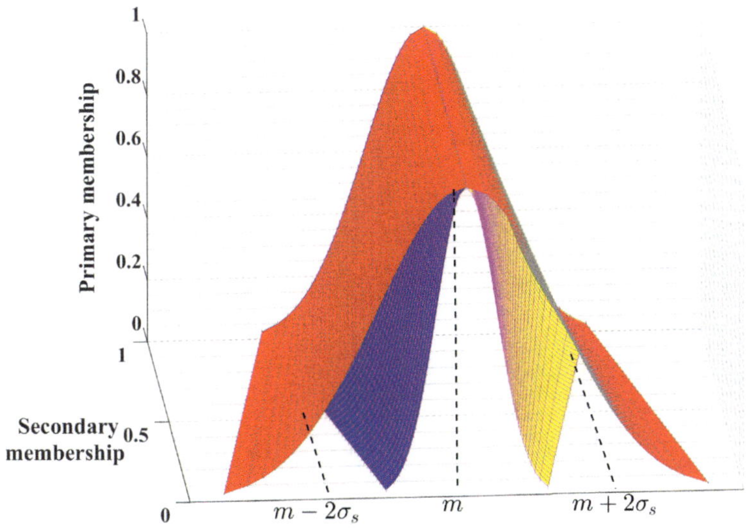

FIGURE 10.2 Schematic diagram of the GTT2FN $\tilde{\tilde{A}} = (m, \sigma_p, \sigma_s)$.

$\tilde{\tilde{B}}$. The associated membership is given by

$$\mu_{\tilde{\tilde{B}}_L}(x) = \begin{cases} h_L \frac{x - b1_L}{b2_L - b1_L} & \text{if } b1_L \le x \le b2_L, \\ h_L \frac{b3_L - x}{b3_L - b2_L} & \text{if } b2_L \le x \le b3_L, \\ 0 & \text{otherwise}, \end{cases} \tag{10.11}$$

$$\mu_{\tilde{\tilde{B}}_U}(x) = \begin{cases} h_U \frac{x - b1_U}{b2_U - b1_U} & \text{if } b1_U \le x \le b2_U, \\ h_U \frac{b3_U - x}{b3_U - b2_U} & \text{if } b2_U \le x \le b3_U, \\ 0 & \text{otherwise}, \end{cases} \tag{10.12}$$

where h_L and $h_U \in [0, 1]$.

10.4.1 Perfect interval type-2 triangular fuzzy number (PIT2TFN)

A GIT2TFN $\tilde{\tilde{B}}$ is said to be a perfect interval type-2 fuzzy number, provided $b2_L = b2_U$ and $h_L = h_U = 1$. Readers may go through [7] and references therein for more related information. In Fig. 10.3, the schematic diagram of the PIT2TFN $\tilde{\tilde{B}}$ is shown.

10.5 Derivative of type-2 fuzzy valued functions

Let $\tilde{\tilde{f}}$ be a fuzzy-valued function defined on the interval $[a, b] \subseteq \mathbb{R}$. $\tilde{\tilde{f}}$ is said to be differentiable at x_0 [4], if $\exists \tilde{\tilde{f}}(x_0)$, such that for $h > 0$ and very close to zero.

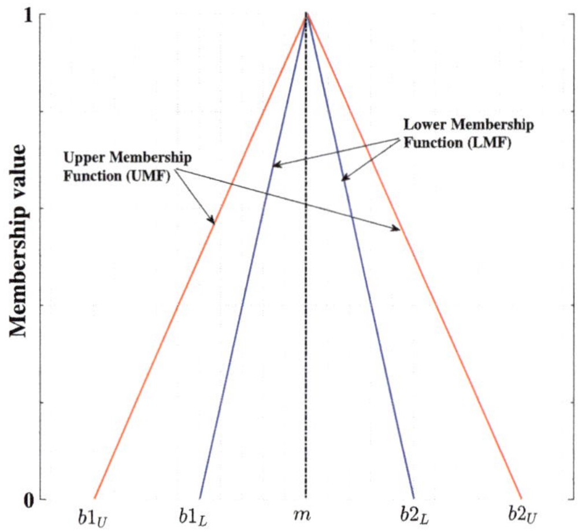

FIGURE 10.3 Schematic diagram of the PIT2TFN $\tilde{\tilde{B}} = (b1_U, b1_L, b2_L, b2_U, b3_L, b3_U)$.

1. The H_2-differences $\tilde{\tilde{f}}(x_0+h) - \tilde{\tilde{f}}(x_0)$ and $\tilde{\tilde{f}}(x_0) - \tilde{\tilde{f}}(x_0-h)$, and the limits

$$\tilde{\tilde{f}}'(x_0) = \lim_{h\to 0^+} \frac{\tilde{\tilde{f}}(x_0+h) - \tilde{\tilde{f}}(x_0)}{h} = \lim_{h\to 0^+} \frac{\tilde{\tilde{f}}(x_0) - \tilde{\tilde{f}}(x_0-h)}{h},$$

or

2. The H_2-differences $\tilde{\tilde{f}}(x_0) - \tilde{\tilde{f}}(x_0+h)$ and $\tilde{\tilde{f}}(x_0-h) - \tilde{\tilde{f}}(x_0)$, and the limits

$$\tilde{\tilde{f}}'(x_0) = \lim_{h\to 0^+} \frac{\tilde{\tilde{f}}(x_0) - \tilde{\tilde{f}}(x_0+h)}{-h} = \lim_{h\to 0^+} \frac{\tilde{\tilde{f}}(x_0-h) - \tilde{\tilde{f}}(x_0)}{-h},$$

exist. Here, the limits are taken in the metric space of all type-2 fuzzy number valued functions [4]. Using the concept of the $\tilde{\alpha}$-plane form and the differentiability of $\tilde{\tilde{f}}$ in the first and second case, one can write $\tilde{\tilde{f}}'$ as $\tilde{\tilde{f}}'(x, \tilde{\alpha}) = (\underline{\tilde{f}}(x, \tilde{\alpha}), \overline{\tilde{f}}(x, \tilde{\alpha}))$.

10.6 Riemann–Liouville integral of the type-2 fuzzy valued function

Let $\tilde{\tilde{f}}$ be a type-2 fuzzy number that is valued, continuous, and a Lebesgue integrable function defined on $[0, a]$, then the Riemann–Liouville integral of $\tilde{\tilde{f}}(t)$ can be given as [8]

$$I^{\beta}\tilde{\tilde{f}}(t) = \frac{1}{\Gamma(\beta)} \int_0^t \frac{\tilde{\tilde{f}}(x)}{(t-x)^{1-\beta}} dx, \tag{10.13}$$

for $\beta \in \mathbf{R}^+$. Further, using the parametric approach the Riemann–Liouville integral can be written as

$$\left[I^{\beta}\tilde{\tilde{f}}(t)\right](\tilde{\alpha}) = \left(I^{\beta}\underline{\tilde{f}}(\tilde{\alpha})(t), I^{\beta}\overline{\tilde{f}}(\tilde{\alpha})(t)\right). \quad (10.14)$$

10.7 Caputo type-2 fuzzy fractional derivative

The fractional derivative of a type-2 fuzzy valued function $\tilde{\tilde{f}}$ of order β in Caputo sense is given by [8]

$$D^{\beta}\tilde{\tilde{f}}(t) = \frac{1}{\Gamma(1-\beta)}\int_0^t \frac{\tilde{\tilde{f}}'(x)}{(t-x)^{\beta}}dx \quad (10.15)$$

where $\tilde{\tilde{f}}$ is continuous and Lebesgue integrable, $\tilde{\tilde{f}}'(x) = \frac{d\tilde{\tilde{f}}}{dx}$ and $\beta \in (0, 1)$.

This chapter thoroughly discusses ideas concerning type-2 fuzzy numbers, as well as the derivatives and integrals of functions valued in type-2 fuzzy numbers. The notions presented in this chapter will be utilized in subsequent chapters to propose solution methodologies for addressing diverse mathematical problems under type-2 fuzzy uncertainty.

References

[1] J.M. Mendel, R.B. John, Type-2 fuzzy sets made simple, IEEE Transactions on Fuzzy Systems 10 (2) (2002) 117–127.
[2] D. Mohapatra, S. Chakraverty, Type-2 fuzzy linear system of equations with application in static problem of structures, Mathematical Methods in the Applied Sciences 46 (1) (2023) 840–866.
[3] H. Hamrawi, Type-2 fuzzy alpha-cuts, De Montfort University, 2011.
[4] M. Mazandarani, M. Najariyan, Differentiability of type-2 fuzzy number-valued functions, Communications in Nonlinear Science and Numerical Simulation 19 (3) (2014) 710–725.
[5] M. Najariyan, M. Mazandarani, R. John, Type-2 fuzzy linear systems, Granular Computing 2 (3) (2017) 175–186.
[6] D. Mohapatra, S. Chakraverty, M. Alshammari, Time fractional heat equation of n + 1-dimension in type-1 and type-2 fuzzy environment, International Journal of Fuzzy Systems (2023) 1–16.
[7] M. Javanmard, H. Mishmast Nehi, Rankings and operations for interval type-2 fuzzy numbers: a review and some new methods, Journal of Applied Mathematics and Computing 59 (2019) 597–630.
[8] M. Mazandarani, M. Najariyan, Type-2 fuzzy fractional derivatives, Communications in Nonlinear Science and Numerical Simulation 19 (7) (2014) 2354–2372.

11

Uncertain static engineering problems

Contents

11.1 Introduction 123
11.2 Type-2 fuzzy linear system of equations 125
11.3 Solution procedure for T2FLSEs and FT2FLSEs 127
11.4 Sample problems 129
11.5 Application problems 135
11.5.1 Rectangular sheet 135
11.5.2 Beam structure 137
11.5.3 Truss structure 139
References 144

Chapter points

- An approach to solve the type-2 fuzzy linear system of equation is discussed.
- Triangularly perfect quasi-type-2 fuzzy numbers (TPQT2FNs) are used to handle the uncertainty.
- Uncertainty is considered in the coefficient matrix, right-hand side vector and in the coefficient matrix and right-hand side vector.
- Numerical examples and application problems related to various engineering structures are provided.

11.1 Introduction

Linear systems of equations are highly effective tools for solving practical problems in several disciplines, including economics, physics, engineering, and mathematics. There are several techniques available in the literature for solving the linear system of equations. The parameters associated with the linear system of equations are typically considered to be deterministic in order to facilitate calculation. However, it is important to acknowledge that uncertainty can arise from a variety of causes, such as measurement mistakes, inadequate information, or intrinsic unpredictability in the system. This amplifies the significance of uncertainty in order to analyze the system in a subtle and detailed way. Probability theory is a generally accepted approach for handling the uncertainty associated with the parameters of a system. Extensive datasets are essential for a more efficient analysis of the uncertain system utilizing the probability technique. The results may be less

Artificial Neural Networks and Type-2 Fuzzy Set. https://doi.org/10.1016/B978-0-44-332894-7.00021-6

accurate due to the lack of a substantial amount of data. Fuzzy numbers and intervals offer an alternative approach to represent uncertainty, particularly when data is limited. They allow for a more flexible description of uncertain parameters by assigning degrees of membership, indicating how likely each value is. When the membership grades themselves are uncertain or imprecise, type-2 fuzzy numbers are used. These provide a more intricate and detailed representation of uncertainty. This chapter is dedicated to thoroughly exploring linear systems of equations in the context of type-2 fuzzy uncertainty, with a particular focus on their applications in structural engineering, where managing uncertainty is often critical for precise modeling and analysis.

Various researchers have studied and proposed different approaches to solve the fuzzy linear system of equations (FLSE). Friedman et al. [1] have solved FLSE by turning the $n \times n$ system to a $2n \times 2n$ crisp system by using the parametric representation of fuzzy numbers. The system of linear equations of the form $\tilde{X} = A\tilde{X} + \tilde{U}$, where A is a crisp matrix and $\tilde{U}$ is a vector of type-1 fuzzy numbers, has been solved using an iterative method [2]. Asady et al. [3] presented a method along with the existence condition for the fuzzy general system of equations. The complex FLSE has been handled by a novel strategy based on the subtraction and addition of the left and right bounds of the unknown fuzzy vector [4]. The steepest descent approach, in conjunction with the convergence analysis, has been successfully employed to solve the FLSE [5]. Otadi and Mosleh have obtained minimal solutions for a non-square FLSE [6]. Ma et al. have studied the duality FLSEs and proposed conditions for the existence of the solutions in their work [7]. Different Artificial Neural Network (ANN) based methods have been proposed in [8] to solve the system of linear equations and various application problems have also been investigated. Affine based approach has been implemented to obtain the closure bounds of the interval and fuzzy linear system of equations in [9]. Behera and Chakraverty [10] have used the concept of fuzzy numbers to analyze the beam, bar, and truss movements, where they have assumed the nodal forces as fuzzy numbers. The applications of fuzzy linear system of equations can be found in the vibration analysis of robotic manipulators [11,12]. The above studies have used only type-1 fuzzy numbers to explain the uncertainty in the parameters. Najariyan et al. have solved the type-2 FLSEs (T2FSLEs), where they have used TPQT2FNs [13].

Additionally, various investigations have been conducted on fully fuzzy linear system of equations (FFLSEs). Single and double parametric form of fuzzy numbers are used [14] to solve the FFLSE by converting the given model to parametric form. A method for solving fully-fuzzy square and non-square systems utilizing a linear programming approach has been established in [15]. Method based on the decomposition of the coefficient matrix has been implemented to solve the FFLSEs in [16]. An computational algorithm has been used in [17] to find the positive solutions of the FFLSEs. Concepts of interval arithmetic has been successfully implemented in [18] to solve the FFLSEs. Mohapatra and Chakraverty [19] have developed an approach based on the double parametric representation of the type-2 fuzzy numbers to solve the fully type-2 fuzzy system of linear equations.

11.2 Type-2 fuzzy linear system of equations

In the type-2 fuzzy linear system of equations, the coefficient matrix is assumed to be crisp, and the unknown and right-hand side vectors are type-2 fuzzy in nature. Specifically, the elements are type-2 fuzzy numbers. TPQT2FNs are employed in this context to address the type-2 fuzzy uncertainty.

Consider the following $n \times n$ type-2 fuzzy linear system of equations (T2FLSEs):

$$
\begin{array}{ccc}
a_{11}\tilde{\tilde{x}}_1 + a_{12}\tilde{\tilde{x}}_2 + & \cdots & + a_{1n}\tilde{\tilde{x}}_n = \tilde{\tilde{b}}_1, \\
a_{21}\tilde{\tilde{x}}_1 + a_{22}\tilde{\tilde{x}}_2 + & \cdots & + a_{2n}\tilde{\tilde{x}}_n = \tilde{\tilde{b}}_2, \\
\vdots & \ddots & \vdots \\
a_{n1}\tilde{\tilde{x}}_1 + a_{n2}\tilde{\tilde{x}}_2 + & \cdots & + a_{nn}\tilde{\tilde{x}}_n = \tilde{\tilde{b}}_n.
\end{array}
\tag{11.1}
$$

The above system can be written in matrix form as $A\tilde{\tilde{X}} = \tilde{\tilde{B}}$, in which $A = [a_{ij}]$, $1 \le i, j \le n$, is the real crisp coefficient matrix, $\tilde{\tilde{X}} = [\tilde{\tilde{x}}_j]$, $1 \le j \le n$ is the type-2 fuzzy unknown vector, and $\tilde{\tilde{B}} = [\tilde{\tilde{b}}_i]$, $1 \le i \le n$ is the type-2 fuzzy right-hand side vector.

The above form of the T2FLSEs in Eq. (11.1) can be written further using the concept of the α-cut of $\tilde{\alpha}$-plane as mentioned in Chapter 10 as

$$
\begin{array}{ccc}
a_{11}\tilde{\tilde{x}}_1(\tilde{\alpha},\alpha) + a_{12}\tilde{\tilde{x}}_2(\tilde{\alpha},\alpha) + & \cdots & + \tilde{a}_{1n}\tilde{\tilde{x}}_n(\tilde{\alpha},\alpha) = \tilde{\tilde{b}}_1(\tilde{\alpha},\alpha), \\
a_{21}\tilde{\tilde{x}}_1(\tilde{\alpha},\alpha) + a_{22}\tilde{\tilde{x}}_2(\tilde{\alpha},\alpha) + & \cdots & + \tilde{a}_{2n}\tilde{\tilde{x}}_n(\tilde{\alpha},\alpha) = \tilde{\tilde{b}}_2(\tilde{\alpha},\alpha), \\
\vdots & \ddots & \vdots \\
a_{n1}\tilde{\tilde{x}}_1(\tilde{\alpha},\alpha) + a_{n2}\tilde{\tilde{x}}_2(\tilde{\alpha},\alpha) + & \cdots & + \tilde{a}_{nn}\tilde{\tilde{x}}_n(\tilde{\alpha},\alpha) = \tilde{\tilde{b}}_n(\tilde{\alpha},\alpha).
\end{array}
\tag{11.2}
$$

Eq. (11.2) can be written in the matrix form as

$$
\begin{bmatrix}
a_{11} & a_{12} & \cdots & a_{1n} \\
a_{21} & a_{22} & \cdots & a_{2n} \\
\vdots & \vdots & \ddots & \vdots \\
a_{n1} & a_{n2} & \cdots & a_{nn}
\end{bmatrix}
\begin{bmatrix}
\tilde{\tilde{x}}_1(\tilde{\alpha},\alpha) \\
\tilde{\tilde{x}}_2(\tilde{\alpha},\alpha) \\
\vdots \\
\tilde{\tilde{x}}_n(\tilde{\alpha},\alpha)
\end{bmatrix}
=
\begin{bmatrix}
\tilde{\tilde{b}}_1(\tilde{\alpha},\alpha) \\
\tilde{\tilde{b}}_1(\tilde{\alpha},\alpha) \\
\vdots \\
\tilde{\tilde{b}}_1(\tilde{\alpha},\alpha)
\end{bmatrix}
\tag{11.3}
$$

$$
\Rightarrow
\begin{bmatrix}
a_{11} & a_{12} & \cdots & a_{1n} \\
a_{21} & a_{22} & \cdots & a_{2n} \\
\vdots & \vdots & \ddots & \vdots \\
a_{n1} & a_{n2} & \cdots & a_{nn}
\end{bmatrix}
\begin{bmatrix}
(\underline{\tilde{x}}_1(\tilde{\alpha},\alpha), \overline{\tilde{x}}_1(\tilde{\alpha},\alpha)) \\
(\underline{\tilde{x}}_2(\tilde{\alpha},\alpha), \overline{\tilde{x}}_2(\tilde{\alpha},\alpha)) \\
\vdots \\
(\underline{\tilde{x}}_n(\tilde{\alpha},\alpha), \overline{\tilde{x}}_n(\tilde{\alpha},\alpha))
\end{bmatrix}
=
\begin{bmatrix}
(\underline{\tilde{b}}_1(\tilde{\alpha},\alpha), \overline{\tilde{b}}_1(\tilde{\alpha},\alpha)) \\
(\underline{\tilde{b}}_2(\tilde{\alpha},\alpha), \overline{\tilde{b}}_2(\tilde{\alpha},\alpha)) \\
\vdots \\
(\underline{\tilde{b}}_n(\tilde{\alpha},\alpha), \overline{\tilde{b}}_n(\tilde{\alpha},\alpha))
\end{bmatrix}
\tag{11.4}
$$

The above matrix equation (Eq. (11.4)) can be written as two interval linear system of equations using the concepts of LMF and UMF and are given in Eqs. (11.5) and (11.6), respectively, as

$$\begin{bmatrix} a_{11} & a_{12} & \dots & a_{1n} \\ a_{21} & a_{22} & \dots & a_{2n} \\ \vdots & \vdots & \ddots & \vdots \\ a_{n1} & a_{n2} & \dots & a_{nn} \end{bmatrix} \begin{bmatrix} \underline{\tilde{x}}_1(\tilde{\alpha},\alpha) \\ \underline{\tilde{x}}_2(\tilde{\alpha},\alpha) \\ \vdots \\ \underline{\tilde{x}}_n(\tilde{\alpha},\alpha) \end{bmatrix} = \begin{bmatrix} \underline{\tilde{b}}_1(\tilde{\alpha},\alpha) \\ \underline{\tilde{b}}_2(\tilde{\alpha},\alpha) \\ \vdots \\ \underline{\tilde{b}}_n(\tilde{\alpha},\alpha) \end{bmatrix} \tag{11.5}$$

$$\begin{bmatrix} a_{11} & a_{12} & \dots & a_{1n} \\ a_{21} & a_{22} & \dots & a_{2n} \\ \vdots & \vdots & \ddots & \vdots \\ a_{n1} & a_{n2} & \dots & a_{nn} \end{bmatrix} \begin{bmatrix} \overline{\tilde{x}}_1(\tilde{\alpha},\alpha) \\ \overline{\tilde{x}}_2(\tilde{\alpha},\alpha) \\ \vdots \\ \overline{\tilde{x}}_n(\tilde{\alpha},\alpha) \end{bmatrix} = \begin{bmatrix} \overline{\tilde{b}}_1(\tilde{\alpha},\alpha) \\ \overline{\tilde{b}}_2(\tilde{\alpha},\alpha) \\ \vdots \\ \overline{\tilde{b}}_n(\tilde{\alpha},\alpha) \end{bmatrix} \tag{11.6}$$

Further, there may be uncertainty in the coefficient matrix A in the above linear system. That may be because of insufficient information about the geometrical or material properties. In those scenarios, the uncertain linear system of the equation under the type-2 fuzzy environment can be coined as fully type-2 fuzzy linear system of equation (FT2FLSEs).

An $n \times n$ FT2FLSEs is given by

$$\begin{matrix} \tilde{\tilde{a}}_{11}\tilde{\tilde{x}}_1 + \tilde{\tilde{a}}_{12}\tilde{\tilde{x}}_2 + & \dots & +\tilde{\tilde{a}}_{1n}\tilde{\tilde{x}}_n = \tilde{\tilde{b}}_1, \\ \tilde{\tilde{a}}_{21}\tilde{\tilde{x}}_1 + \tilde{\tilde{a}}_{22}\tilde{\tilde{x}}_2 + & \dots & +\tilde{\tilde{a}}_{2n}\tilde{\tilde{x}}_n = \tilde{\tilde{b}}_2, \\ \vdots & \ddots & \vdots \\ \tilde{\tilde{a}}_{n1}\tilde{\tilde{x}}_1 + \tilde{\tilde{a}}_{n2}\tilde{\tilde{x}}_2 + & \dots & +\tilde{\tilde{a}}_{nn}\tilde{\tilde{x}}_n = \tilde{\tilde{b}}_n. \end{matrix} \tag{11.7}$$

One can write the above system in matrix form as $\tilde{\tilde{A}}\tilde{\tilde{X}} = \tilde{\tilde{B}}$, in which $\tilde{\tilde{A}} = [\tilde{\tilde{a}}_{ij}]$, $1 \le i, j \le n$ is the real type-2 fuzzy coefficient matrix, $\tilde{\tilde{X}} = [\tilde{\tilde{x}}_j]$, $1 \le j \le n$ is the type-2 fuzzy unknown vector, and $\tilde{\tilde{B}} = [\tilde{\tilde{b}}_i]$, $1 \le i \le n$ is the type-2 fuzzy right-hand side vector.

Using the α-cut of the $\tilde{\alpha}$-plane representation and concepts of LMF and UMF, Eq. (11.7) can be written as the two system of fully interval system of linear equations as

$$\begin{bmatrix} \underline{\tilde{a}}_{11}(\tilde{\alpha},\alpha) & \underline{\tilde{a}}_{12}(\tilde{\alpha},\alpha) & \dots & \underline{\tilde{a}}_{1n}(\tilde{\alpha},\alpha) \\ \underline{\tilde{a}}_{21}(\tilde{\alpha},\alpha) & \underline{\tilde{a}}_{22}(\tilde{\alpha},\alpha) & \dots & \underline{\tilde{a}}_{2n}(\tilde{\alpha},\alpha) \\ \vdots & \vdots & \ddots & \vdots \\ \underline{\tilde{a}}_{n1}(\tilde{\alpha},\alpha) & \underline{\tilde{a}}_{n2}(\tilde{\alpha},\alpha) & \dots & \underline{\tilde{a}}_{nn}(\tilde{\alpha},\alpha) \end{bmatrix} \begin{bmatrix} \underline{\tilde{x}}_1(\tilde{\alpha},\alpha) \\ \underline{\tilde{x}}_2(\tilde{\alpha},\alpha) \\ \vdots \\ \underline{\tilde{x}}_n(\tilde{\alpha},\alpha) \end{bmatrix} = \begin{bmatrix} \underline{\tilde{b}}_1(\tilde{\alpha},\alpha) \\ \underline{\tilde{b}}_2(\tilde{\alpha},\alpha) \\ \vdots \\ \underline{\tilde{b}}_n(\tilde{\alpha},\alpha) \end{bmatrix} \tag{11.8}$$

$$\begin{bmatrix} \overline{\tilde{a}}_{11}(\tilde{\alpha},\alpha) & \overline{\tilde{a}}_{12}(\tilde{\alpha},\alpha) & \dots & \overline{\tilde{a}}_{1n}(\tilde{\alpha},\alpha) \\ \overline{\tilde{a}}_{21}(\tilde{\alpha},\alpha) & \overline{\tilde{a}}_{22}(\tilde{\alpha},\alpha) & \dots & \overline{\tilde{a}}_{2n}(\tilde{\alpha},\alpha) \\ \vdots & \vdots & \ddots & \vdots \\ \overline{\tilde{a}}_{n1}(\tilde{\alpha},\alpha) & \overline{\tilde{a}}_{n2}(\tilde{\alpha},\alpha) & \dots & \overline{\tilde{a}}_{nn}(\tilde{\alpha},\alpha) \end{bmatrix} \begin{bmatrix} \overline{\tilde{x}}_1(\tilde{\alpha},\alpha) \\ \overline{\tilde{x}}_2(\tilde{\alpha},\alpha) \\ \vdots \\ \overline{\tilde{x}}_n(\tilde{\alpha},\alpha) \end{bmatrix} = \begin{bmatrix} \overline{\tilde{b}}_1(\tilde{\alpha},\alpha) \\ \overline{\tilde{b}}_2(\tilde{\alpha},\alpha) \\ \vdots \\ \overline{\tilde{b}}_n(\tilde{\alpha},\alpha) \end{bmatrix} \tag{11.9}$$

11.3 Solution procedure for T2FLSEs and FT2FLSEs

Substituting different values of $\tilde{\alpha}$ and $\alpha \in [0, 1]$ in Eqs. (11.8) and (11.9), we can get different linear system of equations in deterministic and interval environments, as follows:

(a) For $\alpha = 1$ and $\tilde{\alpha} = 1$

In this scenario, both Eqs. (11.8) and (11.9) will result into identical crisp matrix equations given by

$$\begin{bmatrix} n_{11} & n_{12} & \cdots & n_{1n} \\ n_{21} & n_{22} & \cdots & n_{2n} \\ \vdots & \vdots & \ddots & \vdots \\ n_{n1} & n_{n2} & \cdots & n_{nn} \end{bmatrix} \begin{bmatrix} m_1 \\ m_2 \\ \vdots \\ m_n \end{bmatrix} = \begin{bmatrix} n_1 \\ n_2 \\ \vdots \\ n_n \end{bmatrix} \tag{11.10}$$

which represent the center (core) of the type-2 fuzzy system. As the resultant system to be solved is a crisp system, this can be solved by using efficient techniques available for crisp linear system of equations. The solutions of this crisp system represents the center (core) of the type-2 fuzzy solution $\tilde{\tilde{x}}_j, 1 \le j \le n$.

(b) For $\alpha = 0$ and $\tilde{\alpha} = 0$

Now, plugging $\alpha = 0$ and $\tilde{\alpha} = 0$ in Eqs. (11.8) and (11.9), then the resultant two interval systems are given by

$$\begin{bmatrix} [\underline{La}_{11_0}, \underline{Ra}_{11_0}] & [\underline{La}_{12_0}, \underline{Ra}_{12_0}] & \cdots & [\underline{La}_{1n_0}, \underline{Ra}_{1n_0}] \\ [\underline{La}_{21_0}, \underline{Ra}_{21_0}] & [\underline{La}_{22_0}, \underline{Ra}_{22_0}] & \cdots & [\underline{La}_{2n_0}, \underline{Ra}_{2n_0}] \\ \vdots & \vdots & \ddots & \vdots \\ [\underline{La}_{n1_0}, \underline{Ra}_{n1_0}] & [\underline{La}_{12_0}, \underline{Ra}_{n2_0}] & \cdots & [\underline{La}_{nn_0}, \underline{Ra}_{nn_0}] \end{bmatrix} \begin{bmatrix} [\underline{Lx}_{1_0}, \underline{Rx}_{1_0}] \\ [\underline{Lx}_{2_0}, \underline{Rx}_{2_0}] \\ \vdots \\ [\underline{Lx}_{n_0}, \underline{Rx}_{n_0}] \end{bmatrix} = \begin{bmatrix} [\underline{Lb}_{1_0}, \underline{Rb}_{1_0}] \\ [\underline{Lb}_{2_0}, \underline{Rb}_{2_0}] \\ \vdots \\ [\underline{Lb}_{n_0}, \underline{Rb}_{n_0}] \end{bmatrix} \tag{11.11}$$

and

$$\begin{bmatrix} [\overline{La}_{11_0}, \overline{Ra}_{11_0}] & [\overline{La}_{12_0}, \overline{Ra}_{12_0}] & \cdots & [\overline{La}_{1n_0}, \overline{Ra}_{1n_0}] \\ [\overline{La}_{21_0}, \overline{Ra}_{21_0}] & [\overline{La}_{22_0}, \overline{Ra}_{22_0}] & \cdots & [\overline{La}_{2n_0}, \overline{Ra}_{2n_0}] \\ \vdots & \vdots & \ddots & \vdots \\ [\overline{La}_{n1_0}, \overline{Ra}_{n1_0}] & [\overline{La}_{12_0}, \overline{Ra}_{n2_0}] & \cdots & [\overline{La}_{nn_0}, \overline{Ra}_{nn_0}] \end{bmatrix} \begin{bmatrix} [\overline{Lx}_{1_0}, \overline{Rx}_{1_0}] \\ [\overline{Lx}_{2_0}, \overline{Rx}_{2_0}] \\ \vdots \\ [\overline{Lx}_{n_0}, \overline{Rx}_{n_0}] \end{bmatrix} = \begin{bmatrix} [\overline{Lb}_{1_0}, \overline{Rb}_{1_0}] \\ [\overline{Lb}_{2_0}, \overline{Rb}_{2_0}] \\ \vdots \\ [\overline{Lb}_{n_0}, \overline{Rb}_{n_0}] \end{bmatrix}, \tag{11.12}$$

respectively. Eqs. (11.11) and (11.12) are $n \times n$ interval systems of equations. The interval systems in Eqs. (11.11) and (11.12) can be solved by transforming them into the following two $2n \times 2n$ system of linear equations as below:

$$\begin{bmatrix} \underline{La}_{11_0} & \underline{La}_{12_0} & \cdots & \underline{La}_{1n_0} & 0 & 0 & \cdots & 0 \\ 0 & 0 & \cdots & 0 & \underline{Ra}_{11_0} & \underline{Ra}_{12_0} & \cdots & \underline{Ra}_{1n_0} \\ \vdots & \vdots & \ddots & \vdots & \vdots & \vdots & \ddots & \vdots \\ \underline{La}_{n1_0} & \underline{La}_{n2_0} & \cdots & \underline{La}_{nn_0} & 0 & 0 & \cdots & 0 \\ 0 & 0 & \cdots & 0 & \underline{Ra}_{n1_0} & \underline{Ra}_{n2_0} & \cdots & \underline{Ra}_{nn_0} \end{bmatrix} \begin{bmatrix} \underline{Lx}_{1_0} \\ \vdots \\ \underline{Lx}_{n_0} \\ \underline{Rx}_{1_0} \\ \vdots \\ \underline{Rx}_{n_0} \end{bmatrix} = \begin{bmatrix} \underline{Lb}_{1_0} \\ \underline{Rb}_{1_0} \\ \vdots \\ \underline{Lb}_{n_0} \\ \underline{Rb}_{n_0} \end{bmatrix} \tag{11.13}$$

and

$$\begin{bmatrix} \overline{La}_{11_0} & \overline{La}_{12_0} & \cdots & \overline{La}_{1n_0} & 0 & 0 & \cdots & 0 \\ 0 & 0 & \cdots & 0 & \overline{Ra}_{11_0} & \overline{Ra}_{12_0} & \cdots & \overline{Ra}_{1n_0} \\ \vdots & \vdots & \ddots & \vdots & \vdots & \vdots & \ddots & \vdots \\ \overline{La}_{n1_0} & \overline{La}_{n2_0} & \cdots & \overline{La}_{nn_0} & 0 & 0 & \cdots & 0 \\ 0 & 0 & \cdots & 0 & \overline{Ra}_{n1_0} & \overline{Ra}_{n2_0} & \cdots & \overline{Ra}_{nn_0} \end{bmatrix} \begin{bmatrix} \overline{Lx}_{1_0} \\ \vdots \\ \overline{Lx}_{n_0} \\ \overline{Rx}_{1_0} \\ \vdots \\ \overline{Rx}_{n_0} \end{bmatrix} = \begin{bmatrix} \overline{Lb}_{1_0} \\ \overline{Rb}_{1_0} \\ \vdots \\ \overline{Lb}_{n_0} \\ \overline{Rb}_{n_0} \end{bmatrix}, \tag{11.14}$$

respectively. By solving the linear system of equations in (11.13) and (11.14), it will give the left and right bounds of the LMF and UMF, i.e., $\underline{Lx}_{i_0}$, $\underline{Rx}_{i_0}$, $\overline{Lx}_{i_0}$, and $\overline{Rx}_{i_0}$.

(c) For $\tilde{\alpha} = 1$ and $\alpha = 0$

By substituting $\tilde{\alpha} = 1$ and $\alpha = 0$ in Eqs. (11.8) and (11.9), we have the following interval matrix equation:

$$\begin{bmatrix} [La_{11_1}, Ra_{11_1}] & [La_{12_1}, Ra_{12_1}] & \cdots & [La_{1n_1}, Ra_{1n_1}] \\ [La_{21_1}, Ra_{21_1}] & [La_{22_1}, Ra_{22_1}] & \cdots & [La_{2n_1}, Ra_{2n_1}] \\ \vdots & \vdots & \ddots & \vdots \\ [La_{n1_1}, Ra_{n1_1}] & [La_{n2_1}, Ra_{n2_1}] & \cdots & [La_{nn_1}, Ra_{nn_1}] \end{bmatrix} \begin{bmatrix} [Lx_{1_1}, Rx_{1_1}] \\ [Lx_{2_1}, Rx_{2_1}] \\ \vdots \\ [Lx_{n_1}, Rx_{n_1}] \end{bmatrix} = \begin{bmatrix} [Lb_{1_1}, Rb_{1_1}] \\ [Lb_{2_1}, Rb_{2_1}] \\ \vdots \\ [Lb_{n_1}, Rb_{n_1}] \end{bmatrix}, \tag{11.15}$$

which also can be solved by converting it into a $2n \times 2n$ system given by

$$\begin{bmatrix} La_{11_1} & La_{12_1} & \dots & La_{1n_1} & 0 & 0 & \dots & 0 \\ 0 & 0 & \dots & 0 & Ra_{11_1} & Ra_{12_1} & \dots & Ra_{1n_1} \\ \vdots & \vdots & \ddots & \vdots & \vdots & \vdots & \ddots & \vdots \\ La_{n1_1} & La_{n2_1} & \dots & La_{nn_1} & 0 & 0 & \dots & 0 \\ 0 & 0 & \dots & 0 & Ra_{n1_1} & Ra_{n2_1} & \dots & Ra_{nn_1} \end{bmatrix} \begin{bmatrix} Lx_{1_1} \\ \vdots \\ Lx_{n_1} \\ Rx_{1_1} \\ \vdots \\ Rx_{n_1} \end{bmatrix} = \begin{bmatrix} Lb_{1_1} \\ Rb_{1_1} \\ \vdots \\ Lb_{n_1} \\ Rb_{n_1} \end{bmatrix} \tag{11.16}$$

The above system of equations can be solved to obtain the left and right bounds of the principal set of the type-2 fuzzy unknowns, i.e., Lx_{i_1} and Rx_{i_1}. So, all the end points of the type-2 fuzzy unknowns has been obtained. In order to solve the FT2FLSEs, we have considered all the entries of the type-2 fuzzy coefficient matrix $\tilde{\tilde{A}}$ as non-negative. The above approach can be implemented to solve the T2FLSEs, i.e., for crisp coefficient matrix, type-2 fuzzy unknown and right-hand side vector, which is a special case of the FT2FLSEs.

11.4 Sample problems

Here, we will discuss few simple numerical examples of T2FLSEs and FT2FLSEs.

Example 11.1. Let us consider the following 2×2 T2FLSE $\tilde{\tilde{A}}\tilde{\tilde{x}} = \tilde{\tilde{b}}$, where

$$\tilde{\tilde{A}} = \begin{bmatrix} 10 & -4 \\ -4 & 15.5 \end{bmatrix}, \tilde{\tilde{b}} = \begin{bmatrix} (25, 26, 27, 28, 29, 30, 31) \\ (34, 35, 36, 37, 38, 39, 40) \end{bmatrix}. \tag{11.17}$$

Solving the above system by the present method, we have
for $\tilde{\alpha} = \alpha = 1$

$$\begin{bmatrix} 10 & -4 \\ -4 & 15.5 \end{bmatrix} \begin{bmatrix} m_1 \\ m_2 \end{bmatrix} = \begin{bmatrix} 28 \\ 37 \end{bmatrix} \tag{11.18}$$

Solving Eq. (11.18) gives $m_1 = 4.1871$ and $m_2 = 3.4676$.

Again for $\tilde{\alpha} = \alpha = 0$, the type-2 fuzzy system of equations will be

$$\begin{bmatrix} [10, 10] & [-4, -4] \\ [-4, -4] & [15.5, 15.5] \end{bmatrix} \begin{bmatrix} [\underline{Lx}_{1_0}, \underline{Rx}_{1_0}] \\ [\underline{Lx}_{2_0}, \underline{Rx}_{2_0}] \end{bmatrix} = \begin{bmatrix} [27, 29] \\ [36, 38] \end{bmatrix} \tag{11.19}$$

and

$$\begin{bmatrix} [10, 10] & [-4, -4] \\ [-4, -4] & [15.5, 15.5] \end{bmatrix} \begin{bmatrix} [\overline{Lx}_{1_0}, \overline{Rx}_{1_0}] \\ [\overline{Lx}_{2_0}, \overline{Rx}_{2_0}] \end{bmatrix} = \begin{bmatrix} [25, 31] \\ [34, 41] \end{bmatrix} \tag{11.20}$$

The above two 2×2 interval systems can be transformed into 4×4 systems as

$$\begin{bmatrix} 10 & 0 & 0 & -4 \\ 0 & -4 & 10 & 0 \\ 0 & 15.5 & 0 & -4 \\ -4 & 0 & 0 & 15.5 \end{bmatrix} \begin{bmatrix} \underline{Lx}_{1_0} \\ \underline{Lx}_{2_0} \\ \underline{Rx}_{1_0} \\ \underline{Rx}_{2_0} \end{bmatrix} = \begin{bmatrix} 27 \\ 29 \\ 36 \\ 38 \end{bmatrix} \tag{11.21}$$

$$\begin{bmatrix} 10 & 0 & 0 & -4 \\ 0 & -4 & 10 & 0 \\ 0 & 15.5 & 0 & -4 \\ -4 & 0 & 0 & 15.5 \end{bmatrix} \begin{bmatrix} \overline{Lx}_{1_0} \\ \overline{Lx}_{2_0} \\ \overline{Rx}_{1_0} \\ \overline{Rx}_{2_0} \end{bmatrix} = \begin{bmatrix} 25 \\ 31 \\ 34 \\ 41 \end{bmatrix} \tag{11.22}$$

Solving Eqs. (11.21) and (11.22) give $\underline{Lx}_{1_0} = 4.1043$, $\underline{Lx}_{2_0} = 3.4245$, $\underline{Rx}_{1_0} = 4.2698$, $\underline{Rx}_{2_0} = 3.5108$, $\overline{Lx}_{1_0} = 3.9388$, $\overline{Lx}_{2_0} = 3.3381$, $\overline{Rx}_{1_0} = 4.4353$, and $\overline{Rv}_{2_0} = 3.5971$.

Now for $\tilde{\alpha} = 1$ and $\alpha = 0$,

$$\begin{bmatrix} [10, 10] & [-4, -4] \\ [-4, -4] & [15.5, 15.5] \end{bmatrix} \begin{bmatrix} [Lx_{1_1}, Rx_{1_1}] \\ [Lx_{2_1}, Rx_{2_1}] \end{bmatrix} = \begin{bmatrix} [26, 30] \\ [35, 39] \end{bmatrix} \tag{11.23}$$

Again converting Eq. (11.23) into 4×4 system as below:

$$\begin{bmatrix} 10 & 0 & 0 & -4 \\ 0 & -4 & 10 & 0 \\ 0 & 15.5 & 0 & -4 \\ -4 & 0 & 0 & 15.5 \end{bmatrix} \begin{bmatrix} Lx_{1_1} \\ Lx_{2_1} \\ Rx_{1_1} \\ Rx_{2_1} \end{bmatrix} = \begin{bmatrix} 26 \\ 30 \\ 35 \\ 39 \end{bmatrix} \tag{11.24}$$

Solving we have $Lx_{1_1} = 4.0216$, $Lx_{2_1} = 3.3813$, $Rx_{1_1} = 4.3525$, and $Rx_{2_1} = 3.5540$. Finally, the obtained type-2 fuzzy solution can be written as

$$\tilde{\tilde{x}}_1 = (3.9388, 4.0216, 4.1043, 4.1871, 4.2698, 4.3525, 4.4353),$$
$$\tilde{\tilde{x}}_2 = (3.3381, 3.3813, 3.4245, 3.4676, 3.5108, 3.5540, 3.5971).$$

In Figs. 11.1 and 11.2, the plots of the obtained type-2 fuzzy solutions $\tilde{\tilde{x}}_1$ and $\tilde{\tilde{x}}_2$ are shown.

Example 11.3. Consider the 3×3 T2FLSE given by [13],

$$\begin{bmatrix} 280 & 30 & 50 \\ 0 & 30 & 50 \\ 280 & 0 & 50 \end{bmatrix} \begin{bmatrix} \tilde{\tilde{x}}_1 \\ \tilde{\tilde{x}}_2 \\ \tilde{\tilde{x}}_3 \end{bmatrix} = \begin{bmatrix} 83\tilde{\tilde{b}}_1 \\ 65\tilde{\tilde{b}}_2 \\ 785\tilde{\tilde{b}}_3 \end{bmatrix} \tag{11.25}$$

where

$$\tilde{\tilde{b}}_1 = (5, 7, 8, 10, 12, 13, 15),$$
$$\tilde{\tilde{b}}_2 = (1.5, 1.7, 1.8, 2, 2.2, 2.3, 2.5),$$

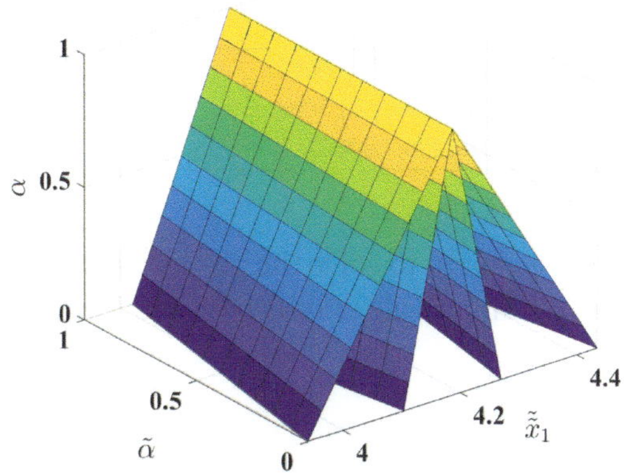

FIGURE 11.1 Plot of the first root $\tilde{\tilde{x}}_1$.

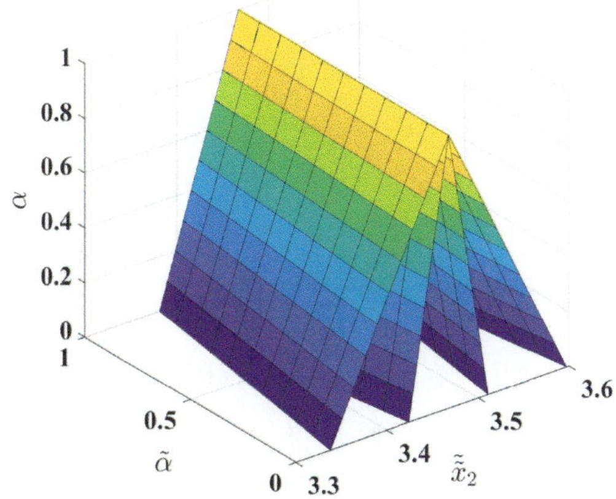

FIGURE 11.2 Plot of the second root $\tilde{\tilde{x}}_2$.

$$\text{and } \tilde{\tilde{b}}_3 = (0.5, 0.7, 0.8, 1, 1.2, 1.3, 1.5).$$

Applying the proposed method to by converting the above T2FLSE into interval systems, we get

$$\tilde{\tilde{x}}_1 = (1.1339, 1.6804, 1.9536, 2.5, 3.0464, 3.3196, 3.8661),$$
$$\tilde{\tilde{x}}_2 = (0.7500, 1.0500, 1.2000, 1.5, 1.8000, 1.9500, 2.2500),$$
$$\tilde{\tilde{x}}_3 = (1.500, 1.5800, 1.6200, 1.7, 1.7800, 1.8200, 1.9000).$$

The obtained type-2 fuzzy solutions are presented in Table 11.1. In Table 11.1, a comparison has been carried out with the result in [13]. From this table, it is clearly evident

Table 11.1 Results by the present method and its comparison with [13].

$\tilde{\tilde{x}}$	Present	Najariyan et al. [13]
$\tilde{\tilde{x}}_1$	(1.1339,1.6804,1.9536, 2.5, 3.0464, 3.3196, 3.8661)	(1.13, 1.68, 1.95, 2.5, 3.05, 3.32, 3.87)
$\tilde{\tilde{x}}_2$	(0.7500,1.0500,1.2000, 1.5,1.8000,1.9500, 2.2500)	(0.75, 1.05, 1.2, 1.5, 1.8, 1.95, 2.25)
$\tilde{\tilde{x}}_3$	(1.500,1.5800,1.6200,1.7,1.7800,1.8200,1.9000)	(1.5, 1.58, 1.62, 1.7, 1.78, 1.82, 1.9)

that the present approach is efficient to solve the given T2FLSEs and also matches with the result in [13]. Further, the obtained values of the type-2 fuzzy unknowns are depicted in Figs. 11.3–11.5.

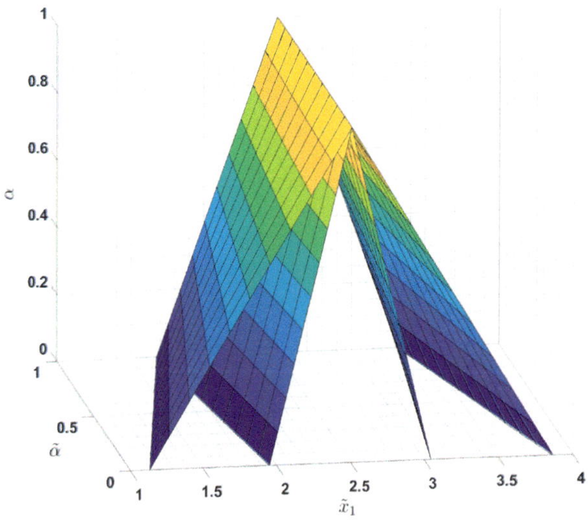

FIGURE 11.3 Plot of the first root $\tilde{\tilde{x}}_1$.

Example 11.5. Consider the 2×2 fully fuzzy type-2 linear system:

$$\begin{bmatrix} (2.7, 2.8, 2.9, 3, 3.1, 3.2, 3.3) & (0.2, 0.3, 0.4, 0.5, 0.6, 0.7, 0.8) \\ (1.7, 1.8, 1.9, 2, 2.1, 2.2, 2.3) & (2.7, 2.8, 2.9, 3, 3.1, 3.2, 3.3) \end{bmatrix} \begin{bmatrix} \tilde{\tilde{x}}_1 \\ \tilde{\tilde{x}}_2 \end{bmatrix} = \begin{bmatrix} (13, 14, 15, 16, 17, 18, 19) \\ (13, 14, 15, 16, 17, 18, 19) \end{bmatrix}$$

By the proposed method, we have for $\tilde{\alpha} = \alpha = 1$,

$$\begin{bmatrix} 3 & 0.5 \\ 2 & 3 \end{bmatrix} \begin{bmatrix} m_1 \\ m_2 \end{bmatrix} = \begin{bmatrix} 16 \\ 16 \end{bmatrix} \tag{11.26}$$

Solving Eq. (11.26), gives $m_1 = 5$ and $m_2 = 2$.

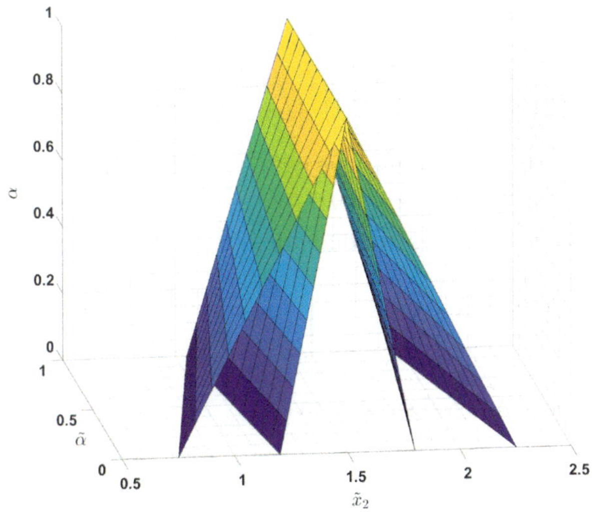

FIGURE 11.4 Plot of the second root $\tilde{\tilde{x}}_2$.

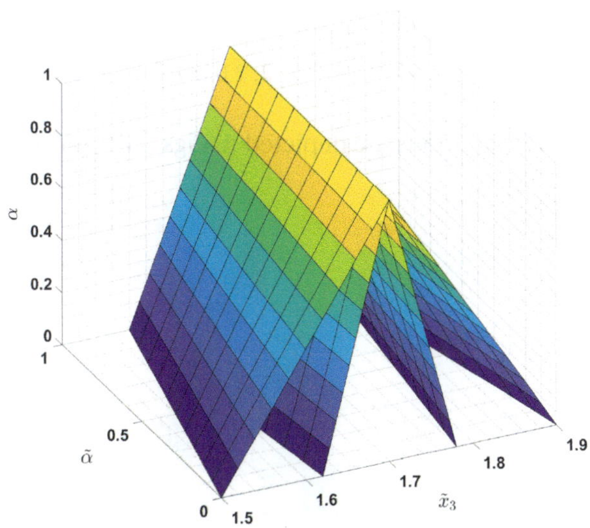

FIGURE 11.5 Plot of the third root $\tilde{\tilde{x}}_3$.

Again for $\tilde{\alpha} = \alpha = 0$, one may have

$$\begin{bmatrix} [2.7, 3.3] & [0.2, 0.8] \\ [1.7, 2.3] & [2.7, 3.3] \end{bmatrix} \begin{bmatrix} [\overline{Lx}_{1_0}, \overline{Rx}_{1_0}] \\ [\overline{Lx}_{2_0}, \overline{Rx}_{2_0}] \end{bmatrix} = \begin{bmatrix} [13, 19] \\ [13, 19] \end{bmatrix} \tag{11.27}$$

and

$$\begin{bmatrix} [2.9, 3.1] & [0.4, 0.6] \\ [1.9, 2.1] & [2.9, 3.1] \end{bmatrix} \begin{bmatrix} [\underline{Lx}_{1_0}, \underline{Rx}_{1_0}] \\ [\underline{Lx}_{2_0}, \underline{Rx}_{2_0}] \end{bmatrix} = \begin{bmatrix} [15, 17] \\ [15, 17] \end{bmatrix} \tag{11.28}$$

Solving the above two interval systems, we get $\overline{Lx}_{1_0} = 4.6763$, $\overline{Rx}_{1_0} = 5.2486$, $\underline{Lx}_{1_0} = 4.9020$, $\underline{Rx}_{1_0} = 5.0898$, $\overline{Lx}_{2_0} = 1.8705$, $\overline{Rx}_{2_0} = 2.0994$, $\underline{Lx}_{2_0} = 1.9608$, and $\underline{Rx}_{2_0} = 2.0359$.

Now for $\tilde{\alpha} = 1$ and $\alpha = 0$, the system becomes

$$\begin{bmatrix} [2.8, 3.2] & [0.3, 0.7] \\ [1.8, 2.2] & [2.8, 3.2] \end{bmatrix} \begin{bmatrix} [Lx_{11}, Rx_{11}] \\ [Lx_{21}, Rx_{21}] \end{bmatrix} = \begin{bmatrix} [14, 18] \\ [14, 18] \end{bmatrix} \tag{11.29}$$

The solution of the above interval system gives

$$Lx_{11} = 4.7945,\ Rx_{11} = 5.1724,\ Lx_{21} = 1.9178$$

and $Rx_{21} = 2.0690$.

Hence the final solution can be obtained as

$$\tilde{\tilde{x}}_1 = (4.6763, 4.7945, 4.9020, 5, 5.0898, 5.1724, 5.2486),$$
$$\tilde{\tilde{x}}_2 = (1.8705, 1.9178, 1.9608, 2, 2.0359, 2.0390, 2.0994).$$

The obtained type-2 fuzzy solutions are depicted in Figs. 11.6 and 11.7.

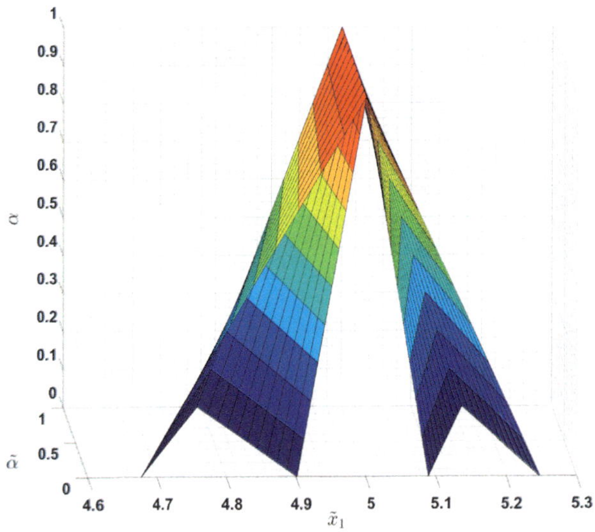

FIGURE 11.6 Plot of the first root $\tilde{\tilde{x}}_1$.

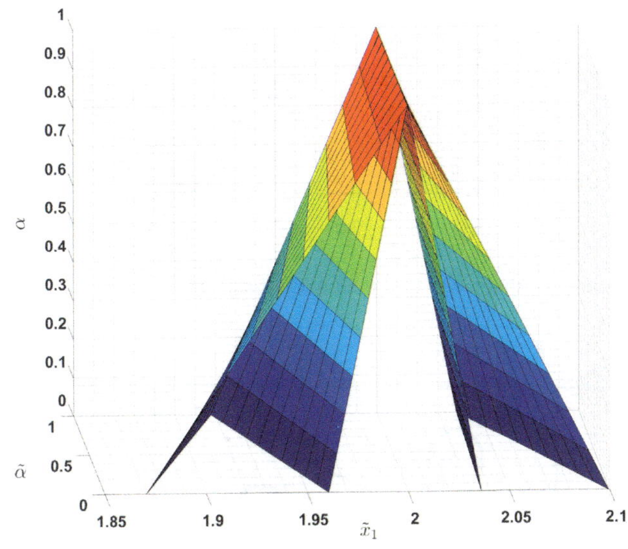

FIGURE 11.7 Plot of the second root $\tilde{\tilde{x}}_2$.

11.5 Application problems

As uncertainty is an important factor to be considered in practical problems. Now let us discuss some application problems related to linear system of equations in the type-2 fuzzy uncertain environment. In particular, structural engineering problems are investigated.

11.5.1 Rectangular sheet

Consider a uniform rectangular sheet, where one end of the sheet is fixed and at the other end an uncertain uniform force $\tilde{\tilde{F}}$ is applied [20] as shown in Figs. 11.8 and 11.9. Suppose the plate is of thickness $h = 1mm$, length $2m$, and width $1m$. Modulus of elasticity and Poisson's ratio of the material of the structure are $E = 206 \times 10^9 N/m^2$ and $\frac{1}{3}$, respectively. Suppose $\tilde{\tilde{x}}_i$ and $\tilde{\tilde{y}}_i$ for $i = 1$ to 4 are the horizontal and vertical type-2 fuzzy displacements at nodes 1 to 4, respectively. We have considered the applied uniform uncertain force as TPQT2FN, $\tilde{\tilde{F}} = (975, 980, 990, 1000, 1010, 1020, 1025)N/m$.

Applying finite element method along with the boundary conditions to the structure at equilibrium, we have

$$K\tilde{\tilde{\delta}} = \tilde{\tilde{F}}, \tag{11.30}$$

where

$$K = \frac{3Eh}{32}\begin{bmatrix} 7 & -4 & -4 & 2 \\ -4 & 13 & 2 & -12 \\ -4 & 2 & 7 & 0 \\ 2 & -12 & 0 & 13 \end{bmatrix} \tag{11.31}$$

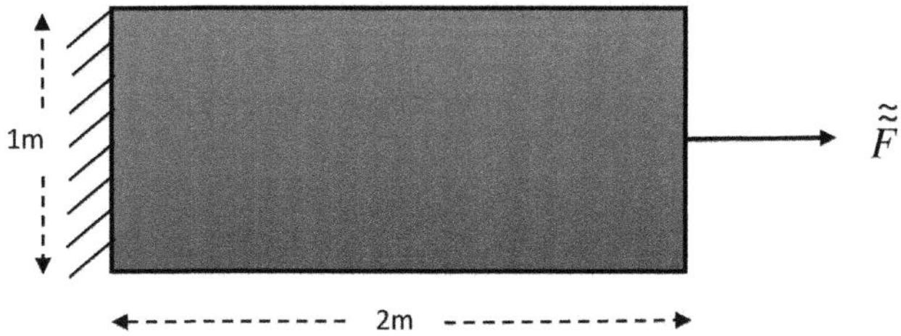

FIGURE 11.8 Uniform rectangular sheet with uncertain type-2 fuzzy force.

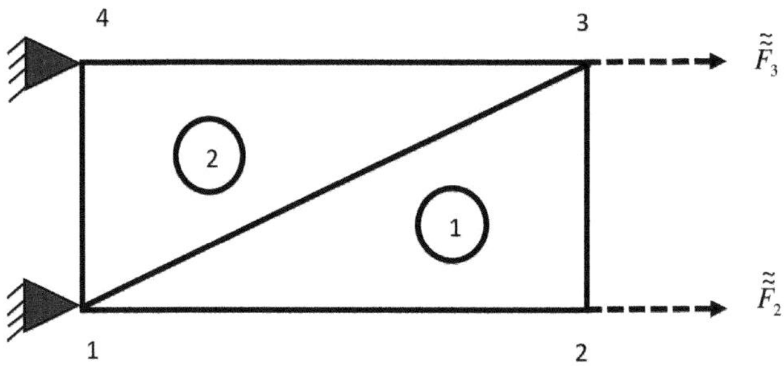

FIGURE 11.9 Elements of rectangular sheet.

$$\tilde{\tilde{F}} = \begin{bmatrix} \frac{\tilde{\tilde{q}}}{2} \\ 0 \\ \frac{\tilde{\tilde{q}}}{2} \\ 0 \end{bmatrix} = \begin{bmatrix} (487.5, 490, 495, 500, 505, 510, 512.5) \\ (0, 0, 0, 0, 0, 0, 0) \\ (487.5, 490, 495, 500, 505, 510, 512.5) \\ (0, 0, 0, 0, 0, 0, 0) \end{bmatrix} \tag{11.32}$$

and

$$\tilde{\tilde{\delta}} = \begin{bmatrix} \tilde{\tilde{x}}_2 \\ \tilde{\tilde{y}}_2 \\ \tilde{\tilde{x}}_3 \\ \tilde{\tilde{y}}_3 \end{bmatrix}. \tag{11.33}$$

Solving the above T2FLSEs using the proposed method, one can obtain the required type-2 fuzzy displacements at nodes 2 and 3, as

$$\tilde{\tilde{x}}_2 = (0.9516, 0.9538, 0.9584, 0.9629, 0.9675, 0.9721, 0.9743) \times 10^{-5},$$
$$\tilde{\tilde{y}}_2 = (0.1508, 0.1552, 0.1641, 0.1730, 0.1819, 0.1907, 0.1952) \times 10^{-5},$$
$$\tilde{\tilde{x}}_3 = (0.8616, 0.8634, 0.8671, 0.8707, 0.8743, 0.8780, 0.8798) \times 10^{-5},$$
$$\tilde{\tilde{y}}_3 = (-0.0072, -0.0035, 0.0040, 0.0115, 0.0190, 0.0235, 0.0303) \times 10^{-5}.$$

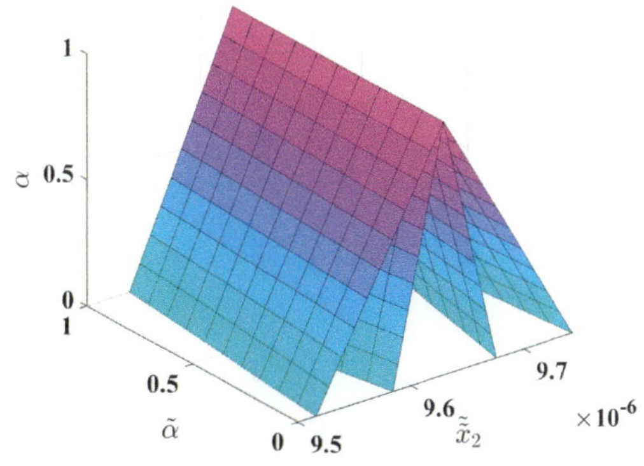

FIGURE 11.10 Plot of the horizontal displacement at node-2.

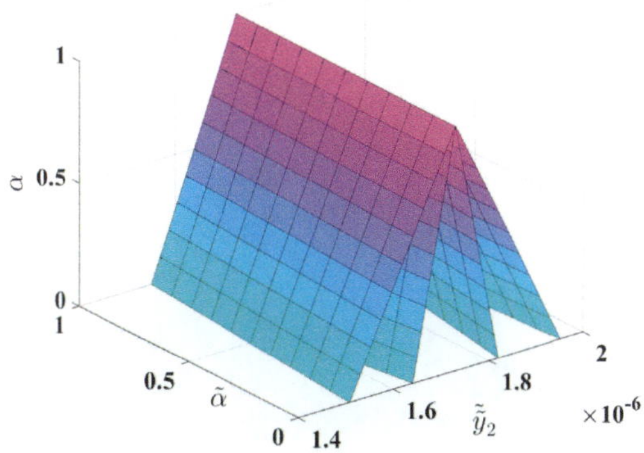

FIGURE 11.11 Plot of the vertical displacement at node-2.

Type-2 fuzzy displacements at nodes 2 and 3 depicted in Figs. 11.10–11.13. The obtained displacements are compared with the solutions by the [13] approach in Table 11.2 and found to be well agreed.

11.5.2 Beam structure

Let us consider a two element beam structure with uniform forces applied on it as shown in Figs. 11.14 and 11.15 [21]. Suppose two type-2 fuzzy uniformly distributed forces $\tilde{\tilde{F}}_1$ and $\tilde{\tilde{F}}_2$ are applied on Elements 1 and 2, respectively. The Young's modulus, moment of inertia, and length of each element of the beam structure is taken as $2 \times 10^8 kN/m^2$, $5 \times 10^{-6} m^4$ and $5m$, respectively. Let $\tilde{\tilde{U}}_1$, $\tilde{\tilde{U}}_3$, and $\tilde{\tilde{U}}_5$ are the linear displacements, and $\tilde{\tilde{U}}_2$, $\tilde{\tilde{U}}_4$, and $\tilde{\tilde{U}}_6$ are the angle of rotations at nodes 1, 2, and 3, respectively. Assume that the applied uni-

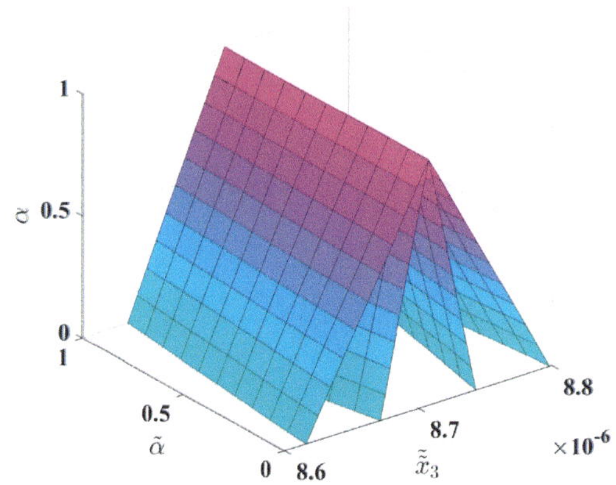

FIGURE 11.12 Plot of the horizontal displacement at node-3.

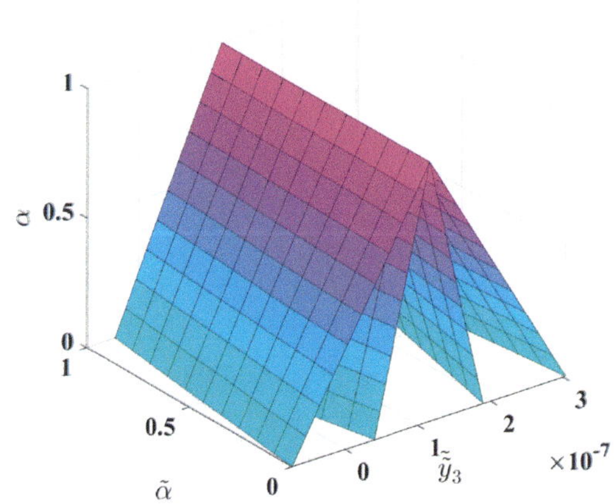

FIGURE 11.13 Plot of the vertical displacement at node-2.

Table 11.2 Obtained horizontal and vertical displacements at nodes 2 and 3 of rectangular sheet.

$\tilde{\tilde{x}}(\tilde{\tilde{y}})$	Present	Najariyan et al. [13]
$\tilde{\tilde{x}}_2$	$(0.9516, 0.9538, 0.9584, 0.9629, 0.9675, 0.9721, 0.9743) \times 10^{-5}$	$(0.9516, 0.9538, 0.9584, 0.9629, 0.9675, 0.9721, 0.9743) \times 10^{-5}$
$\tilde{\tilde{y}}_2$	$(0.1508, 0.1552, 0.1641, 0.1730, 0.1819, 0.1907, 0.1952) \times 10^{-5}$	$(0.1508, 0.1552, 0.1641, 0.1730, 0.1819, 0.1907, 0.1952) \times 10^{-5}$
$\tilde{\tilde{x}}_3$	$(0.8616, 0.8634, 0.8671, 0.8707, 0.8743, 0.8780, 0.8798) \times 10^{-5}$	$(0.8616, 0.8634, 0.8671, 0.8707, 0.8743, 0.8780, 0.8798) \times 10^{-5}$
$\tilde{\tilde{y}}_3$	$(-0.0072, -0.0035, 0.0040, 0.0115, 0.0190, 0.0235, 0.0303) \times 10^{-5}$	$(-0.0072, -0.0035, 0.0040, 0.0115, 0.0190, 0.0235, 0.0303) \times 10^{-5}$

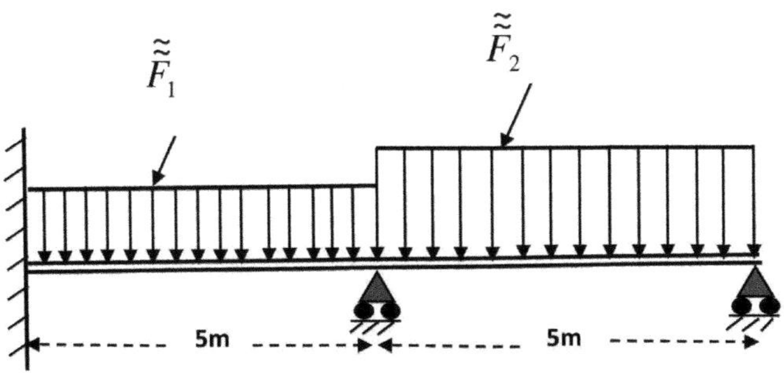

FIGURE 11.14 Beam structure with uniformly applied force.

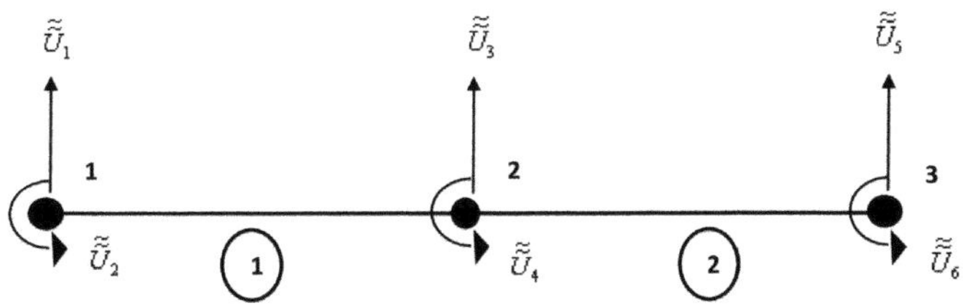

FIGURE 11.15 Elements of beam structure.

formly distributed forces as TPQT2FN in behavior, i.e., $\tilde{\tilde{F}}_1 = (0, 4, 8, 12, 16, 20, 24)kN$ and $\tilde{\tilde{F}}_2 = (16, 20, 22, 24, 26, 28, 30)kN$.

Displacements at each node can be determined by solving the structure's governing equation of motion in the type-2 fuzzy scenario using the proposed methodology. The obtained type-2 fuzzy angular displacements at node-2 and node-3 have been obtained as

$$\tilde{\tilde{U}}_2 = (-0.0565, -0.0506, -0.0431, -0.0357, -0.0283, -0.0208, -0.0104),$$
$$\tilde{\tilde{U}}_4 = (0.0699, 0.0774, 0.0789, 0.0803, 0.0818, 0.0833, 0.0833).$$

Further, the obtained type-2 fuzzy angular displacements at nodes 2 and 3 are shown graphically in Figs. 11.16 and 11.17.

11.5.3 Truss structure

Let us consider the 6-bar truss problem (see Figs. 11.18 and 11.19). From the figures, it can be seen that the structure is divided in to six elements [20]. The material and geometric properties associated with the structure are assumed to be deterministic, whereas the applied loads at different nodes are considered to be type-2 fuzzy in nature as TPQT2FN.

By using finite element method the given problem can be converted into a T2FLSE, given by [22]

$$K\tilde{\tilde{\delta}} = \tilde{\tilde{F}} \tag{11.34}$$

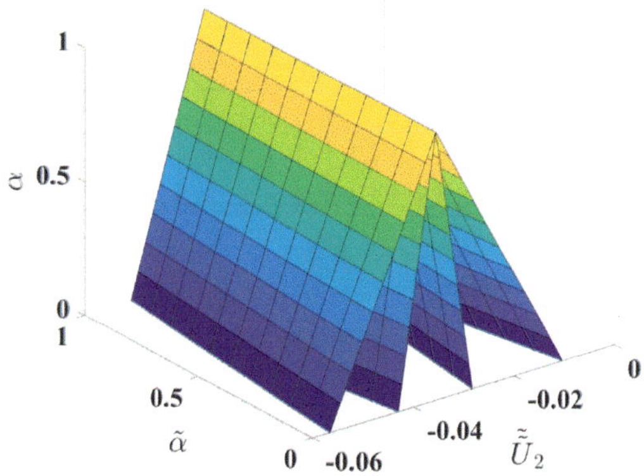

FIGURE 11.16 Plot of type-2 fuzzy angular displacement at node-2.

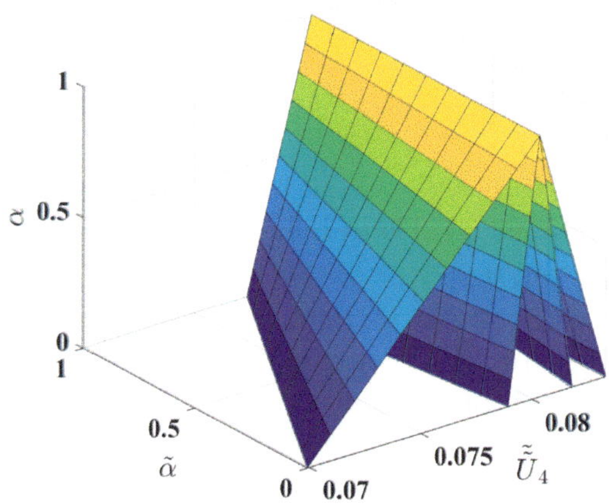

FIGURE 11.17 Plot of type-2 fuzzy angular displacement at node-3.

where K is the stiffness matrix, $\tilde{\tilde{\delta}}$ is the displacement vector and $\tilde{\tilde{F}}$ is the applied load vector.

Here,

$$K=\begin{bmatrix} \frac{E_1A_1}{L_1}+0.36\frac{E_5A_5}{L_5} & -0.48\frac{E_5A_5}{L_5} & -\frac{E_1A_1}{L_1} & 0 \\ -0.48\frac{E_5A_5}{L_5} & \frac{E_3A_3}{L_3}+0.64\frac{E_5A_5}{L_5} & 0 & 0 \\ -\frac{E_1A_1}{L_1} & 0 & \frac{E_1A_1}{L_1}+0.36\frac{E_6A_6}{L_6} & 0.48\frac{E_6A_6}{L_6} \\ 0 & 0 & 0.48\frac{E_6A_6}{L_6} & \frac{E_4A_4}{L_4}+0.64\frac{E_6A_6}{L_6} \end{bmatrix} \tag{11.35}$$

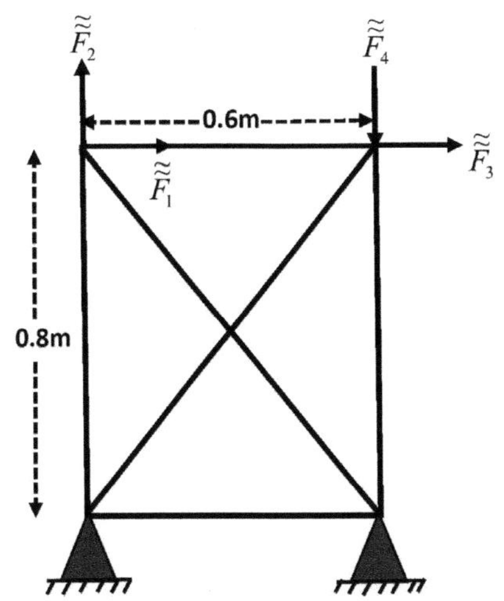

FIGURE 11.18 6-bar truss structure with type-2 fuzzy loads.

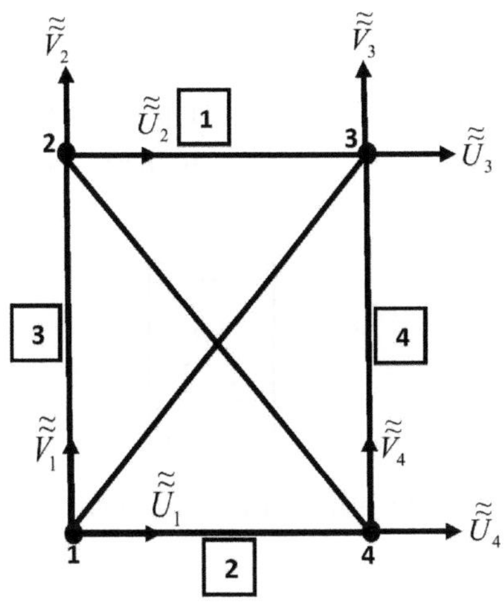

FIGURE 11.19 Elements of 6-bar truss structure.

$$\tilde{\tilde{\delta}} = \begin{bmatrix} \tilde{\tilde{x}}_2 \\ \tilde{\tilde{y}}_2 \\ \tilde{\tilde{x}}_3 \\ \tilde{\tilde{y}}_3 \end{bmatrix} \text{ and } \tilde{\tilde{F}} = \begin{bmatrix} \tilde{\tilde{P}} \\ 2\tilde{\tilde{P}} \\ 2.5\tilde{\tilde{P}} \\ -1.5\tilde{\tilde{P}} \end{bmatrix} \tag{11.36}$$

Now putting $E_i = 2.1 * 10^8 kN/m^2$ for i = 1 to 6, cross-sectional areas A_1, A_2, A_3 and $A_4 = 1 * 10^{-3} m^2$, other cross-sectional areas =1.05 $* \ 10^{-3} m^2$, $\tilde{\tilde{P}} = (19000, 19500, 20000, 20500, 21000, 21500, 22000)$, $L_1, L_2 = 0.6m$, $L_3, L_4 = 0.8m$, and $L_5, L_6 = 1m$ in the above expressions we

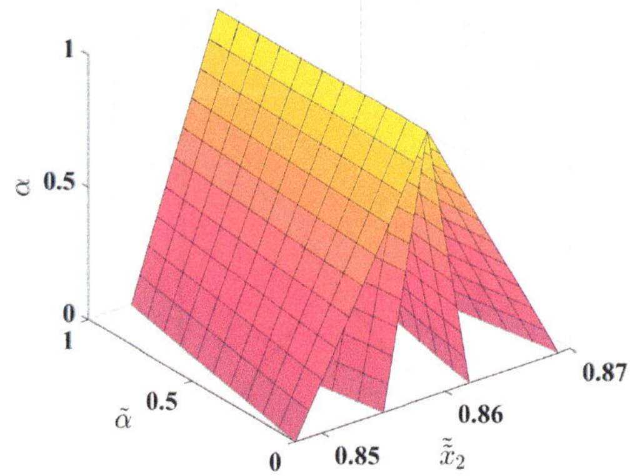

FIGURE 11.20 Plot of the horizontal displacement at node-2.

have

$$K = \begin{bmatrix} 429380 & -105840 & -350000 & 0 \\ -105840 & 403620 & 0 & 0 \\ -350000 & 0 & 429380 & 105840 \\ 0 & 0 & 105840 & 403620 \end{bmatrix} N/m \tag{11.37}$$

and

$$\tilde{\tilde{F}} = \begin{bmatrix} \tilde{\tilde{P}} \\ 2\tilde{\tilde{P}} \\ 2.5\tilde{\tilde{P}} \\ -1.5\tilde{\tilde{P}} \end{bmatrix} \tag{11.38}$$

Solving the proposed method, the horizontal and vertical displacements at node-2 and node-3 are given by

$$\tilde{\tilde{x}}_2 = (0.8479, 0.8514, 0.8549, 0.8585, 0.8619, 0.8655, 0.8690),$$
$$\tilde{\tilde{y}}_2 = (0.3202, 0.3223, 0.3245, 0.3270, 0.3288, 0.3310, 0.3331),$$
$$\tilde{\tilde{x}}_3 = (0.8826, 0.8870, 0.8914, 0.8958, 0.9002, 0.9045, 0.9089),$$
$$\tilde{\tilde{y}}_3 = (-0.3117, -0.3115, -0.3113, -0.3111, -0.3109, -0.3106, -0.3104).$$

In Figs. 11.20–11.23, the obtained type-2 fuzzy displacements are depicted for the better visualization. Also, comparison has been made with the existing interval solution in [22] in a special case, which is shown in Table 11.3.

This chapter addresses type-2 fuzzy linear systems of equations using a methodology founded on the concepts of LMF and UMF of type-2 fuzzy parameters. Various sample problems are addressed using the suggested methodology and contrasted with existing

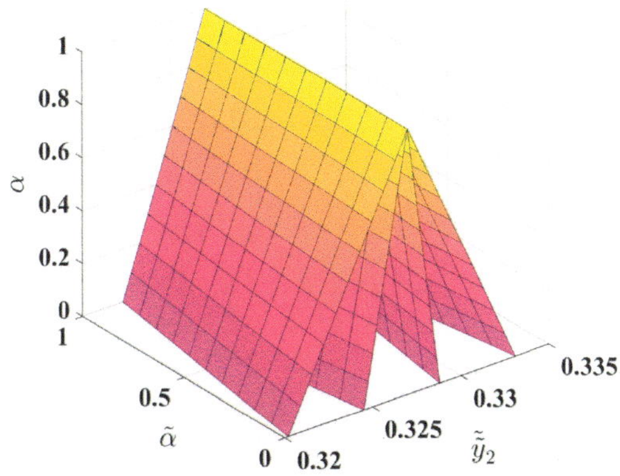

FIGURE 11.21 Plot of the vertical displacement at node-2.

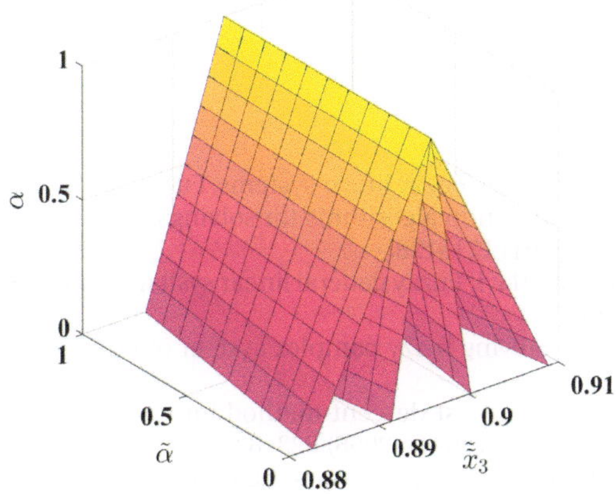

FIGURE 11.22 Plot of the horizontal displacement at node-3.

Table 11.3 Results (type-2) by the proposed method and in [22] (interval).

Displacement	Present (type-2)	Present (reduced interval)	In [22] (interval)
$\tilde{\tilde{x}}_2$	(0.8479, 0.8514, 0.8549, 0.8585, 0.8619, 0.8655, 0.8690)	[0.8514,0.8655]	[0.8514,0.8655]
$\tilde{\tilde{y}}_2$	(0.3202, 0.3223, 0.3245, 0.3270, 0.3288, 0.3310, 0.3331)	[0.3223, 0.3310]	[0.3224, 0.3310]
$\tilde{\tilde{x}}_3$	(0.8826, 0.8870, 0.8914, 0.8958, 0.9002, 0.9045, 0.9089)	[0.8870, 0.9045]	[0.8871, 0.9046]
$\tilde{\tilde{y}}_3$	(−0.3117, −0.3115, −0.3113, −0.3111, −0.3109, −0.3106, −0.3104)	[−0.3115,-0.3106]	[−0.3115,-0.3106]

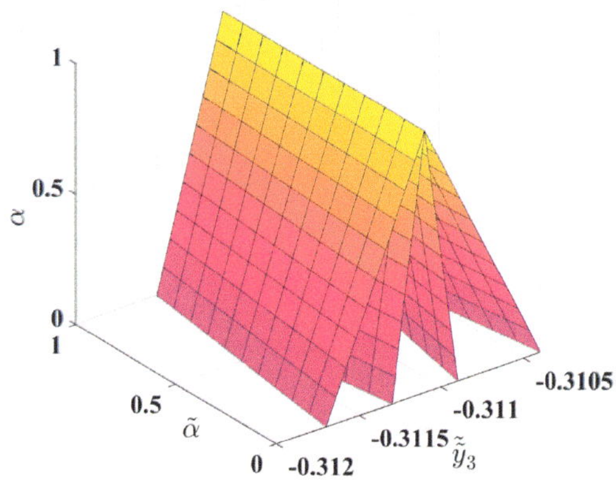

FIGURE 11.23 Plot of the vertical displacement at node-3.

solutions in particular contexts. Furthermore, practical problems pertaining to structural engineering are also effectively examined.

References

[1] M. Friedman, M. Ming, A. Kandel, Fuzzy linear systems, Fuzzy Sets and Systems 96 (2) (1998) 201–209.
[2] X. Wang, Z. Zhong, M. Ha, Iteration algorithms for solving a system of fuzzy linear equations, Fuzzy Sets and Systems 119 (1) (2001) 121–128.
[3] B. Asady, S. Abbasbandy, M. Alavi, Fuzzy general linear systems, Applied Mathematics and Computation 169 (1) (2005) 34–40.
[4] D. Behera, S. Chakraverty, Solving fuzzy complex system of linear equations, Information Sciences 277 (2014) 154–162.
[5] S. Abbasbandy, A. Jafarian, Steepest descent method for system of fuzzy linear equations, Applied Mathematics and Computation 175 (1) (2006) 823–833.
[6] M. Otadi, M. Mosleh, Minimal solution of non-square fuzzy linear systems, Journal of Fuzzy Set Valued Analysis (2012), article ID jfsva-00105.
[7] M. Ma, M. Friedman, A. Kandel, Duality in fuzzy linear systems, Fuzzy Sets and Systems 109 (1) (2000) 55–58.
[8] S. Chakraverty, S.K. Jeswal, Applied Artificial Neural Network Methods for Engineers and Scientists: Solving Algebraic Equations, World Scientific, 2021.
[9] S. Chakraverty, S. Rout, Affine Arithmetic Based Solution of Uncertain Static and Dynamic Problems, Springer Nature, 2022.
[10] D. Behera, S. Chakraverty, Fuzzy finite element analysis of imprecisely defined structures with fuzzy nodal force, Engineering Applications of Artificial Intelligence 26 (10) (2013) 2458–2466.
[11] P. Rao, S. Chakraverty, D. Roy, Vibration analysis of single-link robotic manipulator by polynomial based Galerkin method in uncertain environment, in: Polynomial Paradigms: Trends and Applications in Science and Engineering, IOP Publishing, Bristol, UK, 2022, p. 9-1.
[12] P. Rao, D. Roy, S. Chakraverty, Vibration analysis of single-link flexible manipulator in an uncertain environment, Journal of Vibration Engineering & Technologies 12 (2) (2024) 2677–2694.
[13] M. Najariyan, R. John, M. Mazandarani, Type-2 fuzzy linear systems, Granular Computing 2 (1) (2017) 175–186.
[14] D. Behera, S. Chakraverty, New approach to solve fully fuzzy system of linear equations using single and double parametric form of fuzzy numbers, Sadhana 40 (1) (2015) 35–49.

[15] M. Dehghan, B. Hashemi, M. Ghatee, Computational methods for solving fully fuzzy linear systems, Applied Mathematics and Computation 179 (1) (2006) 328–343.
[16] S. Nasseri, M. Sohrabi, E. Ardil, Solving fully fuzzy linear systems by use of a certain decomposition of the coefficient matrix, International Journal of Computational and Mathematical Sciences 2 (3) (2008) 140–142.
[17] G. Malkaw, N. Ahmad, H. Ibrahim, An algorithm for a positive solution of arbitrary fully fuzzy linear system, Computational Mathematics and Modeling 26 (2015) 436–465.
[18] E. Siahlooei, S.A. Shahzadeh Fazeli, et al., An application of interval arithmetic for solving fully fuzzy linear systems with trapezoidal fuzzy numbers, Advances in Fuzzy Systems, vol. 2018, 2018.
[19] D. Mohapatra, S. Chakraverty, Type-2 fuzzy linear system of equations with application in static problem of structures, Mathematical Methods in the Applied Sciences 46 (1) (2023) 840–866.
[20] D. Behera, S. Chakraverty, H.-Z. Huang, Non-probabilistic uncertain static responses of imprecisely defined structures with fuzzy parameters, Journal of Intelligent & Fuzzy Systems 30 (6) (2016) 3177–3189.
[21] D. Behera, S. Chakraverty, Solving the nondeterministic static governing equations of structures subjected to various forces under fuzzy and interval uncertainty, International Journal of Approximate Reasoning 116 (2020) 43–61.
[22] S. Chakraverty, M. Hladík, D. Behera, Formal Solution of an Interval System of Linear Equations with an Application in Static Responses of Structures with Interval Forces, Applied Mathematical Modelling, vol. 50, Elsevier, 2017, pp. 105–117.

12

Linear dynamical problems with uncertainty

Contents

12.1 Introduction 147
12.2 Type-2 fuzzy linear eigenvalue problems 148
12.3 Solution procedure of type-2 fuzzy linear eigenvalue problem 149
12.3.1 Procedure for T2FSEP 149
12.3.2 Procedure for T2GEP 150
12.4 Sample problems 151
12.5 Application problem 157
12.5.1 Spring-mass system 157
References 163

Chapter points

- Type-2 fuzzy linear eigenvalue problems are studied here.
- An approach based on the triple parametric forms of the type-2 fuzzy entries is presented.
- Application problems related to structural engineering are discussed.
- Comparison studies are provided to show the applicability of the proposed approach.

12.1 Introduction

Eigenvalue problems are fundamental in various fields of science and engineering, involving the determination of characteristic values (eigenvalues) and corresponding characteristic vectors (eigenvectors) of a square matrix. These problems arise in a variety of applications, such as structural analysis, stability studies, and quantum mechanics. In structural engineering, eigenvalue problems help in identifying natural frequencies and modes of vibration of structures. In quantum mechanics, they are used to determine energy levels of quantum systems. Linear eigenvalue problems are categorized into two types, Standard eigenvalue problem (SEP) and Generalized eigenvalue problem (GEP). The general form of SEP is $Ax = \lambda x$, where A is a square matrix, x is the eigenvector, and λ is the eigenvalue. The goal is to find the scalar λ and the vector x that satisfy this equation. The matrix A is often derived from the system's properties, such as stiffness or mass in structural dynamics, whereas the GEP is represented as $Ax = \lambda Bx$, where A and B are square matrices, x is

Artificial Neural Networks and Type-2 Fuzzy Set. https://doi.org/10.1016/B978-0-44-332894-7.00022-8

the eigenvector, and λ is the eigenvalue. The matrix B can be seen as an additional weighting or scaling factor. GEPs often arise in more complex systems where there are multiple interacting matrices, such as in mechanical systems with both stiffness and mass matrices.

In practical applications, material properties, geometric dimensions, and boundary conditions can vary due to manufacturing tolerances, environmental changes, measurement faults, or aging. These variations introduce uncertainty into the system parameters. Probability theory can be used to handle the impreciseness in the parameters. The limitation that lies in the probabilistic approach is that it produces reliable results for large number of data and the results are less effective for small datasets. In such circumstances, this uncertainty can be handled using intervals and fuzzy sets. Various investigations have been carried out by different researchers related to eigenvalue problems incorporating uncertainty in the parameters.

The Rayleigh quotient iteration method has been employed to solve the vibration problem of the structures, governed by the eigenvalue problems, with interval parameters [1]. A perturbation method based on the fundamental perturbation principle and vertex theory has been developed to solve the fuzzy eigenvalue problem [2]. Based on the sufficient regularity condition, Hladik et al. [3] proposed an interval filtering method to approximate interval real eigenvalue bounds iteratively. Leng [4] investigated bounds of the real eigenvalue based on the sufficient regularity condition of interval matrices and has also extended it for the GEP. Artificial neural networks based approach has been developed to solve the fuzzy eigenvalue problems using the concept of α-cut representations of fuzzy numbers [5,6]. An interval filtering approach has been proposed in [7] to solve the interval generalized eigenvalue problem. The same filtering approach also been extended to solve the fuzzy generalized eigenvalue problem. A second-order perturbation method has been proposed to obtain the fuzzy eigenvalues [8]. Identification of stiffness parameters associated with a multi-storey structures has been determined in the fuzzy environment [9]. Eigenvalue bounds of interval matrices have been obtained by Leng and He [10] using the concept of matrix perturbation theory. Chakraverty and Rout has investigated the interval and fuzzy SEPs and GEPs using the affine based approach [11]. The fuzzy filtering method has been used to obtain the closet bounds of the fuzzy eigenvalues of a fuzzy symmetric matrix and application problems related to structural engineering have been investigated [12]. The vibration analysis of flexible robotic manipulators has been investigated in interval and fuzzy uncertain environments using different approaches [13,14], as there may be uncertainty in the membership grade of the fuzzy parameters because of various reasons. In this regard, an approach has been developed in [15] to solve the type-2 fuzzy linear eigenvalue problems.

12.2 Type-2 fuzzy linear eigenvalue problems

Type-2 fuzzy linear eigenvalue problems (T2FLEP) delves into the complexities of eigenvalue analysis in systems where uncertainty is not only present but also extends to the membership grades of fuzzy sets. This section explores the formulation of linear eigenvalue problems within this type-2 fuzzy framework. Based on the classification of the crisp linear eigenvalue problem, T2FLEP may be categorized into two types as follows:

- Type-2 Fuzzy Standard Eigenvalue Problem (T2FSEP)
- Type-2 Fuzzy Generalized Eigenvalue Problem (T2FGEP)

The T2FSEP can be written in mathematical form as

$$\tilde{\tilde{A}}\tilde{\tilde{x}} = \tilde{\tilde{\lambda}}\tilde{\tilde{x}}, \tag{12.1}$$

where $\tilde{\tilde{A}}$ is the type-2 fuzzy square matrix, $\tilde{\tilde{\lambda}}$ is the type-2 fuzzy eigenvalue, and $\tilde{\tilde{x}}$ is the type-2 fuzzy eigenvector, whereas, in T2FGEP, the problem is formulated as

$$\tilde{\tilde{A}}\tilde{\tilde{x}} = \tilde{\tilde{\lambda}}\tilde{\tilde{B}}\tilde{\tilde{x}}, \tag{12.2}$$

where both $\tilde{\tilde{A}}$ and $\tilde{\tilde{B}}$ are square matrices with type-2 fuzzy entries, $\tilde{\tilde{\lambda}}$ and $\tilde{\tilde{x}}$ are the associated type-2 fuzzy eigenvalue and eigenvector, respectively.

12.3 Solution procedure of type-2 fuzzy linear eigenvalue problem

In this section, we present the solution procedure for the type-2 fuzzy linear eigenvalue problem. First, the solution procedure for the T2FSEP is discussed followed by the solution approach for T2FGEP, which is a general case of the T2FSEP.

12.3.1 Procedure for T2FSEP

The TPQT2FN is used to handle the uncertainty in the system, i.e., the entries of the type-2 fuzzy square matrices are taken as TPQT2FN. The β-cut at the α-plane of a TPQT2FN $\tilde{\tilde{W}}$, i.e., $\tilde{\tilde{W}}(\alpha, \beta) = (\underline{\tilde{W}}(\alpha, \beta), \overline{\tilde{W}}(\alpha, \beta))$ is implemented to write the T2FSEP (12.1) in parametric form as

$$\tilde{\tilde{A}}(\alpha, \beta)\tilde{\tilde{x}}(\alpha, \beta) = \tilde{\tilde{\lambda}}(\alpha, \beta)\tilde{\tilde{x}}(\alpha, \beta). \tag{12.3}$$

Now, using the concepts of lower and upper membership functions of TPQT2FN in (12.3), the T2FSEP in (12.3) can be written as two different type-1 fuzzy standard eigenvalue problems as

$$\underline{\tilde{A}}(\alpha, \beta)\underline{\tilde{x}}(\alpha, \beta) = \underline{\tilde{\lambda}}(\alpha, \beta)(\alpha, \beta)\underline{\tilde{x}}(\alpha, \beta), \tag{12.4}$$

and

$$\overline{\tilde{A}}(\alpha, \beta)\overline{\tilde{x}}(\alpha, \beta) = \overline{\tilde{\lambda}}(\alpha, \beta)(\alpha, \beta)\overline{\tilde{x}}(\alpha, \beta). \tag{12.5}$$

The above two type-1 fuzzy eigenvalue problems are in parametric form, depending upon the parameters α and β. Introducing another parameter $\gamma \in [0, 1]$ into these type-1 fuzzy problems separately, these type-1 fuzzy eigenvalue problems can be transformed to

$$\underline{\tilde{A}}(\alpha, \beta, \gamma)\underline{\tilde{x}}(\alpha, \beta, \gamma) = \underline{\tilde{\lambda}}(\alpha, \beta, \gamma)\underline{\tilde{x}}(\alpha, \beta, \gamma), \tag{12.6}$$

and

$$\overline{\tilde{A}}(\alpha, \beta, \gamma)\overline{\tilde{x}}(\alpha, \beta, \gamma) = \overline{\tilde{\lambda}}(\alpha, \beta, \gamma)\overline{\tilde{x}}(\alpha, \beta, \gamma), \tag{12.7}$$

where

$$\begin{aligned}
\underline{\tilde{A}}(\alpha, \beta, \gamma) &= \underline{\tilde{A}}_L((\alpha, \beta) + \gamma(\underline{\tilde{A}}_R((\alpha, \beta) - \underline{\tilde{A}}_L((\alpha, \beta)),\\
\underline{\tilde{x}}(\alpha, \beta, \gamma) &= \underline{\tilde{x}}_L((\alpha, \beta) + \gamma(\underline{\tilde{x}}_R((\alpha, \beta) - \underline{\tilde{x}}_L((\alpha, \beta)),\\
\underline{\tilde{\lambda}}(\alpha, \beta, \gamma) &= \underline{\tilde{\lambda}}_L((\alpha, \beta) + \gamma(\underline{\tilde{\lambda}}_R((\alpha, \beta) - \underline{\tilde{\lambda}}_L((\alpha, \beta)),
\end{aligned} \tag{12.8}$$

and

$$\begin{aligned}
\overline{\tilde{A}}(\alpha, \beta, \gamma) &= \overline{\tilde{A}}_L((\alpha, \beta) + \gamma(\overline{\tilde{A}}_R((\alpha, \beta) - \overline{\tilde{A}}_L((\alpha, \beta)),\\
\overline{\tilde{x}}(\alpha, \beta, \gamma) &= \overline{\tilde{x}}_L((\alpha, \beta) + \gamma(\overline{\tilde{x}}_R((\alpha, \beta) - \overline{\tilde{x}}_L((\alpha, \beta)),\\
\overline{\tilde{\lambda}}(\alpha, \beta, \gamma) &= \overline{\tilde{\lambda}}_L((\alpha, \beta) + \gamma(\overline{\tilde{\lambda}}_R((\alpha, \beta) - \overline{\tilde{\lambda}}_L((\alpha, \beta)).
\end{aligned} \tag{12.9}$$

Eqs. (12.6) and (12.7) can be solved for the LMF and UMF of the type-2 fuzzy eigenvalues in terms of the parameters $\alpha,\ \beta,$ and γ by solving

$$\begin{aligned}
det(\underline{\tilde{A}}(\alpha, \beta, \gamma) - \underline{\tilde{\lambda}}(\alpha, \beta, \gamma)I) = 0,\\
det(\overline{\tilde{A}}(\alpha, \beta, \gamma) - \overline{\tilde{\lambda}}(\alpha, \beta, \gamma)I) = 0,
\end{aligned} \tag{12.10}$$

where I is the identity matrix of same order as of $\tilde{\tilde{A}}$. Substituting the values of $\alpha,\ \beta,$ and $\gamma \in [0, 1]$ different bound points of the type-2 fuzzy eigenvalue $\tilde{\tilde{\lambda}}$ can be obtained.

12.3.2 Procedure for T2GEP

As the generalized eigenvalue problem is the general form of the standard eigenvalue problem, where there is another square matrix B of order A multiplied with the eigenvalue λ in the right-hand side, i.e., in place of the identity matrix I, we have a square matrix B. Here, we have considered this matrix B to be type-2 fuzzy in nature, i.e., $\tilde{\tilde{B}}$. Then using the triple parametric approach as explained in the previous subsection, the T2FGEP will be

$$\tilde{\tilde{A}}(\alpha, \beta, \gamma)\tilde{\tilde{x}}(\alpha, \beta, \gamma) = \tilde{\tilde{\lambda}}(\alpha, \beta, \gamma)\tilde{\tilde{B}}(\alpha, \beta, \gamma)\tilde{\tilde{x}}(\alpha, \beta, \gamma), \tag{12.11}$$

which can be solved separately for the LMF and UMF of the type-2 fuzzy eigenvalue $\tilde{\tilde{\lambda}}$ and the required LMF and UMF bounds of the type-2 fuzzy eigenvalue can be obtained from

$$\begin{aligned}
det(\underline{\tilde{A}}(\alpha, \beta, \gamma) - \underline{\tilde{\lambda}}(\alpha, \beta, \gamma)\tilde{\tilde{B}}(\alpha, \beta, \gamma)) = 0,\\
det(\overline{\tilde{A}}(\alpha, \beta, \gamma) - \overline{\tilde{\lambda}}(\alpha, \beta, \gamma)\tilde{\tilde{B}}(\alpha, \beta, \gamma)) = 0.
\end{aligned} \tag{12.12}$$

These above equations in (12.12) can be solved for $\underline{\tilde{\lambda}}$ and $\overline{\tilde{\lambda}}$ in terms of the parameters α, β, and γ. Further, $\underline{\tilde{\lambda}}$ and $\overline{\tilde{\lambda}}$ can be combined to get the required type-2 fuzzy eigenvalues associated with the given T2FGEP.

12.4 Sample problems

A few sample numerical examples of T2FSEP and T2FGEP are discussed here.

Example 12.1. Let us consider the following type-2 fuzzy matrix:

$$\tilde{\tilde{A}} = \begin{bmatrix} (-1,0,1,2,3,4,5) & (1,2,3,4,5,6,7) \\ (2,4,5,6,7,8,10) & (2,3,4,5,6,7,8) \end{bmatrix} \tag{12.13}$$

and the associated T2FSEP is

$$\tilde{\tilde{A}}\tilde{\tilde{X}} = \tilde{\tilde{\lambda}}\tilde{\tilde{X}}, \tag{12.14}$$

where $\tilde{\tilde{X}} = [\tilde{\tilde{x}}_1, \tilde{\tilde{x}}_2]'$ is the type-2 fuzzy eigenvector associated with the type-2 fuzzy eigenvalue $\tilde{\tilde{\lambda}}$.

Incorporating the β-cut of the α-plane representation of the type-2 fuzzy parameters, Eq. (12.14) will be

$$\tilde{\tilde{A}}(\alpha,\beta)\tilde{\tilde{X}}(\alpha,\beta) = \tilde{\tilde{\lambda}}(\alpha,\beta)\tilde{\tilde{X}}(\alpha,\beta), \tag{12.15}$$

where

$$\tilde{\tilde{A}}(\alpha,\beta) = \begin{bmatrix} \tilde{\tilde{a}}_{11}(\alpha,\beta) & \tilde{\tilde{a}}_{12}(\alpha,\beta) \\ \tilde{\tilde{a}}_{21}(\alpha,\beta) & \tilde{\tilde{a}}_{22}(\alpha,\beta) \end{bmatrix} \tag{12.16}$$

with

$$\begin{aligned}
\tilde{\tilde{a}}_{11}(\alpha,\beta) = (\underline{\tilde{a}}_{11}(\alpha,\beta), \overline{\tilde{a}}_{11}(\alpha,\beta)) = (&[2\beta + (\alpha-1)(\beta-1), \\
&4 - (\alpha-1)(\beta-1) - 2\beta], \\
&[2\beta - (\alpha-1)(\beta-1), \\
&(\alpha-1)(\beta-1) - 2\beta + 4]), \\
\tilde{\tilde{a}}_{12}(\alpha,\beta) = (\underline{\tilde{a}}_{12}(\alpha,\beta), \overline{\tilde{a}}_{12}(\alpha,\beta)) = (&[2\beta + (\alpha-1)(\beta-1) + 2, \\
&6 - (\alpha-1)(\beta-1) - 2\beta], \\
&[2\beta - (\alpha-1)(\beta-1) + 2, \\
&(\alpha-1)(\beta-1) - 2\beta + 6]), \\
\tilde{\tilde{a}}_{21}(\alpha,\beta) = (\underline{\tilde{a}}_{21}(\alpha,\beta), \overline{\tilde{a}}_{21}(\alpha,\beta)) = (&[2\beta + (\alpha-1)(\beta-1) + 4, \\
&8 - (\alpha-1)(\beta-1) - 2\beta], \\
&[2\beta - (2\beta-2)(\alpha-1) + 4, \\
&(2\beta-2)(\alpha-1) - 2\beta + 8]), \\
\tilde{\tilde{a}}_{22}(\alpha,\beta) = (\underline{\tilde{a}}_{22}(\alpha,\beta), \overline{\tilde{a}}_{22}(\alpha,\beta)) = (&[2\beta + (\alpha-1)(\beta-1) + 3, \\
&7 - (\alpha-1)(\beta-1) - 2\beta], \\
&[2\beta - (\alpha-1)(\beta-1) + 3, \\
&(\alpha-1)(\beta-1) - 2\beta + 7]).
\end{aligned} \tag{12.17}$$

Using the concept of LMF and UMF of the TPQT2FN valued parameters in Eq. (12.15) results into the following interval system of SEPs:

$$\begin{bmatrix} \underline{\tilde{a}}_{11}(\alpha,\beta) & \underline{\tilde{a}}_{12}(\alpha,\beta) \\ \underline{\tilde{a}}_{21}(\alpha,\beta) & \underline{\tilde{a}}_{22}(\alpha,\beta) \end{bmatrix} \begin{bmatrix} \underline{\tilde{x}}_1(\alpha,\beta) \\ \underline{\tilde{x}}_2(\alpha,\beta) \end{bmatrix} = \underline{\tilde{\lambda}}(\alpha,\beta) \begin{bmatrix} \underline{\tilde{x}}_1(\alpha,\beta) \\ \underline{\tilde{x}}_2(\alpha,\beta) \end{bmatrix}, \tag{12.18}$$

and

$$\begin{bmatrix} \overline{\tilde{a}}_{11}(\alpha,\beta) & \overline{\tilde{a}}_{12}(\alpha,\beta) \\ \overline{\tilde{a}}_{21}(\alpha,\beta) & \overline{\tilde{a}}_{22}(\alpha,\beta) \end{bmatrix} \begin{bmatrix} \overline{\tilde{x}}_1(\alpha,\beta) \\ \overline{\tilde{x}}_2(\alpha,\beta) \end{bmatrix} = \overline{\tilde{\lambda}}(\alpha,\beta) \begin{bmatrix} \overline{\tilde{x}}_1(\alpha,\beta) \\ \overline{\tilde{x}}_2(\alpha,\beta) \end{bmatrix}. \tag{12.19}$$

Now, using the third parameter $\gamma \in [0,1]$ in Eqs. (12.18) and (12.19), Eqs. (12.18) and (12.19) can be written in triple parametric form as

$$\begin{bmatrix} \underline{\tilde{a}}_{11}(\alpha,\beta,\gamma) & \underline{\tilde{a}}_{12}(\alpha,\beta,\gamma) \\ \underline{\tilde{a}}_{21}(\alpha,\beta,\gamma) & \underline{\tilde{a}}_{22}(\alpha,\beta,\gamma) \end{bmatrix} \begin{bmatrix} \underline{\tilde{x}}_1(\alpha,\beta,\gamma) \\ \underline{\tilde{x}}_2(\alpha,\beta,\gamma) \end{bmatrix} = \underline{\tilde{\lambda}}(\alpha,\beta,\gamma) \begin{bmatrix} \underline{\tilde{x}}_1(\alpha,\beta,\gamma) \\ \underline{\tilde{x}}_2(\alpha,\beta,\gamma) \end{bmatrix}, \tag{12.20}$$

and

$$\begin{bmatrix} \overline{\tilde{a}}_{11}(\alpha,\beta,\gamma) & \overline{\tilde{a}}_{12}(\alpha,\beta,\gamma) \\ \overline{\tilde{a}}_{21}(\alpha,\beta,\gamma) & \overline{\tilde{a}}_{22}(\alpha,\beta,\gamma) \end{bmatrix} \begin{bmatrix} \overline{\tilde{x}}_1(\alpha,\beta,\gamma) \\ \overline{\tilde{x}}_2(\alpha,\beta,\gamma) \end{bmatrix} = \overline{\tilde{\lambda}}(\alpha,\beta,\gamma) \begin{bmatrix} \overline{\tilde{x}}_1(\alpha,\beta,\gamma) \\ \overline{\tilde{x}}_2(\alpha,\beta,\gamma) \end{bmatrix}, \tag{12.21}$$

where

$$\begin{aligned}
\underline{\tilde{a}}_{11}(\alpha,\beta,\gamma) &= 2\beta - \gamma(4\beta + 2(\alpha-1)(\beta-1) - 4) + (\alpha-1)(\beta-1), \\
\underline{\tilde{a}}_{12}(\alpha,\beta,\gamma) &= 2\beta - \gamma(4\beta + 2(\alpha-1)(\beta-1) - 4) + (\alpha-1)(\beta-1) + 2, \\
\underline{\tilde{a}}_{21}(\alpha,\beta,\gamma) &= 2\beta - \gamma(4\beta + 2(\alpha-1)(\beta-1) - 4) + (\alpha-1)(\beta-1) + 4, \\
\underline{\tilde{a}}_{22}(\alpha,\beta,\gamma) &= 2\beta - \gamma(4\beta + 2(\alpha-1)(\beta-1) - 4) + (\alpha-1)(\beta-1) + 3, \\
\overline{\tilde{a}}_{11}(\alpha,\beta,\gamma) &= 2\beta + \gamma(2(\alpha-1)(\beta-1) - 4\beta + 4) - (\alpha-1)(\beta-1), \\
\overline{\tilde{a}}_{12}(\alpha,\beta,\gamma) &= 2\beta + \gamma(2(\alpha-1)(\beta-1) - 4\beta + 4) - (\alpha-1)(\beta-1) + 2, \\
\overline{\tilde{a}}_{21}(\alpha,\beta,\gamma) &= 2\beta + \gamma(2(2\beta-2)(\alpha-1) - 4\beta + 4) - (2\beta-2)(\alpha-1) + 4, \\
\overline{\tilde{a}}_{22}(\alpha,\beta,\gamma) &= 2\beta + \gamma(2(\alpha-1)(\beta-1) - 4\beta + 4) - (\alpha-1)(\beta-1) + 3.
\end{aligned} \tag{12.22}$$

The above two SEPs, i.e., Eqs. (12.20) and (12.21) are solved in terms of the uncertainty handling parameters α, β, and γ to obtain the bounds of the LMF and UMF of the type-2 fuzzy eigenvalues.

Further, the type-2 fuzzy eigenvalues can be written in the traditional componentwise form by substituting the values of α, β, and $\gamma \in [0,1]$ in the obtained triple parametric forms of LMF and UMF of the type-2 fuzzy eigenvalues. The obtained type-2 fuzzy eigenvalues are

$$\begin{aligned}
\tilde{\tilde{\lambda}}_1 &= (-2, -1.7616, -1.7016, -1.6533, -1.6235, -1.6033, -1.5887), \\
\tilde{\tilde{\lambda}}_2 &= (2.5616, 4.7016, 6.6533, 8.6235, 10.603, 12.589, 15).
\end{aligned} \tag{12.23}$$

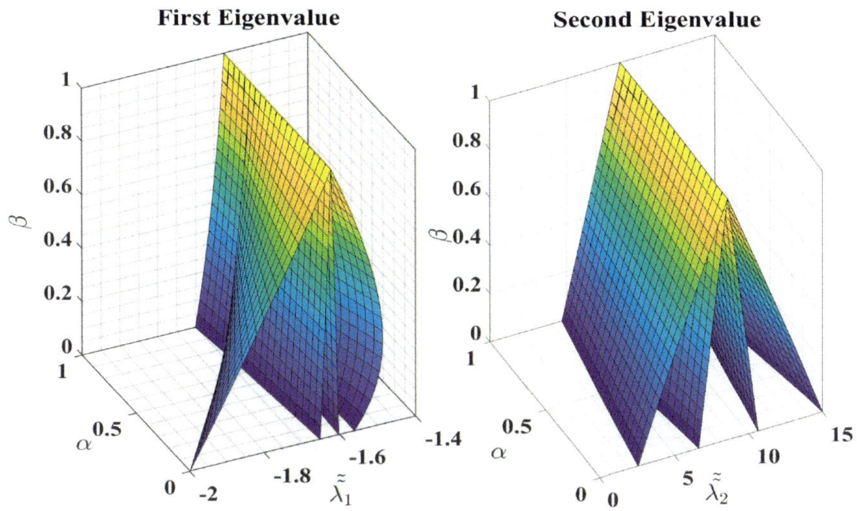

FIGURE 12.1 Plot of the obtained eigenvalues for Example 12.1

The plots of the obtained eigenvalues are shown in Fig. 12.1.

Further, the bounds of the type-2 fuzzy eigenvalues for different values of α and β are shown in Tables 12.1 and 12.2.

Example 12.2. Let us consider the T2FSEP, given by

$$\begin{bmatrix} \tilde{\tilde{a}}_{11} & \tilde{\tilde{a}}_{12} & 0 \\ \tilde{\tilde{a}}_{12} & \tilde{\tilde{a}}_{11} & \tilde{\tilde{a}}_{12} \\ 0 & \tilde{\tilde{a}}_{12} & \tilde{\tilde{a}}_{11} \end{bmatrix} \begin{bmatrix} \tilde{\tilde{x}}_1 \\ \tilde{\tilde{x}}_2 \\ \tilde{\tilde{x}}_3 \end{bmatrix} = \tilde{\tilde{\lambda}} \begin{bmatrix} \tilde{\tilde{x}}_1 \\ \tilde{\tilde{x}}_2 \\ \tilde{\tilde{x}}_3 \end{bmatrix}, \tag{12.24}$$

where

$$\begin{aligned} \tilde{\tilde{a}}_{11} &= (11.25, 11.75, 12.5, 13, 13.5, 14.25, 14.75), \\ \tilde{\tilde{a}}_{12} &= (-4.5, -4, -3.75, -3.25, -3.25, -2.75, -2.25). \end{aligned} \tag{12.25}$$

Now, using the parameters α, β, and γ in the given Eq. (12.24), Eq. (12.24) will be given by the following two SEPs (one for the LMF and another for the UMF),

$$\begin{bmatrix} \underline{\tilde{a}}_{11}(\alpha,\beta,\gamma) & \underline{\tilde{a}}_{12}(\alpha,\beta,\gamma) & 0 \\ \underline{\tilde{a}}_{12}(\alpha,\beta,\gamma) & \underline{\tilde{a}}_{11}(\alpha,\beta,\gamma) & \underline{\tilde{a}}_{12}(\alpha,\beta,\gamma) \\ 0 & \underline{\tilde{a}}_{12}(\alpha,\beta,\gamma) & \underline{\tilde{a}}_{11}(\alpha,\beta,\gamma) \end{bmatrix} \begin{bmatrix} \underline{\tilde{x}}_1(\alpha,\beta,\gamma) \\ \underline{\tilde{x}}_2(\alpha,\beta,\gamma) \\ \underline{\tilde{x}}_3(\alpha,\beta,\gamma) \end{bmatrix} = \underline{\tilde{\lambda}}(\alpha,\beta,\gamma) \begin{bmatrix} \underline{\tilde{x}}_1(\alpha,\beta,\gamma) \\ \underline{\tilde{x}}_2(\alpha,\beta,\gamma) \\ \underline{\tilde{x}}_3(\alpha,\beta,\gamma) \end{bmatrix}, \tag{12.26}$$

and

$$\begin{bmatrix} \bar{\tilde{a}}_{11}(\alpha,\beta,\gamma) & \bar{\tilde{a}}_{12}(\alpha,\beta,\gamma) & 0 \\ \bar{\tilde{a}}_{12}(\alpha,\beta,\gamma) & \bar{\tilde{a}}_{11}(\alpha,\beta,\gamma) & \bar{\tilde{a}}_{12}(\alpha,\beta,\gamma) \\ 0 & \bar{\tilde{a}}_{12}(\alpha,\beta,\gamma) & \bar{\tilde{a}}_{11}(\alpha,\beta,\gamma) \end{bmatrix} \begin{bmatrix} \bar{\tilde{x}}_1(\alpha,\beta,\gamma) \\ \bar{\tilde{x}}_2(\alpha,\beta,\gamma) \\ \bar{\tilde{x}}_3(\alpha,\beta,\gamma) \end{bmatrix} = \bar{\tilde{\lambda}}(\alpha,\beta,\gamma) \begin{bmatrix} \bar{\tilde{x}}_1(\alpha,\beta,\gamma) \\ \bar{\tilde{x}}_2(\alpha,\beta,\gamma) \\ \bar{\tilde{x}}_3(\alpha,\beta,\gamma) \end{bmatrix}, \tag{12.27}$$

Table 12.1 Bounds of first type-2 fuzzy eigenvalue $\tilde{\tilde{\lambda}}_1$ Example 12.1.

α	β	Left bound (LMF)	Right bound (LMF)	Left bound (UMF)	Right bound (UMF)
0	0	−1.6533	−1.6033	−1.5616	−2
0	0.25	−1.6446	−1.6077	−1.4886	−1.8985
0	0.5	−1.6368	−1.6125	−1.5	−1.8007
0	0.75	−1.6298	−1.6177	−1.5512	−1.7082
0	1	−1.6235	−1.6235	−1.6235	−1.6235
0.25	0	−1.6631	−1.5992	−1.5684	−1.8971
0.25	0.25	−1.651	−1.6043	−1.5271	−1.8226
0.25	0.5	−1.6406	−1.61	−1.5365	−1.7512
0.25	0.75	−1.6315	−1.6164	−1.5723	−1.6842
0.25	1	−1.6235	−1.6235	−1.6235	−1.6235
0.5	0	−1.6742	−1.5955	−1.5981	−1.7942
0.5	0.25	−1.6581	−1.6012	−1.5717	−1.7467
0.5	0.5	−1.6446	−1.6077	−1.5743	−1.7017
0.5	0.75	−1.6332	−1.615	−1.5936	−1.6602
0.5	1	−1.6235	−1.6235	−1.6235	−1.6235
0.75	0	−1.6869	−1.592	−1.644	−1.6914
0.75	0.25	−1.6658	−1.5982	−1.621	−1.671
0.75	0.5	−1.6488	−1.6054	−1.6133	−1.6524
0.75	0.75	−1.635	−1.6138	−1.6151	−1.6363
0.75	1	−1.6235	−1.6235	−1.6235	−1.6235
1	0	−1.7016	−1.5887	−1.7016	−1.5887
1	0.25	−1.6742	−1.5955	−1.6742	−1.5955
1	0.5	−1.6533	−1.6033	−1.6533	−1.6033
1	0.75	−1.6368	−1.6125	−1.6368	−1.6125
1	1	−1.6235	−1.6235	−1.6235	−1.6235

where

$$\begin{aligned}
\underline{\tilde{a}}_{11}(\alpha,\beta,\gamma) &= \frac{5\beta}{4} - \gamma\left(\frac{5\beta}{2} + 2\left(\frac{3\beta}{4} - \frac{3}{4}\right)(\alpha-1) - \frac{5}{2}\right) + \left(\frac{3\beta}{4} - \frac{3}{4}\right)(\alpha-1) + \frac{47}{4},\\
\underline{\tilde{a}}_{12}(\alpha,\beta,\gamma) &= \frac{3\beta}{4} + \left(\frac{\beta}{4} - \frac{1}{4}\right)(\alpha-1) - \gamma\left(\frac{5\beta}{4} + \left(\frac{\beta}{2} - \frac{1}{2}\right)(\alpha-1) + \left(\frac{\beta}{4} - \frac{1}{4}\right)(\alpha-1) - \frac{5}{4}\right) - 4,\\
\overline{\tilde{a}}_{11}(\alpha,\beta,\gamma) &= \frac{5\beta}{4} + \gamma\left(2\left(\frac{\beta}{2} - \frac{1}{2}\right)(\alpha-1) - \frac{5\beta}{2} + \frac{5}{2}\right) - \left(\frac{\beta}{2} - \frac{1}{2}\right)(\alpha-1) + \frac{47}{4},\\
\overline{\tilde{a}}_{12}(\alpha,\beta,\gamma) &= \frac{3\beta}{4} + \gamma\left(2\left(\frac{\beta}{2} - \frac{1}{2}\right)(\alpha-1) - \frac{5\beta}{4} + \frac{5}{4}\right) - \left(\frac{\beta}{2} - \frac{1}{2}\right)(\alpha-1) - 4.
\end{aligned} \tag{12.28}$$

Eqs. (12.26) and (12.27) can be solved for the eigenvalues $\underline{\tilde{\lambda}}$ and $\overline{\tilde{\lambda}}$ in terms of the parameters α, β, and γ. These $\underline{\tilde{\lambda}}$ and $\overline{\tilde{\lambda}}$ are correspond to the LMF and UMF of the type-2 fuzzy eigenvalue $\tilde{\tilde{\lambda}}$. Combining the LMF and UMF of the type-2 fuzzy eigenvalues, the required

Table 12.2 Bounds of second type-2 fuzzy eigenvalue $\tilde{\tilde{\lambda}}_2$ Example 12.1.

α	β	Left bound (LMF)	Right bound (LMF)	Left bound (UMF)	Right bound (UMF)
0	0	6.6533	10.603	2.5616	15
0	0.25	7.1446	10.108	3.9886	13.399
0	0.5	7.6368	9.6125	5.5	11.801
0	0.75	8.1298	9.1177	7.0512	10.208
0	1	8.6235	8.6235	8.6235	8.6235
0.25	0	6.1631	11.099	3.0684	14.397
0.25	0.25	6.776	10.479	4.4021	12.948
0.25	0.5	7.3906	9.86	5.7865	11.501
0.25	0.75	8.0065	9.2414	7.1973	10.059
0.25	1	8.6235	8.6235	8.6235	8.6235
0.5	0	5.6742	11.595	3.5981	13.794
0.5	0.25	6.4081	10.851	4.8217	12.497
0.5	0.5	7.1446	10.108	6.0743	11.202
0.5	0.75	7.8832	9.365	7.3436	9.9102
0.5	1	8.6235	8.6235	8.6235	8.6235
0.75	0	5.1869	12.092	4.144	13.191
0.75	0.25	6.0408	11.223	5.246	12.046
0.75	0.5	6.8988	10.355	6.3633	10.902
0.75	0.75	7.76	9.4888	7.4901	9.7613
0.75	1	8.6235	8.6235	8.6235	8.6235
1	0	4.7016	12.589	4.7016	12.589
1	0.25	5.6742	11.595	5.6742	11.595
1	0.5	6.6533	10.603	6.6533	10.603
1	0.75	7.6368	9.6125	7.6368	9.6125
1	1	8.6235	8.6235	8.6235	8.6235

type-2 fuzzy eigenvalues are obtained. Further, plugging different values to the parameters α, β, and γ, the type-2 fuzzy eigenvalues in their standard forms are

$$\begin{aligned}
\tilde{\tilde{\lambda}}_1 &= (11.25, 11.75, 12.5, 13, 13.5, 14.25, 14.75),\\
\tilde{\tilde{\lambda}}_2 &= (5.1631, 6.0931, 7.1966, 8.4038, 8.9038, 10.3609, 11.167),\\
\tilde{\tilde{\lambda}}_3 &= (17.4068, 17.5961, 17.6847, 17.8033, 17.9678, 18.0961, 18.1390).
\end{aligned} \tag{12.29}$$

The three-dimensional plots of the obtained TPQT2FN valued eigenvalues are shown in Fig. 12.2.

Example 12.3. Now, let us consider a T2FGEP, given by

$$\begin{bmatrix} \tilde{\tilde{a}}_{11} & \tilde{\tilde{a}}_{12} \\ \tilde{\tilde{a}}_{12} & \tilde{\tilde{a}}_{22} \end{bmatrix} \begin{bmatrix} \tilde{\tilde{x}}_1 \\ \tilde{\tilde{x}}_2 \end{bmatrix} = \tilde{\tilde{\lambda}} \begin{bmatrix} 300 & 0 \\ 0 & 300 \end{bmatrix} \begin{bmatrix} \tilde{\tilde{x}}_1 \\ \tilde{\tilde{x}}_2 \end{bmatrix}, \tag{12.30}$$

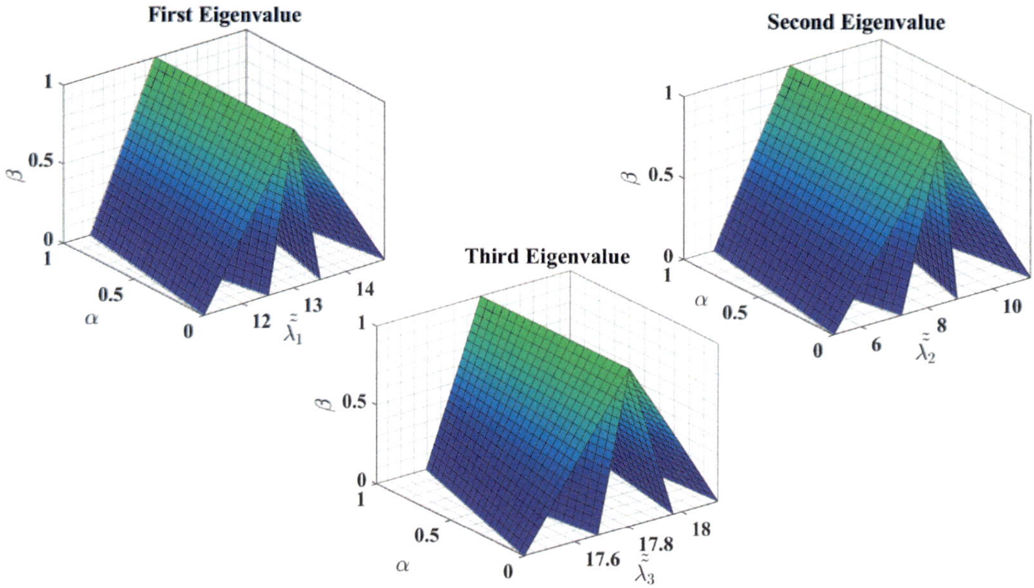

FIGURE 12.2 Plot of the obtained eigenvalues Example 12.2.

where

$$\begin{aligned}\tilde{\tilde{a}}_{11} &= (450, 475, 500, 550, 600, 625, 650),\\ \tilde{\tilde{a}}_{12} &= (-550, -525, -500, -475, -450, -425, -400),\\ \tilde{\tilde{a}}_{22} &= (400, 425, 450, 475, 500, 525, 550).\end{aligned} \tag{12.31}$$

Implementing the triple parametric representation of the TPQT2FN valued parameters in the given T2FGEP, Eq. (12.30) will become two generalized eigenvalue problems, given by

$$\begin{bmatrix}\underline{\tilde{a}}_{11}(\alpha,\beta,\gamma) & \underline{\tilde{a}}_{12}(\alpha,\beta,\gamma)\\ \underline{\tilde{a}}_{12}(\alpha,\beta,\gamma) & \underline{\tilde{a}}_{22}(\alpha,\beta,\gamma)\end{bmatrix}\begin{bmatrix}\underline{\tilde{x}}_1(\alpha,\beta,\gamma)\\ \underline{\tilde{x}}_2(\alpha,\beta,\gamma)\end{bmatrix} = \underline{\tilde{\lambda}}(\alpha,\beta,\gamma)\begin{bmatrix}300 & 0\\ 0 & 300\end{bmatrix}\begin{bmatrix}\underline{\tilde{x}}_1(\alpha,\beta,\gamma)\\ \underline{\tilde{x}}_2(\alpha,\beta,\gamma)\end{bmatrix}, \tag{12.32}$$

and

$$\begin{bmatrix}\tilde{\bar{a}}_{11}(\alpha,\beta,\gamma) & \tilde{\bar{a}}_{12}(\alpha,\beta,\gamma)\\ \tilde{\bar{a}}_{12}(\alpha,\beta,\gamma) & \tilde{\bar{a}}_{22}(\alpha,\beta,\gamma)\end{bmatrix}\begin{bmatrix}\tilde{\bar{x}}_1(\alpha,\beta,\gamma)\\ \tilde{\bar{x}}_2(\alpha,\beta,\gamma)\end{bmatrix} = \tilde{\bar{\lambda}}(\alpha,\beta,\gamma)\begin{bmatrix}300 & 0\\ 0 & 300\end{bmatrix}\begin{bmatrix}\tilde{\bar{x}}_1(\alpha,\beta,\gamma)\\ \tilde{\bar{x}}_2(\alpha,\beta,\gamma)\end{bmatrix}, \tag{12.33}$$

where

$$\begin{aligned}\underline{\tilde{a}}_{11}(\alpha,\beta,\gamma) &= 75\beta - \gamma(150\beta + 2(25\beta - 25)(\alpha - 1) - 150) + (25\beta - 25)(\alpha - 1) + 475,\\ \underline{\tilde{a}}_{12}(\alpha,\beta,\gamma) &= 50\beta - \gamma(100\beta + 2(25\beta - 25)(\alpha - 1) - 100) + (25\beta - 25)(\alpha - 1) - 525,\\ \underline{\tilde{a}}_{22} &= 50\beta - \gamma(100\beta + 2(25\beta - 25)(\alpha - 1) - 100) + (25\beta - 25)(\alpha - 1) + 425,\\ \tilde{\bar{a}}_{11}(\alpha,\beta,\gamma) &= 75\beta + \gamma(2(25\beta - 25)(\alpha - 1) - 150\beta + 150) - (25\beta - 25)(\alpha - 1) + 475,\end{aligned}$$

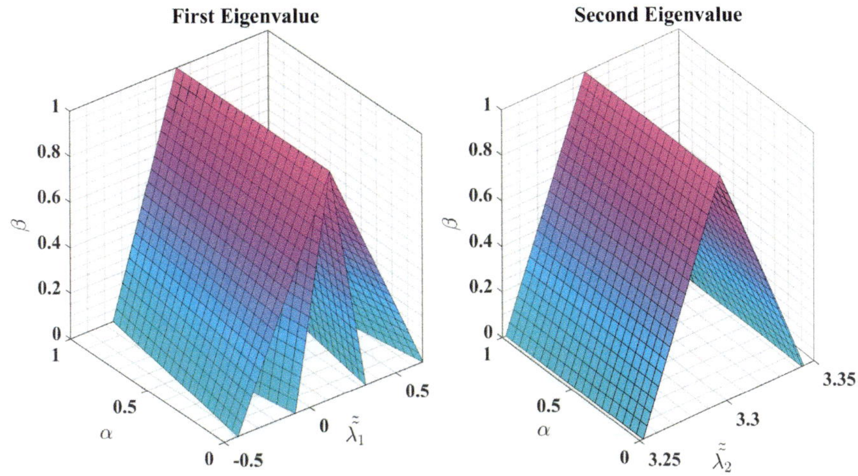

FIGURE 12.3 Plot of the obtained eigenvalues Example 12.3.

$$\bar{\tilde{a}}_{12}(\alpha,\beta,\gamma) = 50\beta + \gamma(2(25\beta - 25)(\alpha - 1) - 100\beta + 100) - (25\beta - 25)(\alpha - 1) - 525,$$
$$\bar{\tilde{a}}_{22}(\alpha,\beta,\gamma) = 50\beta + \gamma(2(25\beta - 25)(\alpha - 1) - 100\beta + 100) - (25\beta - 25)(\alpha - 1) + 425. \quad (12.34)$$

Eqs. (12.34) and (12.34) can be solved for the eigenvalue $\underline{\tilde{\lambda}}$ and $\overline{\tilde{\lambda}}$, respectively. Substituting different values of α, β, and γ and combining the LMF and UMF bounds, the type-2 fuzzy eigenvalues obtained are (see Fig. 12.3)

$$\tilde{\tilde{\lambda}}_1 = (-0.4185, -0.2519, -0.0854, 0.1201, 0.3241, 0.4902, 0.6562),$$
$$\tilde{\tilde{\lambda}}_2 = (3.2518, 3.2519, 3.2520, 3.2965, 3.3425, 3.3431, 3.3437). \quad (12.35)$$

Further, the bounds of the type-2 fuzzy eigenvalues for different values of α and β are shown in Tables 12.3 and 12.4.

12.5 Application problem

In this section, the application problem related to type-2 fuzzy linear eigenvalue problems are discussed.

12.5.1 Spring-mass system

Suppose we have a spring-mass system of five degrees of freedom as shown in Fig. 12.4. Here, we have assumed the mass and stiffness parameters to be uncertain. TPQT2FNs are used to handle the uncertainty in these parameters. To obtain the natural frequencies (eigenvalues) of the system, the T2FGEP associated with the system is

$$\tilde{\tilde{K}}\tilde{\tilde{X}} = \tilde{\tilde{\lambda}}\tilde{\tilde{M}}\tilde{\tilde{X}}, \quad (12.36)$$

Table 12.3 Bounds of first type-2 fuzzy eigenvalue $\tilde{\tilde{\lambda}}_1$ Example 12.3.

α	β	Left bound (LMF)	Right bound (LMF)	Left bound (UMF)	Right bound (UMF)
0	0	−0.085415	0.3241	−0.41856	0.65629
0	0.25	−0.033918	0.27324	−0.28373	0.52253
0	0.5	0.017498	0.22228	−0.14901	0.38856
0	0.75	0.06883	0.17123	−0.014401	0.2544
0	1	0.12007	0.12007	0.12007	0.12007
0.25	0	−0.12706	0.36564	−0.37691	0.61478
0.25	0.25	−0.065143	0.30441	−0.2525	0.49138
0.25	0.5	−0.0033141	0.24307	−0.12819	0.36778
0.25	0.75	0.058426	0.18162	−0.0039965	0.244
0.25	1	0.12007	0.12007	0.12007	0.12007
0.5	0	−0.1687	0.40717	−0.33527	0.57327
0.5	0.25	−0.096368	0.33558	−0.22127	0.46022
0.5	0.5	−0.024126	0.26386	−0.10738	0.347
0.5	0.75	0.048023	0.19202	0.0064075	0.23361
0.5	1	0.12007	0.12007	0.12007	0.12007
0.75	0	−0.21034	0.4487	−0.29363	0.53175
0.75	0.25	−0.12759	0.36674	−0.19005	0.42906
0.75	0.5	−0.044939	0.28464	−0.086565	0.32621
0.75	0.75	0.037619	0.20242	0.016811	0.22321
0.75	1	0.12007	0.12007	0.12007	0.12007
1	0	−0.25198	0.49023	−0.25198	0.49023
1	0.25	−0.15882	0.3979	−0.15882	0.3979
1	0.5	−0.065752	0.30543	−0.065752	0.30543
1	0.75	0.027215	0.21281	0.027215	0.21281
1	1	0.12007	0.12007	0.12007	0.12007

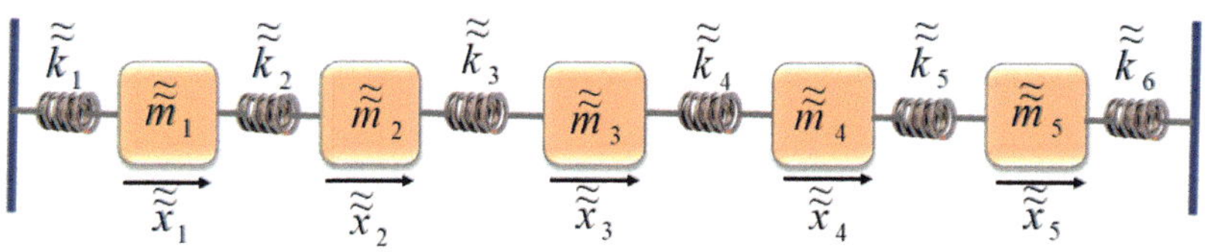

FIGURE 12.4 Schematic diagram of five degrees of freedom spring-mass system.

where

$$\tilde{\tilde{K}} = \begin{bmatrix} \tilde{\tilde{k}}_1 + \tilde{\tilde{k}}_2 & -\tilde{\tilde{k}}_2 & 0 & 0 & 0 \\ -\tilde{\tilde{k}}_2 & \tilde{\tilde{k}}_2 + \tilde{\tilde{k}}_3 & -\tilde{\tilde{k}}_3 & 0 & 0 \\ 0 & -\tilde{\tilde{k}}_3 & \tilde{\tilde{k}}_3 + \tilde{\tilde{k}}_4 & -\tilde{\tilde{k}}_4 & 0 \\ 0 & 0 & -\tilde{\tilde{k}}_4 & \tilde{\tilde{k}}_4 + \tilde{\tilde{k}}_5 & -\tilde{\tilde{k}}_5 \\ 0 & 0 & 0 & -\tilde{\tilde{k}}_5 & \tilde{\tilde{k}}_5 + \tilde{\tilde{k}}_6 \end{bmatrix}, \tilde{\tilde{M}} = \begin{bmatrix} \tilde{\tilde{m}}_1 & 0 & 0 & 0 & 0 \\ 0 & \tilde{\tilde{m}}_2 & 0 & 0 & 0 \\ 0 & 0 & \tilde{\tilde{m}}_3 & 0 & 0 \\ 0 & 0 & 0 & \tilde{\tilde{m}}_4 & 0 \\ 0 & 0 & 0 & 0 & \tilde{\tilde{m}}_5 \end{bmatrix} \tag{12.37}$$

Table 12.4 Bounds of second type-2 fuzzy eigenvalue $\tilde{\tilde{\lambda}}_2$ Example 12.3.

α	β	Left bound (LMF)	Right bound (LMF)	Left bound (UMF)	Right bound (UMF)
0	0	3.2521	3.3426	3.2519	3.3437
0	0.25	3.2631	3.3309	3.2629	3.3316
0	0.5	3.2742	3.3194	3.274	3.3198
0	0.75	3.2853	3.3079	3.2852	3.3081
0	1	3.2966	3.2966	3.2966	3.2966
0.25	0	3.2521	3.3427	3.2519	3.3436
0.25	0.25	3.2631	3.331	3.2629	3.3315
0.25	0.5	3.2741	3.3194	3.274	3.3197
0.25	0.75	3.2853	3.308	3.2852	3.3081
0.25	1	3.2966	3.2966	3.2966	3.2966
0.5	0	3.252	3.3428	3.2519	3.3434
0.5	0.25	3.263	3.3311	3.2629	3.3314
0.5	0.5	3.2741	3.3195	3.274	3.3197
0.5	0.75	3.2853	3.308	3.2853	3.3081
0.5	1	3.2966	3.2966	3.2966	3.2966
0.75	0	3.252	3.343	3.252	3.3432
0.75	0.25	3.263	3.3312	3.263	3.3314
0.75	0.5	3.2741	3.3195	3.2741	3.3196
0.75	0.75	3.2853	3.308	3.2853	3.308
0.75	1	3.2966	3.2966	3.2966	3.2966
1	0	3.252	3.3431	3.252	3.3431
1	0.25	3.263	3.3313	3.263	3.3313
1	0.5	3.2741	3.3196	3.2741	3.3196
1	0.75	3.2853	3.308	3.2853	3.308
1	1	3.2966	3.2966	3.2966	3.2966

The elements of the type-2 fuzzy stiffness and mass matrices are

$$\begin{aligned}
\tilde{\tilde{k}}_1 &= (200, 205, 210, 220, 230, 235, 240), \\
\tilde{\tilde{k}}_2 &= (180, 185, 190, 200, 210, 215, 220), \\
\tilde{\tilde{k}}_3 &= (160, 165, 170, 180, 190, 195, 200), \\
\tilde{\tilde{k}}_4 &= (140, 150, 160, 170, 180, 190, 200), \\
\tilde{\tilde{k}}_5 &= (120, 125, 130, 140, 150, 155, 160), \\
\tilde{\tilde{k}}_6 &= (100, 102.5, 105, 110, 115, 117.5, 120), \qquad (12.38) \\
\tilde{\tilde{m}}_1 &= (10, 12.5, 15, 20, 22.5, 25, 27.5), \\
\tilde{\tilde{m}}_2 &= (12, 13, 14, 15, 16, 17, 18),
\end{aligned}$$

$$\tilde{\tilde{m}}_3 = (14, 14.5, 15, 16, 17, 17.5, 18),$$
$$\tilde{\tilde{m}}_4 = (16, 16.5, 17, 18, 19, 19.5, 20),$$
$$\tilde{\tilde{m}}_5 = (18, 18.5, 19, 20, 21, 21.5, 22).$$

The given T2FGEP in (12.36) can be transformed into the following two generalized eigenvalue problems in terms of the uncertainty handling parameters $\alpha, \beta,$ and γ, as

$$\underline{\tilde{K}}(\alpha,\beta,\gamma)\underline{\tilde{X}}(\alpha,\beta,\gamma) = \underline{\tilde{\lambda}}(\alpha,\beta,\gamma)\underline{\tilde{M}}(\alpha,\beta,\gamma)\underline{\tilde{X}}(\alpha,\beta,\gamma), \tag{12.39}$$

and

$$\overline{\tilde{K}}(\alpha,\beta,\gamma)\overline{\tilde{X}}(\alpha,\beta,\gamma) = \overline{\tilde{\lambda}}(\alpha,\beta,\gamma)\overline{\tilde{M}}(\alpha,\beta,\gamma)\overline{\tilde{X}}(\alpha,\beta,\gamma), \tag{12.40}$$

where the LMF and UMF of the type-2 fuzzy elements in terms of $\alpha, \beta,$ and γ are

$$\underline{\tilde{k}}_1(\alpha,\beta,\gamma) = 15\beta - \gamma\,(30\beta + 2\,(5\beta-5)\,(\alpha-1) - 30) + (5\beta-5)\,(\alpha-1) + 205,$$
$$\underline{\tilde{k}}_2(\alpha,\beta,\gamma) = 15\beta - \gamma\,(30\beta + 2\,(5\beta-5)\,(\alpha-1) - 30) + (5\beta-5)\,(\alpha-1) + 185,$$
$$\underline{\tilde{k}}_3(\alpha,\beta,\gamma) = 15\beta - \gamma\,(30\beta + 2\,(5\beta-5)\,(\alpha-1) - 30) + (5\beta-5)\,(\alpha-1) + 165,$$
$$\underline{\tilde{k}}_4(\alpha,\beta,\gamma) = 20\beta - \gamma\,(40\beta + 2\,(10\beta-10)\,(\alpha-1) - 40) + (10\beta-10)\,(\alpha-1) + 150,$$
$$\underline{\tilde{k}}_5(\alpha,\beta,\gamma) = 15\beta - \gamma\,(30\beta + 2\,(5\beta-5)\,(\alpha-1) - 30) + (5\beta-5)\,(\alpha-1) + 125,$$
$$\underline{\tilde{k}}_6(\alpha,\beta,\gamma) = \frac{15\beta}{2} - \gamma\left(15\beta + 2\left(\frac{5\beta}{2} - \frac{5}{2}\right)(\alpha-1) - 15\right) + \left(\frac{5\beta}{2} - \frac{5}{2}\right)(\alpha-1) + \frac{205}{2},$$
$$\underline{\tilde{m}}_1(\alpha,\beta,\gamma) = \frac{15\beta}{2} - \gamma\left(\frac{25\beta}{2} + 2\left(\frac{5\beta}{2} - \frac{5}{2}\right)(\alpha-1) - \frac{25}{2}\right) + \left(\frac{5\beta}{2} - \frac{5}{2}\right)(\alpha-1) + \frac{25}{2},$$
$$\underline{\tilde{m}}_2(\alpha,\beta,\gamma) = 2\beta - \gamma\,(4\beta + 2(\alpha-1)(\beta-1) - 4) + (\alpha-1)(\beta-1) + 13,$$
$$\underline{\tilde{m}}_3(\alpha,\beta,\gamma) = \frac{3\beta}{2} - \gamma\left(3\beta + 2\left(\frac{\beta}{2} - \frac{1}{2}\right)(\alpha-1) - 3\right) + \left(\frac{\beta}{2} - \frac{1}{2}\right)(\alpha-1) + \frac{29}{2},$$
$$\underline{\tilde{m}}_4(\alpha,\beta,\gamma) = \frac{3\beta}{2} - \gamma\left(3\beta + 2\left(\frac{\beta}{2} - \frac{1}{2}\right)(\alpha-1) - 3\right) + \left(\frac{\beta}{2} - \frac{1}{2}\right)(\alpha-1) + \frac{33}{2},$$
$$\underline{\tilde{m}}_5(\alpha,\beta,\gamma) = \frac{3\beta}{2} - \gamma\left(3\beta + 2\left(\frac{\beta}{2} - \frac{1}{2}\right)(\alpha-1) - 3\right) + \left(\frac{\beta}{2} - \frac{1}{2}\right)(\alpha-1) + \frac{37}{2},$$
$$\overline{\tilde{k}}_1(\alpha,\beta,\gamma) = 15\beta + \gamma\,(2\,(5\beta-5)\,(\alpha-1) - 30\beta + 30) - (5\beta-5)\,(\alpha-1) + 205,$$
$$\overline{\tilde{k}}_2(\alpha,\beta,\gamma) = 15\beta + \gamma\,(2\,(5\beta-5)\,(\alpha-1) - 30\beta + 30) - (5\beta-5)\,(\alpha-1) + 185,$$
$$\overline{\tilde{k}}_3(\alpha,\beta,\gamma) = 15\beta + \gamma\,(2\,(5\beta-5)\,(\alpha-1) - 30\beta + 30) - (5\beta-5)\,(\alpha-1) + 165,$$
$$\overline{\tilde{k}}_4(\alpha,\beta,\gamma) = 20\beta + \gamma\,(2\,(10\beta-10)\,(\alpha-1) - 40\beta + 40) - (10\beta-10)\,(\alpha-1) + 150,$$
$$\overline{\tilde{k}}_5(\alpha,\beta,\gamma) = 15\beta + \gamma\,(2\,(5\beta-5)\,(\alpha-1) - 30\beta + 30) - (5\beta-5)\,(\alpha-1) + 125,$$
$$\overline{\tilde{k}}_6(\alpha,\beta,\gamma) = \frac{15\beta}{2} + \gamma\left(2\left(\frac{5\beta}{2} - \frac{5}{2}\right)(\alpha-1) - 15\beta + 15\right) - \left(\frac{5\beta}{2} - \frac{5}{2}\right)(\alpha-1) + \frac{205}{2},$$

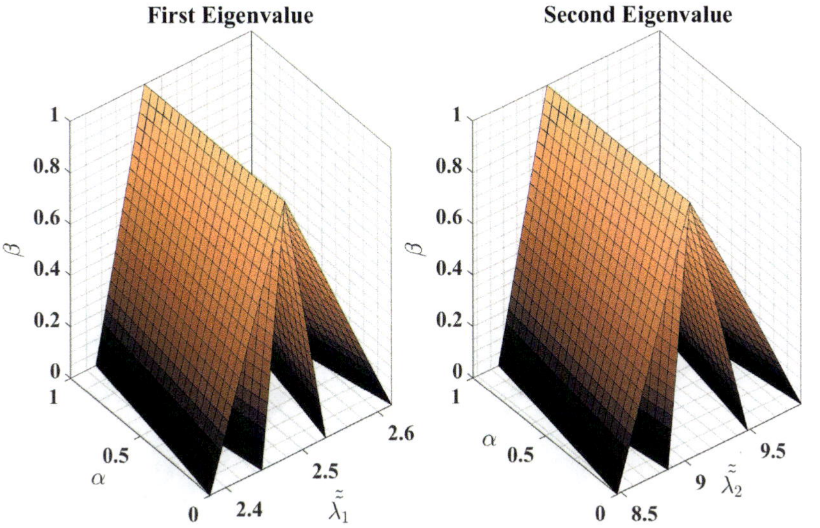

FIGURE 12.5 Plot of the obtained first and second eigenvalues of the spring-mass system.

$$
\begin{aligned}
\overline{\tilde{m}}_1(\alpha,\beta,\gamma) &= \frac{15\beta}{2} + \gamma\left(2\left(\frac{5\beta}{2}-\frac{5}{2}\right)(\alpha-1) - \frac{25\beta}{2} + \frac{25}{2}\right) - \left(\frac{5\beta}{2}-\frac{5}{2}\right)(\alpha-1) + \frac{25}{2},\\
\overline{\tilde{m}}_2(\alpha,\beta,\gamma) &= 2\beta + \gamma\,(2(\alpha-1)(\beta-1) - 4\beta + 4) - (\alpha-1)(\beta-1) + 13,\\
\overline{\tilde{m}}_3(\alpha,\beta,\gamma) &= \frac{3\beta}{2} + \gamma\left(2\left(\frac{\beta}{2}-\frac{1}{2}\right)(\alpha-1) - 3\beta + 3\right) - \left(\frac{\beta}{2}-\frac{1}{2}\right)(\alpha-1) + \frac{29}{2},\\
\overline{\tilde{m}}_4(\alpha,\beta,\gamma) &= \frac{3\beta}{2} + \gamma\left(2\left(\frac{\beta}{2}-\frac{1}{2}\right)(\alpha-1) - 3\beta + 3\right) - \left(\frac{\beta}{2}-\frac{1}{2}\right)(\alpha-1) + \frac{33}{2},\\
\overline{\tilde{m}}_5(\alpha,\beta,\gamma) &= \frac{3\beta}{2} + \gamma\left(2\left(\frac{\beta}{2}-\frac{1}{2}\right)(\alpha-1) - 3\beta + 3\right) - \left(\frac{\beta}{2}-\frac{1}{2}\right)(\alpha-1) + \frac{37}{2}.
\end{aligned}
\tag{12.41}
$$

The generalized eigenvalue problems in (12.39) and (12.40) can be solved to obtain the eigenvalues $\underset{\sim}{\tilde{\lambda}}$ and $\bar{\tilde{\lambda}}$. Combining the solutions of LMF and UMF for different values of α, β, and γ, the required type-2 fuzzy eigenvalues (natural frequencies) are

$$
\begin{aligned}
\tilde{\tilde{\lambda}}_1 &= (2.3788, 2.4119, 2.4466, 2.4774, 2.5307, 2.5732, 2.6179),\\
\tilde{\tilde{\lambda}}_2 &= (8.4660, 8.6598, 8.8613, 9.0342, 9.4774, 9.6957, 9.9033),\\
\tilde{\tilde{\lambda}}_3 &= (16.3706, 16.7064, 17.1043, 17.3883, 18.4144, 19.0372, 19.6829),\\
\tilde{\tilde{\lambda}}_4 &= (26.7605, 27.1123, 27.4704, 27.8939, 29.7373, 30.5905, 31.6152),\\
\tilde{\tilde{\lambda}}_5 &= (39.0340, 39.5938, 40.4249, 41.1365, 43.6481, 46.9143, 52.4146).
\end{aligned}
\tag{12.42}
$$

The plots of the obtained type-2 fuzzy eigenvalues are shown in Figs. 12.5–12.7.

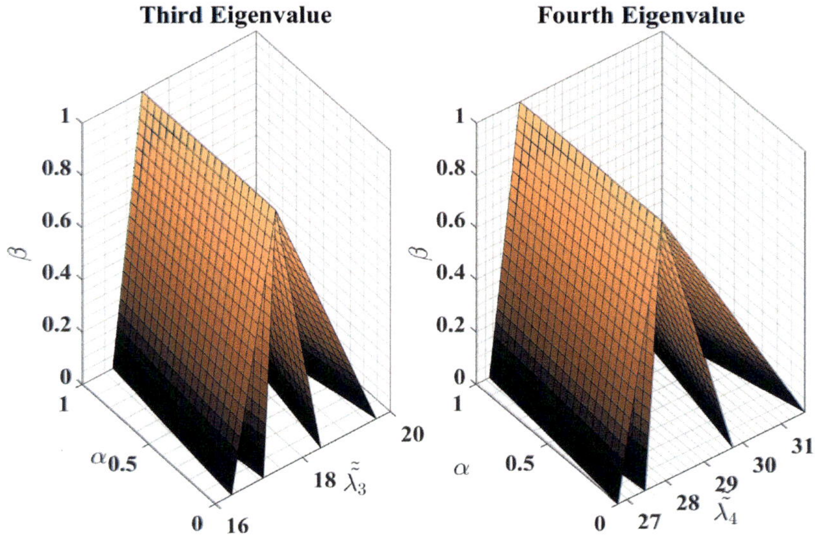

FIGURE 12.6 Plot of the obtained third and fourth eigenvalues of the spring-mass system.

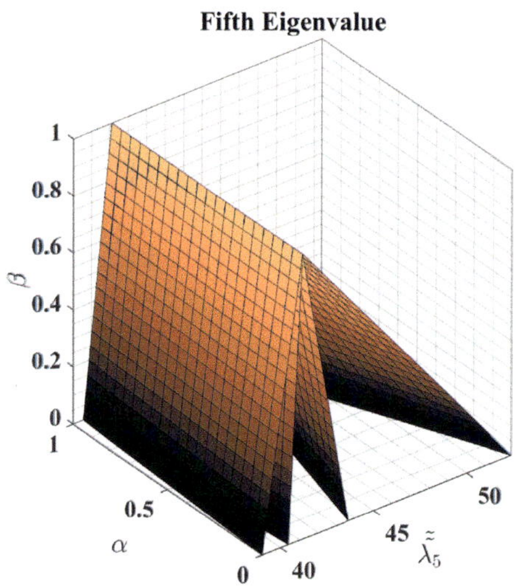

FIGURE 12.7 Plot of the obtained fifth eigenvalue of the spring-mass system.

This chapter discusses type-2 fuzzy linear eigenvalue problems. The concepts of generalized and standard eigenvalue problems are presented briefly. A method utilizing the triple parametric representation of the LMF and UMF for type-2 fuzzy parameters is introduced. Additionally, examples of problems and application problems are effectively handled by the proposed approach to show the applicability of the presented approach.

References

[1] Z. Qiu, S. Chen, H. Jia, The Rayleigh quotient iteration method for computing eigenvalue bounds of structures with bounded uncertain parameters, Computers & Structures 55 (2) (1995) 221–227.

[2] Y. Xia, M. Friswell, Efficient solution of the fuzzy eigenvalue problem in structural dynamics, Engineering Computations 31 (5) (2014) 864–878.

[3] M. Hladík, D. Daney, E. Tsigaridas, A filtering method for the interval eigenvalue problem, Applied Mathematics and Computation 217 (12) (2011) 5236–5242.

[4] H. Leng, Real eigenvalue bounds of standard and generalized real interval eigenvalue problems, Applied Mathematics and Computation 232 (2014) 164–171.

[5] S.K. Jeswal, S. Chakraverty, Fuzzy eigenvalue problems of structural dynamics using ANN, in: New Paradigms in Computational Modeling and Its Applications, Academic Press, 2021, pp. 145–161.

[6] S. Chakraverty, S.K. Jeswal, Applied Artificial Neural Network Methods for Engineers and Scientists: Solving Algebraic Equations, World Scientific, 2021.

[7] N.R. Mahato, S. Chakraverty, Filtering algorithm for real eigenvalue bounds of interval and fuzzy generalized eigenvalue problems, ASCE-ASME Journal of Risk and Uncertainty in Engineering Systems Part B: Mechanical Engineering 2 (4) (2016) 044502.

[8] M. Guo, H. Zhong, Y. Kuan, A second-order perturbation method for fuzzy eigenvalue problems, Engineering Computations 33 (2) (2016).

[9] S. Chakraverty, D. Behera, Parameter identification of multistorey frame structure from uncertain dynamic data, Journal of Mechanical Engineering/Strojniški Vestnik 60 (5) (2014).

[10] H. Leng, Z. He, Computing eigenvalue bounds of structures with uncertain-but-non-random parameters by a method based on perturbation theory, Communications in Numerical Methods in Engineerings 23 (11) (2007) 973–982.

[11] S. Chakraverty, S. Rout, Affine arithmetic based solution of uncertain static and dynamic problems, Springer Nature (2022).

[12] N.R. Mahato, S. Chakraverty, Filtering algorithm for eigenvalue bounds of fuzzy symmetric matrices, Engineering Computations 33 (3) (2016).

[13] P. Rao, S. Chakraverty, D. Roy, Oscillation characteristics of single-link flexible manipulator using design parameters in fuzzy domain, Journal of Vibration Engineering & Technologies (2024) 1–19.

[14] P. Rao, S. Chakraverty, D. Roy, Vibration model of slender single link flexible robotic manipulator based on Timoshenko beam theory with interval uncertainty, in: Proceedings of the 2023 6th International Conference on Advances in Robotics, 2023, pp. 1–5.

[15] D. Mohapatra, S. Chakraverty, Type-2 fuzzy linear eigenvalue problems with application in dynamic structures, Soft Computing in Interdisciplinary Sciences (2022) 93–108.

13

Non-linear dynamical problems with uncertainty

Contents

13.1 Introduction 165

13.2 Type-2 fuzzy non-linear eigenvalue problems 167

13.3 Solution procedure of the type-2 fuzzy non-linear eigenvalue problem 168

13.4 Sample problems 170

13.5 Application problems 178

13.5.1 Damped spring-mass system 178

References 185

Chapter points

- Type-2 fuzzy non-linear eigenvalue problems are discussed.
- An extension of the linearization technique is provided to transform the non-linear eigenvalue problem into a linear eigenvalue problem.
- Triple parametric representation of the type-2 fuzzy parameters is utilized.
- Application problems related to structural dynamics is presented.

13.1 Introduction

The presence of non-linear dynamical problems can be found in various fields of science and engineering, namely vibration analysis, wave dynamics, biological models, and many more. Non-linear dynamical problems arise in various fields lead to non-linear eigenvalue problems. Non-linear eigenvalue problems (NEPs) are an extension of traditional eigenvalue problems, where the relationship between the eigenvalues and eigenvectors is non-linear, making them more complex and challenging to solve. These problems arise in many real-world scenarios, such as in the study of vibrations in mechanical systems with non-linear damping, wave propagation in non-linear media, stability analysis in control systems, the micro-electronic mechanical system, and fluid mechanics. Unlike linear eigenvalue problems, where the eigenvalue appears in a straightforward linear form, non-linear eigenvalue problems involve terms where the eigenvalue is part of a more complicated expression, such as polynomial or transcendental functions. Solving these problems is essential for accurately modeling and predicting the behavior of systems that cannot be described adequately by linear assumptions.

Artificial Neural Networks and Type-2 Fuzzy Set. https://doi.org/10.1016/B978-0-44-332894-7.00023-X

In this regard, various approaches have been developed to solve NEPs. Beyn has proposed an numerical approach to compute all eigenvalues of a non-linear holomorphic eigenvalue problem by transforming into linear eigenvalue problem [1]. Multi-level homotopy perturbation and projection techniques have been used by Massa et al. to solve the quadratic eigenvalue problems [2]. In many practical problems, the NEPs such as polynomial, exponential, and rational eigenvalue problems may also occur. In mechanical systems with free vibration having viscoelastic damping, NEPs reduce to rational eigenvalue problems. The Jacobi–Davidson iterative scheme has been used in order to obtain the extreme eigenvalues [3]. An iterative approach, based on the Arnoldi method has been used by Voss [4] to obtain the eigenvalues associated with a rational NEP. A novel connectionist approach has been implemented in order to solve the NEPs. In this work, four-layer ANN architecture has been constructed by Jeswal and Chakraverty to obtain the eigenvalues [5,6]. Numerical solutions of polynomial eigenvalue problems with Hamiltonian and skew-Hamiltonian coefficient matrices have been obtained by Mehrmann and Watkins [7], following the linearization process. Backward errors and condition numbers for the polynomial eigenvalue problem has been obtained by Tissuer [8] by transforming the problem into a generalized eigenvalue problem.

Uncertainty can arise from various sources, such as imprecise measurements, fluctuating material properties, or environmental conditions, making it difficult to model systems with precise values. To address this, fuzzy or interval uncertainty is often introduced, where uncertain parameters are represented as fuzzy numbers or intervals rather than exact values. In the context of non-linear eigenvalue problems, the presence of uncertainty can lead to a range of possible eigenvalues and eigenvectors, rather than a single solution, complicating the analysis and solution process. This integration of uncertainty into non-linear eigenvalue problems is crucial for accurately modeling complex systems in engineering, physics, and other scientific fields. In this regard, various investigations have been carried out to solve the non-linear eigenvalue problems in the uncertain environment.

The Linear Sufficient Regularity Perturbation (LSRP) method, which linearizes the non-linear eigenvalue problem into a generalized eigenvalue problem, and Direct Sufficient Regularity Perturbation (DSRP) method, which provides a direct solution procedure for solving the NEPs, have been used by Chakraverty and Mahato [9] to solve the interval non-linear eigenvalue problems. The fully-fuzzy non-linear eigenvalue problem has been solved using the fuzzy-affine based approach. In order to handle the uncertainty in the parameters, triangular and trapezoidal fuzzy numbers have been used [10,11]. In order to analyze the vibration in dynamical models, the governing eigenvalue problems have been studied in the uncertain environments [12,13], as there may be uncertainty present in the membership grade, too. Keeping this in mind, Mohapatra and Chakraverty have presented an approach to solve the linear and non-linear eigenvalue problem in the type-2 fuzzy uncertain environment. Generalized type-2 fuzzy numbers have been used there [14,15].

13.2 Type-2 fuzzy non-linear eigenvalue problems

Type-2 fuzzy non-linear eigenvalue problems (T2FNEPs) address the challenges of eigenvalue analysis in systems where uncertainty is not only present but also impacts the membership grades of fuzzy sets. This section delves into the formulation of non-linear eigenvalue problems using the type-2 fuzzy framework.

The general form of a T2FNEP may be given as

$$\tilde{\tilde{F}}(\tilde{\tilde{\lambda}})\tilde{\tilde{X}} = 0, \tag{13.1}$$

where $\tilde{\tilde{F}}$ is a non-linear type-2 fuzzy matrix valued function, $\tilde{\tilde{\lambda}}$ is the type-2 fuzzy eigenvalue, and $\tilde{\tilde{X}}$ is the associated type-2 fuzzy eigenvector. Assuming that $\tilde{\tilde{F}}$ is a polynomial type matrix valued function, then the T2FNEP of degree n is given by

$$(\tilde{\tilde{F}}_n\tilde{\tilde{\lambda}}^n + \tilde{\tilde{F}}_{n-1}\tilde{\tilde{\lambda}}^{n-1} + \ldots + \tilde{\tilde{F}}_1\tilde{\tilde{\lambda}} + \tilde{\tilde{F}}_0)\tilde{\tilde{X}} = 0, \tag{13.2}$$

where $\tilde{\tilde{F}}_0, \tilde{\tilde{F}}_1, \cdots, \tilde{\tilde{F}}_n$ are type-2 fuzzy square matrices of same order, say $m \times m$.

Now, using the β-cut at the α-plane level of the type-2 fuzzy entries of each of the type-2 fuzzy matrices, the type-2 fuzzy eigenvalue and type-2 fuzzy eigenvector in Eq. (13.2), and implementing the concept of LMF and UMF, Eq. (13.2) can be written as

$$\begin{aligned}
&\left(\underline{\tilde{F}}_n(\alpha,\beta)\,\underline{\tilde{\lambda}}(\alpha,\beta)^n + \underline{\tilde{F}}_{n-1}(\alpha,\beta)\,\underline{\tilde{\lambda}}(\alpha,\beta)^{n-1} + \cdots + \underline{\tilde{F}}_1(\alpha,\beta)\,\underline{\tilde{\lambda}}(\alpha,\beta) + \underline{\tilde{F}}_0(\alpha,\beta)\right)\underline{\tilde{X}}(\alpha,\beta) = 0,\\
&\left(\overline{\tilde{F}}_n(\alpha,\beta)\,\overline{\tilde{\lambda}}(\alpha,\beta)^n + \overline{\tilde{F}}_{n-1}(\alpha,\beta)\,\overline{\tilde{\lambda}}(\alpha,\beta)^{n-1} + \cdots + \overline{\tilde{F}}_1(\alpha,\beta)\,\overline{\tilde{\lambda}}(\alpha,\beta) + \overline{\tilde{F}}_0(\alpha,\beta)\right)\overline{\tilde{X}}(\alpha,\beta) = 0.
\end{aligned} \tag{13.3}$$

The first equation in Eq. (13.3) is associated with the LMF and the second equation is associated with the UMF. The uncertain parameters in Eq. (13.3) resembles with the parametric representation of fuzzy numbers. Further, introducing another parameter $\gamma \in [0, 1]$, for simplifying the above interval equations as

$$\begin{aligned}
&\left(\underline{\tilde{F}}_n(\alpha,\beta,\gamma)\,\underline{\tilde{\lambda}}(\alpha,\beta,\gamma)^n + \underline{\tilde{F}}_{n-1}(\alpha,\beta,\gamma)\,\underline{\tilde{\lambda}}(\alpha,\beta,\gamma)^{n-1} + \cdots\right.\\
&\left.+\underline{\tilde{F}}_1(\alpha,\beta,\gamma)\,\underline{\tilde{\lambda}}(\alpha,\beta,\gamma) + \underline{\tilde{F}}_0(\alpha,\beta,\gamma)\right)\underline{\tilde{X}}(\alpha,\beta,\gamma) = 0,\\
&\left(\overline{\tilde{F}}_n(\alpha,\beta,\gamma)\,\overline{\tilde{\lambda}}(\alpha,\beta,\gamma)^n + \overline{\tilde{F}}_{n-1}(\alpha,\beta,\gamma)\,\overline{\tilde{\lambda}}(\alpha,\beta,\gamma)^{n-1} + \cdots\right.\\
&\left.+\overline{\tilde{F}}_1(\alpha,\beta,\gamma)\,\overline{\tilde{\lambda}}(\alpha,\beta,\gamma) + \overline{\tilde{F}}_0(\alpha,\beta,\gamma)\right)\overline{\tilde{X}}(\alpha,\beta,\gamma) = 0,
\end{aligned} \tag{13.4}$$

where

$$\begin{aligned}
\underline{\tilde{\Omega}}(\alpha,\beta,\gamma) &= \underline{\tilde{\Omega}}_L(\alpha,\beta) + \gamma\left(\underline{\tilde{\Omega}}_R(\alpha,\beta) - \underline{\tilde{\Omega}}_L(\alpha,\beta)\right),\\
\overline{\tilde{\Omega}}(\alpha,\beta,\gamma) &= \overline{\tilde{\Omega}}_L(\alpha,\beta) + \gamma\left(\overline{\tilde{\Omega}}_R(\alpha,\beta) - \overline{\tilde{\Omega}}_L(\alpha,\beta)\right).
\end{aligned} \tag{13.5}$$

Here, $\underline{\tilde{\Omega}}$ and $\overline{\tilde{\Omega}}$ represent the fuzzy parameters in the equations associated with LMF and UMF, respectively.

13.3 Solution procedure of the type-2 fuzzy non-linear eigenvalue problem

Motivated from the linearization process given [9], assume the following substitutions:

$$
\begin{aligned}
\underline{\tilde{X}}(\alpha,\beta,\gamma) &:= \underline{\tilde{X}}_1(\alpha,\beta,\gamma),\\
\underline{\tilde{X}}_2(\alpha,\beta,\gamma) &:= \underline{\tilde{\lambda}}(\alpha,\beta,\gamma)\underline{\tilde{X}}_1(\alpha,\beta,\gamma),\\
\underline{\tilde{X}}_3(\alpha,\beta,\gamma) &:= \underline{\tilde{\lambda}}(\alpha,\beta,\gamma)\underline{\tilde{X}}_2(\alpha,\beta,\gamma)\\
&= \underline{\tilde{\lambda}}(\alpha,\beta,\gamma)^2\underline{\tilde{X}}(\alpha,\beta,\gamma),\\
&\vdots\\
\underline{\tilde{X}}_n(\alpha,\beta,\gamma) &:= \underline{\tilde{\lambda}}(\alpha,\beta,\gamma)\underline{\tilde{X}}_{n-1}(\alpha,\beta,\gamma)\\
&= \underline{\tilde{\lambda}}(\alpha,\beta,\gamma)^n\underline{\tilde{X}}(\alpha,\beta,\gamma),
\end{aligned}
\tag{13.6}
$$

and

$$
\begin{aligned}
\overline{\tilde{X}}(\alpha,\beta,\gamma) &:= \overline{\tilde{X}}_1(\alpha,\beta,\gamma),\\
\overline{\tilde{X}}_2(\alpha,\beta,\gamma) &:= \overline{\tilde{\lambda}}(\alpha,\beta,\gamma)\overline{\tilde{X}}_1(\alpha,\beta,\gamma),\\
\overline{\tilde{X}}_3(\alpha,\beta,\gamma) &:= \overline{\tilde{\lambda}}(\alpha,\beta,\gamma)\overline{\tilde{X}}_2(\alpha,\beta,\gamma)\\
&= \overline{\tilde{\lambda}}(\alpha,\beta,\gamma)^2\overline{\tilde{X}}(\alpha,\beta,\gamma),\\
&\vdots\\
\overline{\tilde{X}}_n(\alpha,\beta,\gamma) &:= \overline{\tilde{\lambda}}(\alpha,\beta,\gamma)\overline{\tilde{X}}_{n-1}(\alpha,\beta,\gamma)\\
&= \overline{\tilde{\lambda}}(\alpha,\beta,\gamma)^n\overline{\tilde{X}}(\alpha,\beta,\gamma).
\end{aligned}
\tag{13.7}
$$

Plugging these above expressions in Eq. (13.4), Eq. (13.4) will become

$$
\begin{aligned}
&\underline{\tilde{F}}_n(\alpha,\beta,\gamma)\,\underline{\tilde{\lambda}}(\alpha,\beta,\gamma)\underline{\tilde{X}}_n(\alpha,\beta,\gamma)+\underline{\tilde{F}}_{n-1}(\alpha,\beta,\gamma)\,\underline{\tilde{\lambda}}(\alpha,\beta,\gamma)\underline{\tilde{X}}_{n-1}(\alpha,\beta,\gamma)\\
&\quad+\cdots+\underline{\tilde{F}}_1(\alpha,\beta,\gamma)\,\underline{\tilde{\lambda}}(\alpha,\beta,\gamma)\underline{\tilde{X}}_1(\alpha,\beta,\gamma)+\underline{\tilde{F}}_0(\alpha,\beta,\gamma)\underline{\tilde{X}}_1(\alpha,\beta,\gamma)=0,\\
&\overline{\tilde{F}}_n(\alpha,\beta,\gamma)\,\overline{\tilde{\lambda}}(\alpha,\beta,\gamma)\overline{\tilde{X}}_n(\alpha,\beta,\gamma)+\overline{\tilde{F}}_{n-1}(\alpha,\beta,\gamma)\,\overline{\tilde{\lambda}}(\alpha,\beta,\gamma)\overline{\tilde{X}}_{n-1}(\alpha,\beta,\gamma)\\
&\quad+\cdots+\overline{\tilde{F}}_1(\alpha,\beta,\gamma)\,\overline{\tilde{\lambda}}(\alpha,\beta,\gamma)\overline{\tilde{X}}_1(\alpha,\beta,\gamma)+\overline{\tilde{F}}_0(\alpha,\beta,\gamma)\overline{\tilde{X}}_1(\alpha,\beta,\gamma)=0.
\end{aligned}
\tag{13.8}
$$

Both of the equations in (13.8) are linear eigenvalue problems. Using Eqs. (13.6)–(13.8), the following two system of linear eigenvalue problems can be obtained,

$$
\begin{aligned}
&-\underline{\tilde{F}}_0(\alpha,\beta,\gamma)\underline{\tilde{X}}_1(\alpha,\beta,\gamma)=\underline{\tilde{\lambda}}(\alpha,\beta,\gamma)\Big(\underline{\tilde{F}}_n(\alpha,\beta,\gamma)\,\underline{\tilde{X}}_n(\alpha,\beta,\gamma)\\
&\qquad\qquad+\underline{\tilde{F}}_{n-1}(\alpha,\beta,\gamma)\,\underline{\tilde{X}}_{n-1}(\alpha,\beta,\gamma)+\cdots+\underline{\tilde{F}}_1(\alpha,\beta,\gamma)\,\underline{\tilde{X}}_1(\alpha,\beta,\gamma)\Big),\\
&\underline{\tilde{X}}_2(\alpha,\beta,\gamma)=\underline{\tilde{\lambda}}(\alpha,\beta,\gamma),\\
&\vdots\\
&\underline{\tilde{X}}_n(\alpha,\beta,\gamma)=\underline{\tilde{\lambda}}(\alpha,\beta,\gamma)\underline{\tilde{X}}_{n-1}(\alpha,\beta,\gamma).
\end{aligned}
\tag{13.9}
$$

$$
\begin{aligned}
&-\overline{\tilde{F}}_0(\alpha,\beta,\gamma)\overline{\tilde{X}}_1(\alpha,\beta,\gamma)=\overline{\tilde{\lambda}}(\alpha,\beta,\gamma)\Big(\overline{\tilde{F}}_n(\alpha,\beta,\gamma)\,\overline{\tilde{X}}_n(\alpha,\beta,\gamma)\\
&\qquad\qquad+\overline{\tilde{F}}_{n-1}(\alpha,\beta,\gamma)\,\overline{\tilde{X}}_{n-1}(\alpha,\beta,\gamma)+\cdots+\overline{\tilde{F}}_1(\alpha,\beta,\gamma)\,\overline{\tilde{X}}_1(\alpha,\beta,\gamma)\Big),\\
&\overline{\tilde{X}}_2(\alpha,\beta,\gamma)=\overline{\tilde{\lambda}}(\alpha,\beta,\gamma),\\
&\vdots\\
&\overline{\tilde{X}}_n(\alpha,\beta,\gamma)=\overline{\tilde{\lambda}}(\alpha,\beta,\gamma)\overline{\tilde{X}}_{n-1}(\alpha,\beta,\gamma).
\end{aligned}
\tag{13.10}
$$

Rewriting, Eqs. (13.9) and (13.10) in matrix form, we have

$$
\begin{aligned}
&\begin{bmatrix}-\underline{\tilde{F}}_0(\alpha,\beta,\gamma) & 0 & \cdots & 0\\ 0 & I & \cdots & 0\\ \vdots & \vdots & \ddots & \vdots\\ 0 & 0 & \cdots & I\end{bmatrix}\begin{bmatrix}\underline{\tilde{X}}_1(\alpha,\beta,\gamma)\\ \underline{\tilde{X}}_2(\alpha,\beta,\gamma)\\ \vdots\\ \underline{\tilde{X}}_n(\alpha,\beta,\gamma)\end{bmatrix}\\
&=\underline{\tilde{\lambda}}(\alpha,\beta,\gamma)\begin{bmatrix}\underline{\tilde{F}}_1(\alpha,\beta,\gamma) & \cdots & \underline{\tilde{F}}_{n-1}(\alpha,\beta,\gamma) & \underline{\tilde{F}}_n(\alpha,\beta,\gamma)\\ I & \cdots & 0 & 0\\ \vdots & \ddots & \vdots & \vdots\\ 0 & \cdots & I & 0\end{bmatrix}\begin{bmatrix}\underline{\tilde{X}}_1(\alpha,\beta,\gamma)\\ \underline{\tilde{X}}_2(\alpha,\beta,\gamma)\\ \vdots\\ \underline{\tilde{X}}_n(\alpha,\beta,\gamma)\end{bmatrix}
\end{aligned}
\tag{13.11}
$$

and

$$
\begin{aligned}
&\begin{bmatrix}-\overline{\tilde{F}}_0(\alpha,\beta,\gamma) & 0 & \cdots & 0\\ 0 & I & \cdots & 0\\ \vdots & \vdots & \ddots & \vdots\\ 0 & 0 & \cdots & I\end{bmatrix}\begin{bmatrix}\overline{\tilde{X}}_1(\alpha,\beta,\gamma)\\ \overline{\tilde{X}}_2(\alpha,\beta,\gamma)\\ \vdots\\ \overline{\tilde{X}}_n(\alpha,\beta,\gamma)\end{bmatrix}\\
&=\overline{\tilde{\lambda}}(\alpha,\beta,\gamma)\begin{bmatrix}\overline{\tilde{F}}_1(\alpha,\beta,\gamma) & \cdots & \overline{\tilde{F}}_{n-1}(\alpha,\beta,\gamma) & \overline{\tilde{F}}_n(\alpha,\beta,\gamma)\\ I & \cdots & 0 & 0\\ \vdots & \ddots & \vdots & \vdots\\ 0 & \cdots & I & 0\end{bmatrix}\begin{bmatrix}\overline{\tilde{X}}_1(\alpha,\beta,\gamma)\\ \overline{\tilde{X}}_2(\alpha,\beta,\gamma)\\ \vdots\\ \overline{\tilde{X}}_n(\alpha,\beta,\gamma)\end{bmatrix}
\end{aligned}
\tag{13.12}
$$

Eqs. (13.11) and (13.12) are generalized linear eigenvalue problems involving the uncertainty handling parameters α, β, and γ. Both of these equations can be solved as discussed in Chapter 12 to obtain the LMF and UMF of the type-2 fuzzy eigenvalues associated with the original T2FNEP. Further, substituting particular values for α, β, and $\gamma \in [0, 1]$, different bounds of the type-2 fuzzy eigenvalues can be acquired.

13.4 Sample problems

Non-linear eigenvalue problems, in particular, Quadratic eigenvalue problems (QEPs) are frequently associated with dynamical challenges, particularly in mechanical and structural systems that include vibrations, stability, or dynamic response. In this regard, we will first discuss some numerical examples of quadratic eigenvalue problems under the type-2 fuzzy uncertain environment.

Example 13.1. Let us consider the following quadratic eigenvalue problem,

$$(\tilde{\tilde{F}}_0 + \tilde{\tilde{F}}_1\tilde{\tilde{\lambda}} + \tilde{\tilde{F}}_2\tilde{\tilde{\lambda}}^2)\tilde{\tilde{X}} = 0, \tag{13.13}$$

where

$$\tilde{\tilde{F}}_0 = \begin{bmatrix} \tilde{\tilde{f}}_{011} & \tilde{\tilde{f}}_{012} \\ \tilde{\tilde{f}}_{012} & \tilde{\tilde{f}}_{011} \end{bmatrix}, \tilde{\tilde{F}}_1 = \begin{bmatrix} \tilde{\tilde{f}}_{111} & \tilde{\tilde{f}}_{112} \\ \tilde{\tilde{f}}_{112} & \tilde{\tilde{f}}_{111} \end{bmatrix} \text{ and } \tilde{\tilde{F}}_2 = \begin{bmatrix} \tilde{\tilde{f}}_{211} & 0 \\ 0 & \tilde{\tilde{f}}_{211} \end{bmatrix}. \tag{13.14}$$

The entries are given by

$$\begin{aligned}
\tilde{\tilde{f}}_{011} &= (1, 2, 3, 4, 5, 6, 7), \\
\tilde{\tilde{f}}_{012} &= (-4.5, -4, -3.5, -3, -2.5, -2, -1.5, -0.5), \\
\tilde{\tilde{f}}_{111} &= (11.55, 11.7, 11.85, 12, 12.15, 12.3, 12.45), \\
\tilde{\tilde{f}}_{112} &= (-4.15, -4.1, -4.05, -4, -3.95, -3.9, -3.85), \\
\tilde{\tilde{f}}_{112} &= (1.7, 1.8, 1.9, 2, 2.1, 2.2, 2.2, 2.3).
\end{aligned} \tag{13.15}$$

Using the β-cut at α-plane representation of the type-2 fuzzy entries in the quadratic eigenvalue problem in Eq. (13.13), Eq. (13.13) will become

$$\begin{aligned}
&(\underline{\tilde{F}}_0(\alpha, \beta) + \underline{\tilde{F}}_1(\alpha, \beta)\underline{\tilde{\lambda}}(\alpha, \beta) + \underline{\tilde{F}}_2(\alpha, \beta)\underline{\tilde{\lambda}}^2(\alpha, \beta))\underline{\tilde{X}}(\alpha, \beta) = 0, \\
&(\overline{\tilde{F}}_0(\alpha, \beta) + \overline{\tilde{F}}_1(\alpha, \beta)\overline{\tilde{\lambda}}(\alpha, \beta) + \overline{\tilde{F}}_2(\alpha, \beta)\overline{\tilde{\lambda}}^2(\alpha, \beta))\overline{\tilde{X}}(\alpha, \beta) = 0.
\end{aligned} \tag{13.16}$$

The above two eigenvalue problems correspond to interval quadratic eigenvalue problems. Introducing another parameter $\gamma \in [0, 1]$, the interval problems in parametric form will be

$$\begin{aligned}
&(\underline{\tilde{F}}_0(\alpha, \beta, \gamma) + \underline{\tilde{F}}_1(\alpha, \beta, \gamma)\underline{\tilde{\lambda}}(\alpha, \beta, \gamma) + \underline{\tilde{F}}_2(\alpha, \beta, \gamma)\underline{\tilde{\lambda}}^2(\alpha, \beta, \gamma))\underline{\tilde{X}}(\alpha, \beta, \gamma) = 0, \\
&(\overline{\tilde{F}}_0(\alpha, \beta, \gamma) + \overline{\tilde{F}}_1(\alpha, \beta, \gamma)\overline{\tilde{\lambda}}(\alpha, \beta, \gamma) + \overline{\tilde{F}}_2(\alpha, \beta, \gamma)\overline{\tilde{\lambda}}^2(\alpha, \beta, \gamma))\overline{\tilde{X}}(\alpha, \beta, \gamma) = 0,
\end{aligned} \tag{13.17}$$

where

$$\begin{aligned}
\underline{\tilde{F}}_0(\alpha,\beta,\gamma) &= \begin{bmatrix} \underline{\tilde{f}}_{011}(\alpha,\beta,\gamma) & \underline{\tilde{f}}_{012}(\alpha,\beta,\gamma) \\ \underline{\tilde{f}}_{012}(\alpha,\beta,\gamma) & \underline{\tilde{f}}_{011}(\alpha,\beta,\gamma) \end{bmatrix}, \\
\underline{\tilde{F}}_1(\alpha,\beta,\gamma) &= \begin{bmatrix} \underline{\tilde{f}}_{111}(\alpha,\beta,\gamma) & \underline{\tilde{f}}_{112}(\alpha,\beta,\gamma) \\ \underline{\tilde{f}}_{112}(\alpha,\beta,\gamma) & \underline{\tilde{f}}_{111}(\alpha,\beta,\gamma) \end{bmatrix}, \\
\underline{\tilde{F}}_2(\alpha,\beta,\gamma) &= \begin{bmatrix} \underline{\tilde{f}}_{211}(\alpha,\beta,\gamma) & 0 \\ 0 & \underline{\tilde{f}}_{211}(\alpha,\beta,\gamma) \end{bmatrix},
\end{aligned} \tag{13.18}$$

$$\begin{aligned}
\overline{\tilde{F}}_0(\alpha,\beta,\gamma) &= \begin{bmatrix} \overline{\tilde{f}}_{011}(\alpha,\beta,\gamma) & \overline{\tilde{f}}_{012}(\alpha,\beta,\gamma) \\ \overline{\tilde{f}}_{012}(\alpha,\beta,\gamma) & \overline{\tilde{f}}_{011}(\alpha,\beta,\gamma) \end{bmatrix}, \\
\overline{\tilde{F}}_1(\alpha,\beta,\gamma) &= \begin{bmatrix} \overline{\tilde{f}}_{111}(\alpha,\beta,\gamma) & \overline{\tilde{f}}_{112}(\alpha,\beta,\gamma) \\ \overline{\tilde{f}}_{112}(\alpha,\beta,\gamma) & \overline{\tilde{f}}_{111}(\alpha,\beta,\gamma) \end{bmatrix}, \\
\overline{\tilde{F}}_2(\alpha,\beta,\gamma) &= \begin{bmatrix} \overline{\tilde{f}}_{211}(\alpha,\beta,\gamma) & 0 \\ 0 & \overline{\tilde{f}}_{211}(\alpha,\beta,\gamma) \end{bmatrix}.
\end{aligned} \tag{13.19}$$

The entries associated with above equations are given by

$$\begin{aligned}
\underline{\tilde{f}}_{011}(\alpha,\beta,\gamma) &= 2\beta - \gamma(4\beta + 2(\alpha-1)(\beta-1) - 4) + (\alpha-1)(\beta-1) + 2, \\
\overline{\tilde{f}}_{011}(\alpha,\beta,\gamma) &= 2\beta + \gamma(2(\alpha-1)(\beta-1) - 4\beta + 4) - (\alpha-1)(\beta-1) + 2, \\
\underline{\tilde{f}}_{012}(\alpha,\beta,\gamma) &= \beta - \gamma\left(\frac{5\beta}{2} + \left(\frac{\beta}{2} - \frac{1}{2}\right)(\alpha-1) + (\alpha-1)(\beta-1) - \frac{5}{2}\right) \\
&\quad + \left(\frac{\beta}{2} - \frac{1}{2}\right)(\alpha-1) - 4, \\
\overline{\tilde{f}}_{012}(\alpha,\beta,\gamma) &= \beta + \gamma\left(\left(\frac{\beta}{2} - \frac{1}{2}\right)(\alpha-1) - \frac{5\beta}{2} + (\alpha-1)(\beta-1) + \frac{5}{2}\right) \\
&\quad - \left(\frac{\beta}{2} - \frac{1}{2}\right)(\alpha-1) - 4, \\
\underline{\tilde{f}}_{111}(\alpha,\beta,\gamma) &= \frac{3\beta}{10} - \gamma\left(\frac{3\beta}{5} + 2\left(\frac{3\beta}{20} - \frac{3}{20}\right)(\alpha-1) - \frac{3}{5}\right) \\
&\quad + \left(\frac{3\beta}{20} - \frac{3}{20}\right)(\alpha-1) + \frac{117}{10}, \\
\overline{\tilde{f}}_{111}(\alpha,\beta,\gamma) &= \frac{3\beta}{10} + \gamma\left(2\left(\frac{3\beta}{20} - \frac{3}{20}\right)(\alpha-1) - \frac{3\beta}{5} + \frac{3}{5}\right) \\
&\quad - \left(\frac{3\beta}{20} - \frac{3}{20}\right)(\alpha-1) + \frac{117}{10}, \\
\underline{\tilde{f}}_{112}(\alpha,\beta,\gamma) &= \frac{\beta}{10} - \gamma\left(\frac{\beta}{5} + 2\left(\frac{\beta}{20} - \frac{1}{20}\right)(\alpha-1) - \frac{1}{5}\right)
\end{aligned} \tag{13.20}$$

$$+\left(\frac{\beta}{20}-\frac{1}{20}\right)(\alpha-1)-\frac{41}{10},$$

$$\overline{\tilde{f}}_{112}(\alpha,\beta,\gamma)=\frac{\beta}{10}+\gamma\left(2\left(\frac{\beta}{20}-\frac{1}{20}\right)(\alpha-1)-\frac{\beta}{5}+\frac{1}{5}\right)$$
$$-\left(\frac{\beta}{20}-\frac{1}{20}\right)(\alpha-1)-\frac{41}{10},$$

$$\underline{\tilde{f}}_{211}(\alpha,\beta,\gamma)=\frac{\beta}{5}-\gamma\left(2\left(\frac{\beta}{10}-\frac{1}{10}\right)(\alpha-1)-\frac{2\beta}{5}+\frac{2}{5}\right)$$
$$-\left(\frac{\beta}{10}-\frac{1}{10}\right)(\alpha-1)+\frac{9}{5},$$

$$\overline{\tilde{f}}_{211}(\alpha,\beta,\gamma)=\frac{\beta}{5}+\gamma\left(2\left(\frac{\beta}{10}-\frac{1}{10}\right)(\alpha-1)-\frac{2\beta}{5}+\frac{2}{5}\right)$$
$$-\left(\frac{\beta}{10}-\frac{1}{10}\right)(\alpha-1)+\frac{9}{5}.$$

Now, following the linearization process, the above quadratic eigenvalue problems will become

$$\begin{bmatrix}-\underline{\tilde{F}}_0(\alpha,\beta,\gamma) & 0\\ 0 & I\end{bmatrix}\begin{bmatrix}\underline{\tilde{X}}_1(\alpha,\beta,\gamma)\\ \underline{\tilde{X}}_2(\alpha,\beta,\gamma)\end{bmatrix}=\underline{\tilde{\lambda}}(\alpha,\beta,\gamma)\begin{bmatrix}\underline{\tilde{F}}_1(\alpha,\beta,\gamma) & \underline{\tilde{F}}_2(\alpha,\beta,\gamma)\\ I & 0\end{bmatrix}\begin{bmatrix}\underline{\tilde{X}}_1(\alpha,\beta,\gamma)\\ \underline{\tilde{X}}_2(\alpha,\beta,\gamma)\end{bmatrix} \tag{13.21}$$

and

$$\begin{bmatrix}-\overline{\tilde{F}}_0(\alpha,\beta,\gamma) & 0\\ 0 & I\end{bmatrix}\begin{bmatrix}\overline{\tilde{X}}_1(\alpha,\beta,\gamma)\\ \overline{\tilde{X}}_2(\alpha,\beta,\gamma)\end{bmatrix}=\overline{\tilde{\lambda}}(\alpha,\beta,\gamma)\begin{bmatrix}\overline{\tilde{F}}_1(\alpha,\beta,\gamma) & \overline{\tilde{F}}_2(\alpha,\beta,\gamma)\\ I & 0\end{bmatrix}\begin{bmatrix}\overline{\tilde{X}}_1(\alpha,\beta,\gamma)\\ \overline{\tilde{X}}_2(\alpha,\beta,\gamma)\end{bmatrix}. \tag{13.22}$$

The above generalized eigenvalue problems can be solved for the eigenvalue $\underline{\tilde{\lambda}}(\alpha,\beta,\gamma)$ and $\overline{\tilde{\lambda}}(\alpha,\beta,\gamma)$ in terms of α, β, and γ. Combining the LMF and UMF solution of the eigenvalue, and substituting different values for α, β, and γ the type-2 fuzzy eigenvalues can be obtained.

The acquired type-2 fuzzy eigenvalues are

$$\begin{aligned}\tilde{\tilde{\lambda}}_1&=(-1.0515,-0.6445,-0.3333,-0.1291,0.0631,0.2485,0.4304),\\ \tilde{\tilde{\lambda}}_2&=(-0.4982,-0.4964,-0.4946,-0.4644,-0.4310,-0.3977,-0.3647),\\ \tilde{\tilde{\lambda}}_3&=(-4.7833,-4.4707,-4.1683,-3.8708,-3.5714,-3.1736,-2.6876),\\ \tilde{\tilde{\lambda}}_4&=(-8.8705,-8.3800,-7.9374,-7.5355,-7.1684,-6.8672,-6.5923).\end{aligned} \tag{13.23}$$

The plots of the obtained eigenvalues are illustrated in Fig. 13.1. Further, the bounds of the third and fourth eigenvalues, i.e., $\tilde{\tilde{\lambda}}_3$ and $\tilde{\tilde{\lambda}}_4$ are shown in Tables 13.1 and 13.2 for different values of α and β.

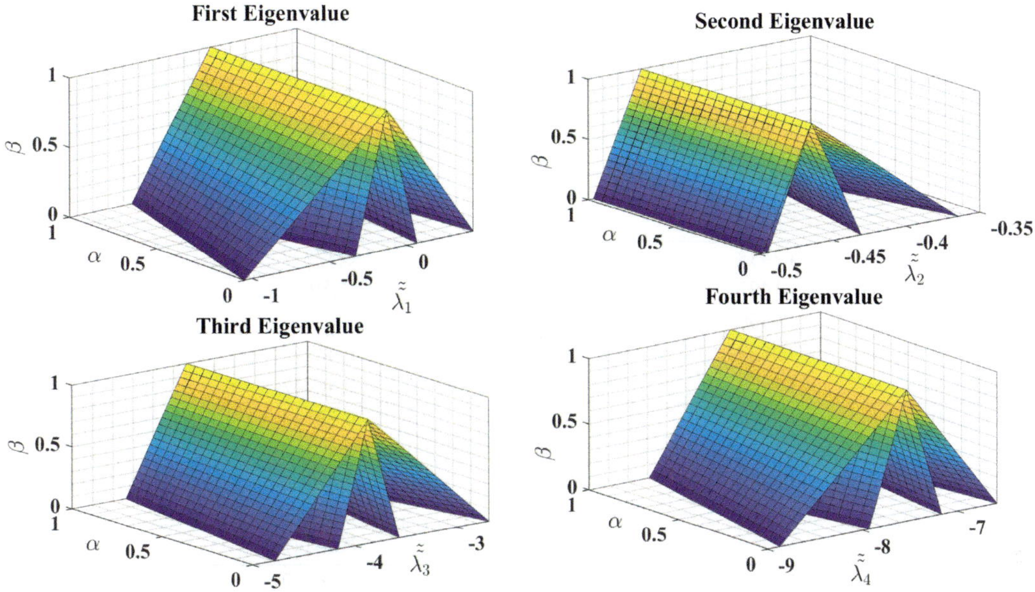

FIGURE 13.1 Plot of the obtained eigenvalues for Example 13.1.

Example 13.2. Suppose we have a type-2 fuzzy quadratic eigenvalue problem, given by

$$(\tilde{\tilde{F}}_0 + \tilde{\tilde{F}}_1\tilde{\tilde{\lambda}} + \tilde{\tilde{F}}_2\tilde{\tilde{\lambda}}^2)\tilde{\tilde{X}} = 0, \tag{13.24}$$

where

$$\tilde{\tilde{F}}_0 = \begin{bmatrix} \tilde{\tilde{f}}_{011} & \tilde{\tilde{f}}_{012} & 0 \\ \tilde{\tilde{f}}_{012} & \tilde{\tilde{f}}_{011} & \tilde{\tilde{f}}_{012} \\ 0 & \tilde{\tilde{f}}_{012} & \tilde{\tilde{f}}_{011} \end{bmatrix}, \quad \tilde{\tilde{F}}_1 = \begin{bmatrix} \tilde{\tilde{f}}_{111} & \tilde{\tilde{f}}_{112} & 0 \\ \tilde{\tilde{f}}_{112} & \tilde{\tilde{f}}_{111} & \tilde{\tilde{f}}_{112} \\ 0 & \tilde{\tilde{f}}_{112} & \tilde{\tilde{f}}_{111} \end{bmatrix}, \quad \tilde{\tilde{F}}_2 = \begin{bmatrix} \tilde{\tilde{f}}_{211} & 0 & 0 \\ 0 & \tilde{\tilde{f}}_{222} & 0 \\ 0 & 0 & \tilde{\tilde{f}}_{233} \end{bmatrix}, \tag{13.25}$$

and

$$\begin{aligned} \tilde{\tilde{f}}_{011} &= (8.94, 8.96, 8.98, 9, 9.02, 9.04, 9.06), \\ \tilde{\tilde{f}}_{012} &= (-3.03, -3.02, -3.01, -3, -2.99, -2.98, -2.97), \\ \tilde{\tilde{f}}_{111} &= (11.94, 11.96, 11.98, 12, 12.02, 12.04, 12.06), \\ \tilde{\tilde{f}}_{112} &= (-4.03, -4.02, -4.01, -4, -3.99, -3.98, -3.97), \\ \tilde{\tilde{f}}_{211} &= (1.97, 1.98, 1.99, 2, 2.01, 2.02, 2.03), \\ \tilde{\tilde{f}}_{022} &= (1.96, 1.97, 1.98, 1.99, 2, 2.01, 2.02), \\ \tilde{\tilde{f}}_{033} &= (1.85, 1.87, 1.89, 1.91, 1.93, 1.95, 1.97). \end{aligned} \tag{13.26}$$

Table 13.1 Bounds of type-2 fuzzy eigenvalue $\tilde{\tilde{\lambda}}_3$ for Example 13.1.

α	β	Left bound (LMF)	Right bound (LMF)	Left bound (UMF)	Right bound (UMF)
0	0	−4.1684	−3.5714	−0.36472	−0.49465
0	0.25	−4.0938	−3.6469	−0.38949	−0.48708
0	0.5	−4.0194	−3.7219	−0.41436	−0.47953
0	0.75	−3.9451	−3.7965	−0.43935	−0.47199
0	1	−3.8708	−3.8708	−0.46447	−0.46447
0.25	0	−4.2433	−3.4762	−0.37297	−0.49509
0.25	0.25	−4.1497	−3.5766	−0.3957	−0.48741
0.25	0.5	−4.0566	−3.6756	−0.41852	−0.47975
0.25	0.75	−3.9637	−3.7735	−0.44143	−0.4721
0.25	1	−3.8708	−3.8708	−0.46447	−0.46447
0.5	0	−4.3186	−3.3786	−0.38123	−0.49554
0.5	0.25	−4.2058	−3.5052	−0.40192	−0.48775
0.5	0.5	−4.0938	−3.6289	−0.42268	−0.47997
0.5	0.75	−3.9822	−3.7505	−0.44352	−0.47221
0.5	1	−3.8708	−3.8708	−0.46447	−0.46447
0.75	0	−4.3944	−3.2781	−0.38949	−0.49598
0.75	0.25	−4.2621	−3.4326	−0.40814	−0.48808
0.75	0.5	−4.1311	−3.5818	−0.42684	−0.48019
0.75	0.75	−4.0008	−3.7275	−0.44561	−0.47232
0.75	1	−3.8708	−3.8708	−0.46447	−0.46447
1	0	−4.4708	−3.1737	−0.39777	−0.49643
1	0.25	−4.3186	−3.3584	−0.41436	−0.48841
1	0.5	−4.1684	−3.5342	−0.431	−0.48041
1	0.75	−4.0194	−3.7043	−0.4477	−0.47243
1	1	−3.8708	−3.8708	−0.46447	−0.46447

Now, using the triple parametric representation of the type-2 fuzzy numbers in the given type-2 fuzzy quadratic eigenvalue problem, the given problem will be

$$\begin{aligned}
&(\underline{\tilde{F}}_0(\alpha,\beta,\gamma)+\underline{\tilde{F}}_1(\alpha,\beta,\gamma)\underline{\tilde{\lambda}}(\alpha,\beta,\gamma)+\underline{\tilde{F}}_2(\alpha,\beta,\gamma)\underline{\tilde{\lambda}}^2(\alpha,\beta,\gamma))\underline{\tilde{X}}(\alpha,\beta,\gamma)=0,\\
&(\overline{\tilde{F}}_0(\alpha,\beta,\gamma)+\overline{\tilde{F}}_1(\alpha,\beta,\gamma)\overline{\tilde{\lambda}}(\alpha,\beta,\gamma)+\overline{\tilde{F}}_2(\alpha,\beta,\gamma)\overline{\tilde{\lambda}}^2(\alpha,\beta,\gamma))\overline{\tilde{X}}(\alpha,\beta,\gamma)=0,
\end{aligned} \tag{13.27}$$

where

$$\underline{\tilde{F}}_0(\alpha,\beta,\gamma)=\begin{bmatrix}\underline{\tilde{f}}_{011}(\alpha,\beta,\gamma) & \underline{\tilde{f}}_{012}(\alpha,\beta,\gamma) & 0\\ \underline{\tilde{f}}_{012}(\alpha,\beta,\gamma) & \underline{\tilde{f}}_{011}(\alpha,\beta,\gamma) & \underline{\tilde{f}}_{012}(\alpha,\beta,\gamma)\\ 0 & \underline{\tilde{f}}_{012}(\alpha,\beta,\gamma) & \underline{\tilde{f}}_{011}(\alpha,\beta,\gamma)\end{bmatrix},$$

$$\underline{\tilde{F}}_1(\alpha,\beta,\gamma)=\begin{bmatrix}\underline{\tilde{f}}_{111}(\alpha,\beta,\gamma) & \underline{\tilde{f}}_{112}(\alpha,\beta,\gamma) & 0\\ \underline{\tilde{f}}_{112}(\alpha,\beta,\gamma) & \underline{\tilde{f}}_{111}(\alpha,\beta,\gamma) & \underline{\tilde{f}}_{112}(\alpha,\beta,\gamma)\\ 0 & \underline{\tilde{f}}_{112}(\alpha,\beta,\gamma) & \underline{\tilde{f}}_{111}(\alpha,\beta,\gamma)\end{bmatrix}, \tag{13.28}$$

Table 13.2 Bounds of type-2 fuzzy eigenvalue $\tilde{\tilde{\lambda}}_4$ for Example 13.1.

α	β	Left bound (LMF)	Right bound (LMF)	Left bound (UMF)	Right bound (UMF)
0	0	−7.9374	−7.1685	−8.8706	−6.5923
0	0.25	−7.8334	−7.2572	−8.4978	−6.8051
0	0.5	−7.7318	−7.348	−8.1532	−7.0321
0	0.75	−7.6325	−7.4407	−7.8334	−7.275
0	1	−7.5355	−7.5355	−7.5355	−7.5355
0.25	0	−8.044	−7.0905	−8.743	−6.6588
0.25	0.25	−7.9112	−7.1972	−8.4092	−6.8582
0.25	0.5	−7.7823	−7.3068	−8.0983	−7.07
0.25	0.75	−7.6571	−7.4195	−7.8078	−7.2953
0.25	1	−7.5355	−7.5355	−7.5355	−7.5355
0.5	0	−8.1532	−7.0143	−8.6188	−6.7267
0.5	0.25	−7.9904	−7.1381	−8.3222	−6.9123
0.5	0.5	−7.8334	−7.2661	−8.044	−7.1083
0.5	0.75	−7.6819	−7.3985	−7.7823	−7.3157
0.5	1	−7.5355	−7.5355	−7.5355	−7.5355
0.75	0	−8.2652	−6.9399	−8.4978	−6.7962
0.75	0.25	−8.071	−7.0802	−8.2369	−6.9673
0.75	0.5	−7.8851	−7.226	−7.9904	−7.147
0.75	0.75	−7.7068	−7.3776	−7.757	−7.3362
0.75	1	−7.5355	−7.5355	−7.5355	−7.5355
1	0	−8.38	−6.8672	−8.38	−6.8672
1	0.25	−8.1532	−7.0232	−8.1532	−7.0232
1	0.5	−7.9374	−7.1863	−7.9374	−7.1863
1	0.75	−7.7318	−7.3568	−7.7318	−7.3568
1	1	−7.5355	−7.5355	−7.5355	−7.5355

$$\underline{\tilde{F}}_2(\alpha,\beta,\gamma)=\begin{bmatrix}\underline{\tilde{f}}_{211}(\alpha,\beta,\gamma) & 0 & 0\\ 0 & \underline{\tilde{f}}_{222}(\alpha,\beta,\gamma) & 0\\ 0 & 0 & \underline{\tilde{f}}_{233}(\alpha,\beta,\gamma)\end{bmatrix}.$$

,

$$\overline{\tilde{F}}_0(\alpha,\beta,\gamma)=\begin{bmatrix}\overline{\tilde{f}}_{011}(\alpha,\beta,\gamma) & \overline{\tilde{f}}_{012}(\alpha,\beta,\gamma) & 0\\ \overline{\tilde{f}}_{012}(\alpha,\beta,\gamma) & \overline{\tilde{f}}_{011}(\alpha,\beta,\gamma) & \overline{\tilde{f}}_{012}(\alpha,\beta,\gamma)\\ 0 & \overline{\tilde{f}}_{012}(\alpha,\beta,\gamma) & \overline{\tilde{f}}_{011}(\alpha,\beta,\gamma)\end{bmatrix},$$

$$\overline{\tilde{F}}_1(\alpha,\beta,\gamma)=\begin{bmatrix}\overline{\tilde{f}}_{111}(\alpha,\beta,\gamma) & \overline{\tilde{f}}_{112}(\alpha,\beta,\gamma) & 0\\ \overline{\tilde{f}}_{112}(\alpha,\beta,\gamma) & \overline{\tilde{f}}_{111}(\alpha,\beta,\gamma) & \overline{\tilde{f}}_{112}(\alpha,\beta,\gamma)\\ 0 & \overline{\tilde{f}}_{112}(\alpha,\beta,\gamma) & \overline{\tilde{f}}_{111}(\alpha,\beta,\gamma)\end{bmatrix}, \tag{13.29}$$

$$\overline{\tilde{F}}_2(\alpha,\beta,\gamma)=\begin{bmatrix}\overline{\tilde{f}}_{211}(\alpha,\beta,\gamma) & 0 & 0\\ 0 & \overline{\tilde{f}}_{222}(\alpha,\beta,\gamma) & 0\\ 0 & 0 & \overline{\tilde{f}}_{233}(\alpha,\beta,\gamma)\end{bmatrix},$$

and

$$\begin{aligned}
\underline{\tilde{f}}_{011}(\alpha,\beta,\gamma)&=\frac{\beta}{25}-\gamma\left(\frac{2\beta}{25}+2\left(\frac{\beta}{50}-\frac{1}{50}\right)(\alpha-1)-\frac{2}{25}\right)+\left(\frac{\beta}{50}-\frac{1}{50}\right)(\alpha-1)+\frac{224}{25},\\
\underline{\tilde{f}}_{012}(\alpha,\beta,\gamma)&=\frac{\beta}{50}-\gamma\left(\frac{\beta}{25}+2\left(\frac{\beta}{100}-\frac{1}{100}\right)(\alpha-1)-\frac{1}{25}\right)+\left(\frac{\beta}{100}-\frac{1}{100}\right)(\alpha-1)-\frac{151}{50},\\
\underline{\tilde{f}}_{111}(\alpha,\beta,\gamma)&=\frac{\beta}{25}-\gamma\left(\frac{2\beta}{25}+2\left(\frac{\beta}{50}-\frac{1}{50}\right)(\alpha-1)-\frac{2}{25}\right)+\left(\frac{\beta}{50}-\frac{1}{50}\right)(\alpha-1)+\frac{299}{25},\\
\underline{\tilde{f}}_{112}(\alpha,\beta,\gamma)&=\frac{\beta}{50}-\gamma\left(\frac{\beta}{25}+2\left(\frac{\beta}{100}-\frac{1}{100}\right)(\alpha-1)-\frac{1}{25}\right)+\left(\frac{\beta}{100}-\frac{1}{100}\right)(\alpha-1)-\frac{201}{50},\\
\underline{\tilde{f}}_{211}(\alpha,\beta,\gamma)&=\frac{\beta}{50}+(\alpha-1)\left(\frac{\beta}{100}-\frac{1}{100}\right)-\gamma\left(\frac{\beta}{25}+2(\alpha-1)\left(\frac{\beta}{100}-\frac{1}{100}\right)-\frac{1}{25}\right)+\frac{99}{50},\\
\underline{\tilde{f}}_{222}(\alpha,\beta,\gamma)&=\frac{\beta}{50}-\gamma\left(\frac{\beta}{25}+2\left(\frac{\beta}{100}-\frac{1}{100}\right)(\alpha-1)-\frac{1}{25}\right)+\left(\frac{\beta}{100}-\frac{1}{100}\right)(\alpha-1)+\frac{197}{100},\\
\underline{\tilde{f}}_{233}(\alpha,\beta,\gamma)&=\frac{\beta}{25}-\gamma\left(\frac{2\beta}{25}+2\left(\frac{\beta}{50}-\frac{1}{50}\right)(\alpha-1)-\frac{2}{25}\right)+\left(\frac{\beta}{50}-\frac{1}{50}\right)(\alpha-1)+\frac{187}{100},\\
\overline{\tilde{f}}_{011}(\alpha,\beta,\gamma)&=\frac{\beta}{25}+\gamma\left(2\left(\frac{\beta}{50}-\frac{1}{50}\right)(\alpha-1)-\frac{2\beta}{25}+\frac{2}{25}\right)-\left(\frac{\beta}{50}-\frac{1}{50}\right)(\alpha-1)+\frac{224}{25},\\
\overline{\tilde{f}}_{012}(\alpha,\beta,\gamma)&=\frac{\beta}{50}+\gamma\left(2\left(\frac{\beta}{100}-\frac{1}{100}\right)(\alpha-1)-\frac{\beta}{25}+\frac{1}{25}\right)-\left(\frac{\beta}{100}-\frac{1}{100}\right)(\alpha-1)-\frac{151}{50},\\
\overline{\tilde{f}}_{111}(\alpha,\beta,\gamma)&=\frac{\beta}{25}+\gamma\left(2\left(\frac{\beta}{50}-\frac{1}{50}\right)(\alpha-1)-\frac{2\beta}{25}+\frac{2}{25}\right)-\left(\frac{\beta}{50}-\frac{1}{50}\right)(\alpha-1)+\frac{299}{25},\\
\overline{\tilde{f}}_{112}(\alpha,\beta,\gamma)&=\frac{\beta}{50}+\gamma\left(2\left(\frac{\beta}{100}-\frac{1}{100}\right)(\alpha-1)-\frac{\beta}{25}+\frac{1}{25}\right)-\left(\frac{\beta}{100}-\frac{1}{100}\right)(\alpha-1)-\frac{201}{50},\\
\overline{\tilde{f}}_{211}(\alpha,\beta,\gamma)&=\frac{\beta}{50}+\gamma\left(2\left(\frac{\beta}{100}-\frac{1}{100}\right)(\alpha-1)-\frac{\beta}{25}+\frac{1}{25}\right)-\left(\frac{\beta}{100}-\frac{1}{100}\right)(\alpha-1)+\frac{99}{50},\\
\overline{\tilde{f}}_{222}(\alpha,\beta,\gamma)&=\frac{\beta}{50}+\gamma\left(2\left(\frac{\beta}{100}-\frac{1}{100}\right)(\alpha-1)-\frac{\beta}{25}+\frac{1}{25}\right)-\left(\frac{\beta}{100}-\frac{1}{100}\right)(\alpha-1)+\frac{197}{100},\\
\overline{\tilde{f}}_{233}(\alpha,\beta,\gamma)&=\frac{\beta}{25}+\gamma\left(2\left(\frac{\beta}{50}-\frac{1}{50}\right)(\alpha-1)-\frac{2\beta}{25}+\frac{2}{25}\right)-\left(\frac{\beta}{50}-\frac{1}{50}\right)(\alpha-1)+\frac{187}{100}.
\end{aligned}\tag{13.30}$$

Now, following the linearization process separately on the equations in (13.27), the nonlinear eigenvalue problems can be transformed into two generalized eigenvalue problems. Solving these generalized eigenvalue problems, one can obtain the LMF and UMF of the type-2 fuzzy eigenvalues in terms of α, β, and γ. Combining the LMF and UMF solutions

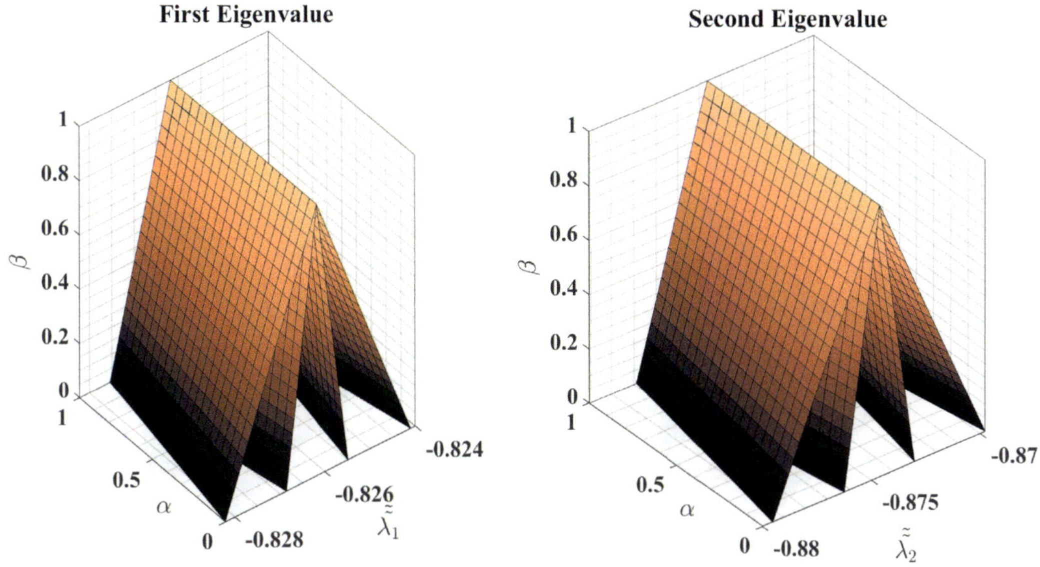

FIGURE 13.2 Plot of the first and second eigenvalues for Example 13.2.

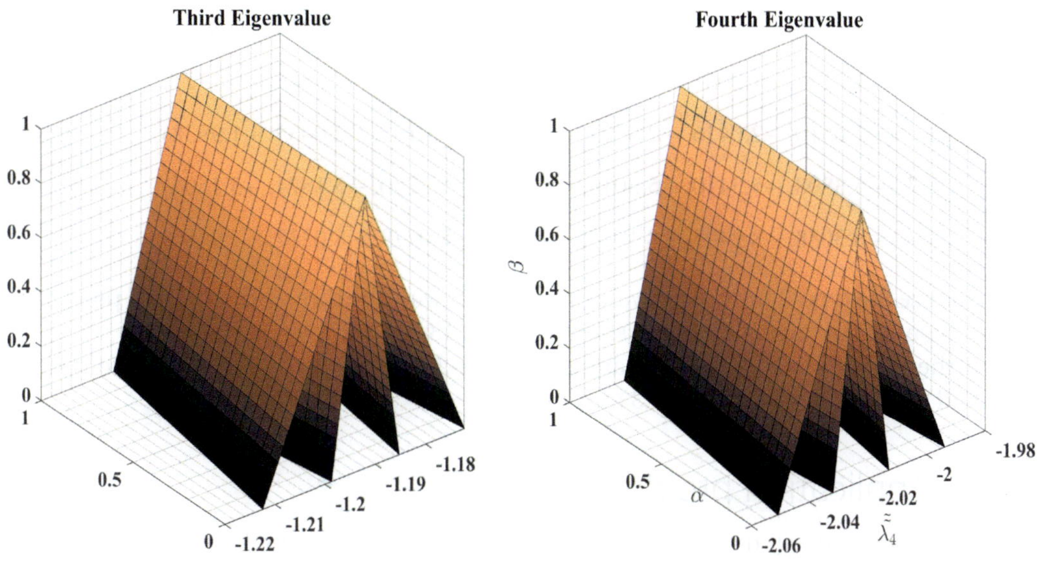

FIGURE 13.3 Plot of the third and fourth eigenvalues for Example 13.2.

and substituting different values to α, β, and γ, the obtained type-2 fuzzy eigenvalues are

$$\tilde{\tilde{\lambda}}_1 = (-0.8282, -0.8275, -0.8268, -0.8261, -0.8254, -0.8248, -0.8241),$$

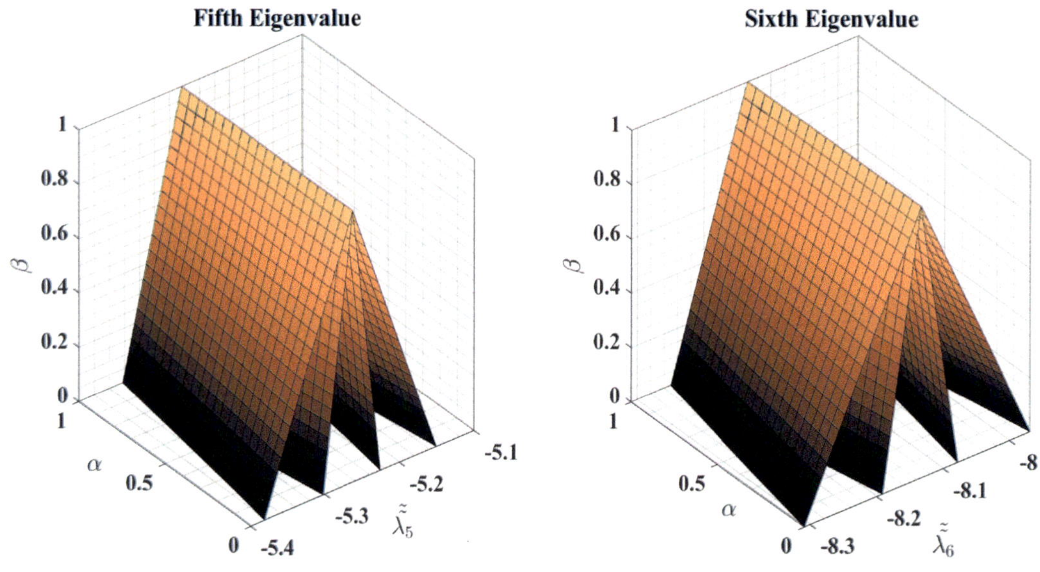

FIGURE 13.4 Plot of the fifth and sixth eigenvalues for Example 13.2.

$$
\begin{aligned}
\tilde{\tilde{\lambda}}_2 &= (-0.8795, -0.8778, -0.8762, -0.8746, -0.8730, -0.8713, -0.8697),\\
\tilde{\tilde{\lambda}}_3 &= (-1.2124, -1.2055, -1.1986, -1.1919, -1.1852, -1.1786, -1.1721),\\
\tilde{\tilde{\lambda}}_4 &= (-2.0510, -2.0416, -2.0322, -2.0227, -2.0132, -2.0035, -1.9938),\\
\tilde{\tilde{\lambda}}_5 &= (-5.3808, -5.3410, -5.3018, -5.2632, -5.2250, -5.1874, -5.1504),\\
\tilde{\tilde{\lambda}}_6 &= (-8.3088, -8.2495, -8.1913, -8.1341, -8.0779, -8.0227, -7.9685).
\end{aligned}
\tag{13.31}
$$

To visualize the type-2 fuzzy eigenvalues in a better way, the three-dimensional plots of the above type-2 fuzzy eigenvalues are shown in Figs. 13.2–13.4.

Further, the bounds of the fifth and sixth type-2 fuzzy eigenvalues for different values of α and β are shown in Tables 13.3 and 13.4.

13.5 Application problems

In this section, we will discus application problems related to the non-linear eigenvalue problems in the type-2 fuzzy uncertain environment using the proposed approach.

13.5.1 Damped spring-mass system

Let us consider a damped spring mass system as shown in Fig. 13.5. Here, we have considered the stiffness, mass, and the damping factors as uncertain. To handle the uncertainty in the model TPQT2FNs are used. Let $\tilde{\tilde{m}}_i$, for $i = 1, 2, 3, 4$ be the type-2 fuzzy mass of the

Table 13.3 Bounds of type-2 fuzzy eigenvalue $\tilde{\tilde{\lambda}}_5$ for Example 13.2.

α	β	Left bound (LMF)	Right bound (LMF)	Left bound (UMF)	Right bound (UMF)
0	0	−5.3019	−5.2251	−5.3808	−5.1504
0	0.25	−5.2922	−5.2346	−5.3514	−5.1786
0	0.5	−5.2825	−5.2441	−5.3220	−5.2068
0	0.75	−5.2729	−5.2537	−5.2926	−5.2350
0	1	−5.2632	−5.2632	−5.2632	−5.2632
0.25	0	−5.3117	−5.2157	−5.3709	−5.1597
0.25	0.25	−5.2996	−5.2276	−5.3440	−5.1856
0.25	0.5	−5.2874	−5.2394	−5.3170	−5.2114
0.25	0.75	−5.2753	−5.2513	−5.2901	−5.2373
0.25	1	−5.2632	−5.2632	−5.2632	−5.2632
0.5	0	−5.3215	−5.2063	−5.3609	−5.1689
0.5	0.25	−5.3069	−5.2205	−5.3365	−5.1925
0.5	0.5	−5.2923	−5.2347	−5.3121	−5.2161
0.5	0.75	−5.2778	−5.2490	−5.2876	−5.2396
0.5	1	−5.2632	−5.2632	−5.2632	−5.2632
0.75	0	−5.3313	−5.1969	−5.3510	−5.1782
0.75	0.25	−5.3143	−5.2135	−5.3291	−5.1995
0.75	0.5	−5.2972	−5.2300	−5.3071	−5.2207
0.75	0.75	−5.2802	−5.2466	−5.2852	−5.2420
0.75	1	−5.2632	−5.2632	−5.2632	−5.2632
1	0	−5.3411	−5.1875	−5.3411	−5.1875
1	0.25	−5.3216	−5.2064	−5.3216	−5.2064
1	0.5	−5.3021	−5.2253	−5.3021	−5.2253
1	0.75	−5.2827	−5.2443	−5.2827	−5.2443
1	1	−5.2632	−5.2632	−5.2632	−5.2632

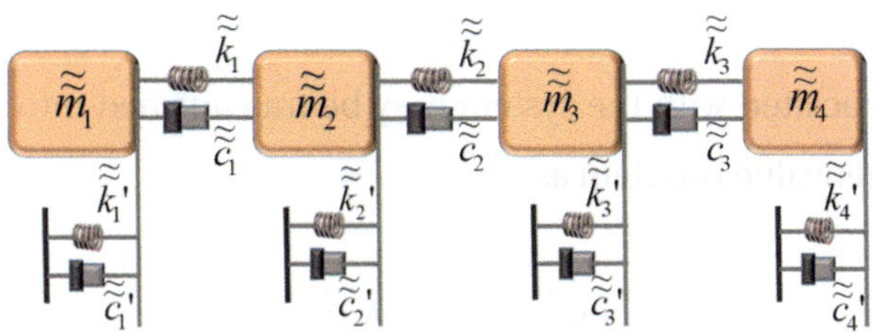

FIGURE 13.5 Schematic diagram of four degrees of freedom damped spring-mass system.

ith object. Let $\tilde{\tilde{k}}_i$ and $\tilde{\tilde{c}}_i$ be the type-2 fuzzy spring constant of the string and type-2 fuzzy damping constant of the damper that connects the object of mass $\tilde{\tilde{m}}_i$ with the object of mass $\tilde{\tilde{m}}_{i+1}$. Further, each object is grounded by springs and dampers, which are also assumed to be uncertain. Suppose $\tilde{\tilde{k}}_i'$ and $\tilde{\tilde{c}}_i'$ are the spring constant and damping constants of the spring and damper that connects the mass $\tilde{\tilde{m}}_i$ with the ground. The governing differ-

Table 13.4 Bounds of type-2 fuzzy eigenvalue $\tilde{\tilde{\lambda}}_6$ for Example 13.2.

α	β	Left bound (LMF)	Right bound (LMF)	Left bound (UMF)	Right bound (UMF)
0	0	−8.1913	−8.0779	−8.3088	−7.9685
0	0.25	−8.1770	−8.0920	−8.2652	−8.0099
0	0.5	−8.1627	−8.1060	−8.2215	−8.0513
0	0.75	−8.1484	−8.1201	−8.1778	−8.0927
0	1	−8.1341	−8.1341	−8.1341	−8.1341
0.25	0	−8.2059	−8.0642	−8.2940	−7.9821
0.25	0.25	−8.1879	−8.0816	−8.2540	−8.0201
0.25	0.5	−8.1700	−8.0991	−8.2141	−8.0581
0.25	0.75	−8.1521	−8.1166	−8.1741	−8.0961
0.25	1	−8.1341	−8.1341	−8.1341	−8.1341
0.5	0	−8.2204	−8.0504	−8.2792	−7.9957
0.5	0.25	−8.1988	−8.0713	−8.2429	−8.0303
0.5	0.5	−8.1773	−8.0922	−8.2067	−8.0649
0.5	0.75	−8.1557	−8.1132	−8.1704	−8.0995
0.5	1	−8.1341	−8.1341	−8.1341	−8.1341
0.75	0	−8.2350	−8.0366	−8.2644	−8.0092
0.75	0.25	−8.2098	−8.0610	−8.2318	−8.0404
0.75	0.5	−8.1845	−8.0853	−8.1992	−8.0717
0.75	0.75	−8.1593	−8.1097	−8.1667	−8.1029
0.75	1	−8.1341	−8.1341	−8.1341	−8.1341
1	0	−8.2495	−8.0228	−8.2495	−8.0228
1	0.25	−8.2207	−8.0506	−8.2207	−8.0506
1	0.5	−8.1918	−8.0784	−8.1918	−8.0784
1	0.75	−8.1630	−8.1063	−8.1630	−8.1063
1	1	−8.1341	−8.1341	−8.1341	−8.1341

ential equation associated with the system may be transformed into the following type-2 fuzzy quadratic eigenvalue problem as

$$(\tilde{\tilde{M}}\tilde{\tilde{\lambda}}^2 + \tilde{\tilde{C}}\tilde{\tilde{\lambda}} + \tilde{\tilde{K}})\tilde{\tilde{x}} = 0, \tag{13.32}$$

where

$$\tilde{\tilde{C}} = \begin{bmatrix} \tilde{\tilde{c}}_{11} & \tilde{\tilde{c}}_{12} & 0 & 0 \\ \tilde{\tilde{c}}_{12} & \tilde{\tilde{c}}_{11} & \tilde{\tilde{c}}_{12} & 0 \\ 0 & \tilde{\tilde{c}}_{12} & \tilde{\tilde{c}}_{11} & \tilde{\tilde{c}}_{12} \\ 0 & 0 & \tilde{\tilde{c}}_{12} & \tilde{\tilde{c}}_{11} \end{bmatrix}, \quad \tilde{\tilde{K}} = \begin{bmatrix} \tilde{\tilde{k}}_{11} & \tilde{\tilde{k}}_{12} & 0 & 0 \\ \tilde{\tilde{k}}_{12} & \tilde{\tilde{k}}_{11} & \tilde{\tilde{k}}_{12} & 0 \\ 0 & \tilde{\tilde{k}}_{12} & \tilde{\tilde{k}}_{11} & \tilde{\tilde{k}}_{12} \\ 0 & 0 & \tilde{\tilde{k}}_{12} & \tilde{\tilde{k}}_{11} \end{bmatrix}, \quad \tilde{\tilde{M}} = 2I_4, \tag{13.33}$$

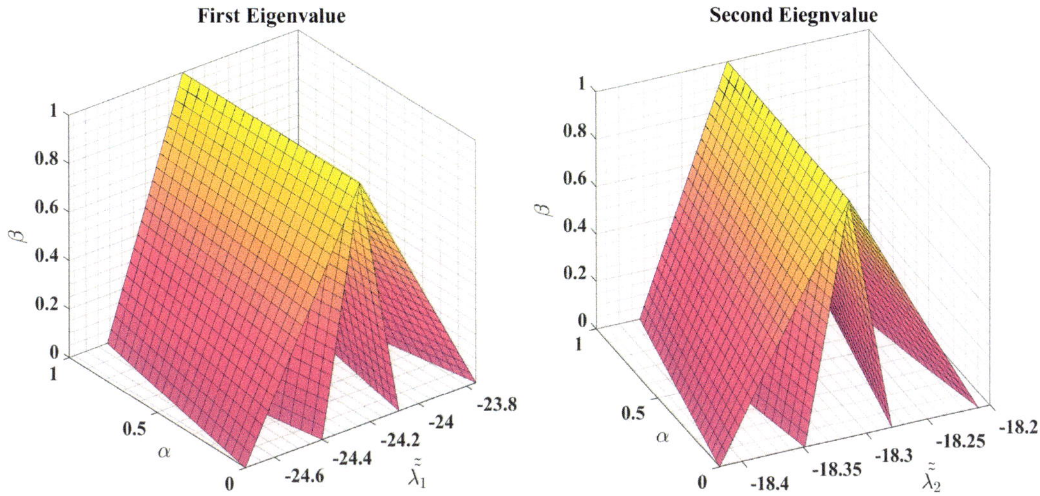

FIGURE 13.6 Plot of the first and second eigenvalues of the damped spring-mass structure.

and

$$\begin{aligned}
\tilde{\tilde{c}}_{11} &= (30, 30.1, 30.2, 30.3, 30.4, 30.5, 30.6),\\
\tilde{\tilde{c}}_{12} &= (-12.5, -12.25, -12, -11.75, -11.5, -11.25, -11),\\
\tilde{\tilde{k}}_{11} &= (14.5, 14.75, 15, 15.25, 15.5, 15.75, 16),\\
\tilde{\tilde{k}}_{12} &= (-3.03, -3.02, -3.01, -3, -2.99, -2.98, -2.97).
\end{aligned} \tag{13.34}$$

Using the triple parametric form, and concepts of LMF and UMF, the given type-2 fuzzy quadratic eigenvalue problem will be

$$\begin{aligned}
&(\underline{\tilde{M}}(\alpha,\beta,\gamma)\underline{\tilde{\lambda}}(\alpha,\beta,\gamma)^2 + \underline{\tilde{C}}(\alpha,\beta,\gamma)\underline{\tilde{\lambda}}(\alpha,\beta,\gamma) + \underline{\tilde{K}}(\alpha,\beta,\gamma))\underline{\tilde{x}}(\alpha,\beta,\gamma) = 0,\\
&(\overline{\tilde{M}}(\alpha,\beta,\gamma)\overline{\tilde{\lambda}}(\alpha,\beta,\gamma)^2 + \overline{\tilde{C}}(\alpha,\beta,\gamma)\overline{\tilde{\lambda}}(\alpha,\beta,\gamma) + \overline{\tilde{K}}(\alpha,\beta,\gamma))\overline{\tilde{x}}(\alpha,\beta,\gamma) = 0.
\end{aligned} \tag{13.35}$$

Further, using the linearization technique as discussed in the preceding section, both the equations in (13.35) can be written as the following generalized eigenvalue problems:

$$\begin{bmatrix} -\underline{\tilde{K}}(\alpha,\beta,\gamma) & 0 \\ 0 & I \end{bmatrix} \begin{bmatrix} \underline{\tilde{x}}_1(\alpha,\beta,\gamma) \\ \underline{\tilde{x}}_2(\alpha,\beta,\gamma) \end{bmatrix} = \underline{\tilde{\lambda}}(\alpha,\beta,\gamma) \begin{bmatrix} \underline{\tilde{C}}(\alpha,\beta,\gamma) & \underline{\tilde{M}}(\alpha,\beta,\gamma) \\ I & 0 \end{bmatrix} \begin{bmatrix} \underline{\tilde{x}}_1(\alpha,\beta,\gamma) \\ \underline{\tilde{x}}_2(\alpha,\beta,\gamma) \end{bmatrix} \tag{13.36}$$

and

$$\begin{bmatrix} -\overline{\tilde{K}}(\alpha,\beta,\gamma) & 0 \\ 0 & I \end{bmatrix} \begin{bmatrix} \overline{\tilde{x}}_1(\alpha,\beta,\gamma) \\ \overline{\tilde{x}}_2(\alpha,\beta,\gamma) \end{bmatrix} = \overline{\tilde{\lambda}}(\alpha,\beta,\gamma) \begin{bmatrix} \overline{\tilde{C}}(\alpha,\beta,\gamma) & \overline{\tilde{M}}(\alpha,\beta,\gamma) \\ I & 0 \end{bmatrix} \begin{bmatrix} \overline{\tilde{x}}_1(\alpha,\beta,\gamma) \\ \overline{\tilde{x}}_2(\alpha,\beta,\gamma) \end{bmatrix}. \tag{13.37}$$

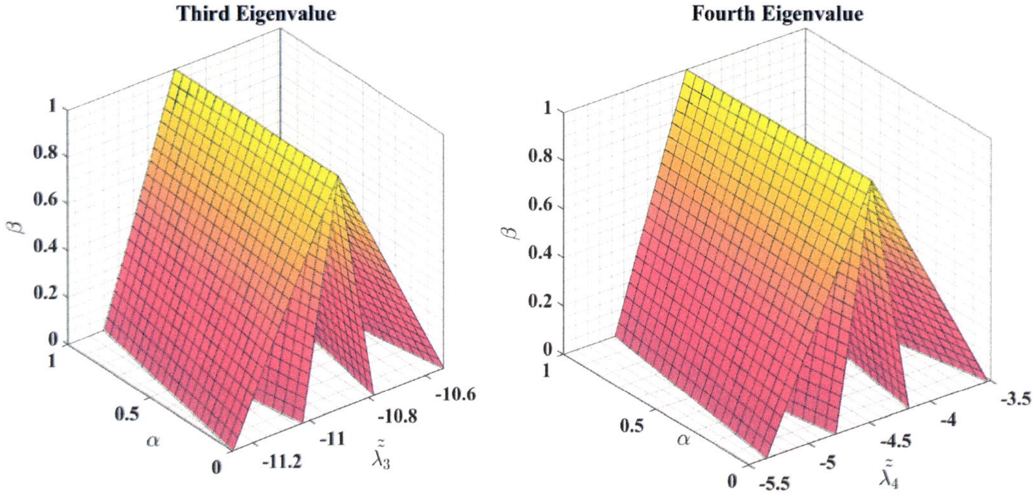

FIGURE 13.7 Plot of the third and fourth eigenvalues of the damped spring-mass structure.

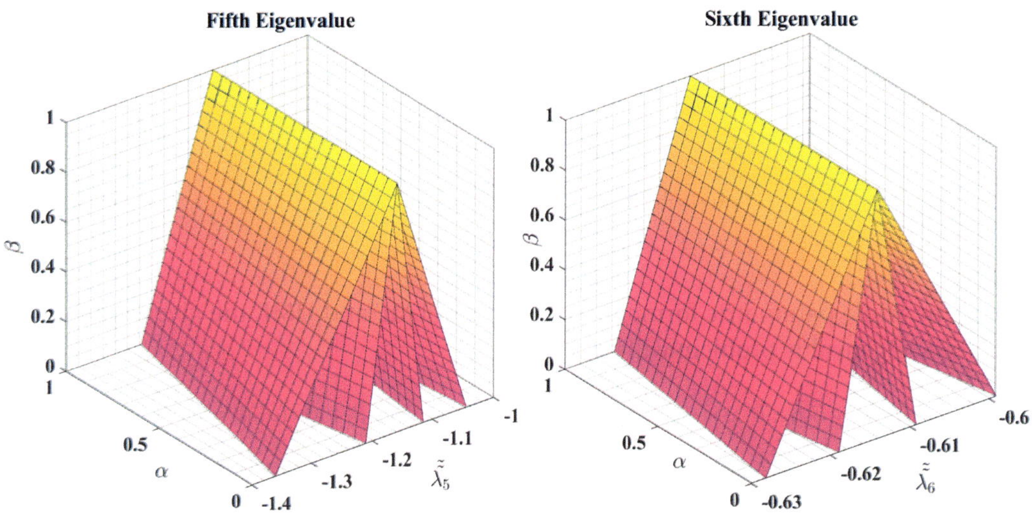

FIGURE 13.8 Plot of the fifth and sixth eigenvalues of the damped spring-mass structure.

By solving Eqs. (13.36) and (13.37), we can obtain the LMF and UMF of the type-2 fuzzy eigenvalues in terms of α, β, and γ. Further, substituting different values to these uncertainty handling parameters and combining the LMF and UMF bounds, the obtained type-2 fuzzy eigenvalues are

$$\tilde{\tilde{\lambda}}_1 = (-24.72026, -24.5607, -24.4010, -24.2412, -24.0814, -23.9214, -23.7613),$$

$$\tilde{\tilde{\lambda}}_2 = (-18.4182, -18.3835, -18.3487, -18.3139, -18.2791, -18.2443, -18.2094),$$

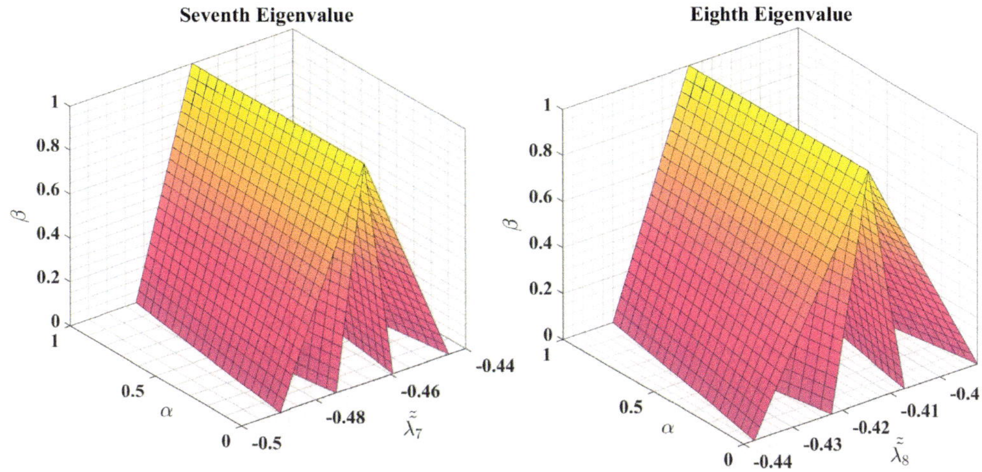

FIGURE 13.9 Plot of the seventh and eighth eigenvalues of the damped spring-mass structure.

Table 13.5 Bounds of type-2 fuzzy eigenvalue $\tilde{\tilde{\lambda}}_1$ of the damped spring-mass structure.

α	β	Left bound (LMF)	Right bound (LMF)	Left bound (UMF)	Right bound (UMF)
0	0	−24.401	−24.081	−24.720	−23.761
0	0.25	−24.361	−24.121	−24.601	−23.881
0	0.5	−24.321	−24.161	−24.481	−24.001
0	0.75	−24.281	−24.201	−24.361	−24.121
0	1	−24.241	−24.241	−24.241	−24.241
0.25	0	−24.441	−24.041	−24.680	−23.801
0.25	0.25	−24.391	−24.091	−24.571	−23.911
0.25	0.5	−24.341	−24.141	−24.461	−24.021
0.25	0.75	−24.291	−24.191	−24.351	−24.131
0.25	1	−24.241	−24.241	−24.241	−24.241
0.5	0	−24.481	−24.001	−24.640	−23.841
0.5	0.25	−24.421	−24.061	−24.541	−23.941
0.5	0.5	−24.361	−24.121	−24.441	−24.041
0.5	0.75	−24.301	−24.181	−24.341	−24.141
0.5	1	−24.241	−24.241	−24.241	−24.241
0.75	0	−24.521	−23.961	−24.601	−23.881
0.75	0.25	−24.451	−24.031	−24.511	−23.971
0.75	0.5	−24.381	−24.101	−24.421	−24.061
0.75	0.75	−24.311	−24.171	−24.331	−24.151
0.75	1	−24.241	−24.241	−24.241	−24.241
1	0	−24.561	−23.921	−24.561	−23.921
1	0.25	−24.481	−24.001	−24.481	−24.001
1	0.5	−24.401	−24.081	−24.401	−24.081
1	0.75	−24.321	−24.161	−24.321	−24.161
1	1	−24.241	−24.241	−24.241	−24.241

Table 13.6 Bounds of type-2 fuzzy eigenvalue $\tilde{\tilde{\lambda}}_2$ of the damped spring-mass structure.

α	β	Left bound (LMF)	Right bound (LMF)	Left bound (UMF)	Right bound (UMF)
0	0	−18.349	−18.279	−18.418	−18.209
0	0.25	−18.340	−18.288	−18.392	−18.236
0	0.5	−18.331	−18.297	−18.366	−18.262
0	0.75	−18.323	−18.305	−18.340	−18.288
0	1	−18.314	−18.314	−18.314	−18.314
0.25	0	−18.357	−18.270	−18.410	−18.218
0.25	0.25	−18.347	−18.281	−18.386	−18.242
0.25	0.5	−18.336	−18.292	−18.362	−18.266
0.25	0.75	−18.325	−18.303	−18.338	−18.290
0.25	1	−18.314	−18.314	−18.314	−18.314
0.5	0	−18.366	−18.262	−18.401	−18.227
0.5	0.25	−18.353	−18.275	−18.379	−18.249
0.5	0.5	−18.340	−18.288	−18.357	−18.270
0.5	0.75	−18.327	−18.301	−18.336	−18.292
0.5	1	−18.314	−18.314	−18.314	−18.314
0.75	0	−18.375	−18.253	−18.392	−18.236
0.75	0.25	−18.360	−18.268	−18.373	−18.255
0.75	0.5	−18.344	−18.284	−18.353	−18.275
0.75	0.75	−18.329	−18.299	−18.334	−18.294
0.75	1	−18.314	−18.314	−18.314	−18.314
1	0	−18.384	−18.244	−18.384	−18.244
1	0.25	−18.366	−18.262	−18.366	−18.262
1	0.5	−18.349	−18.279	−18.349	−18.279
1	0.75	−18.331	−18.297	−18.331	−18.297
1	1	−18.314	−18.314	−18.314	−18.314

$$\tilde{\tilde{\lambda}}_3 = (-11.2725, -11.1498, -11.0272, -10.9048, -10.7824, -10.6602, -10.5381),$$
$$\tilde{\tilde{\lambda}}_4 = (-5.3557, -5.0710, -4.7813, -4.4851, -4.1801, -3.8628, -3.5265),$$
$$\tilde{\tilde{\lambda}}_5 = (-1.3607, -1.2767, -1.2116, -1.1589, -1.1149, -1.0775, -1.0450),$$
$$\tilde{\tilde{\lambda}}_6 = (-0.6282, -0.6236, -0.6190, -0.6142, -0.6093, -0.6042, -0.5991),$$
$$\tilde{\tilde{\lambda}}_7 = (-0.4897, -0.4821, -0.4745, -0.4669, -0.4594, -0.4519, -0.4444),$$
$$\tilde{\tilde{\lambda}}_8 = (-0.4378, -0.4299, -0.4222, -0.4146, -0.4071, -0.3997, -0.3924). \quad (13.38)$$

Further, to visualize the type-2 fuzzy eigenvalues in a better way, the three-dimensional plots of the type-2 fuzzy eigenvalues are shown in Figs. 13.6–13.9. Also, the bounds of the first two type-2 fuzzy eigenvalues are shown in Tables 13.5 and 13.6 for different values of the uncertainty handling parameters α and β for $\gamma = 0$ and 1.

In this chapter, type-2 fuzzy non-linear eigenvalue problems are studied with a solution procedure based upon the triple parametric representation followed by the extension of the linearization approach in the uncertain environment. Numerical examples and application problems are also successfully solved in order to show the applicability of the proposed approach.

References

[1] W.J. Beyn, An integral method for solving nonlinear eigenvalue problems, Linear Algebra and Its Applications 436 (10) (2012) 3839–3863.

[2] F. Massa, B. Lallemand, T. Tison, Multi-level homotopy perturbation and projection techniques for the reanalysis of quadratic eigenvalue problems: the application of stability analysis, Mechanical Systems and Signal Processing 52 (2015) 88–104.

[3] G.L.G. Sleijpen, H.A. Van der Vorst, A Jacobi–Davidson iteration method for linear eigenvalue problems, SIAM Review 42 (2) (2000) 267–293.

[4] H. Voss, An Arnoldi method for nonlinear eigenvalue problems, BIT Numerical Mathematics 44 (2004) 387–401.

[5] S.K. Jeswal, S. Chakraverty, Neural network approach for solving nonlinear eigenvalue problems of structural dynamics, Neural Computing & Applications 32 (2020) 10669–10677.

[6] S. Chakraverty, S.K. Jeswal, Applied Artificial Neural Network Methods for Engineers and Scientists: Solving Algebraic Equations, World Scientific, 2021.

[7] V. Mehrmann, D. Watkins, Polynomial eigenvalue problems with Hamiltonian structure, ETNA. Electronic Transactions on Numerical Analysis [electronic only] 13 (2002) 106–118.

[8] F. Tisseur, Backward error and condition of polynomial eigenvalue problems, Linear Algebra and Its Applications 309 (2000) 339–361.

[9] S. Chakraverty, N.R. Mahato, Nonlinear interval eigenvalue problems for damped spring-mass system, Engineering Computations 35 (6) (2018) 2272–2286.

[10] S. Chakraverty, Solving fully fuzzy nonlinear eigenvalue problems of damped spring-mass structural systems using novel fuzzy-affine approach, Computer Modeling in Engineering & Sciences 121 (3) (2019) 947–980.

[11] S. Chakraverty, S. Rout, Affine Arithmetic Based Solution of Uncertain Static and Dynamic Problems, Springer Nature, 2022.

[12] P. Rao, S. Chakraverty, D. Roy, Oscillation characteristics of single-link flexible manipulator using design parameters in fuzzy domain, Journal of Vibration Engineering & Technologies (2024) 1–19.

[13] P. Rao, S. Chakraverty, D. Roy, Vibration model of slender single link flexible robotic manipulator based on Timoshenko beam theory with interval uncertainty, in: Proceedings of the 2023 6th International Conference on Advances in Robotics, 2023, pp. 1–5.

[14] D. Mohapatra, S. Chakraverty, Type-2 fuzzy linear eigenvalue problems with application in dynamic structures, Soft Computing in Interdisciplinary Sciences (2022) 93–108.

[15] D. Mohapatra, S. Chakraverty, Non-linear dynamic problems with uncertainty in type-2 fuzzy environment, in: Modeling and Computation in Vibration Problems, Volume 2: Soft Computing and Uncertainty, IOP Publishing, Bristol, UK, 2021, p. 10-1.

14

Type-2 fuzzy initial value problems with applications

Contents

14.1 Introduction **187**
14.2 Problem discussion and proposed methodology **189**
14.3 Sample problems **190**
14.4 Application problems **198**
14.4.1 Logistic model 199
14.4.2 Electric circuit 199
14.4.3 Spring-mass system 204
References **206**

Chapter points

- Type-2 fuzzy initial value problems are studied using generalized type-2 fuzzy sets.
- Uncertainty is considered in the initial condition associated with the problem.
- An approach based on the triple parametric form is presented to obtain the solution.
- Application problems related to electric circuits, population models, and spring-mass systems are discussed.

14.1 Introduction

Initial value problems (IVPs) are a fundamental class of differential equations where the solution to the equation is determined by specifying the value of the unknown function at a particular point, known as the initial condition. Such problems are commonly employed in physics, engineering, biology, and economics. Focusing on the widespread application of the IVP, it is crucial to solve and analyze the solution. In this regard, various analytical methods and numerical methods are employed to solve IVPs, depending on the complexity of the problem.

It may be noted that traditional mathematical models often rely on exact values and well-defined relationships, which can be limiting when the available information is incomplete, vague, or subject to fluctuations. In practice, uncertainty can stem from various sources, such as measurement errors, subjective human judgment, environmental variability, and imprecise data. Classical models are not well suited to handle such situations because they assume crisp values for parameters and initial conditions. To deal with this

Artificial Neural Networks and Type-2 Fuzzy Set. https://doi.org/10.1016/B978-0-44-332894-7.00024-1

uncertainty, fuzzy sets/numbers can be helpful, which describe values as ranges with varying degrees of membership rather than fixed points.

A variety of approaches have been employed to address fuzzy differential equations (FDEs) and fuzzy initial value problems (FIVPs) in various research endeavors. Dubois and Prade introduced the derivative of fuzzy-valued functions in 1982 [1]. Later on, the concepts of Hukuhara derivatives were presented by Puri and Ralescu [2]. Further, various other ideas have been presented by different scientists for the fuzzy derivative [3,4]. In order to solve the linear FIVP of nth order, two distinct methodologies have been devised in [5]. The concept of α-cut has been employed to solve second-order FIVPs with fuzzy coefficients in [6]. Higher-order FIVPs have been resolved in a generalized Hukuhara derivative sense by employing the properties of the linear transformations [7]. The approximate solution of the FIVP of first order has been obtained using the classical Euler method and parametric form [8]. The solutions of linear and non-linear FIVPS have been obtained in [9] using an improved Euler method. Artificial neural network approaches have been successfully used to solve the FDEs [10]. Various applications of FDEs can be found in the book by Chakraverty et al. [11], where they have discussed different applications of FDEs along with analytical and numerical solution approaches. Applications of FDEs in the vibration problems of different dynamical systems, namely beams, flexible links have been studied by different researches [12–14].

Type-1 fuzzy sets provide a framework for modeling uncertainty through a membership function where each element of the set has a degree of membership between 0 and 1. However, in many real-world scenarios, the uncertainty involved is more complex and cannot be fully captured by a single membership function. Type-2 fuzzy sets allow for additional degrees of uncertainty by introducing a fuzzy membership function, rather than a crisp one, in which each membership value itself is a fuzzy set. This flexibility is essential when the information or data used to construct the fuzzy model is imprecise or when the system under study experiences high levels of uncertainty. The added layer of fuzziness in type-2 fuzzy sets accounts for uncertainty in the membership function, enabling the model to handle higher levels of uncertainty more effectively. In a type-2 fuzzy differential equation (T2FDE), the involved variables, coefficients, conditions (initial and boundary) are assumed to be type-2 fuzzy numbers. Different approaches and concepts have been developed related to T2FDEs in the recent years. The differentiability of type-2 fuzzy valued functions has been presented in the work by [15], referred to as H_2-differentiability, which is founded on Hukuhara differentiability. Mohapatra and Chakraverty [16] have employed the notion of H_2 differentiability to obtain analytical solutions for the initial value problems of the nth-order linear type-2 fuzzy initial value problems (T2FIVPs). Further, the concept of granular derivative of fuzzy values functions has been extended to develop the granular derivative of type-2 fuzzy valued function. Using the above differentiability concept, type-2 fuzzy initial value problems have been investigated [17].

14.2 Problem discussion and proposed methodology

Let us consider the following nth-order differential equation,

$$\frac{d^n y}{dx^n} + a_0(x)\frac{d^{n-1} y}{dx^{n-1}} + a_1(x)\frac{d^{n-2} y}{dx^{n-2}} + \cdots + a_{n-1}(x)y = f(x), \tag{14.1}$$

subject to the initial conditions $y(0) = m_0, \cdots, \frac{d^{n-1}y}{dx^{n-1}}|_0 = m_{n-1}$. The governing equation of many practical application problems are differential equations, in particular, initial value problems and complete information about the parameters associated with the system must be known for better modeling and understanding of the system. But it may not be always possible to observe all the parameters accurately or there may be some error during the experimental set up. In this regard, the role of uncertainty is very crucial, and considering such uncertainty in the model using type-2 fuzzy numbers is sometimes beneficial where the complete information about the membership grade is also unclear. Extending the concept of the initial value problem in the type-2 fuzzy scenario, the initial value problem in Eq. (14.1) can be written as

$$\frac{d^n \tilde{\tilde{y}}}{dx^n} + \tilde{\tilde{a}}_0\frac{d^{n-1} \tilde{\tilde{y}}}{dx^{n-1}} + \tilde{\tilde{a}}_1\frac{d^{n-2} \tilde{\tilde{y}}}{dx^{n-2}} + \cdots + \tilde{\tilde{a}}_{n-1}\tilde{\tilde{y}} = \tilde{\tilde{f}}(x), \tag{14.2}$$

subject to the type-2 fuzzy initial conditions $\tilde{\tilde{y}}(0) = \tilde{\tilde{m}}_0, \cdots, \frac{d^{n-1}\tilde{\tilde{y}}}{dx^{n-1}}|_0 = \tilde{\tilde{m}}_{n-1}$. In this chapter, we have employed TPQT2FN to handle the uncertain parameetrs in the governing equation and uncertainty is considered in the associated initial conditions.

Now, using the concept of β-cut of α-plane representation in Eq. (14.2), Eq. (14.2) can be written as

$$\frac{d^n \underline{\tilde{y}}(x;\alpha,\beta)}{dx^n} + \underline{\tilde{a}}_0(x;\alpha,\beta)\frac{d^{n-1} \underline{\tilde{y}}(x;\alpha,\beta)}{dx^{n-1}} + \underline{\tilde{a}}_1(x;\alpha,\beta)\frac{d^{n-2} \underline{\tilde{y}}(x;\alpha,\beta)}{dx^{n-2}} + \cdots + \underline{\tilde{a}}_{n-1}(x;\alpha,\beta)$$
$$\underline{\tilde{y}}(x;\alpha,\beta) = \underline{\tilde{f}}(x;\alpha,\beta), \text{ where } \underline{\tilde{y}}(0;\alpha,\beta) = \underline{\tilde{m}}_0(\alpha,\beta), \cdots, \left.\frac{d^{n-1} \underline{\tilde{y}}(x;\alpha,\beta)}{dx^{n-1}}\right|_0 = \underline{\tilde{m}}_{n-1}(\alpha,\beta),$$

and

$$\frac{d^n \overline{\tilde{y}}(x;\alpha,\beta)}{dx^n} + \overline{\tilde{a}}_0(x;\alpha,\beta)\frac{d^{n-1} \overline{\tilde{y}}(x;\alpha,\beta)}{dx^{n-1}} + \overline{\tilde{a}}_1(x;\alpha,\beta)\frac{d^{n-2} \overline{\tilde{y}}(x;\alpha,\beta)}{dx^{n-2}} + \cdots + \overline{\tilde{a}}_{n-1}(x;\alpha,\beta)$$
$$\overline{\tilde{y}}(x;\alpha,\beta) = \overline{\tilde{f}}(x;\alpha,\beta), \text{ where } \overline{\tilde{y}}(0;\alpha,\beta) = \overline{\tilde{m}}_0(\alpha,\beta), \cdots, \left.\frac{d^{n-1} \overline{\tilde{y}}(x;\alpha,\beta)}{dx^{n-1}}\right|_0 = \overline{\tilde{m}}_{n-1}(\alpha,\beta). \tag{14.3}$$

The above two equations are corresponding to type-1 fuzzy differential equations in parametric form. Implementing the triple parametric representation as discussed in Chapter 12, Eq. (14.3) will be

$$\begin{aligned}
&\frac{d^n\underline{\tilde{y}}(x;\alpha,\beta,\gamma)}{dx^n}+\underline{\tilde{a}}_0(x;\alpha,\beta,\gamma)\frac{d^{n-1}\underline{\tilde{y}}(x;\alpha,\beta,\gamma)}{dx^{n-1}}+\underline{\tilde{a}}_1(x;\alpha,\beta,\gamma)\frac{d^{n-2}\underline{\tilde{y}}(x;\alpha,\beta,\gamma)}{dx^{n-2}}+\cdots\\
&\quad+\underline{\tilde{a}}_{n-1}(x;\alpha,\beta,\gamma)\underline{\tilde{y}}(x;\alpha,\beta,\gamma)=\underline{\tilde{f}}(x;\alpha,\beta,\gamma),\\
&\text{where } \underline{\tilde{y}}(0;\alpha,\beta,\gamma)=\underline{\tilde{m}}_0(\alpha,\beta,\gamma),\cdots,\left.\frac{d^{n-1}\underline{\tilde{y}}(x;\alpha,\beta,\gamma)}{dx^{n-1}}\right|_0=\underline{\tilde{m}}_{n-1}(\alpha,\beta,\gamma),
\end{aligned}\tag{14.4}$$

$$\begin{aligned}
&\frac{d^n\overline{\tilde{y}}(x;\alpha,\beta,\gamma)}{dx^n}+\overline{\tilde{a}}_0(x;\alpha,\beta,\gamma)\frac{d^{n-1}\overline{\tilde{y}}(x;\alpha,\beta,\gamma)}{dx^{n-1}}+\overline{\tilde{a}}_1(x;\alpha,\beta,\gamma)\frac{d^{n-2}\overline{\tilde{y}}(x;\alpha,\beta,\gamma)}{dx^{n-2}}+\cdots\\
&\quad+\overline{\tilde{a}}_{n-1}(x;\alpha,\beta,\gamma)\overline{\tilde{y}}(x;\alpha,\beta,\gamma)=\overline{\tilde{f}}(x;\alpha,\beta,\gamma),\\
&\text{where } \overline{\tilde{y}}(0;\alpha,\beta,\gamma)=\overline{\tilde{m}}_0(\alpha,\beta,\gamma),\cdots,\left.\frac{d^{n-1}\overline{\tilde{y}}(x;\alpha,\beta,\gamma)}{dx^{n-1}}\right|_0=\overline{\tilde{m}}_{n-1}(\alpha,\beta,\gamma).
\end{aligned}\tag{14.5}$$

Both the initial value problems in Eqs. (14.4) and (14.5) can be solved in terms of the parameters α, β, and $\gamma\in[0,1]$ to obtain the LMF and UMF solution, respectively. Further, substituting different values for α and β in the acquired LMF and UMF solutions for $\gamma=0,1$ different bounds (left and right) of the LMF and UMF solution can be achieved.

14.3 Sample problems

Example 14.1. Let us consider the following first-order type-2 fuzzy initial value problem:

$$\begin{aligned}
&\frac{d\tilde{\tilde{y}}}{dx}+\tilde{\tilde{y}}\sin(x)=0,\\
&\text{where } \tilde{\tilde{y}}(0)=(1,2,3,4,5,6,7).
\end{aligned}\tag{14.6}$$

Using the β-cut at the α-plane of the type-2 fuzzy parameter $\tilde{\tilde{y}}$ in the given differential equation and initial condition, the above initial value problem (14.6) can be written as

$$\begin{aligned}
&\frac{d\tilde{\tilde{y}}(\alpha,\beta)}{dx}+\tilde{\tilde{y}}(\alpha,\beta)\sin(x)=0,\\
&\text{where } \tilde{\tilde{y}}(0;\alpha,\beta)=(\underline{\tilde{y}}(0;\alpha,\beta),\overline{\tilde{y}}(0;\alpha,\beta)).
\end{aligned}\tag{14.7}$$

Here, $\underline{\tilde{y}}(0;\alpha,\beta)$ and $\overline{\tilde{y}}(0;\alpha,\beta)$ represent the LMF and UMF of the type-2 fuzzy initial condition. Further, using the definition of LMF and UMF of the type-2 fuzzy parameters in the given differential Eq. (14.7), the following two initial value problems can be obtained:

$$\frac{d\underline{\tilde{y}}(\alpha,\beta)}{dx}+\underline{\tilde{y}}(\alpha,\beta)\sin(x)=0,\tag{14.8}$$

and

$$\frac{d\bar{\tilde{y}}(\alpha,\beta)}{dx}+\bar{\tilde{y}}(\alpha,\beta)\sin(x)=0, \tag{14.9}$$

with the associated initial conditions as $\underline{\tilde{y}}(0;\alpha,\beta)$ and $\bar{\tilde{y}}(0;\alpha,\beta)$. Here, Eq. (14.8) represents the equation associated with the LMF and Eq. (14.9) represents the equation associated with the UMF of the type-2 fuzzy unknown $\tilde{\tilde{y}}$. Eqs. (14.8) and (14.9) correspond to the parametric forms of two different type-1 fuzzy differential equations.

Now, introducing another parameter $\gamma\in[0,1]$ as mentioned in the proposed approach, Eqs. (14.8) and (14.9) will be transformed into

$$\begin{gathered}\frac{d\underline{\tilde{y}}(\alpha,\beta,\gamma)}{dx}+\underline{\tilde{y}}(\alpha,\beta,\gamma)\sin(x)=0,\\ \text{with initial condition } \underline{\tilde{y}}(0;\alpha,\beta,\gamma),\end{gathered} \tag{14.10}$$

and

$$\begin{gathered}\frac{d\bar{\tilde{y}}(\alpha,\beta,\gamma)}{dx}+\bar{\tilde{y}}(\alpha,\beta,\gamma)\sin(x)=0,\\ \text{with initial condition}\bar{\tilde{y}}(0;\alpha,\beta,\gamma).\end{gathered} \tag{14.11}$$

Eqs. (14.10) and (14.11) can be solved in terms of the parameters to obtain the LMF and UMF of the required type-2 fuzzy unknown. The obtained LMF and UMF are

$$\begin{aligned}\underline{\tilde{y}}(x;\alpha,\beta,\gamma)&=\exp\left(\cos(x)-1\right)\left(2\beta-\gamma\left(4\beta+2(\alpha-1)(\beta-1)-4\right)+(\alpha-1)(\beta-1)+2\right),\\ \bar{\tilde{y}}(x;\alpha,\beta,\gamma)&=\exp\left(\cos(x)-1\right)\left(2\beta+\gamma\left(2(\alpha-1)(\beta-1)-4\beta+4\right)-(\alpha-1)(\beta-1)+2\right).\end{aligned}$$

Substituting $\gamma=0$ and 1 in the above triple parametric representations, the left and right bounds of the LMF ($\underline{\tilde{y}}$) and UMF ($\bar{\tilde{y}}$) can be obtained in terms of α and β, and given by

$$\begin{aligned}\underline{\tilde{y}}_{left}&=\exp\left(\cos(x)-1\right)\left(2\beta+(\alpha-1)(\beta-1)+2\right),\\ \underline{\tilde{y}}_{right}&=-\exp\left(\cos(x)-1\right)\left(2\beta+(\alpha-1)(\beta-1)-6\right),\\ \bar{\tilde{y}}_{left}&=\exp\left(\cos(x)-1\right)\left(2\beta-(\alpha-1)(\alpha-1)+2\right),\\ \bar{\tilde{y}}_{right}&=\exp\left(\cos(x)-1\right)\left((\alpha-1)(\beta-1)-2\beta+6\right).\end{aligned}$$

The required type-2 fuzzy solution can be obtained using the left and right bounds of LMF and UMF. For the better visualization purpose, the obtained type-2 fuzzy solution is shown graphically in Fig. 14.1, where we have taken the value of $x=0.5$. Also, the footprint of uncertainty is illustrated in Fig. 14.2 to study the behavior of the type-2 fuzzy solution. Further, different values has been substituted for α and β to find different boundary points of the type-2 fuzzy solution, and the values are presented in Table 14.1. For the validation purpose of the present approach, the present solution is compared with the previously existing solution in Table 14.2.

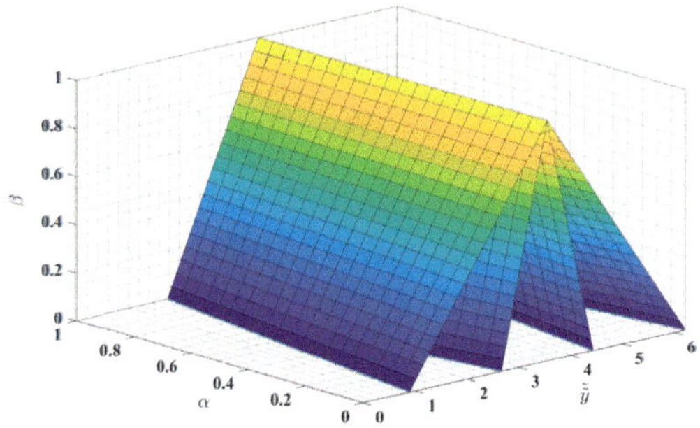

FIGURE 14.1 Plot of the type-2 fuzzy solution $\tilde{\tilde{y}}$ of Example 14.1 at $x = 0.5$.

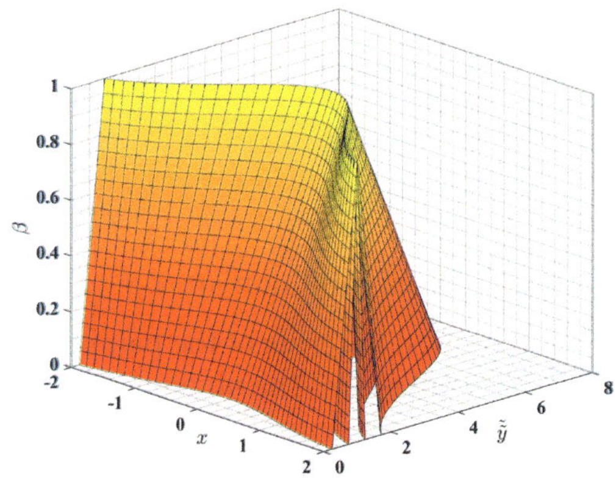

FIGURE 14.2 Footprint of uncertainty of type-2 fuzzy solution $\tilde{\tilde{y}}$ of Example 14.1.

Example 14.2. Let us encounter a second-order type-2 fuzzy initial value problem, given by

$$\frac{d^2\tilde{\tilde{y}}}{dx^2} = -\tilde{\tilde{y}} + 2x, \tag{14.12}$$

with the associated initial conditions as

$$\begin{aligned} \tilde{\tilde{y}}(0) &= (0.7, 0.8, 0.9, 1, 1.1, 1.2, 1.3), \\ \tilde{\tilde{y}}'(0) &= (1.7, 1.8, 1.9, 2, 2.1, 2.2, 2.3). \end{aligned} \tag{14.13}$$

Using the β-cut at the α-plane representation of the type-2 fuzzy parameters in Eq. (14.12) and in the type-2 fuzzy initial condition (14.13), one can obtain the following pair of type-1 fuzzy initial value problems:

$$\frac{d^2\underline{\tilde{y}}(\alpha, \beta)}{dx^2} = -\underline{\tilde{y}}(\alpha, \beta) + 2x, \tag{14.14}$$

with associated initial values $\underline{\tilde{y}}(0; \alpha, \beta)$ and $\underline{\tilde{y}}'(0; \alpha, \beta)$,

Table 14.1 Bounds of the type-2 fuzzy solution $\tilde{\tilde{y}}$ of Example 14.1 at $x = 0.5$.

α	β	Left bound (LMF)	Right bound (LMF)	Left bound (UMF)	Right bound (UMF)
0	0	2.6543	4.4239	0.8848	6.1935
0	0.25	2.8755	4.2027	1.5484	5.5299
0	0.5	3.0967	3.9815	2.2119	4.8663
0	0.75	3.3179	3.7603	2.8755	4.2027
0	1	3.5391	3.5391	3.5391	3.5391
0.25	0	2.4331	4.6451	1.1060	5.9723
0.25	0.25	2.7096	4.3686	1.7143	5.3640
0.25	0.5	2.9861	4.0921	2.3225	4.7557
0.25	0.75	3.2626	3.8156	2.9308	4.1474
0.25	1	3.5391	3.5391	3.5391	3.5391
0.5	0	2.2119	4.8663	1.3272	5.7511
0.5	0.25	2.5437	4.5345	1.8802	5.1981
0.5	0.5	2.8755	4.2027	2.4331	4.6451
0.5	0.75	3.2073	3.8709	2.9861	4.0921
0.5	1	3.5391	3.5391	3.5391	3.5391
0.75	0	1.9908	5.0875	1.5484	5.5299
0.75	0.25	2.3778	4.7004	2.0461	5.0322
0.75	0.5	2.7649	4.3133	2.5437	4.5345
0.75	0.75	3.1520	3.9262	3.0414	4.0368
0.75	1	3.5391	3.5391	3.5391	3.5391
1	0	1.7696	5.3087	1.7696	5.3087
1	0.25	2.2119	4.8663	2.2119	4.8663
1	0.5	2.6543	4.4239	2.6543	4.4239
1	0.75	3.0967	3.9815	3.0967	3.9815
1	1	3.5391	3.5391	3.5391	3.5391

Table 14.2 Comparison of LMF and UMF bounds of type-2 fuzzy solution (Example 14.1).

Solution	Left Bound	Right Bound
	LMF	
Present	$\exp(\cos(x)-1)(2\beta+(\alpha-1)(\beta-1)+2)$	$-\exp(\cos(x)-1)(2\beta+(\alpha-1)(\beta-1)-6)$
[16]	$\exp(\cos(x)-1)(2\beta+(\alpha-1)(\beta-1)+2)$	$-\exp(\cos(x)-1)(2\beta+(\alpha-1)(\beta-1)-6)$
	UMF	
Present	$\exp(\cos(x)-1)(2\beta-(\alpha-1)(\alpha-1)+2)$	$\exp(\cos(x)-1)((\alpha-1)(\beta-1)-2\beta+6)$
[16]	$\exp(\cos(x)-1)(2\beta-(\alpha-1)(\alpha-1)+2)$	$\exp(\cos(x)-1)((\alpha-1)(\beta-1)-2\beta+6)$

and

$$\frac{d^2\overline{\overline{y}}(\alpha,\beta)}{dx^2} = -\overline{\overline{y}}(\alpha,\beta) + 2x, \tag{14.15}$$

with associated initial values $\overline{\overline{y}}(0;\alpha,\beta)$ and $\overline{\overline{y}}'(0;\alpha,\beta)$.

Here, Eqs. (14.14) and (14.15) correspond to the initial value problems associated with the LMF and UMF of the type-2 fuzzy unknown $\tilde{\tilde{y}}$.

Now, introducing another parameter $\gamma \in [0, 1]$, in Eqs. (14.14) and (14.15), results into

$$\frac{d^2\underline{\tilde{y}}(\alpha, \beta, \gamma)}{dx^2} = -\underline{\tilde{y}}(\alpha, \beta, \gamma) + 2x, \tag{14.16}$$
with associated initial values $\underline{\tilde{y}}(0; \alpha, \beta, \gamma)$ and $\underline{\tilde{y}}'(0; \alpha, \beta, \gamma)$,

and

$$\frac{d^2\overline{\tilde{y}}(\alpha, \beta, \gamma)}{dx^2} = -\overline{\tilde{y}}(\alpha, \beta, \gamma) + 2x, \tag{14.17}$$
with associated initial values $\overline{\tilde{y}}(0; \alpha, \beta, \gamma)$ and $\overline{\tilde{y}}'(0; \alpha, \beta, \gamma)$.

Eqs. (14.16) and (14.17) can be solved separately for $\underline{\tilde{y}}(\alpha, \beta, \gamma)$ and $\overline{\tilde{y}}(\alpha, \beta, \gamma)$, i.e., the LMF and UMF of the type-2 fuzzy unknown, in triple parametric form.

The obtained solutions of Eqs. (14.16) and (14.17), in terms of α, β, and γ are given by

$$\begin{aligned}\underline{\tilde{y}}(\alpha, \beta, \gamma) = 2x &+ \cos(x)\left(\frac{\beta}{5} - \gamma\left(\frac{2\beta}{5} + 2\left(\frac{\beta}{10} - \frac{1}{10}\right)(\alpha - 1) - \frac{2}{5}\right)\right.\\ &\left.+\left(\frac{\beta}{10} - \frac{1}{10}\right)(\alpha - 1) + \frac{4}{5}\right)\\ &+ \sin(x)\left(\frac{\beta}{5} - \gamma\left(\frac{2\beta}{5} + 2\left(\frac{\beta}{10} - \frac{1}{10}\right)(\alpha - 1) - \frac{2}{5}\right)\right.\\ &\left.+\left(\frac{\beta}{10} - \frac{1}{10}\right)(\alpha - 1) - \frac{1}{5}\right)\end{aligned} \tag{14.18}$$

$$\begin{aligned}\overline{\tilde{y}}(\alpha, \beta, \gamma) = 2x &+ \cos(x)\left(\frac{\beta}{5} + \gamma\left(2\left(\frac{\beta}{10} - \frac{1}{10}\right)(\alpha - 1) - \frac{2\beta}{5} + \frac{2}{5}\right)\right.\\ &\left.-\left(\frac{\beta}{10} - \frac{1}{10}\right)(\alpha - 1) + \frac{4}{5}\right)\\ &+ \sin(x)\left(\frac{\beta}{5} + \gamma\left(2\left(\frac{\beta}{10} - \frac{1}{10}\right)(\alpha - 1) - \frac{2\beta}{5} + \frac{2}{5}\right)\right.\\ &\left.-\left(\frac{\beta}{10} - \frac{1}{10}\right)(\alpha - 1) - \frac{1}{5}\right)\end{aligned} \tag{14.19}$$

Further, substituting $\gamma = 0$ and 1 in the above triple parametric representations of the LMF and UMF solution, the left and right bounds can be obtained. Graphical results of the obtained type-2 fuzzy solution are shown in Figs. 14.3 and 14.4. In Fig. 14.3, the type-2 fuzzy solution is plotted for $x = 1$ and Fig. 14.4 represents the FOU of the obtained type-2 fuzzy solution. Tabular results are also provided for different values of α and β, for a fixed value of $x = 1$ in Table 14.3.

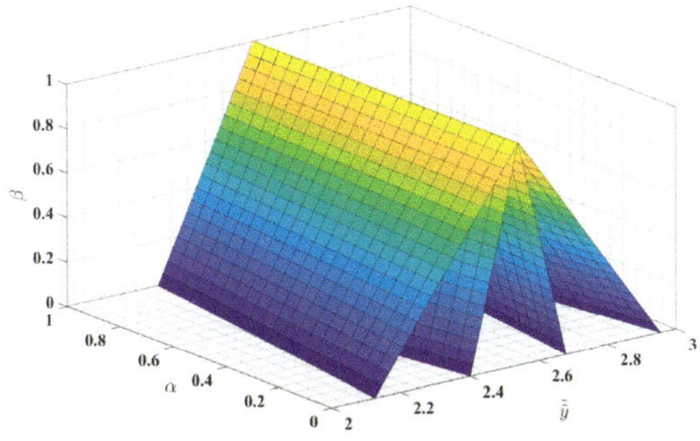

FIGURE 14.3 Plot of the type-2 fuzzy solution $\tilde{\tilde{y}}$ of Example 14.2 at $x = 1$.

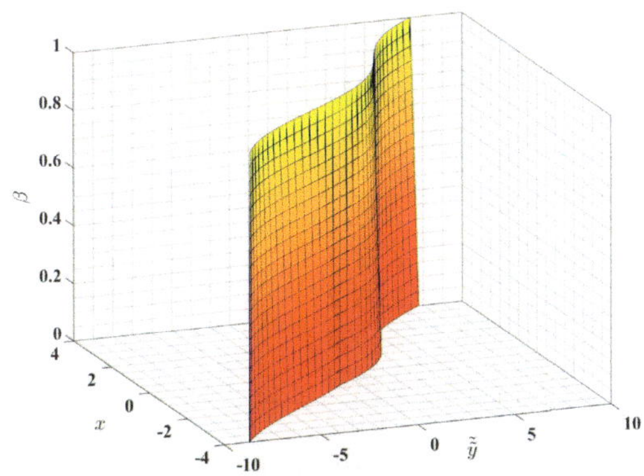

FIGURE 14.4 Footprint of uncertainty of type-2 fuzzy solution $\tilde{\tilde{y}}$ of Example 14.2.

Example 14.3. Let us encounter a fourth-order type-2 fuzzy initial value problem,

$$\frac{d^4\tilde{\tilde{y}}}{dx^4} = -\frac{d^2\tilde{\tilde{y}}}{dx^2} + 2\frac{d\tilde{\tilde{y}}}{dx} + 5x, \tag{14.20}$$

with type-2 fuzzy initial conditions as

$$\begin{aligned}
\tilde{\tilde{y}}(0) &= (2, 3, 4, 5, 6, 7, 8), \\
\tilde{\tilde{y}}'(0) &= (-4, -3.5, -3, -2.5, -2, -1.5, -1), \\
\tilde{\tilde{y}}''(0) &= (8, 8.5, 9, 9.5, 10, 10.5, 11), \\
\tilde{\tilde{y}}'''(0) &= (12, 13, 14, 15, 16, 17, 18).
\end{aligned} \tag{14.21}$$

Using the proposed approach, based on the triple parametric representations of the type-2 fuzzy parameters and initial conditions, the initial value problem given in (14.20) and (14.21) can be solved for LMF and UMF separately. The obtained LMF and UMF solution

Table 14.3 Bounds of the type-2 fuzzy solution $\tilde{\tilde{y}}$ of Example 14.2 at $x = 1$.

α	β	Left bound (LMF)	Right bound (LMF)	Left bound (UMF)	Right bound (UMF)
0	0	2.4021	2.6785	2.1258	2.9548
0	0.25	2.4367	2.6439	2.2294	2.8512
0	0.5	2.4712	2.6094	2.333	2.7476
0	0.75	2.5058	2.5748	2.4367	2.6439
0	1	2.5403	2.5403	2.5403	2.5403
0.25	0	2.3676	2.713	2.1603	2.9203
0.25	0.25	2.4108	2.6698	2.2553	2.8253
0.25	0.5	2.4539	2.6267	2.3503	2.7303
0.25	0.75	2.4971	2.5835	2.4453	2.6353
0.25	1	2.5403	2.5403	2.5403	2.5403
0.5	0	2.333	2.7476	2.1949	2.8857
0.5	0.25	2.3849	2.6958	2.2812	2.7994
0.5	0.5	2.4367	2.6439	2.3676	2.713
0.5	0.75	2.4885	2.5921	2.4539	2.6267
0.5	1	2.5403	2.5403	2.5403	2.5403
0.75	0	2.2985	2.7821	2.2294	2.8512
0.75	0.25	2.3589	2.7217	2.3071	2.7735
0.75	0.5	2.4194	2.6612	2.3849	2.6958
0.75	0.75	2.4798	2.6008	2.4626	2.618
0.75	1	2.5403	2.5403	2.5403	2.5403
1	0	2.2639	2.8167	2.2639	2.8167
1	0.25	2.333	2.7476	2.333	2.7476
1	0.5	2.4021	2.6785	2.4021	2.6785
1	0.75	2.4712	2.6094	2.4712	2.6094
1	1	2.5403	2.5403	2.5403	2.5403

in terms of α, β, and γ are

$$\begin{aligned}\underline{\tilde{y}}(x;\alpha,\beta,\gamma) = {} & \frac{\beta}{4}-\frac{\alpha}{4}+\frac{\gamma}{2}-\frac{5x}{4}+\frac{\alpha\beta}{4}+\frac{\alpha\gamma}{2}-\frac{\beta\gamma}{2} \\ & + e^{x}\left(\frac{5\beta}{8}-\frac{5\alpha}{8}+\frac{5\gamma}{4}+\frac{5\alpha\beta}{8}+\frac{5\alpha\gamma}{4}-\frac{5\beta\gamma}{4}-\frac{5\alpha\beta\gamma}{4}+\frac{11}{2}\right) \\ & -\frac{5x^2}{4}-\frac{\alpha\beta\gamma}{2} \\ & + e^{-x/2}\cos\left(\frac{\sqrt{7}x}{2}\right)\left(\frac{\beta}{8}-\frac{\alpha}{8}+\frac{\gamma}{4}+\frac{\alpha\beta}{8}+\frac{\alpha\gamma}{4}-\frac{\beta\gamma}{4}-\frac{\alpha\beta\gamma}{4}+\frac{5}{8}\right) \\ & -\frac{\sqrt{7}e^{-x/2}\sin\left(\frac{\sqrt{7}x}{2}\right)(\beta-\alpha+2\gamma+\alpha\beta+2\alpha\gamma-2\beta\gamma-2\alpha\beta\gamma+111)}{56}-\frac{17}{8},\end{aligned} \tag{14.22}$$

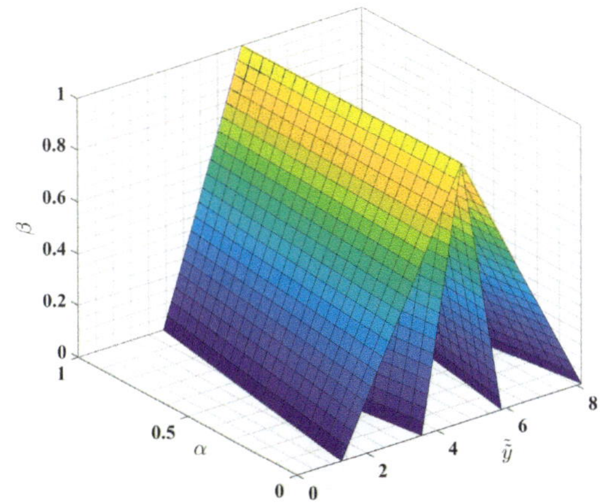

FIGURE 14.5 Plot of the type-2 fuzzy solution $\tilde{\tilde{y}}$ of Example 14.3 at $x = 0.25$.

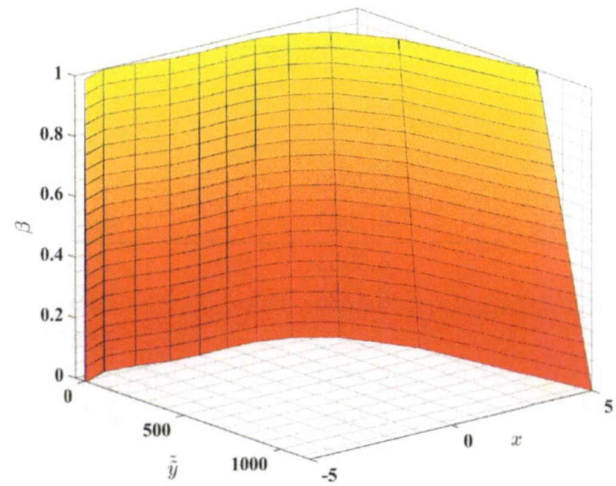

FIGURE 14.6 Footprint of uncertainty of type-2 fuzzy solution $\tilde{\tilde{y}}$ of Example 14.3.

$$\begin{aligned}\bar{\tilde{y}}(x;\alpha,\beta,\gamma) &= \frac{\alpha}{4}+\frac{3\beta}{4}+\frac{3\gamma}{2}-\frac{5x}{4}-\frac{\alpha\beta}{4}-\frac{\alpha\gamma}{2}-\frac{3\beta\gamma}{2}\\ &+e^{x}\left(\frac{5\alpha}{8}+\frac{15\beta}{8}+\frac{15\gamma}{4}-\frac{5\alpha\beta}{8}-\frac{5\alpha\gamma}{4}-\frac{15\beta\gamma}{4}+\frac{5\alpha\beta\gamma}{4}+\frac{17}{4}\right)\\ &-\frac{5x^2}{4}+\frac{\alpha\beta\gamma}{2}\\ &+e^{-x/2}\cos\left(\frac{\sqrt{7}x}{2}\right)\left(\frac{\alpha}{8}+\frac{3\beta}{8}+\frac{3\gamma}{4}-\frac{\alpha\beta}{8}-\frac{\alpha\gamma}{4}-\frac{3\beta\gamma}{4}+\frac{\alpha\beta\gamma}{4}+\frac{3}{8}\right)\\ &-\frac{\sqrt{7}e^{-x/2}\sin\left(\frac{\sqrt{7}x}{2}\right)(\alpha+3\beta+6\gamma-\alpha\beta-2\alpha\gamma-6\beta\gamma+2\alpha+109)}{56}-\frac{21}{8}.\end{aligned} \tag{14.23}$$

Table 14.4 Bounds of the type-2 fuzzy solution $\tilde{\tilde{y}}$ of Example 14.3 at $x = 0.25$.

α	β	Left bound (LMF)	Right bound (LMF)	Left bound (UMF)	Right bound (UMF)
0	0	3.5654	5.852	1.2787	8.1386
0	0.25	3.8512	5.5661	2.1362	7.2811
0	0.5	4.137	5.2803	2.9937	6.4236
0	0.75	4.4228	4.9945	3.8512	5.5661
0	1	4.7087	4.7087	4.7087	4.7087
0.25	0	3.2795	6.1378	1.5646	7.8528
0.25	0.25	3.6368	5.7805	2.3506	7.0667
0.25	0.5	3.9941	5.4232	3.1366	6.2807
0.25	0.75	4.3514	5.066	3.9226	5.4947
0.25	1	4.7087	4.7087	4.7087	4.7087
0.5	0	2.9937	6.4236	1.8504	7.5669
0.5	0.25	3.4224	5.9949	2.565	6.8524
0.5	0.5	3.8512	5.5661	3.2795	6.1378
0.5	0.75	4.2799	5.1374	3.9941	5.4232
0.5	1	4.7087	4.7087	4.7087	4.7087
0.75	0	2.7079	6.7095	2.1362	7.2811
0.75	0.25	3.2081	6.2093	2.7793	6.638
0.75	0.5	3.7083	5.7091	3.4224	5.9949
0.75	0.75	4.2085	5.2089	4.0656	5.3518
0.75	1	4.7087	4.7087	4.7087	4.7087
1	0	2.422	6.9953	2.422	6.9953
1	0.25	2.9937	6.4236	2.9937	6.4236
1	0.5	3.5654	5.852	3.5654	5.852
1	0.75	4.137	5.2803	4.137	5.2803
1	1	4.7087	4.7087	4.7087	4.7087

Substituting $\gamma = 0$ and 1 in Eqs. (14.22) and (14.23), one can obtain the left and right bounds of the LMF and UMF associated with the type-2 fuzzy solution. The obtained type-2 fuzzy solution is illustrated in Fig. 14.5 at $x = 0.25$. Also, for the better understanding of the type-2 fuzzy solution the behavior of the solution is presented graphically using the FOU in Fig. 14.6. Values of left and right bounds of the type-2 fuzzy solution are shown in Table 14.4 for different values of α and β.

14.4 Application problems

In this section, we will encounter some application problems that are governed by differential equations with certain initial conditions. Considering the presence of uncertainty in the practical models, which is obvious, we have solved these application problems in the type-2 fuzzy domain.

14.4.1 Logistic model

The governing equation of the logistic population model is given as

$$\frac{dP}{dt} = rP\left(1 - \frac{P}{k}\right), \tag{14.24}$$

where

P : Population at time t,
r : intrinsic growth rate,
k : Carrying capacity,

and suppose P_0 be the initial population at time $t = 0$.

Implementing the uncertainty factor of higher dimension using the TPQT2FN in the initial population P_0, the governing Eq. (14.24) can be written in the type-2 fuzzy environment as

$$\frac{d\tilde{\tilde{P}}}{dt} = r\tilde{\tilde{P}}\left(1 - \frac{\tilde{\tilde{P}}}{k}\right), \tag{14.25}$$

with the type-2 fuzzy initial condition as $\tilde{\tilde{P}}(0) = \tilde{\tilde{P}}_0 = (0.7, 0.8, 0.9, 1, 1.1, 1.2, 1.3)$.

Solving the type-2 fuzzy logistic model using the proposed approach, the given model can be transformed into two triple parametric form-based initial value problems. Solving separately, the initial value problems associated with the LMF and UMF, the required LMF and UMF solution can be obtained as

$$\underline{\tilde{P}}(t;\alpha,\beta,\gamma) = -\frac{k}{\exp\left(\log\left(1 - \frac{10k}{\beta-\alpha+2\gamma+\alpha\beta+2\alpha\gamma-2\beta\gamma-2\alpha\beta\gamma+9}\right) - rx\right) - 1}, \tag{14.26}$$

$$\overline{\tilde{P}}(t;\alpha,\beta,\gamma) = -\frac{k}{\exp\left(\log\left(1 - \frac{10k}{\alpha+3\beta+6\gamma-\alpha\beta-2\alpha\gamma-6\beta\gamma+2\alpha\beta\gamma+7}\right) - rx\right) - 1}. \tag{14.27}$$

Further, for better understanding purpose, we have considered $r = 0.02$ and $k = 100$, then the type-2 fuzzy solution is shown graphically in Fig. 14.7 for $t = 10$. The FOU of the type-2 fuzzy population is shown in Fig. 14.8 to check the behavior of the population in the type-2 fuzzy uncertain scenario. In Table 14.5, the left and right bounds of the LMF and UMF of the type-2 fuzzy population are shown for different values of α and β.

14.4.2 Electric circuit

Let us consider the electric circuit as shown in Fig. 14.9, consisting of an inductor with inductance (L), a resistor with resistance (R), and a capacitor with capacitance (C). Let $V(t)$ be the applied voltage, then the governing equation of current flow in the circuit is given by

$$L\frac{d^2Q}{dt^2} + R\frac{dQ}{dt} + \frac{Q}{C} = V(t). \tag{14.28}$$

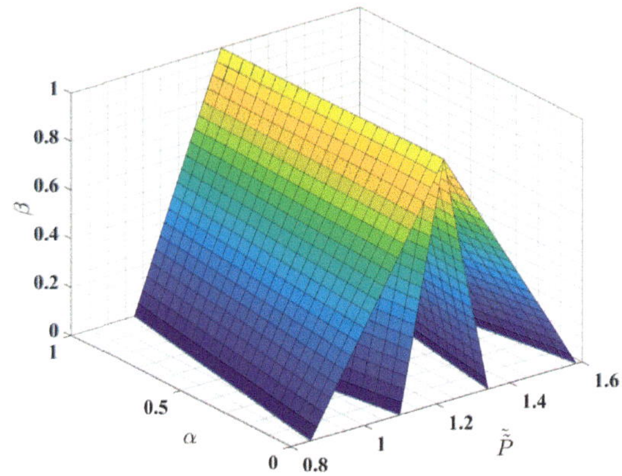

FIGURE 14.7 Plot of the type-2 fuzzy population $\tilde{\tilde{P}}$ at $t = 10$.

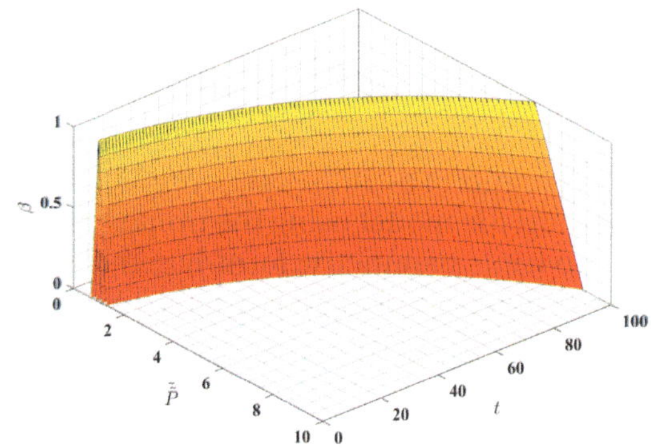

FIGURE 14.8 Footprint of uncertainty of type-2 fuzzy population $\tilde{\tilde{P}}$.

Suppose the amount of charge stored in the capacitor at the moment the circuit starts is Q_0, i.e., $Q(0) = Q_0$, the current flowing through the inductor at $t = 0$ is $I_0 = \frac{dQ}{dt}(0)$.

In the above second-order initial value problem, the parameters are assumed to be deterministic. But there may be uncertainty in the system parameters. Suppose the initial conditions associated with the electric circuit is type-2 fuzzy in nature. Then, the governing equation in the type-2 fuzzy uncertain scenario is

$$L\frac{d^2\tilde{\tilde{Q}}}{dt^2} + R\frac{d\tilde{\tilde{Q}}}{dt} + \frac{\tilde{\tilde{Q}}}{C} = V(t), \tag{14.29}$$

with associated type-2 fuzzy initial conditions $\tilde{\tilde{Q}}_0$ and $\frac{d\tilde{\tilde{Q}}}{dt}(0)$.

Assuming $L = 1$, $R = 2$, $C = 0.25$, and $V(t) = 50\cos(t)$, the governing equation will be

$$\frac{d^2\tilde{\tilde{Q}}}{dt^2} + 2\frac{d\tilde{\tilde{Q}}}{dt} + 4\tilde{\tilde{Q}} = 50\cos(t), \tag{14.30}$$

Table 14.5 Bounds of the type-2 fuzzy population $\tilde{\tilde{P}}$ at $t = 10$.

α	β	Left bound (LMF)	Right bound (LMF)	Left bound (UMF)	Right bound (UMF)
0	0	1.0971	1.3403	0.85366	1.5833
0	0.25	1.1275	1.3099	0.94497	1.4922
0	0.5	1.1579	1.2795	1.0362	1.401
0	0.75	1.1883	1.2491	1.1275	1.3099
0	1	1.2187	1.2187	1.2187	1.2187
0.25	0	1.0667	1.3707	0.8841	1.5529
0.25	0.25	1.1047	1.3327	0.96779	1.4694
0.25	0.5	1.1427	1.2947	1.0515	1.3859
0.25	0.75	1.1807	1.2567	1.1351	1.3023
0.25	1	1.2187	1.2187	1.2187	1.2187
0.5	0	1.0362	1.401	0.91453	1.5225
0.5	0.25	1.0819	1.3555	0.99061	1.4466
0.5	0.5	1.1275	1.3099	1.0667	1.3707
0.5	0.75	1.1731	1.2643	1.1427	1.2947
0.5	1	1.2187	1.2187	1.2187	1.2187
0.75	0	1.0058	1.4314	0.94497	1.4922
0.75	0.25	1.0591	1.3783	1.0134	1.4238
0.75	0.5	1.1123	1.3251	1.0819	1.3555
0.75	0.75	1.1655	1.2719	1.1503	1.2871
0.75	1	1.2187	1.2187	1.2187	1.2187
1	0	0.97539	1.4618	0.97539	1.4618
1	0.25	1.0362	1.401	1.0362	1.401
1	0.5	1.0971	1.3403	1.0971	1.3403
1	0.75	1.1579	1.2795	1.1579	1.2795
1	1	1.2187	1.2187	1.2187	1.2187

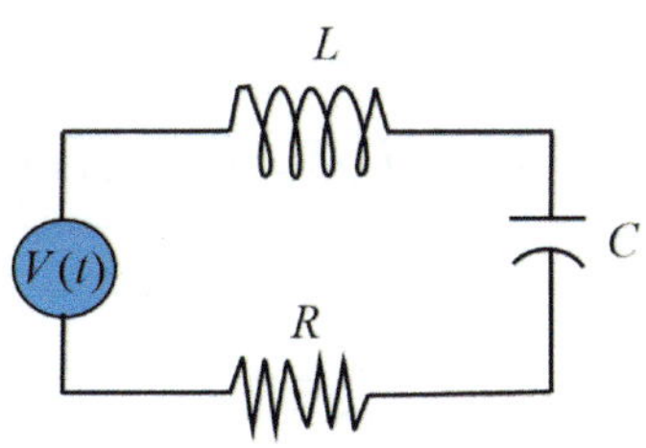

FIGURE 14.9 Schematic diagram of RLC Circuit.

and suppose the type-2 fuzzy initial conditions are $\tilde{\tilde{Q}}_0 = (1.5, 2, 2.5, 3, 3.5, 4, 4.5)$ and $\frac{d\tilde{\tilde{Q}}}{dt}(0) = (0.5, 1, 1.5, 2, 2.5, 3, 3.5)$. Using the proposed approach, LMF and UMF of the type-2 fuzzy charge $\tilde{\tilde{Q}}$ are given by

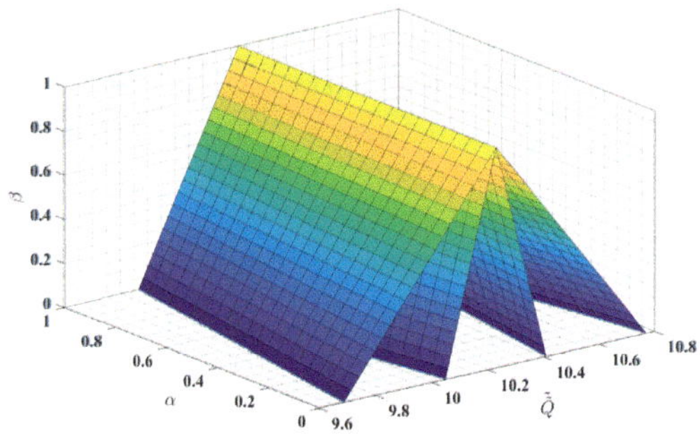

FIGURE 14.10 Plot of the type-2 fuzzy charge $\tilde{\tilde{Q}}$ at $t = 1$.

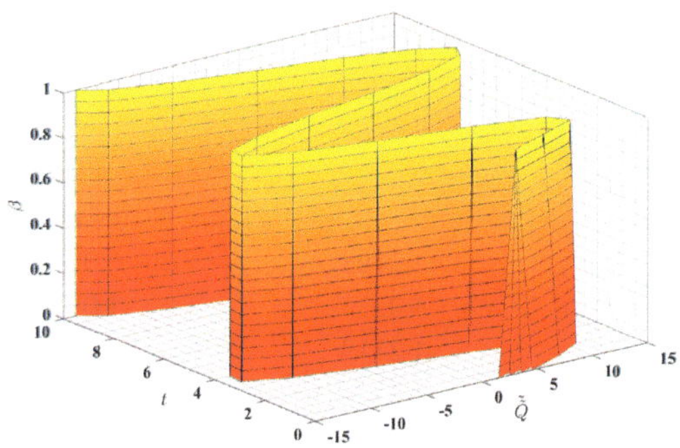

FIGURE 14.11 Footprint of uncertainty of type-2 fuzzy charge $\tilde{\tilde{Q}}$.

$$
\begin{aligned}
\underline{\tilde{Q}}(t;\alpha,\beta,\gamma) = {} & \frac{e^{-x}\cos\left(\sqrt{3}x\right)(13\alpha - 13\beta - 26\gamma - 13\alpha\beta - 26\alpha\gamma + 26\beta\gamma + 26\alpha\beta\gamma + 235)}{2\left(2\sqrt{3}-5\right)\left(2\sqrt{3}+5\right)} \\
& - \frac{25\sqrt{3}\cos\left(\sqrt{3}x\right)}{3}\left[\frac{\sin\left(x\left(\sqrt{3}-1\right)\right) - \cos\left(x\left(\sqrt{3}-1\right)\right)\left(\sqrt{3}-1\right)}{\left(\sqrt{3}-1\right)^2+1}\right. \\
& \left. + \frac{\sin\left(x\left(\sqrt{3}+1\right)\right) - \cos\left(x\left(\sqrt{3}+1\right)\right)\left(\sqrt{3}+1\right)}{\left(\sqrt{3}+1\right)^2+1}\right] \\
& - \frac{\sqrt{3}e^{-x}\sin\left(\sqrt{3}x\right)(13\alpha - 13\beta - 26\gamma - 13\alpha\beta - 26\alpha\gamma + 26\beta\gamma + 26\alpha\beta\gamma + 198)}{39}
\end{aligned}
\tag{14.31}
$$

$$
\overline{\tilde{Q}}(t;\alpha,\beta,\gamma) = \frac{\sqrt{3}e^{-x}\sin\left(\sqrt{3}x\right)(13\alpha + 39\beta + 78\gamma - 13\alpha\beta - 26\alpha\gamma - 78\beta\gamma + 26\alpha\beta\gamma - 224)}{39}
$$

Table 14.6 Bounds of the type-2 fuzzy charge $\tilde{\tilde{Q}}$ at $t = 1$.

α	β	Left bound (LMF)	Right bound (LMF)	Left bound (UMF)	Right bound (UMF)
0	0	10.048	10.408	9.6878	10.768
0	0.25	10.093	10.363	9.8229	10.633
0	0.5	10.138	10.318	9.9579	10.498
0	0.75	10.183	10.273	10.093	10.363
0	1	10.228	10.228	10.228	10.228
0.25	0	10.003	10.453	9.7328	10.723
0.25	0.25	10.059	10.397	9.8566	10.600
0.25	0.5	10.116	10.341	9.9805	10.476
0.25	0.75	10.172	10.284	10.104	10.352
0.25	1	10.228	10.228	10.228	10.228
0.5	0	9.9579	10.498	9.7778	10.678
0.5	0.25	10.025	10.431	9.8904	10.566
0.5	0.5	10.093	10.363	10.003	10.453
0.5	0.75	10.161	10.296	10.116	10.341
0.5	1	10.228	10.228	10.228	10.228
0.75	0	9.9129	10.543	9.8229	10.633
0.75	0.25	9.9917	10.464	9.9242	10.532
0.75	0.5	10.071	10.386	10.025	10.431
0.75	0.75	10.149	10.307	10.127	10.329
0.75	1	10.228	10.228	10.228	10.228
1	0	9.8679	10.588	9.8679	10.588
1	0.25	9.9579	10.498	9.9579	10.498
1	0.5	10.048	10.408	10.048	10.408
1	0.75	10.138	10.318	10.138	10.318
1	1	10.228	10.228	10.228	10.228

$$
\begin{aligned}
&-\frac{25\sqrt{3}\cos\left(\sqrt{3}x\right)}{3}\left[\frac{\sin\left(x\left(\sqrt{3}-1\right)\right)-\cos\left(x\left(\sqrt{3}-1\right)\right)\left(\sqrt{3}-1\right)}{\left(\sqrt{3}-1\right)^2+1}\right.\\
&\left.+\frac{\sin\left(x\left(\sqrt{3}+1\right)\right)-\cos\left(x\left(\sqrt{3}+1\right)\right)\left(\sqrt{3}+1\right)}{\left(\sqrt{3}+1\right)^2+1}\right]\\
&-\frac{e^{-x}\cos\left(\sqrt{3}x\right)(13\alpha+39\beta+78\gamma-13\alpha\beta-26\alpha\gamma-78\beta\gamma+26\alpha\beta\gamma-261)}{2\left(2\sqrt{3}-5\right)\left(2\sqrt{3}+5\right)}
\end{aligned}
\tag{14.32}
$$

Substituting $\gamma = 0$ and 1, in the above triple parametric representations of LMF and UMF, the left and right bounds of the LMF and UMF can be obtained. Further, the type-2 fuzzy solution $\tilde{\tilde{Q}}$ is shown graphically in Fig. 14.10 and the FOU of the type-2 fuzzy solution

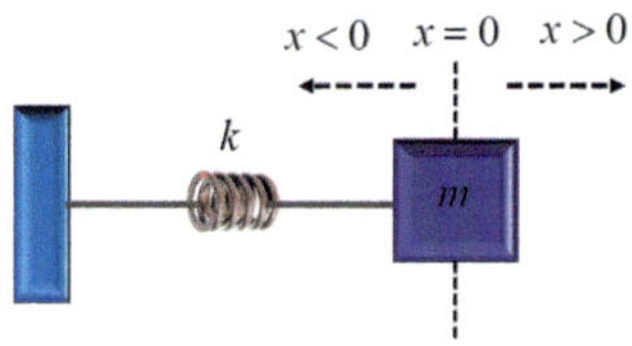

FIGURE 14.12 Schematic diagram of spring-mass system.

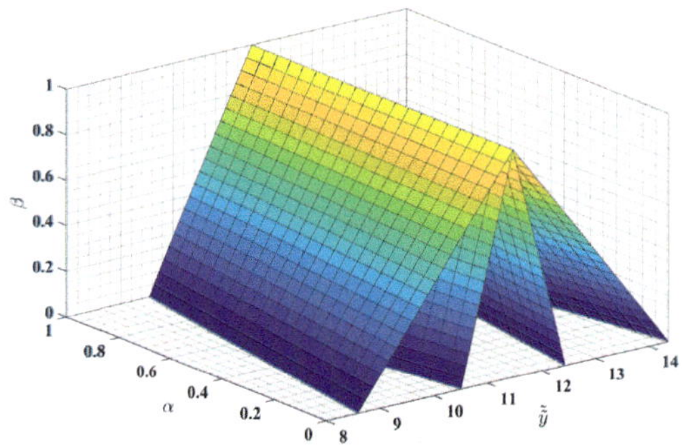

FIGURE 14.13 Plot of the type-2 fuzzy displacement $\tilde{\tilde{y}}$ at $t = 0.5$.

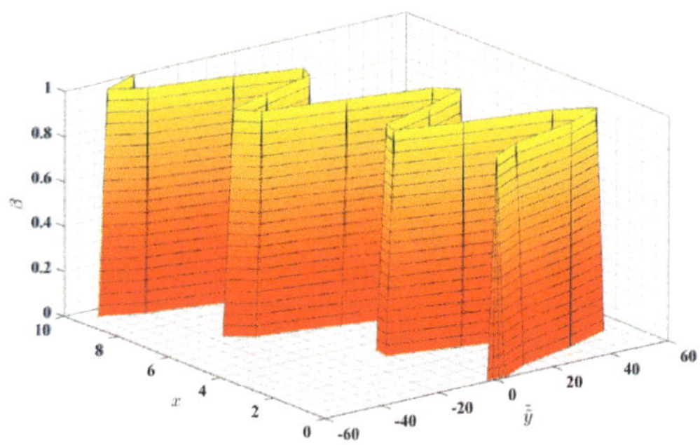

FIGURE 14.14 Footprint of uncertainty of type-2 fuzzy displacement $\tilde{\tilde{y}}$.

is presented in Fig. 14.11. The left and right bounds of the LMF and UMF are shown in Table 14.6 for various values of α and β at $t = 1$.

14.4.3 Spring-mass system

Let us consider the following spring-mass system as shown in Fig. 14.12. Suppose m be the mass of the object, k be the spring constant, and $F(t)$ be the external force applied on the system. The governing equation associated with the displacement $x(t)$ of the object is given by

$$\frac{d^2x}{dt^2} + kx = F(t), \tag{14.33}$$

Table 14.7 Bounds of the type-2 fuzzy displacement $\tilde{\tilde{y}}$ at $t = 0.5$.

α	β	Left bound (LMF)	Right bound (LMF)	Left bound (UMF)	Right bound (UMF)
0	0	10.509	12.431	8.5867	14.353
0	0.25	10.749	12.191	9.3075	13.632
0	0.5	10.989	11.950	10.028	12.911
0	0.75	11.230	11.710	10.749	12.191
0	1	11.470	11.470	11.470	11.470
0.25	0	10.268	12.671	8.8269	14.113
0.25	0.25	10.569	12.371	9.4876	13.452
0.25	0.5	10.869	12.070	10.148	12.791
0.25	0.75	11.169	11.770	10.809	12.131
0.25	1	11.470	11.470	11.470	11.470
0.5	0	10.028	12.911	9.0672	13.872
0.5	0.25	10.389	12.551	9.6678	13.272
0.5	0.5	10.749	12.191	10.268	12.671
0.5	0.75	11.109	11.830	10.869	12.070
0.5	1	11.470	11.470	11.470	11.470
0.75	0	9.788	13.152	9.3075	13.632
0.75	0.25	10.208	12.731	9.848	13.092
0.75	0.5	10.629	12.311	10.389	12.551
0.75	0.75	11.049	11.890	10.929	12.010
0.75	1	11.470	11.470	11.470	11.470
1	0	9.5477	13.392	9.5477	13.392
1	0.25	10.028	12.911	10.028	12.911
1	0.5	10.509	12.431	10.509	12.431
1	0.75	10.989	11.950	10.989	11.950
1	1	11.470	11.470	11.470	11.470

assuming the initial displacement and velocity to be x_0 and $\frac{dx}{dt}(0)$, the governing equation is a second-order initial value problem. Further, considering the presence of uncertainty in the system parameters using type-2 fuzzy numbers, i.e., TPQT2FNs, the governing type-2 fuzzy second-order initial value problem is

$$\frac{d^2\tilde{\tilde{x}}}{dt^2} + k\tilde{\tilde{x}} = F(t), \tag{14.34}$$

with type-2 fuzzy initial conditions $\tilde{\tilde{x}}(0)$ and $\frac{d\tilde{\tilde{x}}}{dt}(0)$. Suppose $k = 4$, $F(t) = 100\cos(0.3x)$ and $\tilde{\tilde{x}}(0) = \frac{d\tilde{\tilde{x}}}{dt}(0) = (-3, -2, -1, 0, 1, 2, 3)$. Using the proposed approach the LMF and UMF of the type-2 fuzzy solution can be obtained in terms of α, β, and γ. The plots of the type-2 fuzzy solutions are given in Figs. 14.13 and 14.14. In Fig. 14.13, the type-2 fuzzy plot is illustrated at $t = 0.5$, whereas Fig. 14.14 is plotted to study the behavior of the type-2 fuzzy solution via the FOU. The bounds of the LMF are shown in tabular form in Table 14.7 for $t = 0.5$ and various values of α and β.

This chapter explores initial value problems under higher-dimensional uncertainty using type-2 fuzzy numbers, with the uncertainty incorporated into the initial conditions of the problems. A solution method is introduced for solving these type-2 fuzzy initial value problems. To demonstrate the applicability and effectiveness of the proposed approach, several numerical examples are provided, followed by real-world application problems from various fields of science and engineering.

References

[1] D. Dubois, H. Prade, Towards fuzzy differential calculus part 3: differentiation, Fuzzy Sets and Systems 8 (3) (1982) 225–233.

[2] M.L. Puri, D.A. Ralescu, Differentials of fuzzy functions, Journal of Mathematical Analysis and Applications 91 (2) (1983) 552–558.

[3] R. Goetschel Jr., W. Voxman, Elementary fuzzy calculus, Fuzzy Sets and Systems 18 (1) (1986) 31–43.

[4] S. Seikkala, On the fuzzy initial value problem, Fuzzy Sets and Systems 24 (3) (1987) 319–330.

[5] J.J. Buckley, T. Feuring, Fuzzy initial value problem for Nth-order linear differential equations, Fuzzy Sets and Systems 121 (2) (2001) 247–255.

[6] Ö. Akın, T. Khaniyev, Ö. Oruç, I.B. Türkşen, An algorithm for the solution of second order fuzzy initial value problems, Expert Systems with Applications 40 (3) (2013) 953–957.

[7] N.A. Gasilov, A.G. Fatullayev, Ş.E. Amrahov, A. Khastan, A new approach to fuzzy initial value problem, Soft Computing 18 (2014) 217–225.

[8] M. Ma, M. Friedman, A. Kandel, Numerical solutions of fuzzy differential equations, Fuzzy Sets and Systems 105 (1) (1999) 133–138.

[9] S. Tapaswini, S. Chakraverty, A new approach to fuzzy initial value problem by improved Euler method, Fuzzy Information and Engineering 4 (2012) 293–312.

[10] S. Effati, M. Pakdaman, Artificial neural network approach for solving fuzzy differential equations, Information Sciences 180 (8) (2010) 1434–1457.

[11] S. Chakraverty, S. Tapaswini, D. Behera, Fuzzy Differential Equations and Applications for Engineers and Scientists, CRC Press, 2016.

[12] P. Rao, D. Roy, S. Chakraverty, Vibration analysis of single-link flexible manipulator in an uncertain environment, Journal of Vibration Engineering & Technologies 12 (2) (2024) 2677–2694.

[13] S.K. Jena, S. Pradyumna, S. Chakraverty, Quantifying uncertainty in free vibration characteristics of nanobeam with one variable first-order shear deformation theory: an analytical investigation, Acta Mechanica (2024) 1–16.

[14] P. Rao, S. Chakraverty, D. Roy, Vibration model of slender single link flexible robotic manipulator based on Timoshenko beam theory with interval uncertainty, in: Proceedings of the 2023 6th International Conference on Advances in Robotics, 2023, pp. 1–5.

[15] M. Mazandarani, M. Najariyan, Differentiability of type-2 fuzzy number-valued functions, Communications in Nonlinear Science and Numerical Simulation 19 (3) (2014) 710–725.

[16] D. Mohapatra, S. Chakraverty, Initial value problems in type-2 fuzzy environment, Mathematics and Computers in Simulation 204 (2023) 230–242.

[17] D. Mohapatra, S. Chakraverty, Type-2 Fuzzy Initial Value Problems Under Granular Differentiability, Mathematics and Computers in Simulation, Elsevier, 2024.

15

Type-2 fuzzy fractional differential equations with applications

Contents

15.1 Introduction 207

15.2 Legendre wavelet method 209

15.2.1 Block-pulse function 209

15.2.2 Fractional-order integration operational matrix 210

15.3 Problem description and implementation of the LWM 210

15.4 Sample problems 211

15.5 Application problems 217

15.5.1 Fractional-order R-L circuit 217

15.5.2 Generalized Bagley–Torvik equation 221

References 228

Chapter points

- Type-2 fuzzy fractional-order differential equations are investigated.
- A numerical approach based on the Legendre wavelets is considered to solve the fractional-order problems.
- Triple parametric representation is used to handle the type-2 fuzzy uncertainty.
- Numerical examples and application problems are explored to check the effectiveness of the wavelet approach.
- Validation of the results are made by using tables and plots.

15.1 Introduction

Fractional differential equations (FDEs) expand the notion of traditional integer-order differentiation and integration to non-integer (fractional) orders, making them an effective tool for modeling a variety of complicated processes in science and engineering. Unlike classic differential equations, which presume that integer-order derivatives dictate system dynamics, fractional derivatives give a more broad framework that includes memory effects and hereditary features. These properties make FDEs ideal for explaining phenomena like anomalous diffusion, viscoelastic materials, signal processing, and control theory. The increased interest in FDEs has resulted in substantial advances in both theoretical and

Artificial Neural Networks and Type-2 Fuzzy Set. https://doi.org/10.1016/B978-0-44-332894-7.00025-3

computational approaches for solving these equations. For a basic overview of fractional calculus and FDEs, see [1–3].

The solutions of FDEs are more intricate compared to their integer-order counterparts due to the non-local nature of fractional derivatives. Analytical methods, such as the Laplace transform [4], Mellin transform [5], and power series expansion [6], are useful for obtaining exact solutions in simpler cases. Special functions, like the Mittag–Leffler function [3], often appear in these solutions, especially for linear FDEs, playing a role similar to the exponential function in classical differential equations. Moreover, fractional differential equations can be solved using more advanced methods like homotopy analysis [7], Adomian decomposition [8], and Laplace–Adomian decomposition [9] methods, which are designed to handle non-linearity and complex boundary conditions effectively. A book on the artificial neural network approach has been written by Mall and Chakraverty [10] to handle fractional-order systems.

The inclusion of uncertainty in FDE-governed models is significant because it represents the intrinsic complexity and unpredictability of many real-world systems. Uncertainties can originate from a variety of causes, including insufficient understanding of system characteristics, external disruptions, measurement mistakes, or environmental changes. In such a scenario, fuzzy theory is combined with fractional calculus, and fuzzy fractional differential equations (FFDEs) have been devised to represent systems with imprecise or ambiguous data. A range of fuzzy time-fractional dynamical models pertaining to diverse biological systems has been examined through the application of various computationally efficient methodologies [11]. The analysis of a fuzzy fractional-order predator–prey model is presented in [12]. The q-homotopy analysis Abodh transform method has been employed to solve the arbitrary-order vibration equation of a large membrane within a fuzzy framework [13]. Researchers have conducted an investigation into the fractional-order COVID-19 model within the context of fuzzy uncertainty [14]. This study employs fixed-point theory to demonstrate both the existence and uniqueness of the solution to the model, while numerical solutions have been obtained through an Euler-based iterative scheme.

The membership grade linked to traditional fuzzy parameters (type-1 fuzzy) is deterministic, which may fail to capture the intricate characteristics of the model being examined, as there may be impreciseness in the membership grade of the fuzzy parameters, too. In this context, type-2 fuzzy numbers are integrated with fractional calculus, resulting in type-2 fuzzy fractional differential equations (T2FFDEs). The concept of fractional derivatives for type-2 fuzzy valued functions was introduced in [15]. A range of mathematical models has been examined through numerical methods within the context of type-2 fuzzy environments. Mohapatra and Chakraverty have addressed different biological models within the context of a type-2 fuzzy uncertain environment by employing effective methodologies [16–18]. The fractional-order heat equation and fluid dynamic model have been examined within the context of a type-2 fuzzy environment [19,20].

15.2 Legendre wavelet method

Legendre wavelets $\phi_{n,m}(t)$ defined on $[0, l)$ are expressed as [21],

$$\phi_{nm}(t) = \begin{cases} \sqrt{m+\frac{1}{2}}2^{\frac{k}{2}} L_m(\frac{2^k t}{l} - \hat{n}), \text{ when } \frac{\hat{n}-1}{2^k} l \le t < \frac{\hat{n}}{2^k} l, \\ 0, \text{ otherwise} \end{cases} \tag{15.1}$$

where $m = 0, 1, 2, ..., M-1$, $n = 1, 2, 3, ..., 2^{k-1}$ (k is a positive integer), $\hat{n} = 2n-1$, $\sqrt{m+\frac{1}{2}}$ is the orthonormality coefficient, 2^{-k} is the dilation parameter, $\hat{n}2^{-k}$ is the translation parameter, and $L_m(t)$ is the Legendre polynomial of degree m.

Legendre wavelets can estimate $f(t)$, a function on $[0, l)$, as

$$f(t) = \sum_{n=1}^{\infty} \sum_{m=0}^{\infty} c_{nm} \phi_{nm}(t), \tag{15.2}$$

where $c_{nm} = \langle f(t), \phi_{nm}(t) \rangle$. Assume that there is an element in $L^2[0, l)$, which is the best approximation of f using a truncated series of Legendre wavelets and can be written as

$$f(t) \equiv \sum_{n=1}^{2^{k-1}} \sum_{m=0}^{M-1} c_{nm} \phi_{nm}(t) = C^T \phi(t) = \hat{f}(t), \tag{15.3}$$

where C and $\phi(t)$ are column vectors of order $2^{k-1}M \times 1$.

Now, taking the collocation points as $t_i = \frac{2i-1}{2^k M} l$, for $i = 1, 2, \ldots 2^{k-1}M$, then the wavelet matrix is defined as

$$\varphi = \left[\phi\left(\frac{l}{2^k M}\right) \quad \phi\left(\frac{3l}{2^k M}\right) \quad \phi\left(\frac{5l}{2^k M}\right) \quad \cdots \quad \phi\left(\frac{(2^k M-1)l}{2^k M}\right) \right]_{2^{k-1}M \times 2^{k-1}M} \tag{15.4}$$

15.2.1 Block-pulse function

The m-set of block-pulse function defined on $[0, l)$ is given by [21,22],

$$b_i(t) = \begin{cases} 1, (i-1)\frac{l}{m} \le t < i\frac{l}{m}, \\ 0, \text{ otherwise}, \end{cases} \tag{15.5}$$

where $i = 0, 1, ..., m$, and $b_i(t)$ are disjoint and orthogonal. An arbitrary function $f(t) \in L^2[0, 1)$ can be written in the block-pulse function as

$$f(t) \approx \sum_{i=1}^{m-1} f_i b_i(t) = f^T B(t), \tag{15.6}$$

where $f_i = \frac{m}{l} \int\limits_0^l f(t) b_i(t) dt$.

Additionally, the block-pulse functions can be used to write Legendre wavelets in the following way:

$$\phi(t) = \varphi_{2^{k-1}M \times 2^{k-1}M} B(t). \tag{15.7}$$

Now, the fractional integral of m sets of block-pulse function vectors is [23],

$$(I^{\nu} B)(t) = F^{\nu}_{2^{k-1}M \times 2^{k-1}M} B(t), \tag{15.8}$$

where ν denotes the fractional order.

15.2.2 Fractional-order integration operational matrix

The Legendre wavelet operational matrix of fractional-order integration ν is [23],

$$P^{\nu}_{2^{k-1}M \times 2^{k-1}M} = \varphi_{2^{k-1}M \times 2^{k-1}M} F^{\nu}_{2^{k-1}M \times 2^{k-1}M} \varphi^{-1}{}_{2^{k-1}M \times 2^{k-1}M}, \tag{15.9}$$

where

$$F_{2^{k-1}M \times 2^{k-1}M} = \left(\frac{l}{2^{k-1}M}\right)^{\nu} \frac{1}{\Gamma(\nu+2)} \begin{bmatrix} 1 & F_2 & F_3 & \cdots & F_{\hat{m}} \\ 0 & 1 & F_2 & \cdots & F_{\hat{m}-1} \\ \vdots & \vdots & \vdots & \ddots & \vdots \\ 0 & 0 & 0 & \cdots & F_2 \\ 0 & 0 & 0 & \cdots & 1 \end{bmatrix},$$

in which [23],

$$F_p = p^{\nu+1} - 2(p-1)^{\nu+1} + (p-2)^{\nu+1}, \; p = 2, 3, ..., 2^{k-1}M.$$

15.3 Problem description and implementation of the LWM

Let us consider the type-2 fuzzy fractional-order differential equation of the form;

$$D^{\nu} \tilde{\tilde{y}}(x) + \tilde{\tilde{F}}(x, \tilde{\tilde{y}}) = 0, \tag{15.10}$$

where $n-1 < \nu < n$ represents the fractional-order derivative in Caputo's sense and $\tilde{\tilde{F}}(x, \tilde{\tilde{y}})$ denotes the remaining term in the fractional-order differential equation. Here, the double tilde parameters signify the type-2 fuzzy uncertainties in the given Eq. (15.10). Using the concept of β-cut of the α-plane, Eq. (15.10) can be written as

$$D^{\nu} \tilde{\tilde{y}}(x; \alpha, \beta) + \tilde{\tilde{F}}(x, \tilde{\tilde{y}}; \alpha, \beta) = 0. \tag{15.11}$$

Further, using the concept of LMF and UMF in Eq. (15.11), results in

$$\begin{aligned} D^{\nu} \underline{\tilde{y}}(x; \alpha, \beta) + \underline{\tilde{F}}(x, \tilde{\tilde{y}}; \alpha, \beta) = 0, \\ D^{\nu} \overline{\tilde{y}}(x; \alpha, \beta) + \overline{\tilde{F}}(x, \overline{\tilde{y}}; \alpha, \beta) = 0. \end{aligned} \tag{15.12}$$

Now, introducing the third parameter $\gamma \in [0, 1]$ as discussed in the preceding chapters to handle the uncertainty in Eq. (15.12), Eq. (15.12) can be written as

$$\begin{aligned} D^{\nu}\underline{\tilde{y}}(x;\alpha,\beta,\gamma)+\underline{\tilde{F}}(x,\underline{\tilde{y}};\alpha,\beta,\gamma)=0,\\ D^{\nu}\overline{\tilde{y}}(x;\alpha,\beta,\gamma)+\overline{\tilde{F}}(x,\overline{\tilde{y}};\alpha,\beta,\gamma)=0. \end{aligned} \tag{15.13}$$

By employing Legendre wavelets to approximate each term in the equations of Eq. (15.13), and utilizing the concept of the fractional-order operation matrix alongside the block-pulse function, it turns out possible to transform both equations into two systems of algebraic equations that are expressed in terms of the uncertainty handling parameters α, β, and γ. The characteristics of the resulting systems of algebraic equations, whether linear or non-linear, are contingent upon the form of the differential equation. Moreover, by addressing the resulting algebraic systems, one can ascertain the unknown coefficient vector. Consequently, an approximate solution for the type-2 fuzzy fractional differential equation can be obtained.

15.4 Sample problems

In this section, two simple numerical examples of type-2 fuzzy fractional initial value problems are discussed. The solution procedure of the sample problems are provided in detail. To handle the uncertainty, TPQT2FNs are used here.

Example 15.1. Let us consider the following T2FFIVP:

$$D^{\nu}\tilde{\tilde{y}}(x)-x\tilde{\tilde{y}}(x)+2\tilde{\tilde{y}}(x)=0,\ 0<\nu\leq 1, \tag{15.14}$$

with the TPQT2FN valued initial condition as $\tilde{\tilde{y}}(0)=(0.7, 0.8, 0.9, 1, 1.1, 1.2, 1.3)$. Using the triple parametric representation of the type-2 fuzzy parameters in the above T2FFIVP, results in

$$D^{\nu}\underline{\tilde{y}}(x;\alpha,\beta,\gamma)-x\underline{\tilde{y}}(x;\alpha,\beta,\gamma)+2\underline{\tilde{y}}(x;\alpha,\beta,\gamma)=0,\ 0<\nu\leq 1, \tag{15.15}$$

where

$$\underline{\tilde{y}}(0;\alpha,\beta,\gamma)=\frac{\beta}{5}-\gamma\left(\frac{2\beta}{5}+2\left(\frac{\beta}{10}-\frac{1}{10}\right)(\alpha-1)-\frac{2}{5}\right)+\left(\frac{\beta}{10}-\frac{1}{10}\right)(\alpha-1)+\frac{4}{5}, \tag{15.16}$$

and

$$D^{\nu}\overline{\tilde{y}}(x;\alpha,\beta,\gamma)-x\overline{\tilde{y}}(x;\alpha,\beta,\gamma)+2\overline{\tilde{y}}(x;\alpha,\beta,\gamma)=0,\ 0<\nu\leq 1, \tag{15.17}$$

where

$$\overline{\tilde{y}}(0;\alpha,\beta,\gamma)=\frac{\beta}{5}+\gamma\left(2\left(\frac{\beta}{10}-\frac{1}{10}\right)(\alpha-1)-\frac{2\beta}{5}+\frac{2}{5}\right)-\left(\frac{\beta}{10}-\frac{1}{10}\right)(\alpha-1)+\frac{4}{5}. \tag{15.18}$$

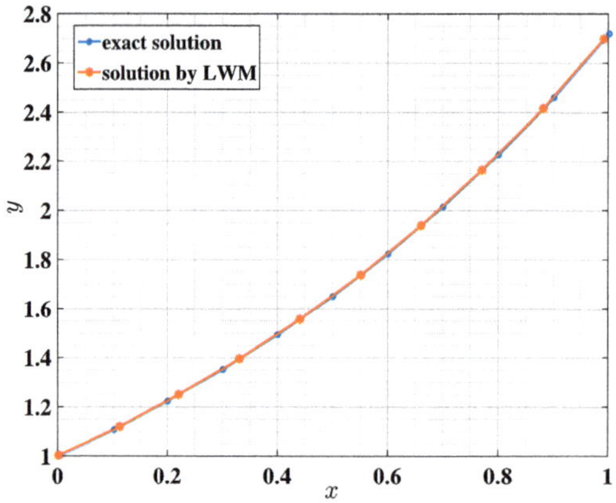

FIGURE 15.1 Comparison of solution of Example 15.1 by the LWM with the exact solution under a crisp condition.

Suppose

$$D^{\nu}\underset{\sim}{\tilde{y}}(x;\alpha,\beta,\gamma)=\underset{\sim}{\tilde{C}}^{T}\phi(x). \tag{15.19}$$

Using the concept of the fractional-order operational matrix, one can obtain

$$\underset{\sim}{\tilde{y}}(x;\alpha,\beta,\gamma)=\underset{\sim}{\tilde{C}}^{T}P^{\nu}\phi(x)+\underset{\sim}{\tilde{y}}(0;\alpha,\beta,\gamma). \tag{15.20}$$

Substituting Eqs. (15.19) and (15.20) in Eq. (15.15) give

$$\underset{\sim}{\tilde{C}}^{T}\phi(x)-x\left(\underset{\sim}{\tilde{C}}^{T}P^{\nu}\phi(x)+\underset{\sim}{\tilde{y}}(0;\alpha,\beta,\gamma)\right)+2\left(\underset{\sim}{\tilde{C}}^{T}P^{\nu}\phi(x)+\underset{\sim}{\tilde{y}}(0;\alpha,\beta,\gamma)\right)=0. \tag{15.21}$$

Taking $2^{k-1}M$ equidistant collocation points, the above equation, i.e., Eq. (15.21) results into a system of linear equations of size $(2^{k-1}M\times 2^{k-1}M)$ in terms of the uncertainty handling parameters α, β, and γ. The system of equations can be solved for the unknown vector $\underset{\sim}{\tilde{C}}$.

Further, substituting the values of $\underset{\sim}{\tilde{C}}$ in Eq. (15.19), the approximate value of the LMF of the required solution of the given type-2 fuzzy fractional-order problem can be obtained.

Proceeding similarly for the UMF equations, i.e., Eqs. (15.17) and (15.18), the UMF solution of the type-2 fuzzy unknown can be attained.

Specifically, for the purpose of validation, the solutions derived using the LWM (for $k=3$ and $M=3$) are compared with the exact solution of the integer-order deterministic model, namely $\nu=1$. The comparative analysis is illustrated in Fig. 15.1. This graphical representation effectively demonstrates the efficacy of the LWM. The numerical comparison is presented in Table 15.1 for different values of k and M. Analysis of the table reveals that the LWM solution progressively approaches the exact solution as the values of k and M are increased. The behavior of the solution for different values of fractional-order differentiation is illustrated in Fig. 15.2.

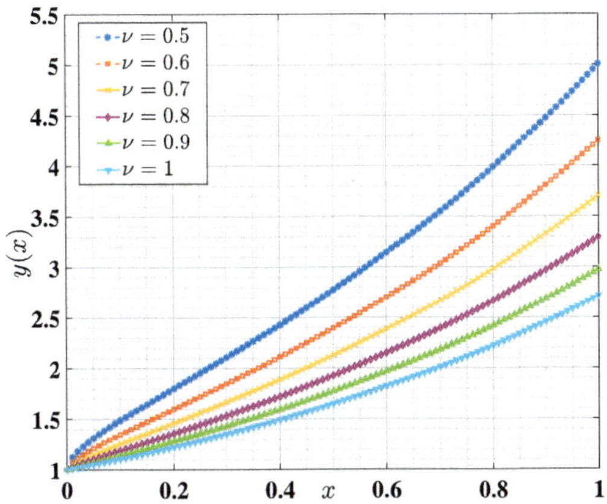

FIGURE 15.2 Solutions of Example 15.1 for different values of the fractional-order derivatives under the crisp condition.

Table 15.1 Solutions of Example 15.1 obtained for different values of k and M and comparison with exact solutions.

x	$k = 1$ and $M = 3$	$k = 2$ and $M = 3$	$k = 3$ and $M = 3$	Exact
0.1	1.1340	1.1100	1.1064	1.1052
0.2	1.2441	1.2268	1.2229	1.2214
0.3	1.3726	1.3569	1.3517	1.3499
0.4	1.5195	1.5003	1.4938	1.4918
0.5	1.6848	1.6571	1.6511	1.6487
0.6	1.8684	1.8343	1.8248	1.8221
0.7	2.0703	2.0254	2.0169	2.0138
0.8	2.2906	2.2397	2.2290	2.2255
0.9	2.5293	2.4771	2.4636	2.4596
1.0	2.7863	2.7377	2.7232	2.7183

The analysis of the derived type-2 fuzzy solution in relation to the precise type-2 fuzzy solution is illustrated in Figs. 15.3 and 15.4. In this analysis, the FOUs of the current LWM solution and the exact solution are presented for $k = 3$, $M = 3$ in the context of the integer-order case. In order to examine the behavior of the type-2 fuzzy solution, the FOUs are illustrated graphically in Figs. 15.5 and 15.6, corresponding to $\nu = 0.9$ and 0.8, respectively. Finally, the bounds of the derived type-2 fuzzy solution are illustrated in Table 15.2 for different values of α and β.

Example 15.2. Let us consider another sample problem as below:

$$D^{\nu}\tilde{\tilde{y}}(x) + \tilde{\tilde{y}}(x) = x + 1, 0 < \nu \leq 1, \tag{15.22}$$

where

$$\tilde{\tilde{y}}(0) = (0.4, 0.6, 0.8, 1, 1.2, 1.4, 1.6). \tag{15.23}$$

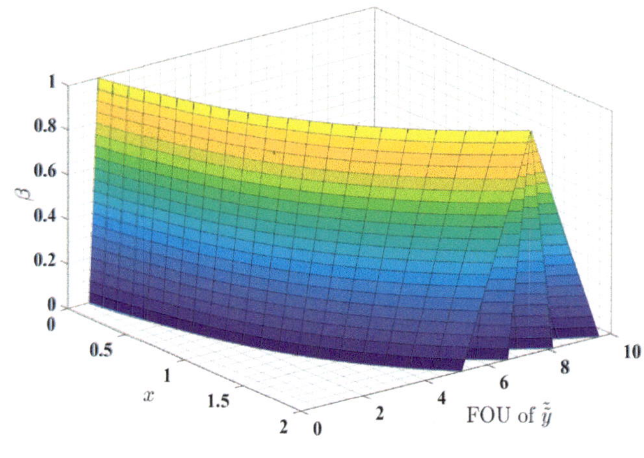

FIGURE 15.3 FOU of the exact type-2 fuzzy solution $\tilde{\tilde{y}}$ of Example 15.1 for $\nu = 1$.

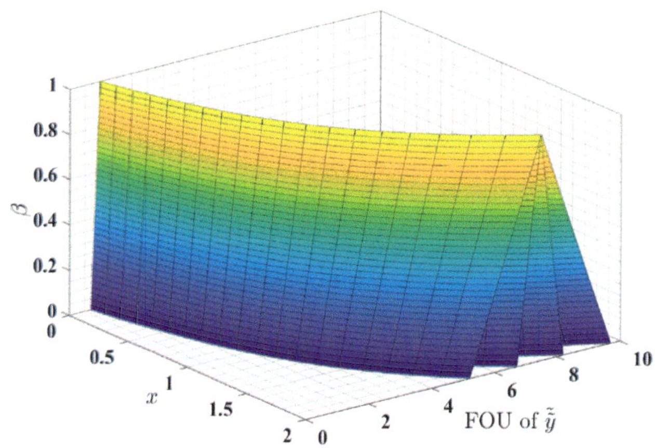

FIGURE 15.4 FOU of the type-2 fuzzy solution $\tilde{\tilde{y}}$ of Example 15.1 for $\nu = 1$ by the LWM.

Using the triple parametric approach, the given fractional-order initial value problems (15.22) and (15.22) can be written as

$$D^{\nu}\underline{\tilde{y}}(x;\alpha,\beta,\gamma)+\underline{\tilde{y}}(x;\alpha,\beta,\gamma)=x+1, 0<\nu\leq 1,$$
$$\text{where } \underline{\tilde{y}}(0;\alpha,\beta,\gamma)=\frac{2\beta}{5}-\gamma\left(\frac{4\beta}{5}+2\left(\frac{\beta}{5}-\frac{1}{5}\right)(\alpha-1)-\frac{4}{5}\right)+\left(\frac{\beta}{5}-\frac{1}{5}\right)(\alpha-1)+\frac{3}{5}, \tag{15.24}$$

and

$$D^{\nu}\overline{\tilde{y}}(x;\alpha,\beta,\gamma)+\overline{\tilde{y}}(x;\alpha,\beta,\gamma)=x+1, 0<\nu\leq 1,$$
$$\text{where } \overline{\tilde{y}}(0;\alpha,\beta,\gamma)=\frac{2\beta}{5}+\gamma\left(2\left(\frac{\beta}{5}-\frac{1}{5}\right)(\alpha-1)-\frac{4\beta}{5}+\frac{4}{5}\right)-\left(\frac{\beta}{5}-\frac{1}{5}\right)(\alpha-1)+\frac{3}{5}. \tag{15.25}$$

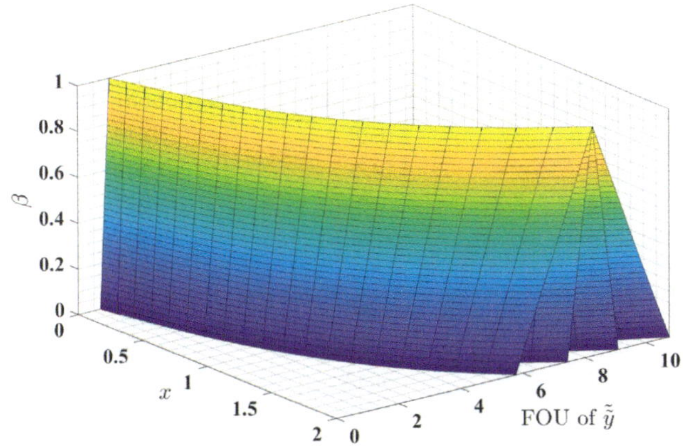

FIGURE 15.5 FOU of the type-2 fuzzy solution $\tilde{\tilde{y}}$ of Example 15.1 for $\nu = 0.9$ by the LWM.

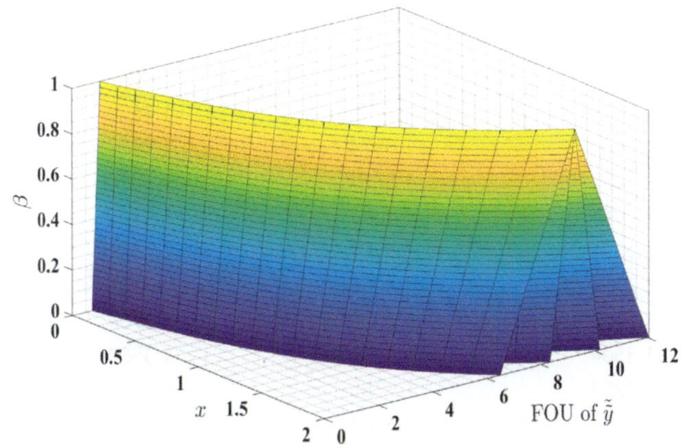

FIGURE 15.6 FOU of the type-2 fuzzy solution $\tilde{\tilde{y}}$ of Example 15.1 for $\nu = 0.8$ by the LWM.

Applying the LWM to the two initial value problems, i.e., Eqs. (15.24) and (15.25) result in the formulation of two systems of linear algebraic equations. By solving these linear systems of equations, one can derive the approximate solutions of Eqs. (15.24) and (15.25). The LMF and UMF are used to derive the required type-2 fuzzy solution $\tilde{\tilde{y}}$ based on the parameters α, β, and γ.

The effectiveness of the LWM is demonstrated by comparing the LWM solution with the exact solution in the crisp scenario for the integer-order case. The validation is illustrated in Fig. 15.7. The graphs illustrating the precise solution for different values of the fractional-order derivative are presented in Fig. 15.8. The convergence of the LWM solution is presented in Table 15.3. The type-2 fuzzy solution derived from the LWM is analyzed in comparison to the type-2 fuzzy exact solution as illustrated in Figs. 15.9 and 15.10. The FOU of the type-2 fuzzy solution is presented in Figs. 15.11 and 15.12 for $\nu = 0.9$ and 0.8, re-

Table 15.2 Bounds of the type-2 fuzzy solution $\tilde{\tilde{y}}$ of Example 15.1 at $x = 0.25$ for $k = 3$, $M = 3$, and $\nu = 0.75$.

α	β	Left bound (LMF)	Right bound (LMF)	Left bound (UMF)	Right bound (UMF)
0	0	1.3504	1.6505	1.0503	1.9506
0	0.25	1.3879	1.6130	1.1628	1.8380
0	0.50	1.4254	1.5755	1.2754	1.7255
0	0.75	1.4629	1.5380	1.3879	1.6130
0	1	1.5004	1.5004	1.5004	1.5004
0.25	0	1.3129	1.6880	1.0878	1.9131
0.25	0.25	1.3598	1.6411	1.1910	1.8099
0.25	0.50	1.4067	1.5942	1.2941	1.7068
0.25	0.75	1.4536	1.5473	1.3973	1.6036
0.25	1	1.5004	1.5004	1.5004	1.5004
0.50	0	1.2754	1.7255	1.1253	1.8756
0.50	0.25	1.3316	1.6692	1.2191	1.7818
0.50	0.50	1.3879	1.6130	1.3129	1.6880
0.50	0.75	1.4442	1.5567	1.4067	1.5942
0.50	1	1.5004	1.5004	1.5004	1.5004
0.75	0	1.2379	1.7630	1.1628	1.8380
0.75	0.25	1.3035	1.6974	1.2472	1.7536
0.75	0.50	1.3692	1.6317	1.3316	1.6692
0.75	0.75	1.4348	1.5661	1.4160	1.5848
0.75	1	1.5004	1.5004	1.5004	1.5004
1	0	1.2004	1.8005	1.2004	1.8005
1	0.25	1.2754	1.7255	1.2754	1.7255
1	0.50	1.3504	1.6505	1.3504	1.6505
1	0.75	1.4254	1.5755	1.4254	1.5755
1	1	1.5004	1.5004	1.5004	1.5004

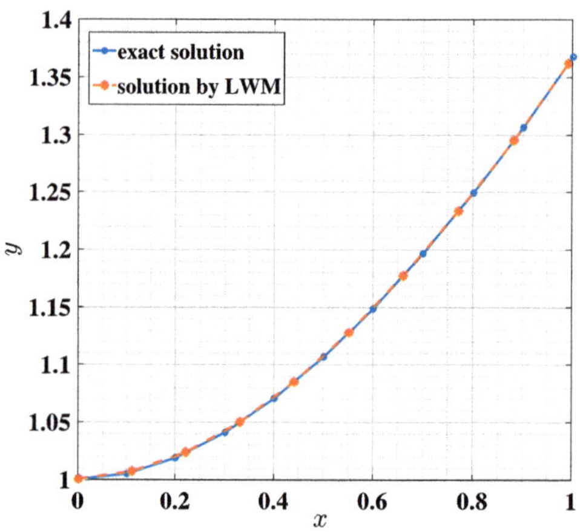

FIGURE 15.7 Comparison of solution of Example 15.2 by the LWM with the exact solution under the crisp condition.

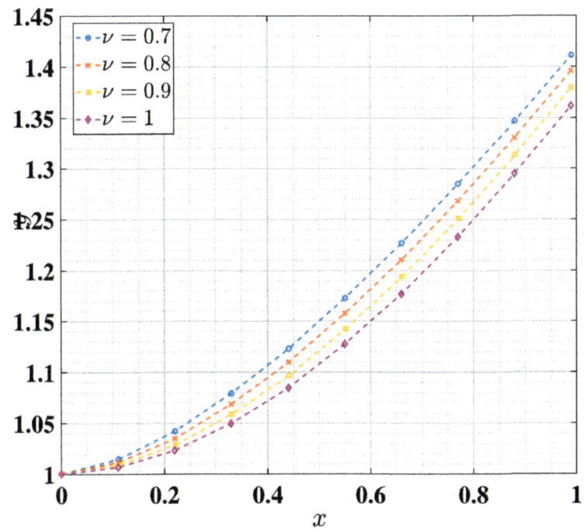

FIGURE 15.8 Solutions of Example 15.2 for different values of the fractional-order derivatives under the crisp condition.

Table 15.3 Solutions of Example 15.2 obtained for different values of k and M and comparison with exact solutions.

x	$k = 1$ and $M = 3$	$k = 2$ and $M = 3$	$k = 3$ and $M = 3$	Exact
0.1	1.0159	1.0085	1.0058	1.0048
0.2	1.0314	1.0220	1.0194	1.0187
0.3	1.0530	1.0432	1.0414	1.0408
0.4	1.0805	1.0721	1.0708	1.0703
0.5	1.1141	1.1087	1.1069	1.1065
0.6	1.1538	1.1499	1.1492	1.1488
0.7	1.1995	1.1979	1.1969	1.1966
0.8	1.2512	1.2503	1.2496	1.2493
0.9	1.3090	1.3071	1.3068	1.3066
1.0	1.3727	1.3684	1.3680	1.3679

spectively. The bounds of the type-2 fuzzy solution are presented in Table 15.4 for different values of α and β.

15.5 Application problems

In this section, we will discuss application problems that are governed by fractional-order initial value problems; further, as the presence of uncertainty is also crucial in practice. In this regard, the fractional-order initial value problems are discussed in the type-2 fuzzy uncertain environment using the LWM.

15.5.1 Fractional-order R-L circuit

The fractional-order RL circuit equation is a generalization of the traditional first-order RL circuit, where the derivative of the current is replaced by a fractional derivative. This

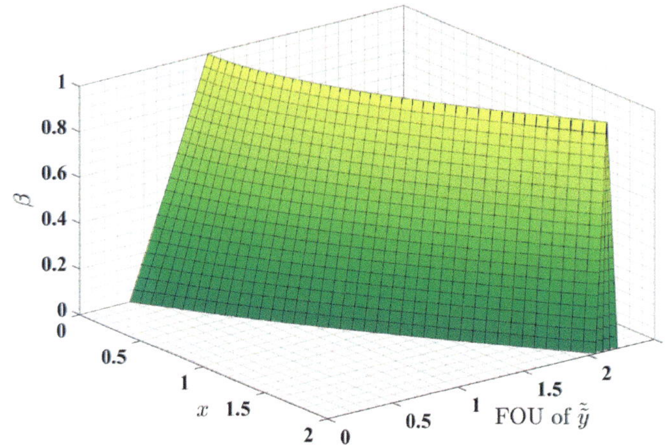

FIGURE 15.9 FOU of the exact type-2 fuzzy solution $\tilde{\tilde{y}}$ of Example 15.2 for $\nu = 1$.

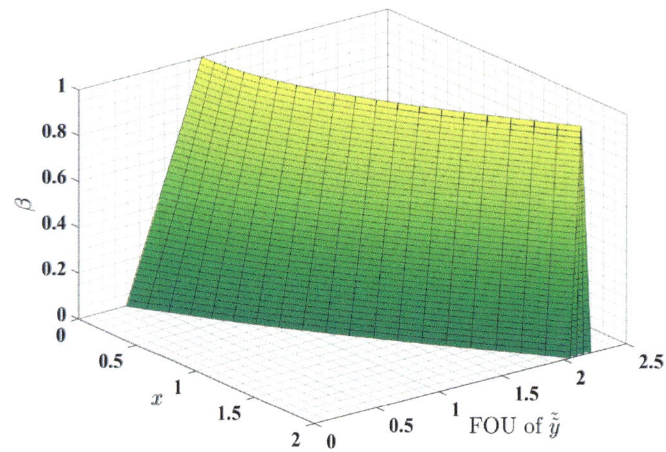

FIGURE 15.10 FOU of the type-2 fuzzy solution $\tilde{\tilde{y}}$ of Example 15.2 for $\nu = 1$ by the LWM.

approach captures more complex dynamics, such as memory effects, which are not represented in standard integer-order systems. In the fractional-order RL circuit, the governing equation is given by [24],

$$LD^{\nu}y(t) + Ry(t) = V(t), \tag{15.26}$$

where L is the inductance, R is the resistance, and $V(t)$ is the applied voltage. Implementing the notion of uncertainty as type-2 fuzzy numbers, in particular, TPQT2FN in the initial condition associated with Eq. (15.26), the type-2 fuzzy R-L circuit of fractional order will be

$$LD^{\nu}\tilde{\tilde{y}}(t) + R\tilde{\tilde{y}}(t) = V(t), \tag{15.27}$$

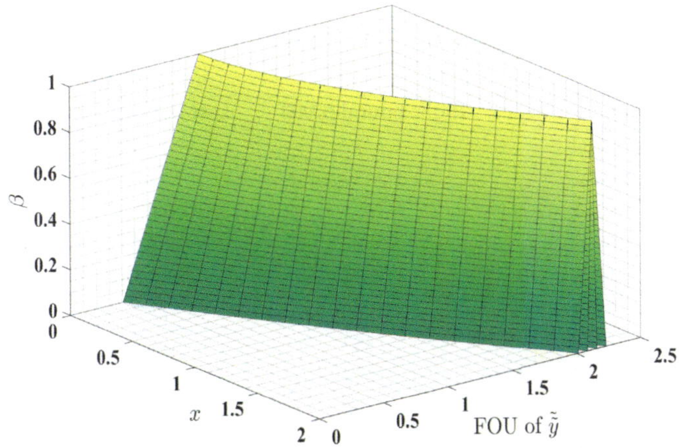

FIGURE 15.11 FOU of the type-2 fuzzy solution $\tilde{\tilde{y}}$ of Example 15.2 for $\nu = 0.9$ by the LWM.

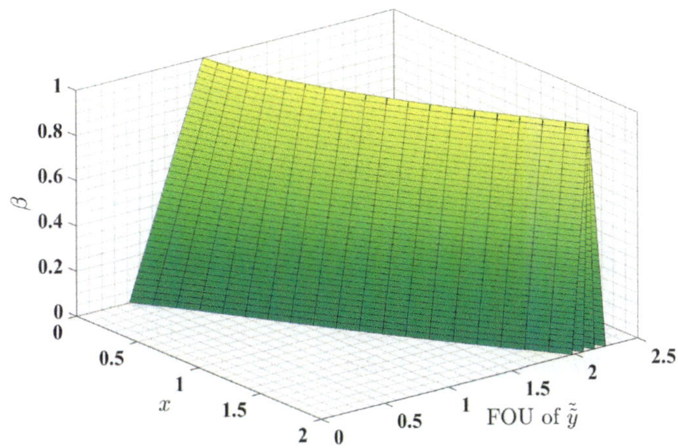

FIGURE 15.12 FOU of the type-2 fuzzy solution $\tilde{\tilde{y}}$ of Example 15.2 for $\nu = 0.8$ by the LWM.

with $\tilde{\tilde{y}}(0) = (0.7, 0.8, 0.9, 1, 1.1, 1.2, 1.3)$. Suppose $L = 1$, $R = 1$, and $V(t) = \sin(t)$, then Eq. (15.27) will be

$$D^{\nu}\tilde{\tilde{y}}(t) + \tilde{\tilde{y}}(t) = \sin(t). \tag{15.28}$$

Using the triple parametric representation and the LWM approach on Eq. (15.28), the LMF and UMF of the type-2 fuzzy solution can be obtained for particular values of the k and M in terms of α, β, and γ.

The obtained LWM solution is compared with the exact solution under the crisp case for the integer-order model as shown in Fig. 15.13. In Table 15.5, the convergence of the LWM solution is shown for $\nu = 1$ under the crisp scenario. Behavior of the crisp solution under different values of the fractional-order derivative is shown in Fig. 15.14.

Table 15.4 Bounds of the type-2 fuzzy solution $\tilde{\tilde{y}}$ of Example 15.2 at $x = 0.5$ for $k = 3$, $M = 3$, and $\nu = 0.85$.

α	β	Left bound (LMF)	Right bound (LMF)	Left bound (UMF)	Right bound (UMF)
0	0	1.0134	1.2423	0.7845	1.4712
0	0.25	1.0420	1.2137	0.8704	1.3854
0	0.5	1.0707	1.1851	0.9562	1.2996
0	0.75	1.0993	1.1565	1.0420	1.2137
0	1	1.1279	1.1279	1.1279	1.1279
0.25	0	0.9848	1.2709	0.8131	1.4426
0.25	0.25	1.0206	1.2352	0.8918	1.3639
0.25	0.5	1.0563	1.1994	0.9705	1.2853
0.25	0.75	1.0921	1.1636	1.0492	1.2066
0.25	1	1.1279	1.1279	1.1279	1.1279
0.5	0	0.9562	1.2996	0.8417	1.4140
0.5	0.25	0.9991	1.2566	0.9133	1.3425
0.5	0.5	1.0420	1.2137	0.9848	1.2709
0.5	0.75	1.0850	1.1708	1.0563	1.1994
0.5	1	1.1279	1.1279	1.1279	1.1279
0.75	0	0.9276	1.3282	0.8704	1.3854
0.75	0.25	0.9777	1.2781	0.9347	1.3210
0.75	0.5	1.0277	1.2280	0.9991	1.2566
0.75	0.75	1.0778	1.1780	1.0635	1.1923
0.75	1	1.1279	1.1279	1.1279	1.1279
1	0	0.8990	1.3568	0.8990	1.3568
1	0.25	0.9562	1.2996	0.9562	1.2996
1	0.5	1.0134	1.2423	1.0134	1.2423
1	0.75	1.0707	1.1851	1.0707	1.1851
1	1	1.1279	1.1279	1.1279	1.1279

Table 15.5 Solutions of the R-L circuit obtained for different values of k and M and the comparison with exact solutions.

t	$k = 1$ and $M = 4$	$k = 2$ and $M = 4$	$k = 3$ and $M = 4$	$k = 4$ and $M = 4$	Exact
0.1	0.9229	0.9130	0.9105	0.9099	0.9097
0.2	0.8486	0.8402	0.8381	0.8376	0.8374
0.3	0.7906	0.7836	0.7819	0.7815	0.7813
0.4	0.7471	0.7415	0.7401	0.7398	0.7397
0.5	0.7166	0.7121	0.7111	0.7108	0.7107
0.6	0.6974	0.6940	0.6932	0.6929	0.6929
0.7	0.6880	0.6854	0.6848	0.6846	0.6846
0.8	0.6868	0.6849	0.6845	0.6844	0.6843
0.9	0.6921	0.6911	0.6908	0.6907	0.6907
1.0	0.7023	0.7025	0.7024	0.7024	0.7024

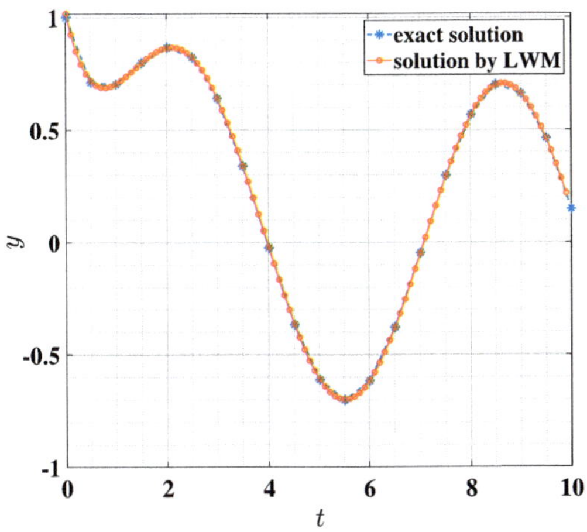

FIGURE 15.13 Comparison of the solution of the R-L circuit by the LWM with the exact solution under the crisp condition.

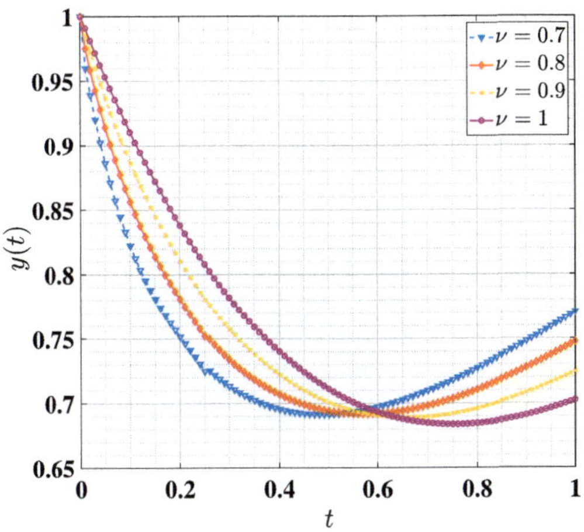

FIGURE 15.14 Solutions of the R-L circuit for different values of the fractional-order derivatives under the crisp condition.

Further, the comparison of the present type-2 fuzzy solution with the exact solution is illustrated graphically in Figs. 15.15 and 15.16. From these two figures, it can be observed that the LWM solution is closed enough with the exact solution. In Figs. 15.17 and 15.18, the FOU of the obtained type-2 fuzzy solution is presented for $\nu = 0.9$ and 0.8. Different bounds of the type-2 fuzzy solution for various values of α and β are shown in Table 15.6.

15.5.2 Generalized Bagley–Torvik equation

The generalized Bagley–Torvik equation is an extension of the classical Bagley–Torvik equation, incorporating fractional-order derivatives to model systems with complex

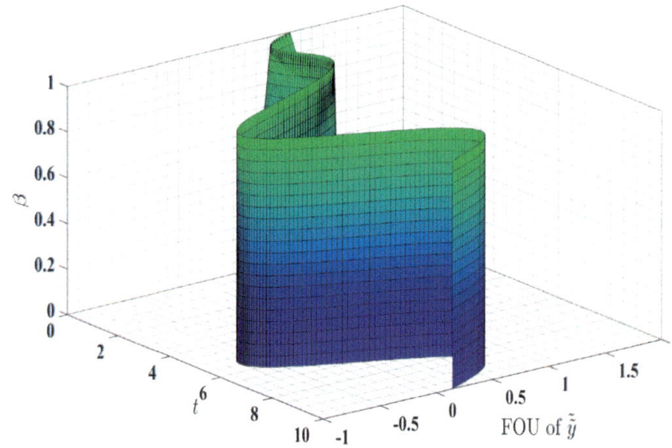

FIGURE 15.15 FOU of the exact type-2 fuzzy solution $\tilde{\tilde{y}}$ of the R-L circuit for $\nu = 1$.

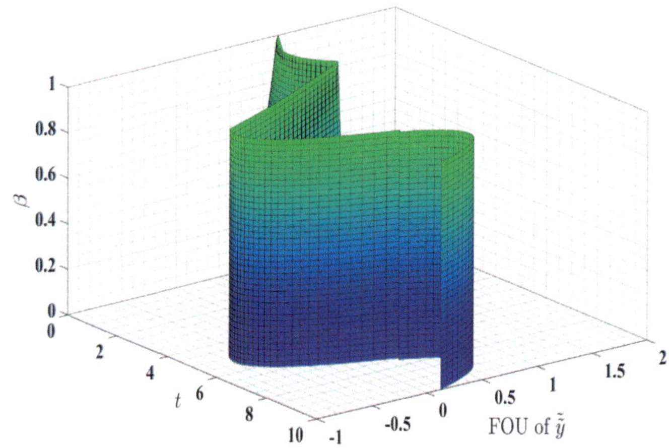

FIGURE 15.16 FOU of the type-2 fuzzy solution $\tilde{\tilde{y}}$ of the R-L circuit for $\nu = 1$ by the LWM.

damping behavior. It is widely used in the study of viscoelastic materials, fluid-structure interaction, and systems exhibiting anomalous diffusion. The generalized Bagley–Torvik equation is given by [25],

$$mD^2x(t) + cD^{\nu}x(t) + kx(t) = F(t), \tag{15.29}$$

where m stands for the mass, c denotes the damping coefficient, k is the stiffness constant, $F(t)$ is the applied external force, and $x(t)$ denotes the displacement function.

Incorporating the concept of uncertainty in the associated initial conditions as TPQT2FNs, the governing equation under the type-2 fuzzy uncertainty is given by

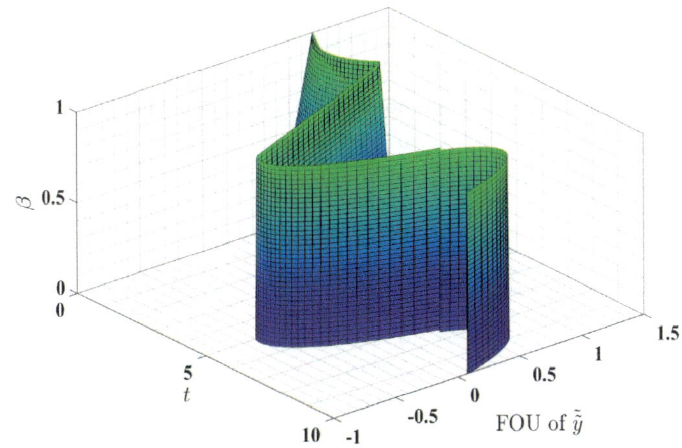

FIGURE 15.17 FOU of the type-2 fuzzy solution $\tilde{\tilde{y}}$ of the R-L circuit for $\nu = 0.9$ by the LWM.

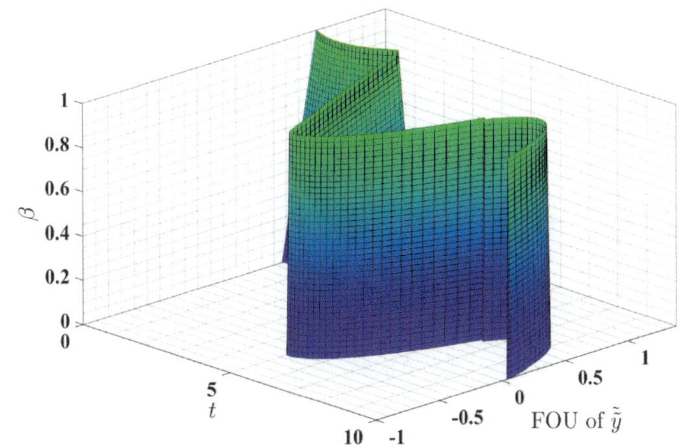

FIGURE 15.18 FOU of the type-2 fuzzy solution $\tilde{\tilde{y}}$ of the R-L circuit for $\nu = 0.8$ by the LWM.

$$mD^2\tilde{\tilde{x}}(t) + cD^{\nu}\tilde{\tilde{x}}(t) + k\tilde{\tilde{x}}(t) = F(t), \tag{15.30}$$

with initial conditions as $\tilde{\tilde{x}}(0)$ and $\tilde{\tilde{x}}'(0)$.

Suppose $m = 1,\ c = 1,\ k = 4,\ F(t) = 10\cos(4t),\ \tilde{\tilde{x}}(0) = (0, 1, 2, 3, 4, 5, 6)$, and $\tilde{\tilde{x}}'(0) = (0, 1, 2, 3, 4, 5, 6)$. Using the triple parametric representation of the type-2 fuzzy parameters in the governing initial value problem and implementing the LWM, LMF, and UMF bounds of the type-2 fuzzy solution can be attained.

In Fig. 15.19, a comparison between the present solution and exact solution for $\nu = 1$ is presented under the deterministic case. It can be observed from this plot that the present solution agreed well with the exact solution. Table 15.7 shows the convergence of the so-

Table 15.6 Bounds of the type-2 fuzzy solution $\tilde{\tilde{y}}$ of the R-L circuit at $t = 0.1$ for $k = 3$, $M = 3$, and $\nu = 0.65$.

α	β	Left bound (LMF)	Right bound (LMF)	Left bound (UMF)	Right bound (UMF)
0	0	0.7291	0.9674	0.5703	1.2850
0	0.25	0.7490	0.9277	0.6299	1.1659
0	0.5	0.7688	0.8879	0.6894	1.0468
0	0.75	0.7887	0.8482	0.7490	0.9277
0	1	0.8085	0.8085	0.8085	0.8085
0.25	0	0.7093	1.0071	0.5902	1.2453
0.25	0.25	0.7341	0.9574	0.6447	1.1361
0.25	0.5	0.7589	0.9078	0.6993	1.0269
0.25	0.75	0.7837	0.8582	0.7539	0.9177
0.25	1	0.8085	0.8085	0.8085	0.8085
0.5	0	0.6894	1.0468	0.6100	1.2056
0.5	0.25	0.7192	0.9872	0.6596	1.1063
0.5	0.5	0.7490	0.9277	0.7093	1.0071
0.5	0.75	0.7788	0.8681	0.7589	0.9078
0.5	1	0.8085	0.8085	0.8085	0.8085
0.75	0	0.6696	1.0865	0.6299	1.1659
0.75	0.25	0.7043	1.0170	0.6745	1.0765
0.75	0.5	0.7390	0.9475	0.7192	0.9872
0.75	0.75	0.7738	0.8780	0.7639	0.8979
0.75	1	0.8085	0.8085	0.8085	0.8085
1	0	0.6497	1.1262	0.6497	1.1262
1	0.25	0.6894	1.0468	0.6894	1.0468
1	0.5	0.7291	0.9674	0.7291	0.9674
1	0.75	0.7688	0.8879	0.7688	0.8879
1	1	0.8085	0.8085	0.8085	0.8085

Table 15.7 Solutions of the Generalised Bargley-Torvik equation obtained for different values of k and M and the comparison with exact solutions.

t	$k = 1$ and $M = 3$	$k = 2$ and $M = 3$	$k = 3$ and $M = 3$	Exact
0.1	−0.0906	0.0586	0.0513	0.0476
0.2	0.1775	0.1897	0.1735	0.1749
0.3	0.3800	0.3332	0.3426	0.3484
0.4	0.5168	0.4889	0.5209	0.5258
0.5	0.5880	0.6570	0.6553	0.6634
0.6	0.5936	0.7000	0.7146	0.7234
0.7	0.5336	0.6415	0.6728	0.6811
0.8	0.4080	0.4991	0.5215	0.5287
0.9	0.2167	0.2730	0.2722	0.2773
1.0	−0.0402	−0.0369	−0.0416	−0.0445

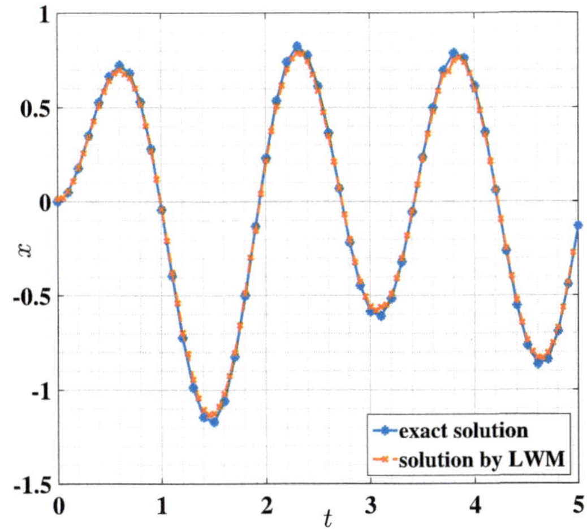

FIGURE 15.19 Comparison of the Generalised Bargley-Torvik equation solution by the LWM with the exact solution under the crisp condition.

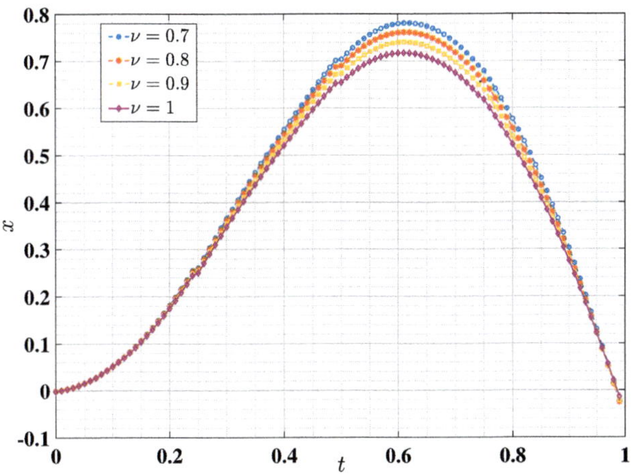

FIGURE 15.20 Solutions of the Generalised Bargley-Torvik equation for different values of the fractional-order derivatives under the crisp condition.

lution toward the exact solution. The behavior of the solution for various values of the fractional-order derivative is shown in Fig. 15.20.

Further, the exact type-2 fuzzy solution and the present type-2 fuzzy solution for the integer case are presented in Figs. 15.21 and 15.22. From these figures, it can be seen that both the plots are identical. The FOUs of the present type-2 fuzzy solution are plotted in Figs. 15.23 and 15.24 for $\nu = 0.9$ and 0.8. Table 15.8 illustrates the bounds of the type-2 fuzzy solution for various values of α and β.

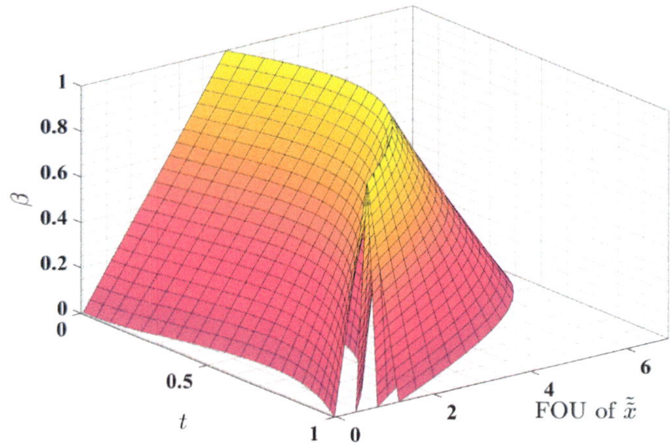

FIGURE 15.21 FOU of the exact type-2 fuzzy solution $\tilde{\tilde{x}}$ of the Generalised Bargley-Torvik equation for $\nu = 1$.

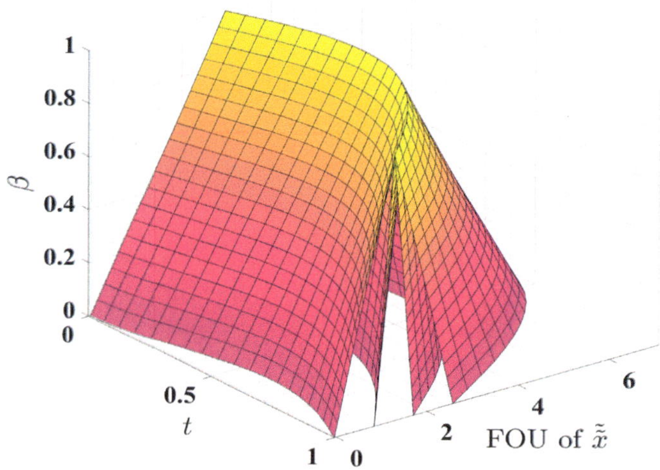

FIGURE 15.22 FOU of the type-2 fuzzy solution $\tilde{\tilde{x}}$ of the Generalised Bargley-Torvik equation for $\nu = 1$ by the LWM.

This chapter examines Type-2 fuzzy fractional differential equations and their applications to real-world problems. The equations are addressed through the application of the triple parametric form of associated type-2 fuzzy parameters, in conjunction by using the Legendre wavelet method. A comparison has been conducted with the exact solution under a specific scenario, and it has been found to be in good agreement.

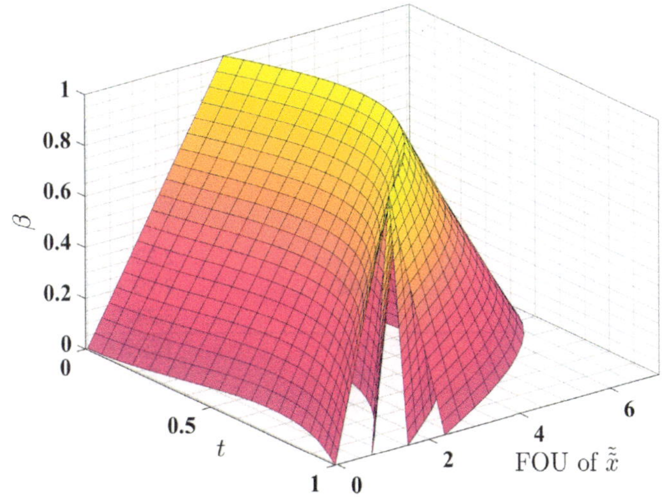

FIGURE 15.23 FOU of the type-2 fuzzy solution $\tilde{\tilde{y}}$ of the Generalised Bargley-Torvik equation for $\nu = 0.9$ by the LWM.

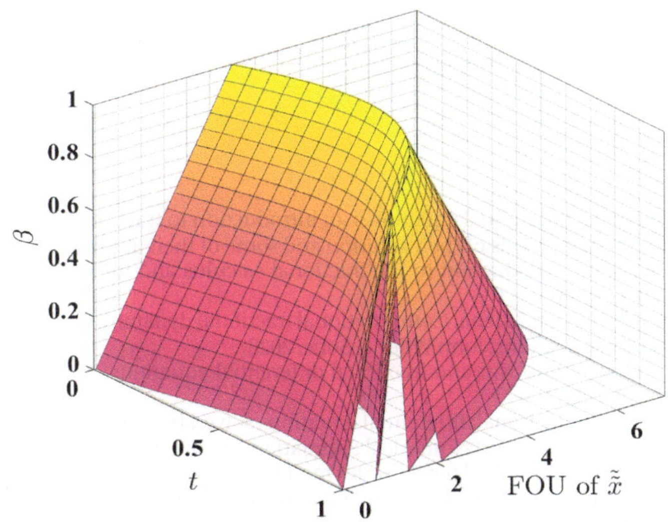

FIGURE 15.24 FOU of the type-2 fuzzy solution $\tilde{\tilde{y}}$ the Generalised Bargley-Torvik equation for $\nu = 0.8$ by the LWM.

Table 15.8 Bounds of the type-2 fuzzy solution $\tilde{\tilde{x}}$ of the Generalised Bargley-Torvik equation at $t = 0.1$ for $k = 3$, $M = 3$, and $\nu = 0.65$.

α	β	Left bound (LMF)	Right bound (LMF)	Left bound (UMF)	Right bound (UMF)
0	0	2.6557	4.8511	0.4603	7.0465
0	0.25	2.9301	4.5766	1.2835	6.2232
0	0.5	3.2045	4.3022	2.1068	5.3999
0	0.75	3.4789	4.0278	2.9301	4.5766
0	1	3.7534	3.7534	3.7534	3.7534
0.25	0	2.3751	5.1107	0.7338	6.7520
0.25	0.25	2.7171	4.7687	1.4861	5.9997
0.25	0.5	3.0590	4.4268	2.2384	5.2474
0.25	0.75	3.4010	4.0848	2.9906	4.4952
0.25	1	3.7429	3.7429	3.7429	3.7429
0.5	0	2.0911	5.3529	1.0039	6.4401
0.5	0.25	2.4989	4.9452	1.6834	5.7606
0.5	0.5	2.9066	4.5374	2.3629	5.0811
0.5	0.75	3.3143	4.1297	3.0425	4.4015
0.5	1	3.7220	3.7220	3.7220	3.7220
0.75	0	1.8020	5.5588	1.2653	6.0954
0.75	0.25	2.2716	5.0892	1.8691	5.4917
0.75	0.5	2.7412	4.6196	2.4728	4.8879
0.75	0.75	3.2108	4.1500	3.0766	4.2841
0.75	1	3.6804	3.6804	3.6804	3.6804
1	0	1.5061	5.6897	1.5061	5.6897
1	0.25	2.0291	5.1667	2.0291	5.1667
1	0.5	2.5520	4.6438	2.5520	4.6438
1	0.75	3.0750	4.1208	3.0750	4.1208
1	1	3.5979	3.5979	3.5979	3.5979

References

[1] I. Podlubny, Fractional differential equations: an introduction to fractional derivatives, fractional differential equations, to methods of their solution and some of their applications, Elsevier, 1998.

[2] K.S. Miller, B. Ross, An introduction to the fractional calculus and fractional differential equations, Wiley-Interscience, 1993.

[3] S. Chakraverty, R.M. Jena, S.K. Jena, Computational fractional dynamical systems: fractional differential equations and applications, John Wiley & Sons, 2022.

[4] K. Li, J. Peng, Laplace transform and fractional differential equations, Applied Mathematics Letters 24 (12) (2011) 2019–2023.

[5] S. Butera, M. Di Paola, Fractional differential equations solved by using Mellin transform, Communications in Nonlinear Science and Numerical Simulation 19 (7) (2014) 2220–2227.

[6] R.M. Jena, S. Chakraverty, Residual power series method for solving time-fractional model of vibration equation of large membranes, Journal of Applied and Computational Mechanics 5 (4) (2019) 603–615.

[7] M. Zurigat, S. Momani, Z. Odibat, A. Alawneh, The homotopy analysis method for handling systems of fractional differential equations, Applied Mathematical Modelling 34 (1) (2010) 24–35.

[8] Q. Wang, Numerical solutions for fractional KdV–Burgers equation by Adomian decomposition method, Applied Mathematics and Computation 182 (2) (2006) 1048–1055.

[9] A. Ali, Z. Gul, W.A. Khan, S. Ahmad, S. Zeb, Investigation of fractional order sine-Gordon equation using Laplace Adomian decomposition method, Fractals 29 (05) (2021) 2150121.

[10] S. Mall, S. Chakraverty, Artificial neural network approach for solving fractional order applied problems, in: New Paradigms in Computational Modeling and Its Applications, Elsevier, 2021, pp. 163–175.
[11] S. Chakraverty, R.M. Jena, S.K. Jena, Time-fractional order biological systems with uncertain parameters, Synthesis Lectures on Mathematics and Statistics 12 (1) (2020) 1–160.
[12] S. Narayanamoorthy, D. Baleanu, K. Thangapandi, S.S.N. Perera, Analysis for fractional-order predator–prey model with uncertainty, IET Systems Biology 13 (6) (2019) 277–289.
[13] R.M. Jena, Arbitrary order vibration equation of large membranes with uncertainty, Modeling and Computation in Vibration Problems, vol. 2, IOP Publishing, 2021, pp. 12-1–12-13.
[14] M. ur Rahman, M. Arfan, K. Shah, J.F. Gómez-Aguilar, Investigating a nonlinear dynamical model of COVID-19 disease under fuzzy caputo, random and ABC fractional order derivative, Chaos, Solitons and Fractals 140 (2020) 110232.
[15] M. Mazandarani, M. Najariyan, Type-2 fuzzy fractional derivatives, Communications in Nonlinear Science and Numerical Simulation 19 (7) (2014) 2354–2372.
[16] D. Mohapatra, S. Chakraverty, Legendre wavelet method based solution of fractional order prey–predator model in type-2 fuzzy environment, Applied Soft Computing 154 (2024) 111370.
[17] D. Mohapatra, S. Chakraverty, Legendre wavelets based approach for the solution of type-2 fuzzy uncertain smoking model of fractional order, Engineering Computations 40 (4) (2023) 868–920.
[18] D. Mohapatra, S. Chakraverty, Fuzzy uncertainty analysis of a fractional order human immunodeficiency virus dynamic model with type-1 and interval type-2 parameters, Journal of Computational and Nonlinear Dynamics 19 (2024) 081001.
[19] D. Mohapatra, S. Chakraverty, M. Alshammari, Time fractional heat equation of n+1-dimension in type-1 and type-2 fuzzy environment, International Journal of Fuzzy Systems 26 (1) (2024) 1–16.
[20] D. Mohapatra, S. Chakraverty, O. Castillo, Numerical investigation of fluid dynamic model in uncertain environment, Applied and Computational Mathematics 22 (3) (2023) 297–316.
[21] M. ur Rehman, R.A. Khan, The Legendre wavelet method for solving fractional differential equations, Communications in Nonlinear Science and Numerical Simulation 16 (11) (2011) 4163–4173.
[22] M. Razzaghi, S. Yousefi, The Legendre wavelets operational matrix of integration, International Journal of Systems Science 32 (4) (2001) 495–502.
[23] A. Kilicman, Z. Zhour, Kronecker operational matrices for fractional calculus and some applications, Applied Mathematics and Computation 187 (1) (2007) 250–265.
[24] A.G. Radwan, K.N. Salama, Fractional-order RC and RL circuits, Circuits, Systems, and Signal Processing 31 (2012) 1901–1915.
[25] H.M. Srivastava, R.M. Jena, S. Chakraverty, S.K. Jena, Dynamic response analysis of fractionally-damped generalized Bagley–Torvik equation subject to external loads, Russian Journal of Mathematical Physics 27 (2020) 254–268.

Index

A

Absolute error, 60–62, 69, 80, 85, 87, 100, 101
Activation functions, 16, 20, 21, 23, 31, 35–37, 57, 58, 73, 93
Adaptive
  learning rates, 25
  solution, 45
Adaptive Moment Estimation (Adam), 25
  optimization, 25, 26, 37, 59, 98
  optimizer, 37, 39, 58
Adjustable parameters, 30, 31, 56, 57, 74
Application problems, 135, 157, 178, 198, 217
Architecture
  ANN, 18
  neural network, 16, 20
  WNNs, 72
Artificial intelligence (AI), 3, 4
Artificial Neural Network (ANN), 16, 24, 31, 35, 124, 148
  approaches, 188, 208
  approximate solution, 30–32, 36, 46, 56, 57
  architecture, 18
  evolution, 15
  history, 16
  learning process, 92
  models, 3, 21, 24, 25, 30, 56, 71, 92
  parameters, 24
  solution, 33, 49
  topology, 17
  training, 46
  trial solution, 36, 37, 43, 48, 51
Automatic differentiation (AD), 94, 96

B

Backpropagation (BP)
  algorithm, 16, 18, 94
  learning algorithm, 19, 58
Batch size, 20, 37, 39, 48, 60, 64
Beam structure, 137, 139
Bias
  correction, 25
  matrices, 93
Block-pulse function, 209–211
Boundary condition (BC), 93, 96
Boundary value problem (BVP), 30
Boxplot, 10–12

C

Caputo
  fractional derivative, 111
  fuzzy fractional derivative, 111
  type-2 fuzzy fractional derivative, 121
Closet bounds, 148
Computational problems, 45
Concept uncertainty, 222
Conventional neural network, 72
Cost function, 24, 31, 36, 47, 58, 61
Crisp
  condition, 212, 213, 216, 217, 221, 225
  linear eigenvalue problem, 148
  scenario, 215, 219
  solution, 219
Curriculum learning, 46, 48, 49, 51, 52
Customized boxplot, 12

D

Damped spring-mass system, 178, 179
Data visualization, 10, 12
Decision model, 18
Deep learning (DL), 19, 25, 77, 89
  application, 92
  architectures, 16
  frameworks, 25
  libraries, 92
Deep neural network, 79, 82, 83
Differentiability concept, 188

Differential equation (DE), 29, 30, 35
Direct Sufficient Regularity Perturbation (DSRP) method, 166
Duffing oscillator
- equations, 56
- problems, 59

Duffing oscillator model (DOE), 58, 59, 64
Duffing–van der Pol oscillator, 56
Dynamical problems, 29, 30

E

Efficacy
- neural model, 48
- SANN, 56

Eigenvalue
- analysis, 167
- bounds, 148
- problems, 147, 148, 150, 165, 170
- problems fuzzy, 148, 149

Electric circuit, 199, 200
ENSE errors, 87
Epochs, 20
Error
- analysis, 52
- calculations, 66
- function, 29, 31–33, 52, 66
- gradient, 19
- graph, 61, 82, 99, 100
- predicted value, 17
- term, 14

Evolutionary computation, 1, 4, 5
Exponential fuzzy number (EFN), 107

F

Fornberg–Whitham (FW) equation, 95, 96, 98, 100
Fractional derivative, 111, 121, 207, 208, 217
Fractional differential equation (FDE), 188, 207, 208
Fractional-order
- integration operational matrix, 210
- R-L circuit, 217

Fully
- fuzzy non-linear eigenvalue problem, 166
- type-2 fuzzy system, 124

Fully fuzzy linear system of equation (FFLSE), 124
Fully type-2 fuzzy linear system of equation (FT2FLSE), 126
Fuzzy
- arithmetic, 110
- coefficients, 188
- derivative, 188
- DEs, 30
- eigenvalue, 148–150, 167
- eigenvalue problems, 148, 149
- eigenvector, 149, 167
- environment, 126, 148, 199, 208
- filtering method, 148
- fractional-order predator–prey model, 208
- framework, 208
- general system, 124
- generalized eigenvalue problems, 148
- inference system, 4
- linear eigenvalue problems, 148, 149, 157, 162
- linear system, 124
- logic, 3, 4
- matrix valued function, 167
- membership function, 188
- model, 188
- numbers, 107–109, 119, 120, 124, 148, 166, 174, 188, 189, 205, 208, 218
  - concept, 124
  - double parametric form, 109
  - parametric form, 124
  - parametric representation, 124, 167
- output, 4
- parameters, 142, 148, 167, 208
- Riemann–Liouville fractional integral, 111
- rules, 4
- set, 3, 4, 107, 113, 114, 148, 188
  - membership grades, 148, 167
  - theory, 1, 3
- solution, 191, 194, 198, 213, 215, 217, 219, 221
- symmetric matrix, 148
- systems, 4, 127, 129
- terms, 3

theory, 208
uncertain
environment, 148, 217
membership grades, 114
scenario, 200
uncertainty, 124, 125, 208, 222
valued functions, 110, 111
valued functions derivative, 110
values, 4
values functions, 188
Fuzzy differential equation (FDE), 188
Fuzzy fractional differential equation (FFDE), 208
Fuzzy initial value problem (FIVP), 188
Fuzzy linear system of equation (FLSE), 124

G
Gaussian fuzzy number (GFN), 107–109
Gaussian triangular type-2 fuzzy number (GTT2FN), 118
General interval type-2 triangular fuzzy number (GIT2TFN), 118, 119
Generalization error, 21
Generalized
Bagley–Torvik equation, 221, 222
linear eigenvalue problems, 169
type-2 fuzzy numbers, 166
Generalized eigenvalue problem (GEP), 147, 148, 166, 172, 176, 181
Global statistical
errors, 80, 86
measures, 89
Google Colab environment, 37, 48, 59, 96
Governing
eigenvalue problems, 166
equation, 47, 55, 58, 59, 74, 76, 139, 189, 199, 200, 204, 218, 222
Gradient descent (GD), 24, 25, 72

H
Hidden layers, 18, 20, 31, 36, 37, 48, 57, 72, 73, 93
Histogram, 11
Hold-out sample validation, 14
Hopfield neural network model, 29
Hyper-parameters, 20, 21, 96

I
Initial condition (IC), 93, 96
Initial value problem (IVP), 187, 194
Interval
arithmetic, 106
parameters, 148
real eigenvalue bounds, 148
uncertainty, 166

K
K-fold cross-validation, 14, 15

L
Lane–Emden
equations, 47
models, 54
Learning
rate, 20, 25, 37, 39, 48, 58, 59, 72, 77, 82, 98
rules, 18
types, 17
Legendre polynomial, 209
Legendre wavelet, 209–211
method, 209, 226
operational matrix, 210
Limited-memory Broyden–Fletcher–Goldfarb–Shanno (L-BFGS), 26, 72
optimization algorithm, 26
optimizers, 25
Linear
eigenvalue problems, 147, 148, 166, 168
FDEs, 208
Linear Sufficient Regularity Perturbation (LSRP) method, 166
Linearization process, 166, 168, 172, 176
Logistic model, 199
Long short-term memory neural network, 56
Loss function, 23, 25, 37, 39, 52, 56–60, 64, 66, 82, 92–95
Lower membership function (LMF), 115
LWM
effectiveness, 215
implementation, 210
solution, 212, 213, 215, 219, 221

M

Machine learning (ML), 4, 10, 12, 91
  algorithms, 45
  model training, 12
  tasks, 5
  techniques, 35
Managing uncertainty, 124
matplotlib library, 11, 12
Matured Deep Learning Libraries, 92
Mean Absolute Error (MAE), 37, 39, 44, 52, 100
Membership
  function, 3, 107, 108, 113, 114, 188
  grade, 114, 124, 148, 166, 189, 208
  value, 3, 4, 188
Mexican Hat mother wavelet function, 73
Mexican Hat wavelet neural network (M_hWNN), 73, 74
Model
  architecture, 20
  parameters, 20
  problems, 37, 48, 60, 78
Modified differential transform method (MDTM), 64, 67, 69
Modified Fornberg–Whitham equation, 95
Multi-layer neural network (MLNN), 37, 43
Multi-layer perceptron (MLP), 29, 30

N

Network
  adaptable parameters, 59
  initial weights, 59
  model, 16
  modeling, 48
  neural, 1, 3, 16–19, 29, 30, 45, 46, 48, 55, 56, 71–73, 92, 93
  parameters, 19, 58
Neural
  approximate solution, 58, 60
  approximation solution, 78, 81, 83
  model efficacy, 48
  network, 1, 3, 16–19, 29, 30, 45, 46, 48, 55, 56, 71–73, 92, 93
    adaptable parameters, 37
    architecture, 16, 20
    behavior, 21
    biases, 20
    development, 16
    efficacy, 35
    input, 65
    model, 18, 21
    output, 21, 32, 52, 66, 74, 93
    parameters, 72
    predicted solutions, 51, 52, 60
    training, 46, 58, 59
    training process, 20
  results, 79, 80
  solutions, 61
Neurons, 16, 18
Non-linear
  financial model, 76
  holomorphic eigenvalue problem, 166
  type-2 fuzzy matrix valued function, 167
Non-linear eigenvalue problem (NEP), 165–167, 170
Numerical solutions, 48, 60, 66, 85, 166, 188, 208

O

Optimization, 24
Optimized hyper-parameters, 95

P

Parameters
  ANN, 24
  fuzzy, 142, 148, 167, 208
  network, 19
  neural network, 72
Parametric
  form, 109, 115, 124, 149, 188, 189, 191
  representation, 109, 124
Partial differential equation (PDE), 91, 92
Pentagonal fuzzy numbers (PFN), 107
Perfect interval type-2 triangular fuzzy number (PIT2TFN), 119
Physics-Informed Neural Network (PINN), 92, 93, 98, 100
  framework, 94
  model, 94, 100
  predictions, 100
  solution effectiveness, 98

Polynomial eigenvalue problem, 166
Practical application problems, 189
Predicted value error, 17
Principle set (PS), 115, 118
Probabilistic reasoning, 1, 4
Python code, 11, 12, 14, 15, 23

Q

Quadratic eigenvalue problem (QEP), 166, 170, 172, 173

R

Radial basis function network (RBFN), 29, 30
Rational eigenvalue problems, 166
Rectangular sheet, 135
Rectifier Linear Unit (Relu), 22, 35
  activation function, 23
Recurrent neural network (RNN), 24
Regularization, 21, 23
Reinforcement learning, 18
Riemann–Liouville
  fractional integral, 110, 111
  integral, 120

S

Sample problems, 129, 151, 170, 190, 211
Scalar multiplication, 117
Scatter plot, 11
Schematic diagram, 14, 15, 31, 107, 108, 115, 118, 119
Scientific Machine Learning (SciML), 92, 100
Secondary membership function, 114
Sigmoid, 21
Sigmoid activation, 21, 44, 71
Sigmoid activation function, 21
Simulation results, 36, 48, 77, 96
Singular value problem (SVP), 47
Soft computing, 1–3
Solution
  ANN, 33
  curve, 82
  fuzzy, 191, 194, 198, 213, 215, 217, 219, 221
  PINNs, 98
  procedure, 127, 149, 168, 211
  process, 166
Spring-mass system, 157, 204
Standard eigenvalue problem (SEP), 147
Standard eigenvalue problems, 162
Stiffness parameters, 148, 157
Stochastic gradient descent (SGD), 72
Supervised learning, 18
Swish, 23
Swish activation function, 23, 36, 37, 39, 44, 48
Symmetric GFN, 109
Symmetry DEs, 30
Symplectic Artificial Neural Network (SANN), 55–57, 60
  algorithm, 57, 59, 66
  efficacy, 56
  model, 66
  modeling, 57
  results, 64
  solutions, 60
Symplectic neural network initial approximate solution, 57

T

Tabular results, 51, 61, 194
Tanh
  activation functions, 21, 37
  function, 21
Target function, 14
Tensorflow deep learning package, 23
Trainable parameters, 74, 82, 94, 95
Training error, 21
Trapezoidal Fuzzy Number (TrFN), 107, 166
Traveling wave solutions, 96
Trial solution, 29, 52
  ANN, 36, 37, 43, 48, 51
Triangular fuzzy number (TFN), 107, 118, 119
Triangularly perfect quasi-type-2 fuzzy number (TPQT2FN), 115, 123–125
Triple parametric
  approach, 214
  form, 152, 181, 194, 226
  representation, 156, 162, 174, 184, 189, 191, 194, 195, 203, 211, 219, 223
Truss structure, 139, 141
Type-1 fuzzy
  differential equations, 191

initial value problems, 192
number, 115
number valued functions, 110
set, 114, 115, 118, 188
standard eigenvalue problems, 149
Type-2 FLSE (T2FSLE), 124
Type-2 fuzzy
coefficient matrix, 129
displacements, 137
eigenvalue, 149, 150, 154, 167
eigenvector, 149, 151, 167
environment, 126, 199, 208
fractional initial value problems, 211
fractional-order differential equation, 210
framework, 148, 167
linear systems, 142
logistic model, 199
matrix, 151
parameters, 192, 211, 223
plot, 205
quadratic eigenvalue problem, 174, 180, 181
scenario, 139
second-order initial value problem, 205
solution, 127, 130, 194, 213, 221, 225
solutions, 131, 134
square matrices, 149
square matrix, 149
systems, 4, 127, 129
uncertain environment, 135, 166, 170, 178, 208
uncertain scenario, 199
uncertainty, 121, 210
unknowns, 129, 132
valued function, 119, 121, 188
Type-2 fuzzy differential equation (T2FDE), 188
Type-2 fuzzy fractional differential equation (T2FFDE), 208, 226
Type-2 Fuzzy Generalized Eigenvalue Problem (T2FGEP), 149
Type-2 fuzzy initial value problem (T2FIVP), 188
Type-2 fuzzy linear eigenvalue problem (T2FLEP), 148, 149, 157, 162
solution procedure, 149
Type-2 fuzzy linear system of equation (T2FLSE), 125, 130–132
Type-2 fuzzy non-linear eigenvalue problem (T2FNEP), 167, 168
Type-2 fuzzy number (T2FN), 115, 118
Type-2 fuzzy set (T2FS), 113–115, 118, 188
vertical slice, 114
Type-2 Fuzzy Standard Eigenvalue Problem (T2FSEP), 149

U

Uncertainty
concept, 222
factor, 199
footprint, 114
fuzzy, 124, 125, 208, 222
handling parameters, 152, 160, 169, 182, 184, 211, 212
quantification, 4
Unforced duffing oscillator problem, 62
Unsupervised
learning, 18
training, 52, 66
Updatable parameters, 57, 75
Upper membership function (UMF), 115
bounds, 150, 157, 182, 223
solutions, 172, 176, 190, 195, 212

V

Validation, 44, 52, 65, 86, 100
loss, 37, 43, 60, 61
set, 14
van der Pol–Mathieu (VdPM) dust plasma model, 60
van der Pol–Mathieu–Duffing Oscillator (VdPM-DO)
model, 58, 59
system, 56
Vertical slice, 114, 115
Vibration problems, 188

W

Wavelet networks, 73
Wavelet neural network (WNN), 72
architecture, 72
model, 71

9780443328947